Other Books by G. Michael Dobbs

Escape. *How Animation Broke into the Mainstream in the 1990's.*

15 Minutes With... *Forty Years of Interviews*

Springfield. *Postcard History of Springfield, Massachusetts*

Tales from the Runway. *Written as Bill Brazil with Danielle Holmes*

Made of Pen & Ink: *Fleischer Studios, The New York years*

What They Didn't Teach You in Journalism School: *The Memoir of an Ink-Stained Wretch*

Made of Pen & Ink: *Fleischer Studios, The Florida years*

The Films and Life of Tom Tyler

Cowboy • Monster • Hero

G. Michael Dobbs

inkwell™
productions

THE FILMS AND LIFE OF **TOM TYLER**

inkwell
productions

Published by
Inkwell Productions
Office of Publication:
17 Spruce Street
Springfield, MA 01105 USA

In association with
Not Dog Books

First Edition: September 2025
ISBN 978-1-7330144-8-9

The Films and Life of Tom Tyler
©2025 G. Michael Dobbs.
All prominently featured characters are trademarks G. Michael Dobbs.
All rights reserved. No text or artwork from or any part
of this book may be reproduced or transmitted in any form or by any means,
electronic or mechanical, including photocopying, recording, or by an
information storage and retrieval system without permission in writing
from the publisher.
All rights reserved. Any similarity to persons living or dead is purely coincidental.
For more information or comments, e-mail us at gmdobbs@comcast.net

Book & cover design ©2025 Mark Masztal.

Table of Contents

Introduction 1
Chapter One: Who was Tom Tyler? 19
Chapter Two: FBO 44
Chapter Three: Immediately After FBO 85
Chapter Four: Reliable Proves Somewhat Reliable 113
Chapter Five: What should have been the big break: Powdersmoke Range and The Last Outlaw 166
Chapter Six: Victory? 180
Chapter Seven: Freelancing 200
Chapter Eight: The Republic Years 283
Chapter Nine: Tom Tyler In Print 161
Chapter Eight: Max and Dave 182
Chapter Nine: Brothers 185
Afterword 338

Dedication

Dedicated to my friend in the movie research trenches, Stephen R. Bissette. An internationally acclaimed cartoonist and film historian (go ahead, look him up), Steve and I have shared endless conversations about the research rabbit holes we have gone down for our various book projects. We have made each other aware of certain movies. We have camped out in the dealers room of the late and lamented Cinefest in Syracuse, NY, going through milk crates full of vintage stills for hours. I'd hold one up and say, "Do you want this?" and he would do the same for me. We knew each other's obsessions. We have sat through movies, old and new, good and bad.

Steve has become part of this project through his conversations and suggestions and now he is indeed part of it with this dedication.

The boys meeting at Smokey Joe's Cigar Lounge in Springfield, MA. From left to right, the ink-stained wretch; illustrator, author and book designer Mark Masztal; Vermont's number one folklorist, Joe Citro; and cartoonist and film historian Stephen R. Bissette.

Acknowledgments

This book is the result of many people helping me and I am appreciative of everyone who contributed in some way.

At the top of the list is my wife Mary who has endured talk about Tom Tyler (as well as Max Fleischer) for more than 46 years. She has always been supportive of my writing career for which I am deeply thankful.

My late parents did not really understand why their son was interested in movies, but they endured/tolerated my obsessions and even supported them by helping me out with my fanzine in my high school and college years where the first version of Tyler's story was published.

My talented friend and designer Mark Masztal has been of enormous assistance. Besides being a talented author and artist, his book designs are wonderful.

I need to acknowledge the Facebook page titled "B Movies and Serials," moderated by a true B western expert Ed Hulse. Several times I've posted questions and received help from the members.

There have been a number of people who allowed me to interview them, most of whom are gone now. I appreciate Calvin Castine, my last interview for this book, for speaking with me about his Tom Tyler comic book project. I especially want to thank the late Molly Redge, one of Tom's sisters, who answered questions at the very beginning of this project more than 40 years ago.

I also want to thank my friends, the late Alex and Richard Gordon, both film producers, both movie fans to their deaths and life-long historians of film. They were both hardcore western fans and their discussions with me were invaluable.

There have been two friends who have been urging me to complete this book because they actually wanted to read it! A tip of my Panama hat to Jon Johnson (the host of "The Pint O' Comics" weekly broadcast over 88.1 WESU – https://spinitron.com/WESU/) and John Dobrydnio (musician and monster kid who co-hosts "Graveyard Cinema" seen on themonsterchannel.com).

Having peers harass you to complete a book is very helpful. Thanks guys!

And I want to thank you for picking up this book. I hope you will enjoy it.

G. Michael Dobbs
City of Firsts, Springfield, MA
August 2025

THE FILMS AND LIFE OF **TOM TYLER**

Introduction

Looking at entertainment from past generations can sometime yield amazing discoveries that continue to amuse and impress or it can deliver something so inexplicable to you that you need to really dig down and put that activity into a historical context in order to understand it.

The B western may fall into the latter category.

These movies were popular theatrically from the 1920s into the mid-1950s when the many changes in the film industry – increasing costs, a migration of audiences to television and changes in American society – made the economic model that governed the production of all B movies obsolete.

These were inexpensive films running for about an hour that could make up a double bill or be the supporting film for a bigger budgeted feature. They were rented for a flat fee – instead of the percentage of the box office gross that A films charged. Studios calculated a flat fee based on the size of the theater which meant for many theaters in smaller towns or in city neighborhoods, the B movie was an important part of the programming.

They were sold in blocks. An independent studio such as Reliable would shoot all of the Tom Tyler films they had scheduled and then sell them as a group to sub-distributors who then in turn booked them into theaters. This method maximized the potential for profitability.

It also served as a way to predict how to gauge a budget for the films. If you know you have 1,000 theaters booking a film for $20 you can see how big your budget should be to make a profit. Decades later the made-direct-to-VHS movies used a similar technique to try to ensure a profit.

The studios made all sorts of B movies but series films proved to be a way to build an audience. B movie series included the Charlie Chan films, Mr. Moto and the Blondie movies based on the comic strip.

While western films are still being made – as well as television series – it's important to note the genre has been a very hardy one since "The Great Train Robbery" was released in 1903. The 13-minute film proved so popular that it spurred other companies to shoot their own versions to take advantage of its popularity.

It also served as the launching pad of the first Western star, Broncho Billy Anderson who made 148 silent westerns.

Although the popularity of Westerns waxed and waned, the genre never really went away. Audiences here and around the world were fascinated by story of the old West – no matter how simplistic or exaggerated they might be.

The classic B western today certainly could inspire some questions among modern audiences. Who are all those guys in hats riding around what appears to be the same group of rocks? The low budgets, the repetition of plots, the continual use of the same sets and locations and the appearances of a group of actors who specialized in the outdoor dramas can give casual viewers the impression that the films are all alike.

George "Gabby" Hayes was a circus performer and vaudevillian who became the best-known sidekick to B westerns heroes, most notably Roy Rogers, Randolph Scott and "Wild" Bill Elliot. He appeared in 174 western features and was beloved by audiences.

While westerns made him money and fame, he was succinct in his opinion about them: "I hate 'em. Really can't stand 'em. They always are the same. You have so few plots – the stagecoach holdup, the rustlers, the mortgage gag, the mine setting and the retired gunslinger."

There was amazing repetition among so many B westerns of storylines, locations and cast members. Regardless, there was a huge audience for them for decades.

And why were they so popular with audiences for nearly 30 years? Part of the appeal was undoubtedly the interest in the folklore of the American West, but much had to do with the star power of the films themselves. People in rural and small-town America where the Western was most popular found it easy to identify with the actors who portrayed characters making their living off the land.

Today, people fail to understand that the bill at the neighborhood movie house changed twice a week and there were special children's matinees and midnight shows. Going to the movies was something many people did on a weekly basis – perhaps twice a week. Theater owners were showmen who created programs, which included a main attraction, a supporting feature film, and short subjects such as cartoons, live-action comedies, and newsreels.

But what distinguished one Western film from another? Hundreds of B westerns were made in the 1930s and '40s. Besides the technical proficiency of the films themselves, the success of the Western rested upon the hero. His appearance and personality were crucial. A gimmick, also, could help.

Consider Gene Autry for a moment.

People today might remember the late Gene Autry more as an accomplished businessman than film star. Autry's success in business was based on his long career in the cinematic saddle. If you have the endurance to make it through Gene Autry's breakout vehicle, Mascot Pictures' serial "The Phantom Empire," you begin to understand how success in B Westerns could be obtained.

The serial is an unpolished piece of work even for 1934, and its hokey lost world plot was aimed squarely at kids. For adults, though, the real attraction was the show's hero Gene Autry, a Western singer who had had success with records and radio at that time but was untested as an actor.

Mascot Pictures was an independent outfit that excelled in making serials in the early 1930s. Its owner, Nat Levine, discovered Autry though his success as a singer and cast him in a supporting role in "In Old Santa Fe" in 1934. This B western was a vehicle for Ken Maynard, an accomplished horseman who was very popular with audiences, but not so much with producers due to his obnoxious temperament and drinking habits.

Autry proved successful in his supporting role and Levine promoted him to be the star of "The Phantom Empire."

Autry sounded like a true son of the West – he was born in Texas – and his down-home singing style compensated for his lack of acting skills. The gimmick of being the first singing cowboy didn't hurt him either.

With his successive films, Autry built up a solid fan base, so much so that he was one of the top box office stars in the country. Although his skills as a performer improved and the quality of his films produced by Republic were among the highest in B Westerns, Autry's overall success was based on his acceptance of his screen personality by audiences.

Autry was a successful performer whose personality overcame the limitations of story and production.

The same can be said for other long-lasting Western stars such as Buck Jones, Tim McCoy, the aforementioned Ken Maynard, Hoot Gibson, and Roy Rogers. Maynard came across like a good old boy from the South. Gibson, a rodeo king, used his self-deprecating sense of humor more than his six-shooter. McCoy was a genuine expert in the culture of Native Americans. No one looked more Western than Jones. Rogers put his own twist on being a singing cowboy.

Western stardom was a double-edged sword. Although it's the goal of every actor to find consistent work and build a reputation, cowboys who were successful frequently found themselves typecast into a sagebrush ghetto. The price of success was a closed door to other kinds of roles.

Take Tom Keene, for example. Keene was a Western star at a number of studios but changed his name twice (to Richard Powers and George Duryea)

THE FILMS AND LIFE OF TOM TYLER

in order to try to break his identification with Westerns. He had some success getting non-Western roles (he was the lead in King Vidor's 1934 socialist drama "Our Daily Bread" and ended his career working in Ed Wood's notorious "Plan Nine from Outer Space") but kept drifting back into Westerns.

B westerns were not the first choice of most of its stars. "Wild" Bill Elliot, who had a lengthy Western career, started out wearing a tuxedo in films such as "Wonder Bar" as Gordon Elliot. Alan "Rocky" Lane also began his career away from the saddle. He pops up in a Charlie Chan film.

For many performers B westerns might be the beginning or end of a career. Buck Jones, Bill Elliot and Tim McCoy all had star turns in non-Westerns, but these roles had little relatively impact on their careers. It wasn't that they weren't competent performers but the expectations of the audience played a role in their acceptance of something different from them.

As a Western character actor, you could find employment in number of films, but as a star you were limited. Once you hit a certain age or had worn out your welcome at the box office, your career was essentially finished.

Western superstars such as Gibson, Maynard and McCoy made rare appearances in films once their glory days were over (the most notable being McCoy in "Around the World in 80 Days").

George Houston was an accomplished opera singer, whose time in the B western saddle was a detour. Fred Scott's career in show business essentially stopped when he left B westerns and he became a successful realtor. Whip Wilson, Sunset Carson, Lash LaRue and others all saw their acting careers end when their studios canceled their series.

Few types of acting careers proved to be as restrictive as B westerns.

Of all the major Western stars of 1930s and '40s just a handful looked at the end of their cowboy careers as the time to pursue other forms of acting. Bob Steele, in a break from cowboy roles, had appeared as Curly in "Of Mice and Men" and later turned up in as a hood tailing Humphrey Bogart in "The Big Sleep." He was a regular on the television series he was on, "F Troop." "But Steele's non-Western appearances could not be compared".

Who? You've heard of William Boyd, Autry and Rogers, but not Tom Tyler? Tyler had an almost 20-year run as the hero in dozens of B westerns. A quick look confirms why Tyler survived as a Western hero from the silent days through the early talkies and into the early 1940s. A tall handsome man, Tyler looked like a textbook definition of a hero. His screen persona included an easy smile and laugh, and his characters never seemed to take themselves too seriously.

Unlike some other screen cowboys, Tyler never went in for elaborate costumes, but frequently wore a tall ten-gallon hat, which made him look seven-feet-tall. He could ride well and had a great physique from his hobby of weight lifting – something that had given him national prominence.

Tyler was different, though, from many other B Western stars. He clearly was interested in acting beyond westerns.

He was unique among Western stars in his ability to switch from hero to villain roles and from stardom in B films and serials to character parts in major films. You would seldom catch one of his peers turning up as a supporting player in a non-western "A" movie.

A signed portrait of Tyler from "Adventures of Captain Marvel." (author's collection)

Tyler appeared in "Gone with the Wind" "Talk of the Town," "Brother Orchid," and "Red River," for example. He was one of the leading serial stars and appeared as the lead in five serials, including "The Adventures of Captain Marvel," considered to be the best serial ever made as well as the adaptation of the popular comic strip, "The Phantom." He was a member of director John Ford's stock company of actors and was in "Stagecoach" "The Grapes of Wrath," "They Were Expendable," "She Wore a Yellow Ribbon," "The Last of the Mohicans" and "What Price Glory" He even appeared as one of the famed Universal Studio monsters, Kharis the Mummy, in "The Mummy's Hand."

Ford must have thought highly of Tyler as he kept employing him.

No other B Western star amassed the kind of credits, as did Tyler. Character roles in major films gave Tyler's acting abilities a kind of workout he wasn't able to get riding the range.

B westerns ended their theatrical life by the mid-1950s. People my age – I just turned 71 – got to know these films through their second life on television during the 1950s and '60s. The extended career of Roy Rogers, as well as the nostalgia boon of the 1970s and '80s kept performers such as Clayton Moore – TV's Lone Ranger – in the public eye.

The emergence of VHS gave B westerns another run at life, with many of them being brought out on home video.

Today, they are easily found on many streaming platforms as well as on DVDs and Blu-rays.

I became seriously interested in film in junior high school when I was drawn to the very films from which my well-meaning mother had shielded me - horror movies. Through late night horror movie shows on local television, I discovered the great gods of classic horror Boris Karloff and Bela Lugosi. My interest in film snowballed when I would watch Karloff in a non-horror film and find other actors I liked. I read every movie magazine I could find, but especially Famous Monsters of Filmland and the more obscure Larry Ivie's Monsters and Heroes. I bought edited and excerpted 8mm versions of classic Hollywood to watch over and over at home.

My favorite in the collection was an edited version of the first chapter of "The Adventures of Captain Marvel." I had watched serials on television and had even seen a chapter or two of the 1943 "Batman" serial as part of my own Saturday matinees in 1962.

But these viewing experiences hadn't prepared me for what the sepia image on my home screen gave me. The version I had may have been missing a soundtrack and eight or so minutes of footage but had all of the sense of wonder.

Who was this guy who played Captain Marvel? Oh, my God, he's the one who played Kharis in one of the mummy movies! And "Monsters and Heroes" – a great but forgotten pop culture magazine – said he was also a cowboy star. As my interest in film grew, so did my fascination in this cowboy actor who wasn't just a cowboy actor. As I learned more, I found a story that was truly American – the son of immigrants who left behind the automobile plants of Detroit to follow a dream of stardom in the movies; a man who bucked the odds and succeeded where so many failed.

Tyler, like so many other cowboy heroes could have drifted into obscurity once his moment in the spotlight had ended, but he continued acting. Despite a crippling disease that changed his appearance, Tyler held onto the dream until almost the very end of his life.

As my studies in film expanded, I realized how unique Tyler's career had been. Tyler had broken the mold more than any other of his contemporaries had, and yet he was relatively forgotten today by many people other than western, serial, and horror film fans.

His story of struggle, accomplishment and loss deserves to be told.

Terms of the trade for this book

The motion picture business through the start of the 20th century to through the 1980s was a very different industry than it is today and some of the phrases I use in the book might be a bit confusing.

How films were made, released and marketed was very different than today. My goal in this section of the book is to offer some context before we ride down the trail too much.

B movie

First let's look at just what a B movie was. At its most simple, the definition describes a movie that is sent out to theater owners on a flat rental fee. Theaters paid a percentage of the box office receipts when showing an A-movie. Rental for a B-western could be as low as $15-$20.

Today almost any low budget genre film is called a "B movie." They are not. They are simply low budget. The closest reincarnation of the B movie came for a relatively brief period when movies destined for the direct-to-video market existed. Like B movie producers of decades past, the producers of a direct-to-video film made money by making a film with exploitable elements as cheaply as they could anticipating just how many VHS tapes they would sell to the rental industry.

B films were a very important building block of the film industry until the advent of television in the 1950s. Most, if not all, of the major studios had B film units. Some studios, such as Republic, Monogram and PRC, made mostly B films to meet the need of theaters.

Western titles

Usually, a title is designed to offer some indication about the nature of the story of a film – not so much in westerns.

Take Tyler's film "Law of the Plains." What does that mean in this multi-generational story of intrigue? I don't know.

All too often, the titles of westerns were more about letting the viewer know he or she was watching a western than referencing what the film was about. Don't put too much faith in the title actually meaning something.

Variety lingo

Variety has long been known as the "bible of show business" and its writers developed a lot of slang that might seem a bit odd today.

"Nabe" was a neighborhood theater. "Hardtops" were indoor theaters while "ozoners" were drive-ins.

Variety writers enjoyed taking a noun and using it with alteration as a verb. Take "canonnerring" for instance, which meant gun play.

A "dualer" means a double bill. "Exhibs" means exhibitors.

Marketing

The way movies are marketed today is a pale shadow of what that process used to be like.

Movie theaters were competitive businesses. Many, many theaters were locally owned. In order to compete, theater owners and managers were very aware that they just weren't showing a movie but instead presenting a show. They used cartoons, newsreels, comedy short subjects, musical short subjects, among other short features, to build an evening of entertainment.

There was more than just one show a week at a theater. Many theaters had special weekend shows for children. In some metro areas there were "grindhouses," which showed the program continuously in order to get different audiences at different times.

The movies could change weekly or twice within a week, again depending upon the theater. Some movies would have just one screening.

Double features were common, especially in smaller theaters. Sometimes it would be two B movies, sometimes it would be a B movie with a bigger budgeted film – an A film.

Theater managers, once they knew which film would be booked, would receive a pressbook from the distributor with the accessories a manager could order to promote the film. These tools included a trailer or preview, one sheet posters, lobby cards to be displayed in the lobby, lobby inserts and over-sized posters called three-sheets and six sheets. The pressbook would also have stories that could be given to local newspapers and radio stations in the hopes they would use them – free advertising – along with layouts for paid ads.

The emphasis was showmanship in order to draw in the audiences.

Window cards were small posters printed on card stock with a blank spot at their top where theater managers could write something like "Playing Tuesday at The Bijou." These cards were frequently in the window of local businesses who would display them in exchange for tickets.

Theater owners and managers would read trade publications such as The Film Daily, Variety and The Motion Picture Herald, in order to assess which films to book and how to promote them.

Distribution

Motion pictures were distributed in four major ways during much of the 20th century.

Major studios – or well-financed smaller studios – maintained booking offices called exchanges in many major cities. Independent Theater managers would contact the exchanges to get a print of a film they wanted to present.

The second means of distribution was the major studios that owned their own theaters.

Until the Supreme Court decision in 1948 – in United States v. Paramount Pictures, Inc. – movie studios were allowed to own theater chains. The studios essentially distributed their product to their own theaters until this decision.

The third means was the states rights system in which producers would sell a film to a sub-distributor with a territory. Those sub-distributors would book the film in as many theaters as possible and as many times as possible within a designated area. This was the preferred way to distribute a film if a small studio did not have exchanges.

Tyler's films for Syndicate, Reliable and Victory in the 1930s were all distributed by states rights.

The fourth way to get a film to an audience was the roadshow. The producer of a film would book a film within a theater at a negotiated rate. Frequently these films were exploitation films, often shown only to adults. Producer Kroger Babb's legendary exploitation film "Mom and Dad" – in which a teenage girl becomes pregnant and the film culminates in birth of a baby footage – made millions through this method.

What was it like to make a B film?

In 1945, director Nick Grinde wrote the following essay for the Saturday Evening Post about making B-movies. He started his directing career in 1928 at MGM with a Tim McCoy western and worked in various genres for Mascot, Republic, Warner Bros. and Columbia. At this point in his career, he was a wily vet who had made some very good low-budget films. It's well worth reading for its insider perspective.

Pictures for Peanuts

Over on Stage 6 a million-dollar picture is starting this morning. The call was for nine – a little well-placed optimism you could say that the epic is beginning to show promise of getting under way. A lot of departments with a whale of a lot of mighty fine technical abilities have been working for weeks toward this very day. Propmen, grips, gaffers, electricians, boom men, recorders, mixers, cameramen, assistant cameramen, a script clerk overflowing her rose-colored slacks, a company clerk, an assistant director, his assistant and his assistant are functioning with the occupational movements that will find each one ready when the moment finally comes to record the suspensive scene where Nancy says, 'I am tired of wearing other people's clothes. From now on I will wear my own or nothing!"

This confused efficiency, laced, of course, with a fine sense of self-preservation, is going on, all unnoticed, around, above and in between the associate producer and the director, who already are trying to see who can stay calm longer. The pattern is familiar to everyone. Too much has been written about the habitat of the colossal picture for anyone to have escaped a willing or unwilling education on the subject.

But over on Stage 3 in this same studio another picture was scheduled to start this morning: at eight-thirty. It's ten-thirty over there, too, and they have exactly two hours' work under their belts. There are no press agents or fan-magazine writers hovering around. No newspaper columnists are harvesting their succulent crop. You'd think it said "Contagious" on the door instead of "Quiet, Please! Shooting!"

The difference is that this is just another little picture. A B picture, if you please. B standing for Bread and Butter, or Buttons, or Bottom Budget. And standing for nearly anything else anyone wants to throw at it. But it's a robust little mongrel and doesn't mind the slurs, because it was weaned on them. If the trade papers give a B the nod at all, they usually sum up their comments by saying it will be good for Duals and Nabes, which is why you'll find them on a double bill in the neighborhood theaters.

A B picture isn't a big picture that just didn't grow up; it's exactly what it started out to be. It's the twenty-two-dollar suit of the clothing business, it's the hamburger of the butcher shops, it's a seat in the bleachers. And there's a big market for all of them.

Only by perpetual corner cutting can these often quite presentable cheaper pictures be made to show the profit that is so very agreeable to the studios which invested their money in them.

Like the less expensive suit of clothes, the cloth from which they are fabricated is not all wool, the buttonholes are machine made, and the buttons themselves are more or less synthetic. But when you are all through, you have a suit or a picture which goes right out into the market with its big brothers and gives pretty good service at that. The trick is to judge them in their class and not by A standards.

In the finer pictures, results are all that are aimed at, let the costs fall where they may. The best possible actors are hired to articulate the finest lines the top writers can conjure up. And the best directors mount the stories in convincing and appropriate settings. Of course, occasionally somebody's aim is a little off, but that's beside the point.

In making a program picture, all this is different. Cheaper raw materials are used and a more thrifty approach is indicated. No expensive best seller or Broadway play is bought. That's out; it's not even thought about. The whole picture will be made for much less than the cost of such a property. The story used will be an original submitted by one of the freelance writers who knows just what and whom he is slanting it for. Or it may be a magazine story from one of the pulps or a fifteen-minute radio program purchased for its basic idea or twist. These properties are then blown up into script form and length by a writer who either works at the studio already or is brought in for the job. If he gets six weeks' work out of it, he's lucky. If he takes much more, he had better buy bonds with the money, because he won't be back very soon.

There are all kinds of ways of writing a story besides good and poor. It can be written up or written down. It can be costly to produce or slanted on the frugal side. If the cast of characters can't be held down in numbers, it's the wrong story for limited money. And if they can't be kept out of busy places like night clubs, railroad depots and football games, look out for the budget.

Beating a Cover Charge

Basic emotions can happen in a quiet place as well as at the Stork Club. If John and Peggy are cast in modest circumstances, they can wear their own wardrobe, and a set suitable for their home can be found already standing somewhere in the studio. It's easy when you get the knack of it. Then, instead of taking her to a bustling restaurant for lunch and having some costly busybodies come by and tell them about the murder, they can be discovered coming out of the restaurant and shutting the door on all that expense. A reasonably priced newsboy can sell them a newspaper, so they can read all about the homicide. John's reaction to the bumping-off of his best friend will be of the same fine stuff out here on the sidewalk as it would have been over a crepe suzette. John, being who he is, naturally has to catch up with the rat who did it before the police do. There's a matter of a good name and a hunk of money involved. But does John's search take him to crowded bars, well-filled hotel lobbies, busy downtown streets, bus stops and other gregarious rendezvous? Not by two budgets. He interviews a rooming-house proprietor who lives in a little standing set at the edge of town, and who is home alone at the moment. Then he talks to a milkman in front of a brownstone set on the old New York street. The milk wagon really isn't expensive when you consider that it hides a big hole in the front of the house where some gangsters dynamited their way out in the second episode of a serial last week.

When John finally gets into the chase at the end of the picture, does he search the affluent Union League club, or a museum, or the zoo? You guessed it, cousin, the scene is shot in an alley with three cops and some dandy shadows. And if it's done properly, it can be plenty thrilling, even if it is mounted in cut-rate atmosphere.

There are comparatively inexpensive ways of larding a story with a semblance of size and scope just waiting for the resourceful producer. One such fellow is a whiz at using stock shots from newsreels or any other fertile source. Whenever a building is blown up, or a bridge blows down, or a forest burns, or a strike riot breaks out, the chances are that someone is right there making a movie of it. If the stuff is good, this producer will buy a batch, paying for it by the foot, and have a whole story written around it or at least an important sequence. If you have a real forest fire to cut to, you can do wonders with a little cabin, a few trees, a wind machine, sun-dry lycopodium torches, and a batch of smoke pots. And you will have avoided the spending of up to $100,000 or more.

If you're lucky and things work out right, you can make quite a dent in your picture right here, and you'll probably come out with a climax that will bring a pleasant look from the front office. If you're real careful and have the wind blowing from the same direction as the wind blew in the original film and watch your smoke density, the real and the staged films will cut together like well-hung wallpaper.

Other stock footages that have inspired important sequences are those of train wrecks, rodeos, the rescue of downed aviators, shipwrecks, kidnap manhunts, and even baby shows. You may not end up with the story you started out to make but look at the wallop your detour gave you. And you can always salvage the abandoned sequences in another lot.

One studio struck oil by buying foreign films that had great scenic values and plenty of long shots. These films were bought outright, negative and all. Then a new story was written around these long shots and American actors hired to play the few reels needed to go with the salvaged scenery. The only demand on the refurbished plot was that the writers had to dream up excuses for their characters to go through the same scenic exteriors in the same groupings and dressed exactly the same as in the original. In that way, all the picturesque entrances and exits could be retained. Shooting the outdoor close-ups and the interior sets for the new version was a routine matter, quickly done. But the total result was very dressy indeed, thanks to the Swiss Alps shot by somebody else and bought for peanuts.

Borrowed Thrills

Another sleight-of-hand trick that's used every day in the B-hives is the so-called montage. That's a series of quick cuts of film borrowed from earlier pictures. It's the Lend-Lease of the studios, Whatever the subject, there is always film available from some other fellow's picture that will add otherwise prohibitive flavor to a sequence.

Say it's a gangster film. Tony and his mob have been terrorizing the city for months. You can't shoot a first-class crime wave on short dough, so you borrow or buy about twenty pieces of thrilling moments from twenty forgotten pictures. A fleeing limousine skids into a streetcar, a pedestrian is socked over the head in an alley, a newspaper office is wrecked by hoodlums, a bomb is thrown into a dry-cleaning truck, a woman screams, a couple of mugs are slapping a little merchant into seeing things their way. And so, on until we end up on a really big explosion. All this, garnished with sound effects and crescendo orchestration, dissolves through to three serious-looking actors in a standing set. One of the men says, "This city has got to be cleaned up. Tony and his mob have got to go." And this is Scene I in the script which will be shot on Stage 3.

Montages can take care of World War I or II, a cross-country journey, a college education, a rise from poverty to riches or anything else too expensive in time and money to photograph. Often the determined face of the leading man is superimposed over this potpourri to remind you it is he who is having all these experiences. Of course, he'll never know how he suffered until he sees the preview.

One producer fell in love with a reel of train wheels. Somebody shot too much of a speeding train one day. Probably the wind on the handcar which was following the engine's underpinning with the camera was so strong that the cameraman couldn't hear the command to cut. Or something. Anyway, here was all that lovely footage of train wheels going somewhere.

The producer never really rested right until he found a story where the characters pursued one another from city to city. Every time Joe thought he was being shadowed he got that don't-fence-me-in look on his face and they dissolved to a hunk of money-saving train wheels. Then, of course, the detective, who either had to get a clue or end the story right there, got his portion of the wheels, and we knew that he was right after Joe again. So, they chased from city to city, using up more and more train wheels, until the picture ended up in a draw between moving drama and galloping wheels.

Stock stuff is not the only thing that is borrowed. Plots are hijacked in broad daylight. The fellows who make the dehydrated films are the most consistent disciples of the biggies. Gold isn't the only thing that's where you find it. If the brand on a cow can be changed with a hot iron, the earmarks of a situation can be camouflaged with a typewriter.

One of the most comforting things about plot lifting is that there are no new plots, and the fellows you raid have no doubt had their own little forays into the published works of even earlier shanghaies. Plagiarism is a nasty word, but only for amateurs.

Several years ago, a major studio made a star picture with a costly scenario wherein a character who was a whaler by trade and went on long trips to sea, as whalers do, was double-crossed during his absences by a landlubber. Things went like this for a while, until one day the whaler had his leg bitten off by a shark who got into the picture somehow. Well, the wife wasn't so much of a heel that she could let him down in his hour of need. So, she nursed him, but during his convalescence he could see which way the prevailing wind was blowing. All of which made for quite a neat triangle Several years later, a producer at the same studio needed a story, but had very little money allowed him with which to get it. He remembered the whale picture and also realized that it was all paid for. So, he told one of his writers how to retread the plot. At the preview of this reclaimed yarn, a lion tamer was being double-crossed by a tightrope walker every time he went in the cage for his act. He suspected it a little, which made him careless, and the lion bit his leg off. Well, the wife wasn't so much of a heel that she could let him down in his hour of need. So, she nursed.... See how it's done?

A beautiful set built for one of the more affluent productions has a pull like gravity to the fellow with the short moneybags. He haunts the side lines, drooling while the aristocrats shoot their leisurely schedule. Then he collars the big boss for permission to get his cast in there for just a few hours. The answer is no, of course. It always is at first.

He explains that the way he will shoot it no one will recognize it for the same set. He'll have his director pick new angles and re-dress the foreground. His picture is all action anyway, so it will feel like a different place entirely and it won't conflict a bit with the A picture; he'll underwrite that. And what a production lift it will give his otherwise barren little efforts. It will save it! He will even agree to shoot at night while the rightful occupants sleep. He'll be in and out, and they'll never know it.

As soon as he has gained his point, he calls the assistant director from his picture and instructs him to change the schedule to accommodate the plucking of this nocturnal plum. Then he drops in on his writers, who are now busy dreaming up a new script and who have already completely forgotten the one now shooting. He tells them to drop everything for an hour or two and whip up a night's work in this set which will involve the principals and maybe up to ten or twelve extras, but no more. They point out that there is no conceivable way in which the characters of this yarn could find themselves in such a lavish set. The producer asks them who is paying their salaries, and would they just go down and take a look at the set, and hurry and write something and not be so touchy. There are at least a thousand reasons why the characters could find themselves in that set. All he asks them to think of is one – but by tomorrow night.

Of course, eventually the results of all this nomadic scheming are dumped into the busy lap of the director. It is he who is expected to manipulate these assorted ingredients into a presentable theatrical offering in what, with practically no understatement, might be called no time at all. The B director has to know more tricks than Harry Houdini did, and he has to pull them out of his hat right now – not after lunch. He has to know a lot about making pictures and be able to toss that knowledge at a situation and hope that some of it will stick. He doesn't have time to do any one thing quite as well as he would like to, because he can't stop and do just that one thing. He is, for the moment, a juggler and must keep his eye on all the Indian clubs.

The scene to be shot is on the process stage. That, as you probably know, is where they put scenery from somewhere else behind you and make you look as though you'd been there – a handy gadget if there ever was one. The set in front of the process screen is a Pullman drawing room. Outside of the train windows will appear, on command, the retreating countryside of Ohio – Can No. 76, Train Backgrounds; Right to Left; Please Return to Vault. In the scene will be the leading man and the leading lady and the Pullman porter, who is to bring them a telegram. It's a short scene and won't take long to shoot. Already the assistant from another company is sticking his nose in to see if shooting is progressing, as his company is scheduled to use this same process background screen in an hour from now. Only when his company arrives it will be Times Square which blossoms behind his heavies and the comic – Can No. 31, New York Streets; Daytime; Stationary; Please Return to Vault.

Assistant No. 1 tells Assistant No. 2 that everything will be on schedule somehow. It always is. The only slight drawback is the fact that the colored actor who is to play the part of the Pullman porter is conspicuously not there yet. Seems he has been contacted, though, and is even now arranging with a friend of his to pick him up where his car broke down and hurry him to the waiting train fragment. While the assistants are still talking, the director, long since indoctrinated to abhor a time vacuum, is having the leading man's right hand blackened. Then, with the porter's white coat on, it will be his hand that is photographed knocking on the drawing-room door. In the hand will be the telegram, and the shot will tell us visually that a porter has a telegram for the occupants of Room B. The shot will be even more effective than seeing the porter approach the door in a long shot as it was written, and, of course, it keeps the company working, which is what those precious fleeting moments were made for in the first place.

When this shot is finished the leading man will resume his original identity, and if the overdue Thespian is still not there, he will be photographed in his individual close-up receiving the telegram from the supposedly offscreen porter and will answer his unspoken questions. By that time the missing actor will surely have arrived and the necessary three-shot of the group will be made, and it will all come out just as though it had been planned to be shot backward in the first place, whereas the only thing that had been planned for sure was to shoot, period. One director returned from a three-day location trip with the full confidence that a New York penthouse would be awaiting his directorial efforts. His script called for a refined high-society argument, followed by the blackmailer's accidental crash through the penthouse window to the street far below. All of which led quite logically to a big courtroom scene which was to be the high spot of the picture.

It had been agreed to spread a bit and to spend a respectable part of the construction money on this particular set and really make something nice out of it. But in the director's absence it seems that, just as work was about to start on the building of the penthouse set, the producer stumbled on a very charming garden pergola and a bright idea at the same time. The structure was set amid potted foliage and real grass mats and had been used for an idyllic love scene in a recent Viennese picture. Why couldn't the accident happen in the arbor of a pseudo-Long Island estate instead of on the roof top of a downtown building? A trifling detail, but a thrifty one. The switch was ordered immediately.

When the director heard about what they had done to him behind his back, he went into a condensed tantrum. By training and instinct, he knew he had to hit his fury fast. He knew he was entitled to anger, wrath and indignation, and he also knew that if he took too long about it, he'd have a hard time getting back on schedule. So, he pulled out all his emotional stops and inquired why, while they were at it, they hadn't switched him to an igloo or a tepee. How, he demanded, could you plunge a man down to his death from the French window of a garden bower?

So, a couple of minutes later, when he started work, a gun was slipped into the struggle, and when the actors had choked all the dialogue out of each other, the darn thing went off, and everyone except the victim, who was now comfortably off the pay roll, turned up in the courtroom as per plan.

Another corner-chopping expedient is premised on the different rates of pay for bit actors, depending on whether or not they speak. A bellboy, for instance, who is not playing a part, but who is just in for the day to take someone's bags to the elevator, will get $16.50 if he remains silent. But this is boosted to $25.00 if he articulates so much as a "Yes, sir" or "Thank you, sir." Nine times out of ten it's awkward to keep him silent, but that's how close these budgets are pruned. The actor says, "Take my bags to my room. I'll go up later." The bellboy nods silently and exits. Eight-fifty saved. Or the lady asks where the phone booths are. The bellboy points mutely, and the lady says, "Oh, thank you," and the bellboy wishes he could have said it. It makes the hotel help look mighty surly, to say the least, but the silent bellboy is here to stay.

One director, who shall be nameless, but whom we'll call Nick, was given a $16.50-bit man who had so much to pantomime that he and everyone else ran out of ideas for suitable gestures. Nods, points, shrugs, smiles and scowls were all tossed to the camera, but there was still more plot and still the order to keep him frugally inaudible. So, like always, something had to be done. He was finally played as a character with laryngitis, and wrote his answers on slips of paper, which were then photographed and cut into the film. The part came out as a nice thrifty novelty.

So by shaving the corners of already clipped corners, by shooting backward and sideways to make budgets and salaries come out even, by re-dressing and doubling the same set three or four times, by shooting only the absolutely necessary footage, by concentrating on speed and novelty and plot pattern rather than on time-consuming characterizations and penetrating emotional studies, you can make a picture that may never get the Academy award, but will, however, have a healthy career and earn money.

Not all A pictures are good; any more than all B pictures are poor. You can get ptomaine at the classiest hotel and you can get a good steak in a dog wagon. Both kinds of pictures can learn something from the other. Today, with continuing manpower and raw-material shortages, it wouldn't be a bad idea at all if the super-supers would funnel a bigger percentage of their efforts onto the screen and not on extracurricular waste motions.

By the same token, the quickies, which have brought the efficiency of getting their money's worth down to a microscopic point, could improve their standing in the community if they would apply the same efficient diligence to seeing that their scenario material was a bit more honest. Fast cutting may hide a weak point in the script, but there is a ceiling on fast cutting. Unlike the V-2 bomb, it mustn't go faster than sound—you guess why. So, the best thing to do is to tighten up the story points with the same sure hand that whittles the budgets.

A bookkeeper hopped up on a stool in the studio lunchroom next to a director a couple of days after he had finished making a fast detective yarn. The double-entry fellow said, "Say, your picture came out swell."

The director, being human, rumors to the contrary, was delighted, and said, "Oh, have you seen it? The cutter told me it wouldn't be ready till tomorrow."

The answer was, "No, I haven't seen it. 1 mean you brought it in a day under schedule and nicely under the budget. Boy, you did a fine job!" Unfortunately, none of this praise comes under the heading of entertainment. When the picture gets to the theaters, its penny-pinching undergarments had best be covered by lace of amusement, or some rude patron of the drama will say, "Your slip is showing."

And now let's see the Hollywood of many years ago through the career of a man who succeeded in becoming part of it.

Chapter One

Who was Tom Tyler?

Being a journalist most of my life, I wish there were several in-depth interviews so I can "hear" the voice of Tom Tyler. I want to know how he would recount his life as the son of immigrants seeking a better life for themselves. I want to know how much courage he had to leave his family, hitchhike to Los Angeles and through luck and a show of will, actually reach his goal of being an actor.

And not just any actor, but one whose career went from 1926 to 1953. He had a career where he worked for directors such as John Ford, William Wyler and Howard Hawks.

Few B-western cowboy stars received the journalistic scrutiny as the A listers did and so conversations with Tyler are few indeed.

Tom Tyler's roots were in the upstate New York area not far from the shores of Lake Champlain. In the 2010 census, Witherbee – a hamlet in the town of Moriah – had a population of 347.

The hamlet is known as the birthplace of baseball pitcher Johnny Podres, who played in the major leagues from 1953 to 1969.

Until local broadcaster Calvin Castine published a comic book about Tyler – "Tom Tyler Tales, one and two" – in the early 2000s, relatively few people knew that he was also from Witherbee, he explained to me.

In a biographical essay in the comic book, Castine wrote, "Destined to become one of the most prolific B western movie stars of the 1930s, Vincent Markowski was born into a Moriah iron mining family on Aug. 9, 1903, the son of Frank and Helen Markowski. The birthplace is generally listed in Port Henry, NY, but one would have to believe that back in 1903, there is a strong possibility that the birth actually took place at the Markowski home in Witherbee.

"Although listed on the Witherbee-Sherman and Republic Steel Corporation records as being of Polish descent, the family is actually Lithuanian, according to Vincent's nephew Mike Tyler. The Markowski family included five children: Frank junior, Vincent, Joe, Maliane (Molly) and Katherine. Frank, Sr. was naturalized on April 22, 1918, with his wife's name listed as 'Hellena.'

Mike Tyler's father told him that Mike's grandmother was of French-Canadian Indian heritage. So, anyone in the southern Quebec-northern New York region with the name 'Montville' in their genealogy might want to explore their possible relationship to Tom Tyler.

"The exact date that the family left the Moriah area to settle in the Detroit suburb of Hamtramck, MI, is subject to debate but evidence would indicate it to be around 1918. The Witherbee-Sherman and Republic Steel Corporation records show that Frank Marco Jr., age 16 Polish laborer at 3 mill, started work June 25, 1917, and left on Sept. 18, 1918. Town of Mariah historian Joan Dabby was unable to find the work dates for Frank Sr. because many of the local records had been lost in fires over the years.

"The year 1918 would put Vincent at roughly age 15. At a later date he and his boyhood friend Emil Karkowski, whose family also had immigrated from Moriah to the Hamtramck area, headed for Hollywood. According to Emil's son Tom, Emil got as far as Colorado. When their money ran short Emil headed back home while Vincent ventured on."

Castine provided an additional interview for B-Westerns.com – an essential website. He wrote, "In the Fall of 1999 and again, in December 2000, I communicated with Tom Karkowski, whose father was a friend of Tyler. In summary, Tom writes, 'My father became a boyhood friend of his. My father, sister and their parents immigrated to this country in October, 1907. We know that they made their first communion together around 1908-10 in a small church in Mineville. Evidently the Markowski's moved to Detroit not much longer after that. My grandfather was a shoemaker in Mineville during that period. They too moved their family to Detroit around the same era as the parents of Vincent did. When he decided to go to Hollywood for fame and fortune he talked my father into going with him. They worked their way across the country, making a stop in Denver, where, as the family story goes, my father lost his wallet and evidently his nerve or desire to become a movie star and returned home to Detroit. He later moved back to the Mineville area, met my mother who was from Vermont, got married and started a family. At one point in time, Tom Tyler did ask my father to come to Hollywood, however, love prevailed and he remained in the area. He passed away in 1963.'"

To give sense of what mining life was like, Patrick F. Farrell pointed out in his book "Through the Light Hole," in 1912, there were 847 men working in the mines in Witherbee. The average daily wage was $2.17. There were 243 lost time injuries that year with eight fatal accidents. Mining wasn't safe and it wasn't profitable.

In 1972, I had the pleasure of speaking with actor James Pierce about his career and Tyler's. Pierce was a college football star who made the jump into acting during the silent period. He was in the cast of "Leatherstocking," along with Tyler in one of his earliest screen roles. Tyler played a Mohawk Indian. Pierce, who was the fourth man to play Tarzan on screen – he also wound up as the son-in-law of Tarzan creator Edgar Rice Burroughs – thought highly of Tyler. "He was a fine physical specimen and kept in great shape. He did most of his own stunts…. He was very sincere and honest on and off the screen." Pierce also noted Tyler had a thick accent.

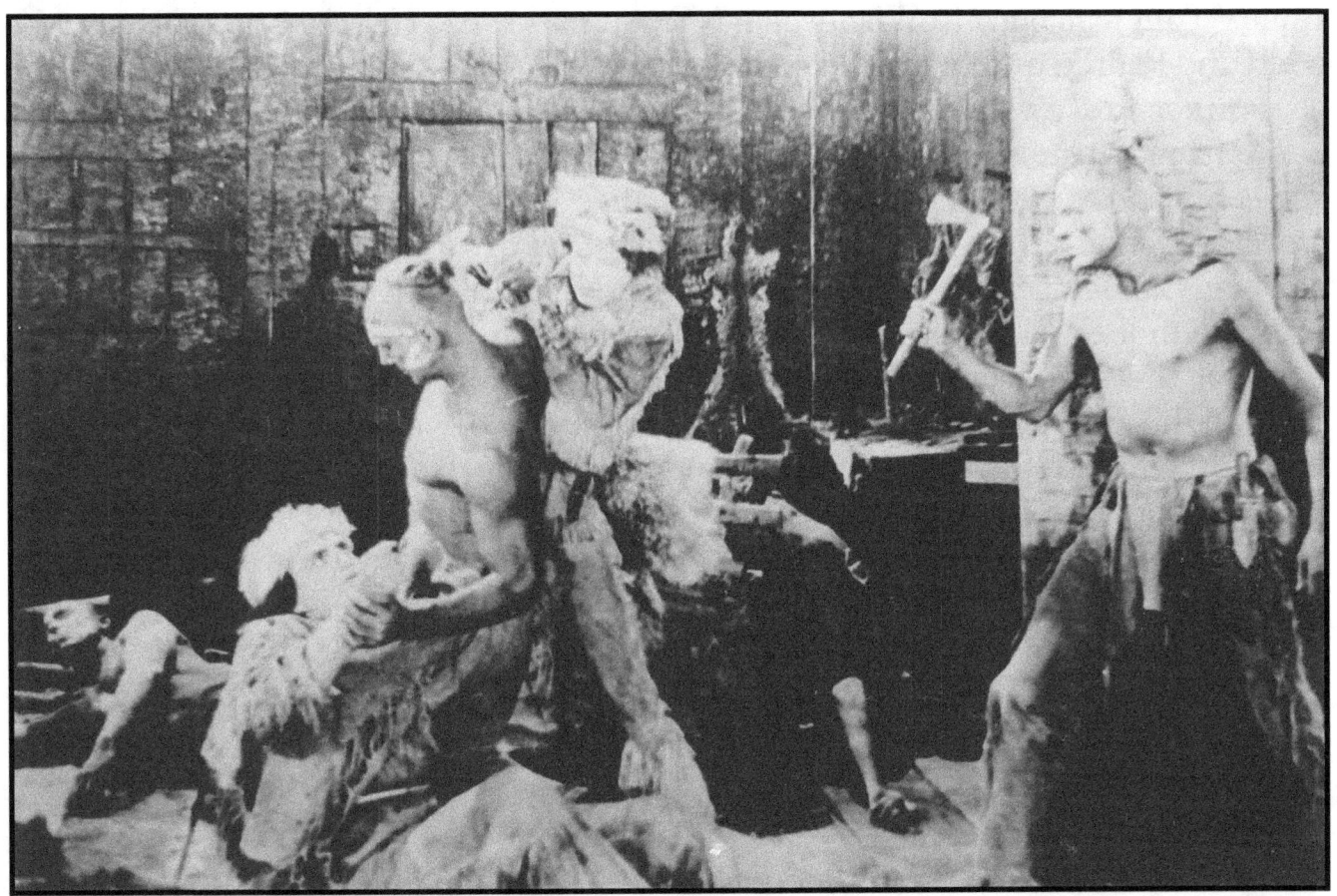

#1. James Pierce on floor with Tyler as a Mohawk native on top of him,. (Courtesy of James Pierce, author's collection)

Getting first-hand information was not as easy as I hoped it would be when I started this project as a college paper for a film class. Also in 1972, I wrote former movie actor and stunt man Joe Bonomo about Tyler as he had co-starred in two serials with him, "Phantom of the West" and "Battling with Buffalo Bill." Bonomo had come out with an autobiography but he offered me nothing about Tyler.

In 1973, I wrote writer and comic strip creator Lee Falk about his reactions to the serial based on his "Phantom" comic strip, in which Tyler starred.

He wrote back, "Unfortunately, or perhaps fortunately, I never saw 'The Phantom' serial Tom Tyler. Perhaps you could give me your opinion of that masterpiece."

When I exchanged the letters with Falk, "The Phantom" was not available for screenings.

Screen contemporary Col. Tim McCoy, who had a long starring career in westerns, told me he knew of Tyler but had never met him.

I had better luck with information when I was able to find one of Tyler's sisters, Molly Redge, in 1973 and she kindly answered some of my many questions. "Tom was born in Witherbee, NY, Aug. 9, 1903. He had two brothers, Joseph and Frank, and two sisters Molly and Catherine. Her father worked in the coal mines in New York. We went to county schools in New York. Our parents came from Lithuania. We moved to Detroit in 1919 because our father didn't want his sons to work in the mines because it was so dangerous. He went to work at Dodge's. He wanted to be an actor and always said he wanted to be a cowboy. So, he decided to go to Hollywood. He didn't have any money so I gave him the money to go. He did hitchhike out there. He went in 1922. When he first got there he worked as a weightlifter; that's how he got into the movies. At first he worked as an extra. His first picture was "Let's go Gallagher." He didn't forget his family, after he made it big. He made his father retire and supported his parents. He came back to Detroit about two times while working. He stayed with us. So many people came to see him we couldn't keep the doors closed. The last time he came back was when he was sick. He didn't want us to know he was sick, but we found out from our brother that was out there with him and we – my sister and I – talked him into coming back here. He was here about one year before he died. He had arthritis. He died at Saint Francis hospital May 1, 1954.

"Tom's real name was William Markowski."

I was shocked at the last line as every reference to his life listed the name "Vincent." This made sense though as Tyler's first stage name was "Bill Burns" and yet every reference about his name listed his first name as "Vincent."

I replied to the letter and asked some more questions. I received an unsigned letter in different handwriting, that read, "I would like to know how come you you're so interested in Tom's life. Don't you think it's kind of personal? To your first question, Tom was married. He wrote regularly to his parents but they never kept any letters. He won the weightlifting award in California. No, he did not regret playing in the westerns and I don't know where you got your information but Tom died of a heart attack, and he was not broke. I don't know why he played the mummy in 'The Mummy's Hand.' He never mentioned it. He was a very nice person, very good to his parents and other people also."

The anonymous writer also sent me Frank Tyler's address but added, "I don't know if it will be any good." After the chilly response and the veiled warning about contacting Frank, I dropped any further correspondence.

According to their Tom Tyler pages on B-westerns.com, Tyler attended St. Florian Grammar School and Hamtramck High.

Hour Detroit published a story about Tyler in 2010 by Richard Bak, and Tyler's nephew Ray Slepski was interviewed.

Bak wrote, "Vincent, one of five siblings, briefly attended Catholic schools, but like many teenagers of the era, he dropped out to enter the workforce. Factory jobs were plentiful in industrial Detroit, and he soon found one. During this period, he became interested in weightlifting and spent much of his free time chiseling his already sturdy 6-foot-2 frame. One weekend, he was competing in a bodybuilding contest at the Martha Washington Theatre on Joseph Campau when a talent agent suggested he try his luck in Hollywood."

Bak wrote the following about Frank, "His brother Frank came to California and decided to stay. He found a studio job as a gaffer and best boy, spending most of his career with Columbia Pictures. Tired of being asked why his and Tom's names were different, he changed his last name to Tyler, too."

Another one of my first attempts at an interview took place in 1974. My instructions were to drive to Witherbee, NY, from my home outside of Springfield, MA. I then had to find the pay phone that stood in the middle of the "town" and call Wesley Cembalski, the man who said he knew Tom Tyler when Tyler's family lived here at the turn of the 20th Century.

The telephone call followed hours of driving into upstate New York.

Cembalski then gave me some additional driving directions and I went to his nearby home. He greeted me with the warning that his retirement job was selling headstones and that he could be called away at any moment to sell someone a grave marker.

He apparently was old enough to have known Tyler's family, the Markowskis personally. He recounted the church in the mining community showed silent films in its basement and this might have been the first time Tyler saw any sort of movie.

He then hinted the family's move to Michigan was brought on by some sort of scandal that involved Tyler's brother Frank. He would say no more unless he got paid.

I was simply a college student working his way through school. There was no extra money to pay for an interview. The visit ended after that.

Tyler did make it to Los Angeles but it took him several years to break into the film industry. Writer Dorothy Calhoun apparently interviewed Tyler for Motion Picture Classic in July 1928. Articles such as these were usually arranged with the studio, in this case FBO but I think there are some truthful statements in it and worthy of reprinting:

The Sucker who Succeeded

His kids sister shrilled, "Mama, Tom's doing it again! Mama, he's got his face all painted funny and he's talking to his self."

His mother said worriedly, "Tom if you put any more of that nasty dirt stuff on your face I'll tell your father and he will give you a licking. Sometimes I think you're crazy, spending good money on that on such trash! It's going to it's going to those awful nickelodeons that's done it.

His father, heavy-handed superintendent of the iron ore mines on Lake Champlain, said grimly, "Not another word do you hear me? My son an actor! Fine business for a healthy man. You're going to learn to be an automotive mechanic and make a decent living."

The letter from the correspondent school said, "Dear Sir, we are sending you the makeup kit. We feel sure you have great talent and will succeed on the screen. Kindly send the second installment, $5 and the next lesson, 'Screen Technique' will be mailed promptly. Yours truly, the [blank] correspondence school of screen acting.

He was 17, tall, gangling. Evenings he would run himself ragged carrying heavy cans of film from one movie house to another two miles away but he barely moved in answer to a call for a bucket of coal for the kitchen stove. He was driving a truck and saving up his money. When he had enough for his fare to California, he was going out to be a movie hero, like Eddie Polo or Hobart Bosworth. But not like Bill Hart. He didn't like westerns. He always walked out when the first shot of sagebrush flashed on the screen. Besides he was scared of horses.

Meanwhile he was learning how to be a movie actor so to be ready. The lessons covered everything: how to make up as an old man; how to register the different emotions, rage grief fear; how to be a comedian; how to dress for society parts. Some of them were sort of hard to do alone but it wasn't safe to ask the family to help. Better lock the door while you practice the lesson on "How to Make Love" and you've got one on screen fighting where you had to choke yourself. It was wiser to do it in the barn where you could make plenty of noise without attracting attention.

This isn't the story of "Merton of the Movies." But it might be. Tom Tyler, cowboy star, tells these things with immense seriousness. His suit fits with suave and expensive perfection over his great muscles and it has been many a year since a maternal voice warned, "Tom, brush your hair. It's a sight!" But he is still the type of earnest youngster who reads success stories and believes in them, who scans advertisements promising to reveal the secret of getting ahead in 12 easy lessons and clips the coupon. He is still the youngster who (rather grimy, not so well pressed) alighted from a freight train in Los Angeles six years ago and looked eagerly around him.

With him he carried his most precious possession a letter from the Johnson Screen Training School to the Hollywood movie magnates beginning "To whom it might concern." The letter went on to assure Mr. Lasky or Mr. Goldwyn that the bearer had completed with honor the course on screen acting and was ready to go to work. "We recommend Mr. Tyler (the name written in the letter.) It went on to reassure any still hesitating producer as "either a hero heavy or comedian and promise you will make no mistake in employing him."

In the course of the next three years this letter was to be laid trustingly and then not quite so trustingly before the delighted gaze of many casting directors until finally it was so worn with handling that it was hardly legible. "By that time, I had sort of lost faith in it." admits Tom, "and I threw it in the waste paper basket.

"I wouldn't wish what I've been through for anyone," he says. "For more than a year I didn't have any room. I sleep on the hillsides and in alleys and packing boxes. I'm hungry most of the time."

The present tense does something startling – vital – to his tale, the commonplace odyssey of a struggling movie extra.

"Between jobs I get other work when I can. I wash dishes and dumps on the Boulevard – they let you eat first. Three times I start to write home and ask for money to come back. But my dad said when I left all right go and keep on going so I tear up the letters. I've lived for months on 15 or 20 cents a day for food. There's still a mission on Spring Street where you can get a bowl of Lima bean soup and all the bread you can eat for six cents. I couldn't eat food like that now and there are other ways. I need to go on those free rubber neck rides the real estate salesman and oil operators give. Had to listen to a lot of hot air but they always serve a free lunch."

For three years Tom Tyler tramped from lot to lot. During all that time he was keeping fit for his chance when it did come. Four times a week he exercised at the YMCA gymnasium though sometimes his knees were so shaky that he could hardly stand. And the YMCA gave him his chance. One day the bored eye of the casting director fell on his biceps. "You in the back there," he shouted, "The husky guy with the black hair come on in."

Tom Tyler had a job. He was hired as an Indian chief for $50 a week for a serial. He was a movie actor at last.

"I write home," says Tom "and tell the folks what I'm making but they don't believe me. And when I send them two stills from the picture showing me with my head shaved and my face painted they know I'm NOT lying!"

After the serial, his broad shoulders won him the part of a Prussian officer in one of Elinor Glyn's pictures. The skin tight uniform showed his YMCA built muscles to such advantage that Madame Glyn's eyes singled him out and he was summoned to her side.

"I'm looking for a man to do a bit in the picture," she told him, "and I believe you've got the build for it. Take off your coat please."

Tom blushed, "I can't do that," he muttered, "because well I haven't got anything on underneath.

"Quite all right," said sweetly the Glyn. "Take it off."

Before 200 extras Tom stripped to the waist and got the part. Then FBO needed a western hero and sent for him. "Can you ride?" they asked and Tom, without flinching answered "Sure."

Tyler is seen here with the studio owner, Joseph P. Kennedy and his director Robert De Lacey on the FBO lot.

Two weeks before his first picture was to start one of the cowboys on the FBO lot was approached by a white-faced youngster whom he recognized as a western star. "I want," he said and swallowed hard, "I want a horse to ride around a little and get in practice."

The cowboy led out "Flashlight." A huge stallion rearing as he came, saddled him and handed the reins to Tom. Clumsily the new Wild West hero scrambled aboard and clung desperately to the horses mane. "Gosh, fella," whistled the cowboy, "how long have you been riding?"

"I've never been on a horse before in my life," Tom Tyler confessed.

Two weeks later he galloped over the crest of the hill in pursuit of the outlaw gang and the director murmured to a newspaper reporter, "Yes a real cowboy, right off the ranch!"

So, let's unpack this a bit. Tyler did the extra work on "Three Weeks," the Elinor Glyn movie in 1924. Glyn was a very well-known author of both books and movie scripts who specialized in sexy romances. She is the one to coin the phrase "It," meaning sex appeal.

His role in "Leatherstocking," in 1924, has been documented.

I have no doubt the recounting of his poverty while trying to establish himself was truthful. Tyler was like thousands of people in the 1920s who thought they could have a career in the movies.

As far as his casting at FBO, he was among a group of candidates and according to other sources, he did not know how to ride a horse.

Tyler's friend, Oliver Drake, recalled Tyler's early years, in his book, "Written Produced & Directed by Oliver Drake." He wrote, "So I ended up in San Bernardino filming 'Means and Motors,' a two-reel comedy and we soon had a goodly crowd of townspeople watching us shoot chase scenes from the bed of a flatbed truck. It was while I was working for Shellcraft that I met a young man by the name of Bill Burns. He was husky, well built, over 6 feet tall, and one of the champion amateur weight lifters of the world. He was sponsored by the Los Angeles Athletic Club but received no food or pay from the members. He lived in a cheap room in Boyle Heights and walked several miles to Hollywood to be at some studio when the gates opened. If he did not get a job at one studio, he'd walk to another. About twice a week, he came by Cosmo Art and was usually hungry so I would take him out for donuts and coffee. While we didn't see each other very much, we met about every other week and ate at a little restaurant near Third and Spring where we could have dinner for 15 cents. Bill was as excited about westerns as I was and talked about becoming a western star. We became pals, and he soon became part of our circle of friends."

Here is a shot of Tyler just after the announcement that he would be the new cowboy star for FBO in August 1925.

This account certainly seems to confirm elements of the fan magazine story. Tyler lived in poverty before his break at FBO and tried his best to work his way into the motion picture business. His career at the studio is discussed in the next chapter.

His name apparently was an issue. FBO certainly didn't want his birth name, and apparently "Bill Burns" was not acceptable either. He was given "Tom Tyler" and then made it legal.

Headline: Gets Irish name for movie parts (Los Angeles Record April 5, 1926).

"'What chance has a fellow with my name winning Irish parts in movies, judge?' appealed Joseph [sic] Markowski to Judge Stevens when he appeared before the court asking that his name be changed. Markowski, according to his statement, was finding it increasingly difficult to convince casting directors that he was just the Irish type they wanted, in spite of the fact that he makes a completely satisfactory son of Erin on the screen. 'I want my name changed to Tom Tyler judge,' Markowski said. Judge Stevens, with a few scratches of his pen, granted the request."

FBO certainly cranked up the publicity machine for Tyler and notices started to appear outside of the trade papers.

(Los Angeles Evening Citizen April 20, 1926) "Tom Tyler, FBO western star, wants to make 10 real pictures instead of the five-reelers they insist on putting him in. Dorothy Dunbar, recently signed by FBO to a long-term contract, is playing opposite him in his current production, 'The Masquerade Bandit,' and now Tom complains that he can't do his stuff properly in a mere 5,000 feet of film.

This is an unusual story as Tyler is still a new "star" but he is interested in more challenging films, something to which he alludes in other publicity to come.

The downside to publicity also made itself known. (May 9, 1928, Los Angeles Times)

"Five weeks ago, Ethlyn Claire was engaged as leading woman for Tom Tyler, western hero of the screen. Yesterday her friends in Hollywood said this meeting five weeks ago has developed into an interesting romance which may end in her signing as the leading woman for life. Miss Claire, a Titian haired beauty, was asked about it. She would neither deny nor affirm the

Tyler's career as a weightlifter reached the top – AAU records and selection to go to the 1928 Olympics. December 1926.

reports but indicated there is a possibility of their being engaged. 'It's a little too early to say anything definite,' Miss Claire said. 'Tom and I are very dear friends but that is all I can say at the present. You had better see me sometime later or ask Tom.' Tyler couldn't be located for his version. Miss Claire came to Hollywood some time ago and played in Century comedies before graduating to Universal as a leading woman. At the expiration of her contract, she went to FBO where she already had completed two pictures as Tyler's leading woman."

It looks like Claire wanted some press.

Tyler's career as a weightlifter received quite a bit of attention during his time at FBO.

Detroit Free Press, June 3, 1928, noted that Tyler was hoping to land a spot on the Olympic weight-lifting team for the Amsterdam games.

(Redondo Daily Breeze, June 20, 1928) "Tom Tyler, western star, is on leave of absence from the flickers to train for the Olympics. He holds the AAU record for weight lifting and tossing 297 pounds."

(Hollywood Daily Citizen Aug. 28, 1926) "Tom Tyler, motion picture actor, today is the new amateur weightlifting champion. In a series of weightlifting contests, Tyler succeeded in beating Dave Willoughby, Jerry Kingsbury, Bill Petrie and Romaine Straight at the Los Angeles Athletic Club. Tyler said a new amateur mark of 206 pounds for the two-handed snatch. He holds records of 218 and 200 and 286 pounds in the one and two hand clean and jerk respectively."

Tyler made the Olympic weightlifting team, however the American Olympic Committee decided not to send the team to the 1928 Amsterdam Olympics. It's interesting to note that two of Tyler's action hero contemporaries, Herman Brix, better known as Bruce Bennett and Buster Crabbe, were at that Olympics and both were medalists.

The merger of FBO into RKO and the dismissal of all of its stars in 1929 meant a major event in Tyler's life and career as is detailed in Chapter Three. He persevered though, landing work at independents Syndicate, Mascot, Monogram and Frueler.

After his dismissal from FBO, Tyler, according to Oliver Drake, sold his car and house. In the 1930 census "26-year-old Thomas Tyler (born New York) was a roomer living with Edward M. and Irene C. Bottar at 212 South Hamilton Drive, Beverly Hills, California. He was single, occupation was 'Actor – Movies,'" reported B-westerns.com from the census.

During his brief stay at Freuler, Tom's by-line appeared in the November 1933, edition of Broadway and Hollywood Movies, a fan magazine.

It's interesting to see a B-western actor working at an indie studio get this kind of publicity. I would guess part of it comes due to his nearly seven years as an actor. Tyler was a known western star. Needless to say, I don't believe for a moment that Tyler actually wrote this story, especially since he had expressed interest in non-western roles.

It's the type of publicity designed to draw attention to these westerns.

Tyler (allegedly) wrote, "It's the John Barrymores who get the orchids but the cowboys get the punches into pictures – and get a great kick out of it!

"I have all the respect and admiration in the world for those real actors who get fat screen roles who are masters of an art and who deserve and receive the adulation of countless thousands of fans in this country – and elsewhere – but honestly I wouldn't change my horse for Romeo's ladder nor would I trade it for the swankiest chaise lounge in the friendliest boudoir that Maurice Chevalier ever sang a theme song!

"'Four-star hits'" may mean something different to the critics but to me it means just that! Giving a guy everything you have in your two clenched fists – and may the blows fall where they may!

"Although I'm not a native westerner having been born at Port Henry NY (and proud of it!) I've been roaming the boundless plains for lo these many years that I seem to feel more at home with a coyote than a pom [Pomeranian] and enjoy sleeping beneath the stars on a treeless rim better than the swellest feather bed set up you could imagine! Honest!

"Gosh, I can remember when I first appeared in a western although I can't recall the incident of all the particulars. I do seem to remember I was one of the 'bad men' and what a stiff fight I put up before the director cautioned me that I was prolonging the footage and I grudgingly realized that I had to 'give in.' Gee I didn't want to! A good thing too that it wasn't a sound film because the director would not have been able to call me the miscellaneous kinds of so and so that he lavished on my too vigorous portrayal. In fact, my distaste for curtailing a fight that went to my boyish heart like wine was brought to an abrupt end when a hero grabbed a stout chair and made contact with my head that gave me my first general idea of what a four-star picture can be! Stars! Boy I saw 'em! Of course it was my own fault, I should have realized that when you're on the wrong side of a story you just got to give in gracefully or take it!

"And I guess the boys who appear in films can do that!

Don't get any idea that the fights we put on are any pink teas! If you're not the equal of the best just forget all about action films – they're not yours. On the other hand, if you've never itched to do Hamlet or can watch Clark Gable without getting a yen to double for him, you'll find acting in westerns more fun than watching them.

"I've fought amateur champions and even fellows who have first rate reputations in the professional class. And they don't know what it means to pull a punch. And I've gotten many a thrill out of it and have enjoyed it so keenly that some of my bruises I've given and taken are pretty near hospital cases! It's all been done in good spirit though and I've yet to meet the man who harbored a grudge when the camera stopped shooting.

"But let me draw off my 10-gallon for a moment to the many pretty ladies whom I've appeared with in countless pictures and who have the stuff of which stardom is made. Take for instance Caryl Lincoln one of the most charming and most beautiful girls who appear on the screen. Miss Lincoln has been borrowed from Paramount to appear opposite me in my latest Monarch production 'War of the Range' (which I hope you'll be seeing soon!)

"Here is a little lady who rides like a veteran in spite of her youthfulness, who, during the film, is required to sit in a wagon when her horses run away and who does so with calm and poise of the most hardened cow lad! No, not for a moment is the field opened alone to men who fight, gals who dare are equally welcome to the fraternity of the West – where men are men – and the girls are heroines!"

After being away from his family for nearly a decade, Tyler came home, as his sister told me. (Detroit Free Press, Dec. 25, 1934) Tyler spent Christmas with his family. "Tyler manufacturers western pictures so fast he doesn't remember the name of the picture he worked in just before leaving California for Detroit. He is, however, sorry he didn't bring his horse he said for he thinks he could probably navigate our slippery streets better on horseback." Newspaper ads showed that Tyler's films played widely in the Detroit area and through Michigan.

The next year he returned. (Jan. 2, 1935, Detroit Free Press) "Tom Tyler, star of western movies, who is visiting his parents in Hamtramck is getting his first taste of cold weather in a long time. He lived in Hamtramck before going to Hollywood where he has made some 65 western pictures and five [at this point he had made four serials. This is the first time he has seen his father, Frank Markowski, in nine years. Tyler stayed at his parents' home on Mitchell Avenue for the holidays on his way to New York. He plans to leave Wednesday and return in several days for a second brief stay. Monday he appeared at a dinner given for 40 boys of poor families by the Opt-Lite club in Saint Ann's community house."

What was his New York vacation like? We have it documented by TV legend Ed Sullivan.

Silver Screen fan magazine October 1935 published a story written by Ed Sullivan – then a New York newspaper columnist and years before his incarnation as a TV variety show host – about Loretta Young visiting New York City for vacation. Young, who was a top star at that point, was accompanied by Dorothy di Frasso, Sullivan and Tyler.

Tyler clearly traveled among the upper echelons of Hollywood.
The NYC vacation was also mentioned in the Jan. 5, 1935, edition of The Film Daily.

Sullivan wrote, "It was on a cold wet day that Dorothy di Frasso, Tom Tyler, Loretta and myself visited the New York aquarium. Dorothy born in New York had never seen the aquarium close up for her only view of the circular squat building at the tip of Manhattan island had been from the deck of the wrecks or Ile de France streaming down the Bay. Tyler, the western star, had never seen it, and neither had Loretta, so I acted as chauffeur and guide.

"The rain was pelting down when I parked the car at Battery Park. Occasionally the driving patches of fog that blotted out the ruffled waters of the harbor lifted long enough to permit a blurred view of the Statue of Liberty. "The aquarium," I said in my best man about town voice, was originally Castle Garden an immigration depot and it was at Castle Garden that Jenny Lind, the Swedish Nightingale sang at her American premiere in September 1850. Miss Young broke in, "Listen, Edwin we came here to see the fishes. The Countess de Frasso said, "My God do you remember that far back?" Tyler grinned sympathetically. I chilled the young girl and the Countess with a look of complete scorn. Furthermore, Loretta, I said the name is not Edwin, it is Edward and she smiled brightly, "I like Edwin better."

Later in the story, Young said she understands how the fish may feel being on display with people staring at them. "I know just how those fishes feel, don't you Tom?" said Miss Young as we halted at an illuminated tank. "Everybody staring at them, no privacy."

Tyler was there with di Frasso, rather than Young. At a party, also conducted in 1936, Tyler is seen in a photo spread with the likes of Richard Barthelmess, Charlie Chaplin, Jack Oakie and other "A" lister Hollywood stars. Standing next to him at the party was the infamous di Frasso, a New Yorker, whose family wealth enabled her of a lifetime of very high living and multiple husbands, as well as multiple lovers, covered by considerable press.

According to The Ancient and Esoteric Order of the Jackalope podcast, "She was married to a count and lived in Italy until she met Gary Cooper and resulting affair propelled her to move to Hollywood, set up an impressive mansion and divorce her husband.

"She also started throwing her legendary parties and became known as a prominent hostess.

"It wasn't long before the Countess di Frasso was the top hostess in Hollywood. If you received an invitation to one of her soirées, you knew you had made it. Guests rubbed shoulders with Hollywood royalty like Fred Astaire, Lionel Barrymore, Charles Boyer, Dolores Del Rio, Marlene Dietrich, Douglas Fairbanks Jr., Clark Gable, Samuel Goldwyn, Frederick March, Norma Shearer, Irving Thalberg, Fay Wray, and Loretta Young. She even extended invitations to that young up-and-comer Cary Grant, much to Cooper's dis-

The Countess Di Frasso, the most popular hostess in Hollywood, with some of her guests at her recent costume party. Jack Oakie, Tom Tyler and Richard Barthelmess are having a good time.

Tyler is among the guests at a costume party hosted by Countess di Frasso as noted by Silver Screen magazine, August 1935.

"In June 1935 she threw a costume party where guests were instructed to come dressed as someone from history they admired. The Countess herself dressed as Stravinsky's Firebird (which is sort of cheating), but her good friend Marlene Dietrich was the one who made headlines by dressing as Leda, a costume that consisted of a skimpy dress in the shape of a swan. [And if that sounds familiar to you, it's because Björk wore a recreation of that dress to the Oscars in 2001.]

"As for her love life, well, the Countess continued to have affairs with everyone in Hollywood who wasn't Gary Cooper. Her sexual conquests included director Johnny Farrow; screenwriters Rowland Brown, Willis Goldbeck, and Ben Hecht; actors Reggie Gardiner, William Powell, Lyle Talbot, and Tom Tyler; Olympic bobsledder Freddie McEvoy; a parade of aristocratic European himbos; and even Cary Grant (I hear he's the new Gary Cooper)."

Tyler was traveling in some pretty racy circles. Pretty impressive for a guy who was making B westerns.

What did his co-stars think of him? The memories of Frank Coghlan Jr. and William "Billy" Benedict are in the chapter about his Republic films. Thanks to interviews conducted by Mike Fitzgerald and Boyd Magers at www.Westernclippings.com (another vital website for the study of westerns), we get an idea of Tyler's reputation.

Louise Currie

Currie was the female lead in "Adventures of Capt. Marvel." "The situations were exciting. I didn't do much except be a victim on most of the cliffhangers. Tom Tyler was a wonderful, but a quiet man…a nice fellow, attractive, a good person, but he was shy! Frank Coghlan Jr., Billy Benedict and I had lots of fun together, but Tom never seemed to join us in our good times. Those two boys are very talented, super to work with. They really knew what they were doing. Such fine young actors. We chatted, laughed and enjoyed working together. Tom stayed by himself, but again, he couldn't have been nicer. It's just too bad he didn't become pals like Frank and Billy and I did."

Barbara Weeks appeared with Tyler in "Two-Fisted Justice."

"Yes, actually that was made before I went to Columbia—it was a little Monogram picture. I remember Yakima Canutt, who was an Indian and who did a lot of stunts. He was a very talented guy. Tom Tyler was the cowboy star…he was a good-looking hunk but dumb as a duck (Laughs). Luckily, I had learned to ride in Central Park in New York, and I had my own horse, named Flapper, in California. So, all the riding scenes were never any trouble for me!"

Roberta Gale – worked with Tyler twice in "Mystery Ranch" and "Terror of the Plains" in her career of 17 films

"Asked about Tom Tyler, she states rather meanly, '"He was tall and handsome and couldn't act. What more is there?" And Bob Steele, her other twice-leading man, "A little shrimp who couldn't act, but could ride those horses well, at least."'

Julie Bishop, also known as Jacqueline Wells, had a very interesting and lengthy career appearing with Buster Crabbe, W.C. Fields, Boris Karloff, Bela Lugosi and Laurel and Hardy, among others. She appeared with Tyler in the Universal serial, "Clancy of the Mounted." "Tom Tyler was so handsome, so tall, and his voice – striking. But he was a man and I was a child playing a grown-up – something that happened quite a bit in those days, for some reason. So, naturally, we never dated or anything like that! I thought the serial was marvelous, incidentally."

Lois Collier, also an actor with a long and varied career, co-starred in many of Tyler's Three Mesquiteers films at Republic.

"Receiving her first real break, Lois was referred to as the 4th Mesquiteer as she played the lead in seven of Republic's Three Mesquiteers B-westerns, more than any other actress. 'I enjoyed them. I was just starting and it was good experience. Of course, I wanted something bigger! The people at Republic were all nice. Tom Tyler later did some 'Boston Blackie's and we'd talk about those old days, making the Mesquiteers. Tom was a real quiet, nice man. Bob Steele was a real westerner. Both were good actors. Horses scared me, they still do. I hated 'em. When we'd be on location, I'd look around and Bob Steele would have made his horse stand directly over my head, as if it were going to kick me. He thought that was so funny. I didn't, as those creatures frighten me. The director yelled they could have a big lawsuit here, but that didn't stop Bob and his practical jokes. Horses are beautiful animals, but if they all disappeared off the face of the earth tomorrow it would be just fine with me. I'd rather have a dog!"

Marion Shilling appeared with Tyler in "Rio Rattler"

"A handsome big mass of muscle. Always prompt and knew his lines but very quiet. He was in the midst of a torrid romance with Marlene Dietrich and during the day was probably 'in recovery'."

Beth Marion appeared with Tyler in two of his Victory productions, "Rip Roaring Buckeroo" and "The Phantom of the Range."

"He was a very handsome fellow. Very happily married. He also drove me back to town one time; we had a nice long visit. I was really shocked to hear he'd died early in life. He had surgery for, I believe, an ulcer and they cut the Vegus nerve. From then on, his health went right down. I always thought, more than over-pronouncing his words, he maybe had a little accent and was trying to overcome that."

So, the general assessment was that Tyler was a professional on set, who was nice but shy with people.

I think it would be interesting to include the observations of Peggy Moran, the female lead of "The Mummy's Hand." She was interviewed for the on-line publication, Monster Kid Magazine (https://gammillustrations.bizland.com/monsterkid2/index.html). Here is the exchange between Moran and the interviewer Domenic Florentino: Do you remember when they first said to you that you were going to be in this picture, 'The Mummy's Hand?'

"No, I don't remember anything about it. I only knew I was making it. I do remember that I didn't know if I was going to scream or not because I had never practiced a scream because the whole neighborhood would have descended upon me, you know. So, I didn't know if I could scream or not. Also, in 'The Mummy's Hand' I never met the actor without his makeup on. I didn't even know his name. They couldn't even introduce me because he couldn't talk. So, we just did scenes together and I never knew who he was.

You never saw him outside the makeup?

"Never saw him. I heard later he was an actor by the name of Tom Tyler. I wouldn't even know him if I saw a picture of him. I don't know if he's still alive."

Although there are certainly gaps in Tyler's private life, his marriage and its dissolve have certainly caused much interest and speculation.

Tyler was married after his stint with Sam Katzman's Victory Pictures was over. Of those eight westerns, his bride-to-be Jeanne Martel had co-starred in two of

HOLLYWOOD COUPLE WED

Tom Tyler, star of western films, shown as he left the altar yesterday with his bride. She is the former Jeanne Martele, also known on stage and screen. (P) photo

Tom Tyler, Cowboy Film Star, Married to Actress at Church

Tyler and his bride appeared in the Los Angeles Times on Sept. 4, 1937.

them. Martel was born Jeanne E. Nelson on March 1, 1915, in Pennsylvania, and passed away April 24, 1980, in the Ventura, California area, according to B-westerns.com.

In his story, Richard Bak wrote, "On Sept. 8, 1937, following a five-month romance, Tyler married actress Jeanne Martel in Los Angeles. The violet-eyed brunette, described as a Joan Crawford look-alike, had lived in Detroit for a time when she was a girl. She was several years younger than Tyler, who told the press he was "mainly interested in Jeanne as the grand wife she is and not the great star she might someday become." He called her "Punky."

Tyler and his soon-to-be wife actress Jeanne Martel from the film "The Lost Ranch." (author's collection)

Los Angeles Evening Citizen News, Sept. 3, 1937, reported, "Tom Tyler, hero of many a western, will be married at 7:00 to Jeanne Martel, screen-actress.
Their romance began 18 months ago when the two met on the RKO lot during the filming of 'The Last Outlaw.' They will be married in formal rights in the little Church of the Flowers in Forest Lawn Memorial Park. Mrs. Edward

Everett Louderback, mother of the bride, will be her only attendant and William Mieklejohn, Tyler's business manager will be his best man. A reception will follow at the home of Doctor and Mrs. Stetson Humphrey. Tomorrow night the actor will fly to Georgia where the actor is to continue a personal appearance tour. 'That won't be over until November so our real honey honeymoon will begin then,' Miss Martell said."

Variety also took note of the nuptials with a story datelined Atlanta, GA and dated Sept.14, "Trekking hither and yon in the smaller burgs of this state via trailer is Jeanne Martel, now the wife of Tom Tyler, horse opera film star, leading attraction of the Wallace Brothers circus. Tyler got leave of absence and left the three-ringer at Rome, GA, flying to Glendale, CA where he married miss Martel. They flew back to Georgia and rejoined the circus in Columbus, [GA], Sept. 6 and have settled down to circus life together. Girl, a native of Allentown, PA, got her chance in films at bridegroom's request and she and Tyler appeared together in a number of westerns before he went out with circus for season Sept. 15, 1937."

Newspaper accounts show that Tyler and his bride visited the family in the Detroit area about two months after their nuptials.

Martel apparently left acting after her marriage. She had appeared in seven roles – three with Tyler at Victory; two at Victory with Herman Brix/ Bruce Bennett; an MGM short titled "What do You Think?' and finally as an uncredited role of a cigarette girl in "Bringing Up Baby" in 1938.

Various researchers have tried to find out more about their marriage, including a date for the divorce. Based on my own research it is apparent that either the family was not told any details or they simply don't want to speak about it in depth.

According to the 1940 Los Angeles census, in 1939, Tyler worked 13 weeks and earned $5,000-plus. No occupation listed for his wife. The census taker visited on May 6, 1940, and Tom and Jean (Jeanne) were still married, again according to B-western.com.

Based on his research, Bak wrote he believes Tyler's development of scleroderma, the rare autoimmune disease for which there is still no cure that ultimately killed him, was in part at least the cause for his marriage failure. Nephew Ray Slepski told him that Martel could not live with the disease. "Tyler's young wife could not live with his condition. 'They got divorced,' Slepski said, "The story we always heard was that she ran off with some other guy."

Bak wrote about the condition Tyler had. "In addition to thickening of the skin, the disease also can wreak havoc with the victim's internal organs. According to literature from the Scleroderma Foundation in Byfield, Mass., 'The same process going on in the skin can enmesh the lungs in strands of scar tissue so dense that the victim struggles for air. Scar tissue in the esophagus makes swallowing painful and troublesome. In the digestive tract it inhibits the absorption of nutrients. Joints all over the body might throb with pain. Kidney involvement is particularly treacherous. It leads to high blood pressure and kidney failure.'"

Here is another part of this mystery. When Republic issued its pressbook for "Adventures of Captain Marvel" – the over-sized booklet sent to theater managers to show them how to market a movie – it carried a brief biography of Tyler. After noting his athletic accomplishments as well as some of his movie credits, the anonymous writer continued, "Tyler is married and has one child. His pet hobbies are golf, tennis and swimming."

A child? Nowhere have I seen that before. Did the Republic press department get something wrong? Did they make something up? Was it a painful memory that family members did not want to bring up?

By the way, in other press accounts, Tyler was described as a homebody who liked to cook and do woodworking.

Bak also quoted Slepski about Tyler's business acumen, "Like many actors, he had displayed little business sense. He and a partner once opened a realty office on North Vine in Hollywood and somehow managed not to make any money during Southern California's real-estate boom. 'One time, some guy wanted him to invest $1,100 in distributing a new lemon-lime soft drink, but he said no,' Slepski says. 'The soft drink was 7 Up.'"

A search indicated that Tyler and a business partner named Willett were in the real estate and insurance business in 1934 as there were many real estate listings for their firm in the classified sections of Los Angeles Times that year.

Tyler did enlist for the draft in World War II with his registration dated Feb. 14, 1942 – "38-year-old Tom Tyler was born August 9, 1903, in Witherbee, New York. He lived at 3096 Lake Hollywood Drive, Los Angeles; employer was Republic Studios; he was 6 feet, 1 inch tall and weighed 200 pounds; and contact was Paul Wilkins, 8853 Sunset Boulevard" from B-westerns.com.

Although as this book will attest, Tyler acted as long as his health circumstances allowed. In a story about Detroit residents succeeding in the movies in the Detroit Free Press on March 16, 1946, Tyler was hailed as an outstanding villain in "San Antonio" with Errol Flynn.

A recurring rumor has been that Tyler's facial features started to look differently about 1947, the year in which he made only one screen appearance in "Cheyenne." Film producer and historian Sam Sherman told me that Tyler had been in a car accident and has received reconstructive surgery on his face. Certainly, the scleroderma was making notable changes in his physique, but I've been unable to find any information to corroborate the rumor about plastic surgery.

Another unconfirmed story is that infamous low-budget director Ed Wood met Tyler by hitting him with his car! According to the story, Wood did not injure Tyler in the traffic accident and after picking him up Wood insisted on giving Tyler, who was walking, a ride. Wood recognized Tyler, who initially wouldn't identify himself. Eventually, Tyler admitted who he was.

If true, this may be how Wood hired Tyler for his half-hour color television pilot "The Crossroads Avenger" in 1953, one of the last acting jobs Tyler had. I have to admit skepticism as it's a strange "meet cute" sort of story. My late friend, film producer and historian Alex Gordon, who knew well of my interest in Tyler, was an associate of Wood's early in Gordon's career. He never once mentioned the story to me.

As the letter from Tyler's sister Molly said, he spent about the last year of his life living with his sister Katherine Slepski in her Hamtramck home. His illness was so severe that he could no longer work and live on his own.

Writer Richard Bak wrote, "He arrived at his sister's house one November day in 1952, virtually penniless. His nephew, then a young teenager, surrendered his bedroom — which was directly across from the only bathroom in the house – and moved into another one down the hall. 'The bathroom had one of those steam cabinets, and he liked to use it,' Slepski says. 'It seemed to help his hands and his skin a little.'"

Bak continued, "In Hamtramck, Tyler spent most days in a chair in the sun room, overlooking a grassy lot. In nice weather, he sometimes would sit on the front porch and patiently answer neighbors' questions about Hollywood and its stars. He shuffled instead of walked, and his gnarled hands had a hard time gripping his favorite summer food, corn on the cob. His lips retracted and his teeth and eyes bulged. His skin was taut, discolored, and leather-like. 'He was not pleasant to look at,' Slepski says. 'It really took a toll on my mother. She was a saintly woman. She never complained and neither did my dad.

In those days, family took care of family. There never was any question that we would take care of Uncle Tom.'"

Actor turned Detroit broadcaster, Tom Kennedy had been introduced to Tyler near the end of his career. Kennedy had worked in B westerns himself. He spoke to Bak about how Gene Autry had hired Tyler on his television show. Bak wrote, "'We all knew that Tom was terminal and that Gene had hired him as a tribute,' Kennedy said in a 1997 interview. 'We loved Gene for this gesture. Tom gave a superlative performance in both segments. We spent a week with Tom, and I got to talk to him about his fascinating career. He knew Doug Fairbanks, Valentino, John Gilbert, Tom Mix, William S. Hart, Chaplin. John Ford liked him, as well as many other famous directors of that time.'"

Tyler's grave marker. Courtesy of https://www.findagrave.com.

Another point of contention in the stories about Tyler was his finances. Some reference that he was "broke" or "penniless" at the time he moved back to live with his sister. The anonymous letter writer told me he was not "broke." Death came to the actor on May 1, 1954. Officially he died from a heart attack, but that was part of the complications due to his scleroderma. Ray Slepski told Bak, "He'd been looking a little better, so it actually was a shock when he died that night,' Slepski says.

"'Word got out that, hey, this was a movie actor,' Slepski says. 'He was laid out at Wysocki Funeral Home on McNichols, a couple blocks from our house.

It was a small funeral parlor, and I remember it being so crowded. People were coming from all over the country. Guys with cowboy hats, old actors, kids who saw him on TV, just a ton of people.'"

"A police escort was needed for the 65-car procession from the funeral home to Mount Olivet Cemetery, where Tyler was buried in the Markowski family plot. A stone marker bears an image of him in a cowboy hat."

Tyler's death was noted by the UPI with an obituary. The obituary's headline read, "Tom Tyler, film cowboy made famous by TV dies.

"Services will be held Wednesday for Tom Tyler, 50, a former motion picture cowboy, who gained a new following among the nation's young television fans. Tyler, his fortune dwindling and his stardom a thing of the past, died of a heart attack Saturday night in Saint Francis Hospital in suburban Hamtramck, his boyhood home. Although he no longer ranked as a Hollywood star, Tyler's fame began to soar in recent years among children who watched his old films on television. But Tyler gained nothing from TV personally. He had neglected to buy the rights to his old pictures. Tyler, whose real name was Vincent Marko, [sic] returned to Detroit 18 months ago and was living at the home of a sister, Mrs. Katherine Slepski. He had given up his Hollywood career eight years ago. Among pictures in which Tyler had feature parts were 'Cheyenne,' 'She wore a Yellow Ribbon,' 'San Antonio' and 'The Beautiful Blonde from Bashful Bend,' 'Younger brothers' and 'Hellfire.' In 1942, he was honored for his audience drawing ability in the Motion Picture Herald's fame poll. To many he was well known as one of The Three Mesquiteers. He was born in Port Henry, NY and entered movies in 1927 and in 1937 he married actress Jean Martel. For 14 years before his entrance into movies he held the world's a weightlifting championship, and in 1928 he qualified for the Olympic Games.

A handsome portrait of Tyler from his FBO film "The Desert Pirate." (author's collection

UPI made a few mistakes here. As far as I could tell Tyler was not in "Hellfire" or "The Beautiful Blonde from Bashful Bend." He entered movies well before 1927 and did not have the weightlifting record for "14 years" before his movie debut.

The UPI reporter was correct about a resurgence in Tyler's fame thanks to television and his westerns. A number of Tyler's films were also being re-released in theaters. In its Aug. 30, 1954, edition, Broadcasting Telecasting reported Tyler's Mascot serial was being released to television. In the mid-1950s, RKO started re-releasing a number of films featuring Tyler. They included "Valley of the Sun," "Blood on the Moon," and "Badman's Territory." "The Adventures of Captain Marvel" was re-released by Republic as "The Return of Captain Marvel" on April 15, 1954, just two weeks before his death. The comic book had ceased publication in 1953.

Variety ran a short obit on May 5, 1954, in which the writer described Tyler as "vet cowboy actor" and reported his last name as "Marko." Motion Picture Daily on May 4, 1954, also ran a brief obituary. It noted his career in westerns and reported he was survived by two sisters and did not mention Frank, his brother.

Chapter Two

FBO

Movie writer, director and producer Oliver Drake remembered how he learned of his friend Bill Burns's good news.

In his autobiography, "Written Produced & Directed by Oliver Drake," Drake wrote, "I hadn't heard from Bill Burns for months and none of my friends had seen or heard from him...Then one Wednesday evening, I came home and there was a message for me that the landlady had taken over the one telephone in the building. It was from Bill Burns. He asked me to call him at a new number at eight o'clock that evening. After having dinner and cleaning up, I went to the hall phone and called him. Bill answered the phone himself and after exchanging greetings, he hit me with a bombshell. He said that her had had several screen tests during the summer and in September had signed for FBO studios as a western star. He had made one picture for them, which they liked, and they picked up his option for three more years and had changed the name to Tom Tyler."

Bill Burns, formerly William Markowski, was now Tom Tyler, a name Drake reported was picked from a book, but other accounts noted it as selected by the owner of the studio, Joseph P. Kennedy.

For Markowski, this must have been a dream come true. After three years of trying to break into motion pictures with minimal success, he had the chance to star in a western produced by the company that made the highly popular Fred Thomson western films.

Markowski didn't forget his friend Drake in the midst of his good fortune. Drake wrote that "'I tried to blurt out my congratulations, but he stopped me with a chuckle. 'This isn't all I called you for,' he said. 'I talked to the top brass here at the studio about your ideas for western stories; and Edwin King, the vice president in charge of production, said he would like to meet you and discuss the idea of your submitting some stories for the studio."

Over the next three years, Drake was able to sell a number of scripts to FBO

Drake was impressed with his first visit to the FBO lot.
"I walked through the door of this magic kingdom and looked around; it was truly a beautiful place. In front of the administration building on the lot side was nothing but lawn, trees and criss-crossing walks that went to various buildings and stages – one of the nicest studios in the business," he wrote.

***

FBO had been founded in 1920, by the British firm of Robertson-Cole, which distributed British automobiles in this country and imported and exported films. Its studio on Gower Street was built in 1922.

By 1925, the studio had changed hands and was bought for $1million by banker and business speculator Joseph P. Kennedy, who had decided that there was money to be made in the picture business.

Kennedy had purchased a group of movie theaters and having a studio that would provide product for them as well as others was a dominant economic model of the film industry until the Supreme Court outlawed the practice in 1949.

What kind of a studio was FBO? An article in the August 8, 1925, edition of Moving Picture World gave readers a glimpse. Like other studios, FBO tried to offer exhibitors a varied line-up of product. The top of the line for the studio was its "Gold Bond" films – a reference to valuable negotiable securities and not the medicated bath powder.

The FBO line-up for 1925-26 included 12 "Gold Bond" productions including "Drusilla with a Million," "Parisian Nights" and "If Marriage Fails?," which, the article noted, all played at the Capitol and Colony theaters in New York City.

Today, the name of a theater means relatively little, but from the 1920s through the end of the 1940s, where a film played could add prestige to the production. Big city theatre owners were looked upon as showmen, as well as businessmen, and if they selected a movie to showcase, other exhibitors took notice.

The choice a theatre owner made was crucial, because in the era many years before the multi-plex, they only had one screen. If an exhibitor made the wrong choice, they were stuck with a dog. Unlike theaters today, runs of a film were not long unless they were a huge hit. The program at many theaters changed several times a week.

FBO is a difficult studio to assess today as the bulk of its films were destroyed when the studio was re-incorporated as RKO. The rule of thumb among archivists is that 75 percent of the silent films made in this country are lost. In some cases, older films were simply stored and ignored by studios – a dangerous practice as the silver nitrate film on which they were printed became volatile with age and literally could explode and burst into flames.
In other cases, the studios actually sold the prints and negatives to companies that would reclaim the silver from them.

At the heart of the issue was the perceived commercial potential of films. Once the sound revolution had taken place in the late 1920s, the box office value of silent films was greatly diminished. In a few cases, such as the sound re-issue of William S. Hart's western epic "Tumbleweeds" (1925) in 1939, there was a nostalgic appeal to a select audience.

In an era in which theater owners had programs twice a week and special children's shows and late-night screenings as well, too many people – often including their producers – considered films an ephemeral art form.

In many ways FBO was like Republic would be a few years later. It specialized in a slate of films aimed at rural and small-town markets. A trade ad for the 1926-1927 season used a baseball metaphor – "Three on base! None out! Score tied! And FBO smashes a homer! Here's what you get from FBO in 1926-27: 56 Showman's features (How they click!) 2 Two-reel series – 12 episodes each (How FBO can make 'em!) 24 Two Reel Comedies (Class of the trade) 52 Animated cartoons."

Westerns, though, were very important to FBO's success.

Under Kennedy, FBO was transformed and instituted an aggressive sales and publicity effort. If you look at a multi-page trade ad from June 23, 1928, you'll see what I means.

The four-page ad emphasized on the bottom of its page that booking an FBO film meant "more net profit with FBO Pictures."

Another headline read "nation's shrewdest showmen unite in smashing booking tribute to FBO. Giant circuits grab trade's best array of outdoor shows."

At the time, the studio had been able to hire cowboy legend Tom Mix, who headed up their schedule of pictures but Tyler and fellow Western star Bob Steele along with Tyler's co-star Frankie Darro were all featured in the ad. Steele's father was Robert Bradbury, a principal director at the studio.

"FBO steals spotlight," another headline proclaimed. "The spot light of publicity blazes steadily on FBO and its brilliant young president, Joseph P. Kennedy."

You can tell that Kennedy probably wrote that copy.

At this point the production head running the studio was William Le Baron. Le Baron stayed with the company until 1931 seeing it through the switch to RKO before going to Paramount where he was production chief from 1936 until 1941. He continued as a major producer until 1947.

Other films in that 1925 season included a newspaper drama "The Last Edition," a railroad melodrama "The Midnight Flyer," and two films based on the popular romance novels of author Laura Jean Libbey

At that time, the studio's stars included western hero Fred Thomson, who eventually went to Paramount before his untimely death in 1929 and actress Evelyn Brent, comic action star Maurice "Lefty" Flynn and stuntman turned star Richard Talmadge.

The studio released a serial that year, "The Adventures of Mazie" and had a series of short comedies starring Hank Mann and Chester Conklin. The studio was also the distributor of the animated cartoons that were produced by the Bray Studios at one point.

Why make low-budget westerns if there was little prestige? The late film historian William K. Everson provided an answer in his book "A Pictorial History of the Western Film," "The market for double bills was growing, Westerns were popular and they were still the cheapest kind of film to make. And since they didn't have to worry about even semi-literate dialogue, clean photography...fast action was all that they had to worry about."

***

Moving Picture World's headline read "FBO announces Tom Tyler as 'surprise' western star" in its August 8, 1925, edition.

The story, which carried no byline, read: "Tom Tyler, a young man who was born as William Burns in Port Henry, NY, just twenty-two years ago, is the new 'surprise star' who has signed by Film Booking Offices to take the lead in a series of western pictures. He strongly resembles George O'Brien, built on a larger and more powerful scale.

"Mr. Tyler, a team star of the Los Angeles Athletic Club, has been appearing on the screen for less than a year. He has, however, already been spotted by film experts, and was offered an attractive contract by Metro-Goldwyn-Mayer just after the day he had been gobbled up by FBO. He appeared in Elinor Glyn's 'The Only Thing' and has supported Fred Thomson. He also played several roles with Joe Brown productions and was featured in The 'Midnight Express.'

"Tyler holds the American and world's record in weightlifting in two events; the one 'clean and jerk' at 240 1/2 pounds and the two hand 'snatch' at 213 pounds, He is an expert horseman and spent much of

Motion Picture News published this review of "Let's Go Gallagher" on Oct. 3, 1925.

47

THE FILMS AND LIFE OF TOM TYLER

his time on his father's ranch in Wyoming. He has won renown at football and is a track and field star.

"FBO seems to be specializing in world's champions. While the personnel of the big Hollywood studios does not include any fistic title holders and there is no disposition on the part of the powers that be within the organization to annex any pugilists, almost every department of athletics is represented by FBO stars who are champions in their lines. Fred Thomson, Maurice 'Lefty' Flynn, Dick Talmadge, Bob Custer and others all hold American or world's record marks and now Tom Tyler has been added to this galaxy of 'outdoor' stars. With his attractive personality, modest disposition, a winning smile, and a great screen presence and with the line-up of rattling stories, which had so far been purchased for him, the new 'surprise star' should be a whale of a pleasant surprise for exhibitors and fans.

Here is the Tom Tyler production crew in May 1928.

"'Let's Go Gallagher!' is the tentative title of the first Tyler production. It is a fast-moving western, replete with action."

Let's unpack that statement. The announcement was part fact and part Hollywood fiction. As we know, Tyler's father did not have a Wyoming ranch and Tyler was not an "expert horseman." According to publicity materials released by Universal to hype Tyler's 1932 serial "Clancy of the Mounted," Tyler accepted the FBO contract "when he couldn't as much mount a horse."

"That time he arose at daybreak everyday for a month and actually learned to be one of the best horsemen of the movies in time to save his job," the press materials continued.

Tyler did become a fine horseman as evident in his films.

There is no mention anywhere that Tyler was a "renown" football and track star, either. Whether or not he was going to be offered a contract at MGM is not known. This writer has never read of any indication that MGM was interested in Tyler. He did appear in an Elinor Glyn film but it was "Three Weeks."

If MGM had been interested, Tyler must have been chagrined, to say the least, that he had signed up with little FBO when he could have been part of the studio that boasted it had "more stars than there are in heaven."

MGM would have a contract Western star in Col. Tim McCoy and later signed a "straight" actor, Johnny Mack Brown, under contract who would later become a fixture on the B-western scene for 20 years.

Tyler's accomplishments as a weight lifter were true, though.

In 1926, an annual publication titled "American Athlete" called Tyler, "a perfect example of the all-around athlete. He scales 197 pounds in trained condition and is surprisingly fast on his feet...Among his other accomplishments, he can perform an astonishing variety of acrobatic tricks and daring stunts on the horizontal bar."

It is interesting to note the emphasis FBO placed on athletic accomplishment. Many sportswriters have called the 1920s "The Golden Age of Sports"

A trade ad from 1926 shows the star power of FBO and current releases at the time. Evelyn Brent would later appear with Tyler in a Three Mesquiteers film and Alberta Vaughn would co-star in one of Tyler's Reliable productions.

when Babe Ruth, Red Grange and Bobby Jones dominated their sports. Perhaps having signed literally one of the strongest men in the country appealed to the company.

According to author Cari Beauchamp in her book "Joseph P. Kennedy's Hollywood Years," the hiring of a new western star was all about profit. She wrote, "Kennedy looked to clone a cheaper version of Fred Thomson and turned to a Detroit weightlifter who had hitchhiked his way to Hollywood and had found a few bit parts under his birth name Vincent Markowski. The 22-year-old six-footer was renamed Tom Tyler, put on a horse for the first time in his life and started churning out westerns that copied Thomson's titles. Tyler's first FBO film was 'Let's Go Gallagher' after Thomson's earlier success 'Galloping Gallagher.' Best of all from Kennedy's point of view, the Tyler films were produced for under $10,000 and the star was happy with his $175-a-week salary."

To put that salary in perspective, today that amount would be $3,154. Annually that would be $164,008. Tyler was making far, far more than the average American at the time even with a salary that saved Kennedy money. The budget of $10,000 would be a little more than $180,000, a low but still respectable amount to make a western.

***

Tyler's first film was "Let's Go Gallagher!" and Moving Picture World's review (Oct. 10, 1925) reported, "More than ordinary interest for the picture patron is attached to the FBO production 'Let's Go Gallagher!' because of the fact that it serves to introduce an entirely new 'Western' star in the person of Tom Tyler. He proves to be a well-built young fellow of pleasing personality, a regular he-man who is an athlete, a good scrapper and a fine rider. In fact, he possesses all of the requirements of this type of role and can hold his own with the majority and outdistance many of his rivals in the field. We feel sure that the fans will like him."

The review continued with "so much material has been worked into the story that there is something doing every minute with no let down. There is action from start to finish. This picture should please the Western fans who have demonstrated that they don't care for familiarity of the situations provided there is plenty of action, good fights and hard riding and a likable star. 'Let's Go Gallagher!' fills this bill to a 'T'."

The trade paper has similar good things to report on Tyler's second film, "The Wyoming Wildcat."

"'The Wyoming Wildcat' should prove a satisfactory attraction where 'westerns' are liked for it contains a good proportion of all of the elements which have proven their popularity in pictures of this kind, plus the appeal of the 'kiddie' angle, which will make it especially alluring to the children."

In a Nov. 26, 1925, trade ad, FBO listed reports from exhibitors about the first Tyler picture. L. Deyo of the Miers Theatre in Schoharie, NY, wrote the film was "a wonderful western feature with a wonder star," while R.A. Preuss of the Arvada Theatre, Arvada, Colorado wrote "a knockout...I hope FBO will star him on another like this."

The ad read "Out of oblivion and into national prominence in three months is an unheard-of procedure. But none can deny that Tom Tyler with little Frankie Darrow [sic] and Napoleon the Mutt has justified the tremendous advance ballyhoo accorded them."

The format for Tyler's films were set with that first film of having Tyler's character interact with a juvenile played by Frankie Darro. The phrases "Tom Tyler and his pals" "Tom Tyler and his buddies," referring to Darro on his

#4 Tyler shows off a bit in "Wyoming Wildcat," 1925. (author's collection)

Shetland pony and Beans the dog, became common on the advertising and promotional material.

***

Having a re-occurring co-star, especially a child, gave the Tyler films a difference among the hundreds of low-budget westerns that were being made at the time and subsequent reviews noted Darro's appeal and contribution to the series.

FBO used Darro quite a bit in non-western productions as well, as detailed in John Gloske's biography of Darro titled "Tough Kid The Life and Films of Frankie Darro."

Franke Darro and Tyler had real chemistry on screen in this arcade card. (author's collection)

Darro went on to a long career in film. As a teen and young adult, he both starred in major studio films such as "Wild Boys of the Road" to low-budget films and serials to walk-ons in many films as a jockey. He later made one series of films at Monogram in the late 1930s and early 1940s in which he was often paired with the black comedian Mantan Moreland and another series which centered around college life co-starring Keye Luke.

Acrobatic and athletic, Darro had an urban energy in his sound era performances and seemed to be cut from the same cloth as James Cagney. If he had been able to land a contract position at a major studio, Darro could have easily played the kind of roles that Mickey Rooney had played at MGM.

Darro came from a show business family whom he apparently supported as a child and had a difficult adult life thanks to a tangle of relationship problems and alcoholism. One career challenge was his short stature, which limited the roles for which he was considered.

On screen Darro and Tyler had true chemistry and seem to genuinely care for one another. As a young man, Gloske met Darro and befriended him in the last four years of Darro's life. Gloske told me that Darro had fond memories of Tyler and that when they crossed paths in Hollywood after the FBO series concluded they were both happy to see each other.

It's a puzzle to me that when Tyler was performing in independent Westerns in the 1930s and when Darro was also a freelancer that no enterprising producer thought to team them back up.

***

FBO ran a trade ad on Feb. 13, 1926, in Moving Picture World that featured a letter from an exhibitor.

H.R. Rehfield of the Royal Theatre in Sioux Falls, South Dakota, wrote the FBO offices "Knowing you to be very interested in how all FBO pictures go over at my house, believe it will interest you to know that Tom Tyler and his gang again broke my Saturday records. You will recall that I did the best Saturday business to date when I played 'Let's Go Gallagher!' and the kids (or grow-ups too for that matter) did not forget what a wonderful picture he made so they all came back again to see 'The Wyoming Wildcat' and believe me they all ate it up as it is sure fire and contains plenty of comedy, hard-riding and several good scraps to say nothing of the big climax where Tom and his horse plunge into the river from a high cliff to rescue the heroine. Little Frankie Darrow sure pleases the kids as he is a very finished little performer and as I previously stated I hope FBO keeps him in the cast."

Interesting to note that Darro's name is spelled by FBO with a "*w*," although in other materials his name is "Darro."

The Bible of show business, Variety, did not get around to reviewing a Tyler film until Dec. 1, 1926, when it ran a review of "Out of the West."

An armful of boy. Tom Tyler looks remarkably paternal in this pose with Frankie Darro. Tom is F. B. O.'s new western star, and is gaining no little popularity.

This photo from the Los Angeles Times on March 6, 1927 shows Tyler and Darro out of uniform. Clearly there was affection between these two performers.

"This 'western' has all the earmarks of a picturized version of a Frank Merriwell. It looks like the old Merriwell stuff with the home run hero at the bat. This may not sound like a 'western,' but it is a western crowd that plays all cowhands with Tom Tyler, the big hero.

"Not much to it, but some rough riding by Tyler and he's a roughrider all over the lot. There are several good laughs, one not intended, but spontaneous just the same. This unexpected laughter came when little Frankie Darro discovers the hero is a captive in a cave on the day of the big game he is to pitch. Little Frankie conceived the idea of attracting the guard outside. As the guard steps into the open, he is socked on the bean from above by a rock or boulder flung downward by Frankie. Tyler is a hard worker. He takes his screen assignment pretty seriously, but he is not afraid to mess up his physiognomy in the rough stuff. Frankie Darro is a child of the movies; he knows his onions right now and he's only a whisper, so to speak."

The plot revolved around neighboring ranches with rival baseball teams. It should be noted that Variety, along with many other critics, viewed westerns, especially those made by studios such as FBO as lesser entertainment. Perhaps it was the repetition of plots or story points or that many westerns emphasized action over characterization that turned off critics.

The screenwriters at FBO seemed to take the challenge seriously of coming up with plots that were set in the West, but didn't necessarily involve crooked bankers, earnest widowers, renegade Native Americans or water rights. Although Tyler's FBO films are full of typical elements such as misunderstandings that lead to the hero having to prove himself innocent of something, one wouldn't expect a film such as "Terror Mountain" from 1928.

The American Film Institute's catalog of silent films includes the following synopsis: "Buddy Roberts, who lives alone with his sister, Lucille, in a deserted house on top of a mountain begins to receive threatening letters and to see apparitions. With no family to turn to, he writes to cowboy star Tom Tyler and asks for assistance. Tom is about to leave for a vacation and gladly comes to help out his desperate young fan. Tom defeats the outlaw gang threatening Buddy and Lucille, restores a large sum of money (hidden by the late uncle) to the children and promises to bring them to Hollywood with him."

Other Tyler westerns had plots that tried to avoid some of the western cliches:
- "The Tyrant of Red Gulch" has Tyler as Tom Masters, a cowboy who helps the prisoners of a mad Russian who controls a mining settlement.
- "Phantom of the Range" was set in contemporary times and had Tyler as an actor stuck in a western town and having to get a job as a cowboy, The plot included real estate swindles and a charge of bigamy. Variety said, "Plenty of action in this better than average western that will more than please the kids in the neighborhood houses. The grownups too will like is as the story is told with directness that reflects credit on director James Dugan."
- "The Masquerade Bandit" (1926) had a story in which Tyler's character inherits a ranch and a hidden treasure from a friend, who is secretly a railroad bandit. The gang wants their booty and the sheriff thinks Tyler is the bandit.
  Moving Picture World's reviewer, C. S. Sewell, noted "Novel plot twist, suspense, and fast action make Tom Tyler Western snappy entertainment."

- "Red Hot Hoofs" (1926) has Tyler breaking his promise not to fight when a boxer comes to the ranch and he needs the prize money to help his girlfriend's brother.
  Sewell called this film, "Entertaining combination of pugilistic and western punch."
- "The Cowboy Cop" (1926) had Tyler playing a cowpuncher who is new to contemporary Los Angeles and becomes a mounted police officer.
  The film's climax, though, involved a chase scene with cars and motorcycles.
- "Lightning Lariats" (1927) had Tyler's character protecting an exiled boy king from a Balkan nation. Darro played the young king. Sewell said, "Tom Tyler's newest is pleasing combination of western and mythical kingdom melodrama."
- "Tom and his Pals" (1927) featured a movie company coming to shoot a film at a real ranch with a lot of jokes at the visitors' expense.
  Variety called the film, "a slight variation from the tried-and-true type of western."
- "Gun Law" (1929) had the heroine of the film refuse Tyler's proposal of marriage and he wins her when he is able to put a valuable marble quarry (!) in her name.

Tyler found himself the lead western star on the lot after Kennedy, as Beauchamp detailed in her book, engineered a deal with Paramount with Thomson. Kennedy lent Thomsen out for a four-picture deal with Paramount even covering Thomson's FBO salary, saving Kennedy quite a bit of money. Thomson remained under contract to Kennedy and FBO. To bolster its western line-up, Bob Steele, the son of director Robert Bradbury, was hired along with a young actor named Buzz Barton.

Frankle Darro steals a scene from "The Desert Pirate," 1927. (author's collection)

Beauchamp explained that with these three stars, FBO now could offer a new western to theater owners nearly every week.

Tyler helps Darro ski in "Terror Mountain," 1928. (author's collection)

So, what was a Tom Tyler FBO western really like? Sinister Cinema (www.sinistercinema.com) had made available one Tyler FBO available for viewing, "Texas Tornado" (1928). Taken from an original print from Europe, the Sinister version has missing footage but is extant enough to get a sense of the direction and production value of these films.

The film has been removed from the company's website, but it can be seen on YouTube.

First the title, like many Western titles, has little to no connection with the plot, other than the film is set in Texas.

The second thing one notices is that with a running time of about an hour, FBO wastes little time in telling the story. In an "adult" Western, there would be back-story and motivation to set up the plot. Here the viewers are thrown right into the story with little preparation. This story-telling shorthand is undoubtedly what irritated so many reviewers about the program western.

"Texas Tornado" opens with the Briscoe family being held captive by the evil Latimer. It seems that if Latimer stalls them long enough they won't make it to the bank in time to renew the lease on their ranch. Oil has been discovered on Latimer's neighboring ranch and he wants the chance to drill on this ranch.

When it looks the bleakest, in rides Tom King (Tom Tyler) to visit the ranch. Perhaps he was there to help renew the lease since apparently he helped set it up. However, he is able to rescue the Briscoe family – which includes a child Buddy (Darro) who is King's nephew – over-power Latimer and set off for the bank.

With Latimer close behind, King takes off for the bank. He doesn't know that Latimer has positioned men along the trail to town to stop everyone and they ambush King.

King fights them off and is aided by his daughter and young Buddy.

King makes it to the bank on time and renews the lease and secretly arranges with the bank to underwrite the loans made to Briscoe for the exploration of oil on the ranch.

Latimer later attacks Briscoe, which places him in a coma, and implies King who breaks out of jail. He learns that Buddy has been kidnapped and tracks the boy down. Escaping from Latimer and his men, King is shot by the heroine, who thinks that King has kidnapped Buddy.

She and Buddy try to escape from Latimer and Buddy climbs into a box suspended over a canyon to reach the other side. The box opens accidentally and Buddy is hanging over the canyon.

Luckily, King has just been grazed by the bullet and manages to rescue Buddy and punch out Latimer once more. Latimer recovers quickly enough to draw down on King, but then the sheriff, who has been tracking King since his jail break shows up and reluctantly has to bring him back to jail.

Rufus, the ranch's cook, shows up at that moment to tell the sheriff that Briscoe has regained consciousness and has revealed that Latimer was his attacker. The sheriff has his man, the daughter has a new boyfriend, and Buddy gets to meet his long-lost uncle, who is, of course, King.

The plot has so many unanswered questions that one almost doesn't want to consider them. What is the relationship between King and Briscoe that motivates King to do everything he does? Why is Buddy in care of the Briscoes? Why does King happen along to the Briscoe ranch at this time?

With this kind of film, it's best not to consider those questions, but rather to marvel at its construction. This film's great pace obscures these concerns. Instead, we get some great riding footage with close-up from camera trucks, and several wonderfully staged fight scenes.

Some writers have noted in assessing Tyler's career that he didn't seem to be able to throw an effective looking punch on camera during his low-budget series in the 1930s. While the fights in the Poverty Row Reliable Pictures series were often less than satisfying, one could see that in this FBO Tyler was a very effective stuntman.

Besides the action sequences, Tyler's performance was under-stated at a time when the demands of silent film making often had actors over-playing their pantomime. Tyler and Darro are very appealing together and Darro shines in his role.

All in all, "Texas Tornado" has many of the elements one wants from a low-budget Western.

YouTube had a grainy 90-second clip from "Phantom of the Range" as an advertisement for a company the purports to have the entire film. The clip doesn't really give any real taste of the film – no action or riding sequences. It has since been removed.

※※※

In another trade ad featuring remarks from an exhibitor, "Born to Battle" (1926) was featured and notes the action content of this FBO production.

"Tom Tyler – I never did see a title fit like this one did. If he doesn't battle, I have failed to ever see a battle and to carry out the title the kid has a battle that absolutely sets the kids wild...Out of the 800 that is made every year I do not believe I could have selected anything that would have filled the bill as good as this one did. I used 'Born to Battle' for the kids' Christmas morning [show], but I had oodles of adults ask me after the show if I wouldn't run it in the afternoon instead of [Harold Lloyd's] 'The Freshman' which I was using – C.E. Longacre, Dixie Theatre, Dickson Tenn."

Several things should be noted here. A well-made low budget western such as this one can be more entertaining to the right audience than one of the classics of silent comedy. Budget didn't mean much to this audience. What they wanted to get from a western, "Born to Battle" obviously delivered. A well-made B-film could easily match his more expensive cousin in entertaining an audience.

The second point is that Tyler's films, again like those of his sagebrush colleagues, were considered entertainment for kids and for less discriminating adults. Already there was a distinction between "adult" westerns and "non-adult" westerns. Adult westerns, like "The Iron Horse," "The Covered Wagon" or "Tumbleweeds" usually featured better known stars in stories that emphasized adult situations usually told on an epic scale. An adult western was bound to have more scenes involving character and plot than action.

Tyler's star was on the rise, though Moving Picture World, June 11, 1927, reported "...With Tom Tyler rapidly taking the place recently vacated by Fred Thomson, FBO's program of western pictures is taking a place second to none in the industry.

"Tyler has made rapid strides during his two years with FBO and with his horse 'Flash' and dog 'Beans' has become one of the leading favorites on the screen."

Even Variety was occasionally expressing a positive opinion on a Tyler western. "A pleasing mixture of those western ingredients which patrons of the adventure stand to enjoys and expect. Contains speed, constant action, unpretentious love theme, and a rippling of comedy through out. Consequently, it can't fail to click in the places where they crave lots of pepper in their film fares, even at the expense of reasonability," wrote the reviewer about "Cyclone of the Range" on May 4, 1927.

FBO publicized its releases heavily to theater owners and managers as this January 1927 trade ad attests.

The Variety review of "Splitting the Breeze" indicates what kind of play the FBO westerns received in some theaters. It was viewed on a double bill for a single day at the Arena Theater in New York City.

"Plenty of riding and gun play in a fast-moving western that will appease the customers of the one, two, and three-day grinds." In other words, theaters that changed their bills after one, two, or three days.

The review continued, "And 'Splitting the Breeze' is a box office picture for houses using this type of cowboy drama."

Variety, though, could damn with faint praise as it did with its review of "The Flying 'U' Ranch" on Nov. 2, 1927.

"Average horsey aroma for the cowboy addicts...Tyler's pictures seem to be selling well in their certain market, so there is no use suggesting that his director deviate from aged cowboy stories. The customers seem not to notice they've seen each picture anywhere from several times to several hundred. Photographed clearly and directed simply. Very simply."

And then Variety could blast a film with both barrels: "One of the Woolworth plots of the plains. Story padded in way so unusual as to be obvious to grind audiences; the only one who will sit through 'The Avenging Rider.'

"Director apparently had bunch of female extras on pay roll. Used them with ridiculous comparison to cut-in and drag along customary ranch murder case. Dames in dusty country and bearded men flitted around barn in classic veils or high cut bathing outfits.

"Tom Tyler forces rough expression and grabs the close-up which make it monotonous. Thing is generally nonsensical and abnormally hacked." (Nov. 14, 1928)

Toward the end of the 1920s, some people in the film industry seemed to think that westerns were falling out of favor with audiences and critics alike and the Variety review of "Trail of the Horse Thieves" reflects this change in taste.

"This western takes the usual tack where the hero is believed in the wrong by ingenious friends. It is just one of those which are gradually dying in the grinds.

"Tom Tyler overacts to a painful degree and Little Frankie [Darro] seems to be aping him. Cave effects and quicksand substitute as the applause point for the flat lands and the noose. Change is somewhat of a relief." (Feb. 20, 1929)

Yet exhibitors who sent their reports into the Feb. 2, 1929, edition of the trade paper Exhibitors Herald-World generally had good things to say.

A beautiful trade ad from 1928 featuring the team of Tyler and Darro.

"Terror Mountain: Tom Tyler – not a straight western, but a pleasing picture – J.L. Seiter, Selma Theater, Selma, Cal."

"Terror Mountain: Tom Tyler – December 20... Wow! Whadda you know about that! Our leading moneymaker for 1927 and 1928 not making expenses – not only that but losing money for us. Well, it was a disagreeable rainy night so much so in fact that even the manager stayed at home by the radio rather than face the elements. Our operator [projectionist] said it was an average Tyler picture. – H.B. Grice, Aiken Mills theater, Bath, S.C."

"Tyrant of Red Gulch" Tom Tyler…An out of the ordinary Western that should have general appeal. A supposed idiot furnishes good comedy throughout the picture. Yes, Frankie Darro is in this picture, too… H.B. Grice, Aiken Mills theater, Bath S.C."

"The Phantom of the Range: Tom Tyler …One of Tom's best Westerns…J.P. Johnson, S. of N. theater, Ambrose, N.D."

Even though Tyler's career would appear to be solid, several events out of his control changed his professional life.

By mid-1928, Kennedy had acquired control of another small studio, Pathé, and the once prestigious theater chain Keith, Albee-Orpheum. By Aug. 22, 1928, Kennedy had signed a deal with RCA to use that company's sound system at his studios. The contract also gave RCA the option to buy FBO.

The first sound FBO film, "The Perfect Crime" starring Clive Brook, was released on August 6, 1928. RCA decided to exercise its option to buy the studio in late October 1928.

The Film Booking Office now became Radio-Keith-Orpheum and eventually RKO. The company's initial features were called "Radio Pictures."

What would this mean to the stable of FBO stars such as Tyler and Bob Steele? Unemployment.

David Sarnoff, the head of RCA, wasn't interested in having his new subsidiary make low-budget program films.

The new administration even sold the horses Tyler and Steele used, according to Beauchamp.

An indication of just how low the stock of the once well-regarded FBO westerns could be seen in the Variety review of "Pride of the Pawnee" on June 19, 1929.

"This was made after Radio Pictures decided westerns were passé and it shows it, Just the old hoke with all of the tricks and bad enough to show the public that Radio was right in quitting this kind of stuff…"

And so, The Exhibitors Herald-World reported that on Jan. 29, 1929, that "Tom Tyler ended three years at RKO studios today. He not only leaves the company but also leaves the Western field to do straight roles. He will use another name in all his future work, but what the name will be is undecided. "Tyler built up a great following throughout the world in the Western pictures he has made during the past 36 months."

THE FILMS AND LIFE OF TOM TYLER

For the first time since 1925 Tyler was facing uncertain times and his friend Oliver Drake wrote about it in his autobiography:

"Things were tough in the picture business, but my friend Tom Tyler was having it tougher. He had a slight Lithuanian accent and it seemed no one wanted to hire him for a talkie. He moved out of his house in Beverly Hills, sold his big car and was slowly going down the drain. I finally convinced him to get with my friend J. Frank Glendon and see if Frank could help him lose his accent. I got them together and they began work. Frank liked Tom very much and continued coaching him over the next few months, long after Tom's money ran out."

Tyler did find employment but not in non-westerns as he had hoped.

He was not off the screen for very long.

This 1929 trade ad coming before the creation of RKO shows the status of FBO's western lineup, which now included for a brief time the legendary Tom Mix.

Chapter Three

Immediately After FBO

Alden P. Armagnac wrote in the September 1928 edition of Popular Science Monthly, "Will talking movies, newest competitor of the silent drama, eventually usurp its place? That is the question on the lips of everyone who has watched its phenomenal spread throughout the country. Today, the movies you can see and hear are presented in more than 400 theaters – from the Roxy in New York, seating 6,200 to the Sun Tower in Los Angeles with a seating capacity of 900 – and by the first of the year, it is expected that such theaters will number a thousand. For the first time in their spectacular history the 'movies' are being made over…

"The small cities and towns have talking movies, too. Aberdeen, N.D., Aberdeen, Wash., Akron, O., Albany, NY. – the list of towns and cities that have theaters equipped to show them reads like an encyclopedia.

"'In five years, there will be no silent pictures,' says Jesse L. Laskey, vice president of the Paramount-Famous-Laskey Corporation. 'Motion pictures are as much entitled to embrace sound as is the stage,' D. W. Griffith, independent motion picture producer declares…"

With the success of "The Jazz Singer" in 1928, the motion picture industry was turned upside down. Today many people think that it was primarily the stars who couldn't adjust to sound who were affected, however the sound revolution had a deep impact.

Theater owners had to not only wire their auditoriums for sound, but there was debate about which sound system was to prevail as the standard of the industry. Warner Brothers Vitaphone synchronized the image on the film with the sound on a separate large record. The sound system used by William Fox had a technology that put the sound on the side of the film print itself. The way of making films at the studios had to be changed. With silent films, sets from different films could be alongside one another without affecting their production. Directors could give their orders to the actors and camera operators while the film was rolling. Sound meant building stages that were sound proof.

The musicians, who provided the music and the sound effects in every theater in America, were also about to lose their jobs.

And the importing and exporting of films became a far more expensive proposition. With silent films all was needed was to film new title cards in a different language. In the early years of sound, producers made multiple versions of a film with the star learning his or her dialogue phonetically and supported by a cast fluent in a particular language.

FBO, while not the biggest studio in Hollywood, did have one of the most ambitious owners in the form of Joseph P. Kennedy. By mid-1928, Kennedy had acquired control of another small studio, Pathé, and the once prestigious theater chain Keith, Albee-Orpheum. By Aug. 22, 1928, Kennedy had signed a deal with RCA to use that company's sound system at his studios. The contract also gave RCA the option to buy FBO.

David Sarnoff, the head of RCA, was a key asset in the business arrangement. He saw the new studio as a market for the RCA motion picture sound system.

The first sound FBO film, "The Perfect Crime" starring Clive Brook, was released on August 6, 1928. RCA decided to exercise its option to buy the studio in late October 1928.

The Film Booking Office now became Radio-Keith-Orpheum, RKO. The company's initial features were called "Radio Pictures."

What would this mean to the stable of FBO stars such as Tyler, Bob Steele, Bob Custer and Ranger the dog? Unemployment.

David Sarnoff, the head of RCA, wasn't interested in having his new subsidiary make low-budget program films.

An indication of just how low the stock of the once well-regarded FBO westerns could be seen in the Variety review of "Pride of the Pawnee" on June 19, 1929.

"This was made after Radio Pictures decided westerns were passé and it shows it, Just the old hoke with all of the tricks and bad enough to show the public that Radio was right in quitting this kind of stuff..."

And so, The Exhibitors Herald-World reported that on Jan. 29, 1929, that "Tom Tyler ended three years at RKO studios today. He not only leaves the company but also leaves the Western field to do straight roles. He will use another name in all his future work, but what the name will be is undecided. "Tyler built up a great following throughout the world in the Western pictures he has made during the past 36 months."

This is truly a turning point in Tyler's life. It's interesting to note that he was considering literally starting over as an actor with a new name, something others had done.

For the first time since 1925 Tyler was facing uncertain times and his friend writer and director Oliver Drake wrote about it in his autobiography, "Things were tough in the picture business, but my friend Tom Tyler was having it tougher. He had a slight Lithuanian accent and it seemed no one wanted to hire him for a talkie. He moved out of his house in Beverly Hills, sold his big car and was slowly going down the drain. I finally convinced him to get with my friend J. Frank Glendon and see if Frank could help him lose his accent. I got them together and they began work. Frank liked Tom very much and continued coaching him over the next few months, long after Tom's money ran out."

At this point in Tyler's career there were two significant opportunities for him that dissolved through no fault of his own. The first happened in the summer of 1929 when Tyler was scheduled to star in the new film proposed by famed German director F.W. Murnau and documentarian Robert Flaherty. The Hollywood Filmograph reported in its July 27, 1929, edition that "Tom Tyler is leaving for South America on Aug. 10 to play the lead in a feature production. F. W. Murnau will direct the picture."

That film was to be "Tabu."

This was a fantastic break for Tyler as it would put him in a non-western production directed by the famed German director. Plus, he needed the job. Using a cowboy star for a non-western role was nothing new for Murnau who had used George O'Brien as the male lead in "Sunrise," one of his best films. The issue, as Professor Mark Langer explained in his commentary on the "Tabu" Blu-ray, was there was a conflict between Murnau and Flaherty about the nature of the film. Flaherty was soon pushed out and Murnau decided to bring the production of the film to the South Seas and use non-actors – with the exception of one person – in his story.

Tyler did a get a job though. It was about as far from working with an acclaimed director in a non-western film as he could get.

On April 18, 1929, The Film Daily announced Tyler and Bob Custer were signed to make westerns for Syndicate. Tyler was back in the saddle as the star of a series of very low-budget westerns released by Syndicate Pictures.

Tyler was slated to star in F.W. Murnau's 'Tabu,' but it didn't happen.

The team of Trem Carr and W. Ray Johnston are seen in this publicity photo for their Monogram release, "Lost in the Stratosphere" in 1934.

W. Ray Johnston, a producer active in the silent era, formed Rayart Productions in 1925 with Trem Carr working with him. That company evolved into Syndicate Pictures in 1929. Carr was the production manager at Syndicate.

Although not a major studio by any means, Johnston reported in an article in Exhibitors Herald World dated June 21, 1930, that working as an independent producer distributing his films through the state's right method was indeed profitable, even in the Depression.

"A robust condition is presented by the independent film exchanges of the count in figures just released by W. Ray Johnston who distributes independent product through those channels. An average yearly gross of $3,478,897 for the past two years is given in the Johnston statistics for exchanges selling his product which number only about half those in the United States."

In the state's rights system, a guy like Johnston didn't have to have offices or exchanges in major cities supply theaters with prints, which was the system used by the major studios. Producers like his level couldn't afford that overhead. Instead, they would partner with local distributors who would, for a fee, rent the movies to theaters.

A Motion Picture Herald article dated Jan 27, 1934, paid tribute to Ray Johnston's 20 years in films. "In 1931, the distributors of his product [Syndicate] in the field joined with the Johnston producing and distributing affiliates in the formation of the Monogram Pictures Corporation…"

"W. Ray Johnston, who was making many silent features under the company and brand of Rayart, allied himself with Trem Carr, independent producer in Hollywood, to make 24 cowboy thrillers in silent form to service the thousands of theatres which appeared to be in need of this kind of product while the large companies were trying to learn the intricacies of the new talker technique and were acquiring equipment and rebuilding their studios."

This is a polite way of saying the silent films were produced for theaters that had not yet changed to sound, Syndicate could supply them with low-cost westerns.

When Syndicate dissolved Johnston helped form Monogram in 1931. Carr took up the offer of Herbert J. Yates to merge Monogram into other independent companies to create Republic studios in 1935. In 1936, Carr broke away to re-form Monogram where he remained until his death in 1946.

The movies made by Syndicate and other low-budget producers would be classified as "B movies." Although today any low-budget film is called that, the term means something in particular. A classic B movie means the film was offered to theaters on a flat rental fee based on the size of the theater. In the 1930s that fee, depending upon the movie, could be as low as $10. Keep in mind admission costs to see these films could also be as low as a dime.

As B.western.com noted, "From a cowboy film perspective, this meant that a George O'Brien western for RKO or a Johnny Mack Brown for Universal would make more money and play at better theaters than a Tom Tyler oater for Reliable Pictures or a Reb Russell cheapy done by producer Willis Kent. And a Tom Tyler Reliable would get more play dates than a film from a bottom-of-the-barrel producer such as Robert J. Horner or Denver Dixon (Victor Adamson) … During the 1930s, there were various low budget producers and companies trying to peddle their movies and this created some competition. For example, a distributor would place a higher value on films with popular cinema stalwarts such as Tom Tyler and Bob Steele, but had limited interest in the likes of Bill Cody, Reb Russell, Buffalo Bill, Jr., etc."

Saving money in production was the name of the B western game as that could increase grosses.

Although companies specializing in B film made other kinds of movies but Westerns were popular for several reasons. There seems to be a fairly steady interest in the genre from audiences. There was a production infrastructure for westerns from actors, locations, horse services, etc. Since many of the scenes in a western are outdoors, which also saved money on soundstage rental, as many companies didn't really own their own physical studio.

Low budget moviemaking was a risky business. Again B-western.com explained, "The bulk of the so-called Poverty Row or Gower Gulch B movie producers and production companies could not afford their own distribution networks and certainly did not own any theaters. To get their film product into movie houses, they furnished their output to independent exchanges and distributors who handled films for a variety of companies. These were the 'states rights distributors' and 'states rights exchanges.' Basically, the Poverty Row producer/production company sold the exhibition rights to their film for a flat fee and for a given period of time. In return, the exchange could book the picture an unlimited number of times in as many theaters as they could … Sales people from these exchanges interfaced with the theaters in their distribution area and arranged for contracts on the films. For cowboy films, the negotiations afforded the theater owner the option of selecting which range hero was popular and would generate maximum ticket sales. When all of this was completed, the exchanges ordered the number of prints they needed (and they, not the film producer, generally paid for the prints). This practice allowed the distributors to minimize the number of prints of a film."

Tyler made films for Syndicate in 1929, 1930 and 1931. In 1929 they were "The Man from Nevada," "Law of the Plains," "The Phantom Rider," "'Neath

Heralds were inexpensively printed handouts theaters would use to announce an up-coming movie or a weekly schedule. This herald was unused as the area in which the theater and showing information would be shown is blank. (author's collection)

there was "Call of the Desert" and "Canyon of Missing Men" and in 1931, "West of Cheyenne," "God's Country and the Man" and "Riders of the Plains."

The first Syndicate production that made it to Variety was "Man from Nevada" on Sept. 18. 1929.

Thanks to the considerable effort by Tyler historian Mary Della Valle (https://www.aventurasdetomtyler.com), this film, as well as "Law of the Plains," are once again available for assessment. Della Valle and Ben Model of Undercrank Productions led a restoration project that brought these two films to Blu-ray in pristine condition. For any serious Western or Tyler fan, the Blu-ray is essential viewing as it helps fill in the history of Tyler's work at Syndicate, soon to be Monogram.

"The Man from Nevada" concerns itself with the plight of a hapless settler, his adult daughter and two mischievous sons, Wart, and Wiggles, who provide comedy relief. They are living in a shack on property that is coveted by villainous Al Ferguson. Tyler is a neighboring rancher who takes up their cause. There is one scene in which Tyler tries to teach the lazy, shiftless father of the family, how to stick to for himself and fight.

In the course of writing this book and watching as many of Tyler's films as possible to me, I have to say that J.P. McGowan has been a hit or miss director. While well photographed, this film is not among his best but is better than some of his other Syndicate productions.

Variety wrote, "J. P. McGowan is turning out a lot better stuff. This one with Tom Tyler called 'The Man from Nevada' has it all over anything J.P. has released in months. It's all the old hoke, but it's tied together better. Technically from the camera and the lighting points of view, it's

Tyler's first sound role was part of what was marketed as "Rodeo Comedies" produced by Pathé. His old FBO director, Robert Delacey, helmed this short.

above McGowan's average. The quickest grinds and the cheaper third runs will appreciate these improvements.

"Tom Tyler, ex-FBOite, just liked to do good. Fortunately for the theme (and McGowan has never been known to think one up without plenty of wild socking) Tom has a chance to bowl over the strong bad gents at hysterical tempo. There is some cold shooting, but minor wounds are the only development. J.P. plays to the kid angle and a timid papa who finally keeps his land after learning from Tom that a jilt on the chin is better than good penmanship in sticking to a land claim.

"There's a girl, Natalie Joyce, in the motherless big sister role. Not much for love stuff, J.P. is all for men. Plenty of hard riding with the audience not so often forgetting what it is all about."

The films ran 55 minutes and played one day in New York at Loew's one day as part of a double bill."

The name of J.P. McGowan is a prominent one in low budget westerns in the 1920s and '30s. An immigrant from Australia he was a triple threat of actor, producer and director. He started directing movies in 1912 and specialized in westerns and other action films.

His films featured lead actors such as Buzz Barton, Wally Wales and Lane Chandler. He continued directing until 1938 – his last film was a Jack Randall western at Monogram – but then he concentrated on acting. From 1938 to 1951, he was executive secretary of the Screen Directors Guild and died in 1952.

He was obviously a favorite of Trem Carr who carried him over after Syndicate evolved into assignments for Monogram.

For Tyler, McGowan extended his relationship into his next studio following Monogram, Monarch/Freuler Film Associates.

It's important to decode another term that might be misunderstood. "Grinds" refer to grindhouses, which were theaters that ran its program of films continuously through the day. There was a hierarchy in exhibition with films appearing initially in first-run theaters, after which a second-run theater, most often one found in neighborhoods, could get the film. Third runs would be theaters below that, meaning not a very selective spot for a movie to play.

Did these cheap westerns get play in the big cities? Yes some did. Tyler's "The Phantom Rider" was seen on a double bill in New York City in 1929 at Loew's Theater. It played exactly one day, a Tuesday, according to The Film Daily.

This is probably a good place to explain that theaters did not hold films as we see today. The economic model today is the longer a movie theater has a film, the sliding rental scale allows them to make more money. The term in the industry is that a film has "legs."

Years ago, many of the movie going public attended theaters more than

THE FILMS AND LIFE OF TOM TYLER

MASCOT MASTER SERIALS

THE Mascot name on a serial is a guarantee of an outstanding quality product. "The King of the Kongo," "Vultures of the Sea," "The Vanishing West," "Heroes of the Wild," and "The Fatal Warning" are typical of the long line of Mascot Master Serial successes. They are typical of high standard attractions that we are offering you this season in "The Lone Defender," "The Phantom of the West" and "King of the Wild." Recorded, of course, on film and disc.

Rin-Tin-Tin

RIN-TIN-TIN, the greatest dog star in screen history, is at the peak of his popularity to-day. He has just completed a sensationally successful vaudeville tour of the RKO theatres throughout the country, further enhancing his already outstanding value as a box office attraction. "The Lone Defender" is Rin-Tin-Tin's first serial. The story, written for him, offers, for the first time, a production in which all of his varied talents will have their full play.

MASCOT Pictures Corporation confidently predicts that "The Lone Defender" will set a new mark for serial business.

Tom Tyler

TOM TYLER is a well-known star of Western feature productions. His following is second to none among the lovers of virile, outdoor dramas. In "The Phantom of the West" he has a story that affords unusual opportunities for his extraordinary versatility. Tom Tyler will be supported by a typical Mascot cast of outstanding Western stars.

"King of the Wild"

"KING OF THE WILD" is another Mascot wild animal serial, a sequel to "King of the Kongo," one of the most successful wild animal serials ever made. This production, which will offer the most unusual group of wild animals ever seen in a motion picture, will have a cast of stellar players whose box office value will assure record business wherever it is shown.

MASCOT MASTER SERIALS

MASCOT PICTURES CORPORATION

NAT LEVINE President
Telephone Circle 2564

1650 Broadway, New York, N.Y.
Cable Address, LEVPIC, N.Y.

The Beekman Press, Inc.

Tyler's second talking film was the Mascot serial, "Phantom of the West," as promoted by these ads for the trade.

once a week. Theater owners changed their bill often to keep patrons coming back. Depending upon the market, there would be shows aimed at entertaining workers getting out of late-night shifts, as well as Saturday programs for kids.

"The Law of the Plains" (1929) is the second movie on the Blu-ray and it is odd in that MacGowan seems to have more resources but what he does with them is almost puzzling.

Tom plays a double role here: father and son. As the father he is a former U.S. marine and now the owner of a ranch in a central American country. The elder Tyler is preparing to sell the property when there is a U.S. invasion to stop rebels. At the same time the villain (played with too much relish by McGowan) and his associates manages to kill the older Tyler and take over the property and his estate.

This section of the film is complete with scenes involving quite a number of extras as rebels and U.S. marines, as well as the ship that delivers the Marines. These actually impressive scenes don't really tie into the plot of McGowan plotting to steal Tyler's ranch and money.

Fast-forward to the American West and at least 15 years later, and the son also played by Tyler is now a cowhand who gets involved with saving McGowan's niece from the control of her criminal uncle as well as being married to someone she can't stand.

There is a lot going on in this film – way too much – and it really doesn't tie together satisfactory.

Variety didn't like the next film very, "The Phantom Rider." Its review said, "Tom Tyler has little to do in this one. JP McGowan, who directed the film, copped all of the acting space. He's about in every sequence, which doesn't make this fireman's opera any better. McGowan has used all his stuff in this filmfoto except a fire. He's got the stuttering grass plower, the tough criminal, windblown ranch owner and a purty [sic] girl.

"But it's a tough tamale of a picture even for McGowan's sort of stuff. The story runs away from the camera more than a half dozen times, only to be reined in by the captions, written it seems to tell the customers why something is going to happen. Besides the title is useless to the film. Customers never see the rider doing his phantoming except once, and then he is off the horse."

"'Neath Western Skies" received this review in The Film Daily on Dec. 15, 1929: "Fair Western carries some good thrill stuff with Tyler, a likable hero. Nice love story. Okay for the Western fans. The story follows the routine

This herald promoted Tyler's first serial. (author's collection)

lines and is made interesting by the skilled direction of the veteran director J.P.McGowan, who knows how to give the fans the good old hoke they like. Tom Tyler is the owner of oil property and of course the gang is out to spoil his chances of getting the drilling under way, They steal his drills and through a mix-up the drills get into procession of the gal. Along comes Tom and the girl and himself works out the plot to the point where they have the game properly licked and recover the drills eventually. The action is there with sufficient fight stuff to satisfy the regular crowds. There is a good amount of plot that is plausibly worked out and this one will satisfy 'em …. Direction: smooth, photography: okay."

This review was one of three silent productions of a page of films described as "All-Talker." The other silent was a Bob Custer western produced by Syndicate and the other was an import from Great Britain.

Motion Picture News on Jan. 25, 1930, also had a review, which read in part, "Just Another Film. Tom Tyler has a following and on the strength of that this may get by as a double-feature offering. It's pretty crude otherwise and nothing to get excited about there are several fights, some hard riding and a sprinkling of comedy to make up for its other shortcoming. Except for Tyler, the cast is just so-so; director McGowan playing a comedy part … For houses which play this type of western, this will get by chiefly as a Tom Tyler vehicle. The star is a good-looking chap and has been appearing in out-door pictures for years, which should invest him with a certain amount of box-office value. Plenty of support is needed to hold up the bill."

If the FBO films had received little respect from some reviewers, these silent Syndicate productions seemed more and more like antiques with the passing of each week. Although in the fall of 1929 there were still quite a number of silent films being produced, it was clear to even the casual observer that industry insiders considered sound to the dominant form of the medium. It should be noted the critics for Variety were well known for their general disdain for westerns, which their reviewers often criticized for productions values, scripts and acting.

From Variety's review of Syndicate's "Pioneers of the West" (Jan. 29, 1930): "Spotted [placed] best on double grind bills. Being silent makes it doubtful of exploitation draw except as a novelty relief from talkers and for western fans especially."

Syndicate was still releasing silent films into the spring of 1930. "Call of the Desert" (available through Sinister Cinema) has its moments but is not memorable. Tyler plays a young man with his deceased father's map to a gold claim and inexplicably teams up with a total stranger to help him find the

claim. Naturally since its veteran movie bag guy Bud Osborne we know that he is up to no good. Osborne grabs the map and leaves Tyler for dead. Tyler is rescued by a prospector and brought to a nearby ranch to recover. Naturally the heroine falls in love with him and also to be expected Osborne is her uncle. She helps Tom eventually reclaim what is his.

The film does open with an unusual setting: what is a described as a freak snowstorm in the desert. Since I can't imagine Syndicate would have the budget to replicate snow in an outdoor setting so I can guess they simply wrote it into the script.

Tyler astride his horse in "Phantom of the West" and looking appropriately apprehensive as the hero.

"Call of the Desert," although competent on its own terms looks like "Citizen Kane" next to Tyler's next Syndicate film, "Canyon of Missing Men."

On April 2, 1930, Variety noted that Syndicate's new production "Canyon of Missing Men" came with "disc orchestration" or a recorded musical track. "…The music is funeral when the cowboys go gallivanting over the hills in search of the missing Jane and it's staccato in its punchlines when the boys pummel their way into a victory that needs no count of 10 slow or otherwise." "Canyon of Missing Men" is available today. Alpha (oldies.com) has a DVD that features a very worn print. It is an incredibly slow-moving film involving a cattle rustler who is reformed by the love of the daughter of a local rancher whose cows he and his gang have been stealing. The film is essentially without any action with the exception of a climactic fight at the story's end. The fight is photographed in a long shot, making it even less exciting.

It is one of the crudest, cheapest films from a technical viewpoint one would see in 1929. Remember the silent film had reached great heights in acting, photography and editing but McGowan was either hampered by his budget and schedule or just decided to phone it in and failed as a director in telling this story.

Tyler has little to do and less story in which to work.

The soundtrack on the Alpha disc is not the original score.

The next Syndicate release didn't fare well, either. "The Lone Horseman" was eviscerated by reviewer Robert Hage in the Motion Picture News (Aug. 2, 1930). J.P. McGowan directed and produced the film which Hage described as "a quickie, apparently shot from the cuff in a couple of days and combining all the worst features of the western cycle. Three men sitting in the vicinity of the reviewer slept through most of it.

"It looks as if they cut expenses on this one. J.P. McGowan the producer and director has a fat role as the villain and the assistant director is in the cast, too. McGowan's performance, like that of most of the cast was ham to 'nth degree."

To remain competitive, Syndicate had to convert to sound. Its first sound film was a western released in the fall of 1930, "The Lonesome Trail" starring Charles Delaney. The film was released, according to its ad, in two sound versions, "sound on film and disc," acknowledging the competition that still existed between sound technologies.

A trade ad from Aug. 26, 1930, in the Film Daily proclaimed the Syndicate Pictures line-up. The ad noted, "the big drive is on to bring the children and the adults back to the theatres. They want action pictures. Syndicate Pictures takes pleasure in presenting their program for the season of 1930-31."

The films included "16 All Talking Outdoor Classics and 18 Alice Comedy Cartoons."

A note in the Sept. 27, 1930, edition of the Exhibitors Herald-World showed the factory-like way Syndicate made its films. The studio had three units supervised by Trem Carr making films. "One picture is scheduled to go into production each week until the 16 planned are completed."

Tyler would make three more films for Syndicate, all sound films, "West of Cheyenne," "God's Country and the Man" and "Riders of the Plains," but first he was going before the microphones.

In 1930, Tyler made his talkie debut by appearing in a short subject produced by Pathé titled "Half Pint Polly." It was part of a series called "Rodeo Comedies" and the film was directed by Robert De Lacey, the director who made many of Tyler's FBO films.

In a story in the Exhibitors Herald World on April 12, 1930, about the new series of shorts, it was noted, "The Western star is coming back into his own is exemplified in the signing of Tom Tyler to play the lead in 'Half Pint Polly.' Like many of the other Western stars, Tyler felt the marked slack in cowboy picture production after the advent of talkies, for this innovation first necessitated producers confining the greater part of their production to interiors.

"Tyler has a role in 'Half Pint Polly' that calls for him to do some of his former hard-rising and thrilling stunts which now enhanced by the talkie medium discloses a fertile and bigger field for this particular type of talent."

The short received a fair amount of attention for its use of music and for rising stunts performed by Jimmy Casey and Tyler.

A brief in The Film Daily (Oct. 1, 1930) reported, "Tom Tyler sez that 'Half Pint Polly,' two-reeler just released by Pathé is the first western in which he did not have to fight the villain in at least one scene."

Tom is the actor receiving top billing but the real star is the rather inexplicable Mona Ray, an actress of very short stature, best known for her blackface role in the 1927 "Uncle Tom's Cabin." Ray is Half-Pint Polly, who returns to her father's ranch from school back east. Her father is participating in a horse race with this foreman as the rider, played by Tyler. The rancher with whom he has a bet had his men kidnap Tyler in order to win the race and Polly with the help of two young trick riders manages to rescue him. Naturally he wins the race.

There's a lot of silly slapstick in the film, which perhaps audiences in 1930 may have liked but seems artless now. This film is available also from Alpha.

Tyler's IMBD page lists that he was in an uncredited role in the drama "Her Man" in 1930. The film was released in the fall of that year and as an ad in several of the trades testified (Oct. 15, 1930) critics loved it.

If you're interested in Pre-Code movies, then you must watch this film. Directed by Tay Garnett and made by Pathé, the film tells the story of a young American prostitute played by Helen Twelvetrees working in a bar in Cuba. She is controlled by a pimp named Johnny portrayed with appropriate oiliness by Richard Cortez. She and a sailor named Dan (Phillips Holmes) fall in love and have to escape from the pimp and his goons.

The film shows just how well the movie industry had adjusted to sound by 1930. The film expertly uses sound effects to help support the story. Garnett and his camera operator use a lot of tracking shots as well as early and effective rear projection. The film's sets and use of extras also shows the budget and the care paid to this production.

I greatly enjoyed it and recommend it. Check it out at https://www.youtube.com/watch?v=AnCfXJckDRk

Now, does Tyler actually turn up? Yes, he does in a crowd of sailors coming to the hero's rescue at the end of the film. Watch for him at the concluding fight of the film. His appearance is fleeting.

Of course, the question that must be asked is why would he be part of an uncredited crowd scene? I'm pretty confident this was a one-day or two-day job and in 1930 for Tyler a paycheck was a paycheck. It's interesting to note that he made "Half-Pint Polly" for Pathé and this film was also a Pathé production. Was he on the lot and decided to make some quick money when asked?

Speaking of inexplicable, Pathé remade the comedy the same year, renaming it "Pardon My Gun." Both films are on the Alpha disc. Whole bits of business were repeated but this version has much more western music in it. The male lead is played by George Duryea, better known to western fans as Tom Keene. It is as thankless a role as Tyler had.

The good news is that Tyler's voice registered well on camera. Author Don Miller, whose books on B movies are essential, wrote in "Hollywood Corral," "The intriguing thing about Tyler was his somewhat sinister attitude underlined by piercing eyes and a deep but repressed speaking voice as if the sounds were coming from the shadows."

It is appropriate at this time to discuss Tom's second appearance in a sound picture, his first serial, "Phantom of the West." Produced by Nat Levine and his Mascot Pictures Corp., the serial was announced in a trade ad in the Film Daily July 31, 1930. The multi-page ad also announced "The Lone Defender" starring Rin-Tin-Tin, and "King of the Kongo that featured Boris Karloff in a pre- "Frankenstein" role.

The Rin-Tin Tin serial – yes, a trained dog had proven to be a big box office draw during the silent era – was popular enough for Levine to order 106 prints of it to service the demand as reported by The Film Daily on Oct. 8, 1930.

The ad stated, "Tom Tyler is a well-known star of Western feature productions His following is second to none among the lovers of virile, outdoor dramas. In 'The Phantom of the West,' he has a story that affords unusual opportunities for his extraordinary versatility. Tom Tyler will be supported by a typical Mascot cast of outstanding Western stars."

This was going to be Mascot's first all-talkie serial.

Levine produced action films and serials. He has figured prominently among Western fans for his discovery of Gene Autry and his early casting of John Wayne in several serials after his starring debut in "The Big Trail."
He was one of the founders of Republic, merging Mascot with Monogram and other several other small studios to form a new larger one in 1935. Despite his success and experience he was out of Republic by 1938 due to clashes with Herbert Yates, the company's president.

As noted on the excellent website B-westerns.com, Levine's pro-

> **Famous Western Director for New Tom Tyler Release**
>
> « »
>
> **TREM CARR**
> PRODUCING MANAGER
> of
> **SYNDICATE PICTURES**
>
> ANNOUNCES
>
> The selection of J. P. McCARTHY, former Metro Director and Director of "OUT OF THE DUST," "THE OKLAHOMA CYCLONE," "LAND OF MISSING MEN" and other Box Office Successes to Direct
>
> **TOM TYLER**
> IN
> **A RIDER OF THE PLAINS**
>
> Recorded by the Famous BALSLEY and PHILLIPS Noiseless Sound System
>
> « »
>
> All Tom Tyler Productions are under the personal supervision of
>
> **TREM CARR**
>
> Distributed by
> SYNDICATE PICTURES

Trem Carr was so excited about J.P. McCarthy on as a director, he took out a trade ad to announce it.

This trade ad from December 1930 announces the new line-up of Tyler's Syndicate talkies.

duction techniques for making serials were passed along to Republic. "His cliffhangers established the pattern which was adopted and fine-tuned by other studios and production companies. While Levine did not create the approach, he perfected the use of two directors and two separate filming units, with one shooting the main players and dialog while a second unit cared for stunts, action sequences, location shots with doubles, etc."

Another point made there is "The primary reason for Republic's early success was due to Mascot personnel and the Mack Sennett lot that Levine had acquired."

Levine heralded the release date of "Phantom" as Dec. 1, 1930, in an ad in the Film Daily (Nov. 3, 1930).

In the column "Seen and Heard in Dark Places," (Exhibitor's Daily Review and Motion Pictures Today, Dec. 5, 1930) author "J.L.K." wrote about Mascot's latest serial. "Nat Levine yesterday previewed the first two episodes of 'The Phantom of the West' If your patrons have an itch for rip-tearing, knock down and drag out action, out where the cactus sprouts, book this one for the works – ten chapters in two spindles each ...listen to this – wild horse stampeding; a hotel fire in which the hero is tumbled several stories by the Phantom; the ridingest little girl since Texas Guinan quit the western silents, Dorothy Gulliver, and cute; and action without end – just a few thrills crammed into the first two chapters."

The author concludes, "Tom Tyler is the star. We've kept Tom out of this until now because the 'story's the thing,' not Tom."

In the same publication and edition, Levine reports with recent bookings, he has "established what he believes to be new precedents for this type of attraction," meaning "The Phantom of the West."

According to The Films Daily, one of Levine's distributors booked the serial "to the various large New York circuits including RKO, Fox, Warner, Century and others."

Levine certainly hyped the production with trade ad after trade ad proclaiming which theater chain was showing the serial.

He managed to book the film into several theater chains for a seven-day screening – the whole 10 chapters in seven screenings.

The Film Daily (Dec. 7, 1930) reviewed the serial and stated, "With a western setting it gives full play for the cowboy actions material. This one reverts to the old thrill serial material and has been capably directed ... The grown-ups may find some of the action poorly motivated and not altogether plausible. But this type of serial is made for the kids and to put over the good old hoke meller. This one meets the standard."

As a whole, serials have convoluted plots and "Phantom" is no exception. Tyler plays Jim Lester, whose father has been murdered 15 years previous. The man tried for the murder has escaped from prison and appeals to Lester so he can help prove not just his innocence but also who actually killed Lester's father.

The red herrings and suspects are legion in this serial and the plot is complicated by a mysterious villain known as "The Phantom." Having seen many serials, I have to say this is not a good one. Tyler is fine in the film. He handles his dialogue well considering this is his second sound outing and there are some action sequences that show off his stunt skills.

The problem is the villain himself. He is absolutely god-like in this serial. He communicates to the rest of the characters by throwing a dart near them with a message wrapped around it wherever the serial is set, straining credibility There is absolutely no logic in this gimmick and when one discovers just who The Phantom is, that device seems even more ludicrous.

Director D. Ross Ledermann may have been a little more competent than J.P. McGowan and seemed to have more resources in this production than anything McGowan did, but the film is bit of a mess at times.

Audiences seemed to respond well to it, as noted in the Motion Picture Herald which reported, "Seven hundred kids lined up two hours before the doors opened! That's what Edward Seletter, former manager of the Arcadia Theatre, Portsmouth, NH, experienced when he started the serial 'Phantom of the West.'"

He had promised the first 50 kids would be admitted free.

Tyler then returned to Syndicate with two sound productions under his belt.

Action is what helped sell a B western to an audience and more than gun battles, fights were often the highpoint of an action sequence. Tyler has received criticism that he didn't do well in fights, despite his previous work as a stunt man as well as his athletic ability. There are many instances that show he was very capable in doing stunt fight work but Tyler, like most of his contemporaries, was at a disadvantage – a lack of planning and an understanding how a fight scene should be filmed.

It wasn't until the legendary stunt performer Yakima Canutt, while working with John Wayne, that the modern fight scene started to take shape. B-westerns.com offers this explanation, "Canutt is credited with the development of the choreographed screen brawl (where, in earlier films, the hero and baddie threw unrealistic punches at each other and wrestled/flailed around).

"The Canutt screen fight involved the positioning of the camera at angles to the participants (rather than straight on), and the camera would often face one of the participants. That camera angle gave the perception of bone-crushin' punches landing on the jaw. Many writers and fans also note that Canutt did much of this development during his many appearances with John Wayne in Wayne's oaters for Paul Malvern's Lone Star productions of the 1930s. Wayne and Canutt would remain friends for life."

Although this eventually became the norm, but initially not all directors or stuntmen understood this technique.

Richard Talmadge was a stuntman turned action star. He made both silents and talkies and several of his mid-1930s low-budget action films are on YouTube. If you watch them, you see that Talmadge did essentially what we would call parkour. He was well skilled at jumps and falls. Fighting, though, was another matter. Talmadge, despite his skill and experience, produced fight scenes that looked awful and amateurish.

To watch Tyler's capabilities, watch his film "Light of the Western Skies" from 1940. His brawl with Victor Jory is very impressive, but this is after the development of modern screen fight techniques.

The other person who developed the modern fight scene was director William Witney. After watching director Busby Berkley direct and choreograph a dance scene, Witney (who explained this in his essential memoir "In a Door, Into a Fight, Out of a Door, Into a Chase") realized he could use the same techniques in staging and photographing a fight.

These two men quite literally changed action films, making it safer for stuntmen and more exciting for audiences.

"West of Cheyenne" (1931) is another re-working of a familiar western trope: the good guy who infiltrates a band of outlaws to save a person unjustly accused of a crime.

In this case, Tyler's rancher father is convicted of a murder committed by the mysterious Laramie Kid. The Kid resides in a guarded town used by outlaws as a hide-out.

Tyler must convince the crooks that he is one of them and stages a fight that concludes with the shooting of a sheriff. The "sheriff" is actually his buddy Banty, played by Ben Corbett.

Corbett – actually a working cowboy at one point – appeared with Tyler several times and was seen as comic relief of sorts. He had a lengthy career in film, but usually played part of a gang or was an uncredited extra as his IMBD pages reveals. His greatest prominence came in the "Bud and Ben" western short subject series made by Reliable Pictures.

This trade ad announces Tyler's second serial, the first for Universal.

Harry Webb directed the film and his work here is quite perfunctory. The one aspect of the film that truly surprised me was the fact the outlaws kept a group of women hostages in the town for sexual purposes. Although definitely a Pre-Code film, none-the-less that kind of sexual element doesn't appear many times in a B western.

The second of the two missed chances for Tyler came in 1931. That year, MGM acquired the movie rights to Tarzan. As author Gabe Esso described in his book "Tarzan of the Movies," MGM leadership was impressed with the grosses of "Trader Horn," and was interested in another jungle-based adventure. Edgar Rice Burrough's creation Tarzan was available after many silent film productions.

Director William S. Van Dyke started looking for someone to play the character. Esso quoted Van Dyke saying, "What I want is a man who is young, strong, well-built, reasonably attractive but not necessarily handsome and a competent actor. The most important thing is that he has a good physique. And I can't find him." Apparently he considered, Joel McCrea, Johnny Mack Brown, Clark Gable, among others. "I want someone like Jack Dempsey, only younger. Tom Tyler is the best so far, but he's not muscular enough."

Van Dyke finally settled on Olympic champion Herman Brix, but Brix had injured himself while working on his first film. Van Dyke eventually chose Johhny Weissmuller. Brix later starred as Tarzan in a serial several years later. Tyler had the build – he was an AAU champion weightlifter – he certainly was handsome and he could act. It must have been a blow not to get that part since he could have easily done it. Weissmuller, although beloved, was not the actor Tyler was.

In 1931's "God's Country and the Man," Tyler plays a Texas Ranger named Rawlins assigned to go to a small town known for its violence. He requests as his partner Stingaree Kelly, a recently jailed outlaw, played by the one and only George "Gabby" Hayes before his well-known set of whiskers. Hayes plays the role with an Irish accent.

Tyler is supposed to stop the gunrunning from this town to a rebelling Mexican general. He is warned by his superior not to get involved with any women. Of course, viewers know he will and his character falls for Rose, played by Betty Mack with a fake Mexican accent.

The town is controlled by Livermore, played by Al Bridge, an actor who pops up in many westerns. His bad guy plays the violin and performs a dirge before he murders someone and wears a white tuxedo with a cummerbund at his rustic saloon.

The renegade Mexican General Gomez is played by Juan Rivero, another familiar face to western fans, appearing with Tyler several times. Ted Adams is a Mexican government agent undercover to thwart the general.

Rose turns out to be a U.S. government agent working against Livermore as well. So, the plot has three undercover agents trying to stop this guy. When her true allegiances are discovered, Livermore gives her over to Gomez with the implication she will be raped.

Tyler rescues the girl and Kelly, although shot, rides out and reports to Tyler that he has killed Livermore and the pictures end with the sidekick's death.

There is far more plot than action in this movie. Compared to his other Syndicate films, director J.P. McGowan seemingly makes more an effort, including some moving camera shots that are decidedly different than his usual compositions. At least it has an interesting gimmick for the villain.

Between takes on location "Battling with Buffalo Bill" are Lucille Brown, Rex Bell and Tyler.

Motion Picture Times (May 12, 1931) carried a brief story about Syndicate's success. "That Syndicate bunch is certainly doing its part towards putting independent productions on the map. The National Board of Review has placed Syndicate's 'God's Country and the Man,' a Tom Tyler western on the selected list for April. All who have seen this western feel that it is the best independent production in many, many months."

"Rider of the Plains" (1931) is actually a very respectable low budget western, largely because of its plot. Tyler plays an outlaw who is the adopted father of sorts to a boy who idolizes him. Coming into a town for supplies, Tyler falls in love with a pretty store owner and discovers a former outlaw colleague is now the town's minister (Ted Adams). The influence of his love interest and the action of the minister helps convince Tyler he must give up the boy so he can be raised by the minister. By the end of the movie Tyler's character is reformed and he is reunited with the boy.

Director John McCarthy (also billed as J.P. McCarthy) was another who labored hard and long in the low budget film world starting in 1920 and ended his career making a Cisco Kid western at Monogram in 1945. His work on this film showed more ambition and attention to characterization than many other Syndicate offerings.

Trem Carr thought so much of McCarthy that he took out an ad in The Film Daily on Feb 9, 1930, to announce that "Famous Western Director for new Tom Tyler release." The ad continued that McCarthy was a former director for Metro and had many box offices successes.

Tyler finally had a role from Syndicate that allows him to act outside of the normal tropes of the good guy. Although the good bad man or the bad man who finds redemption are standard western plots, what helps this film is the interplay between Tyler and Andy Shuford who plays "Silent Sandy," his sort-of son. Shuford appeared in a number of films from 1927 to 1933 after which he left acting and he does a good job. Under the Monogram brand, he was paired up with Bill Cody for a series of westerns several years later.

This was Tyler's last film for Syndicate before it would transform itself to Monogram.

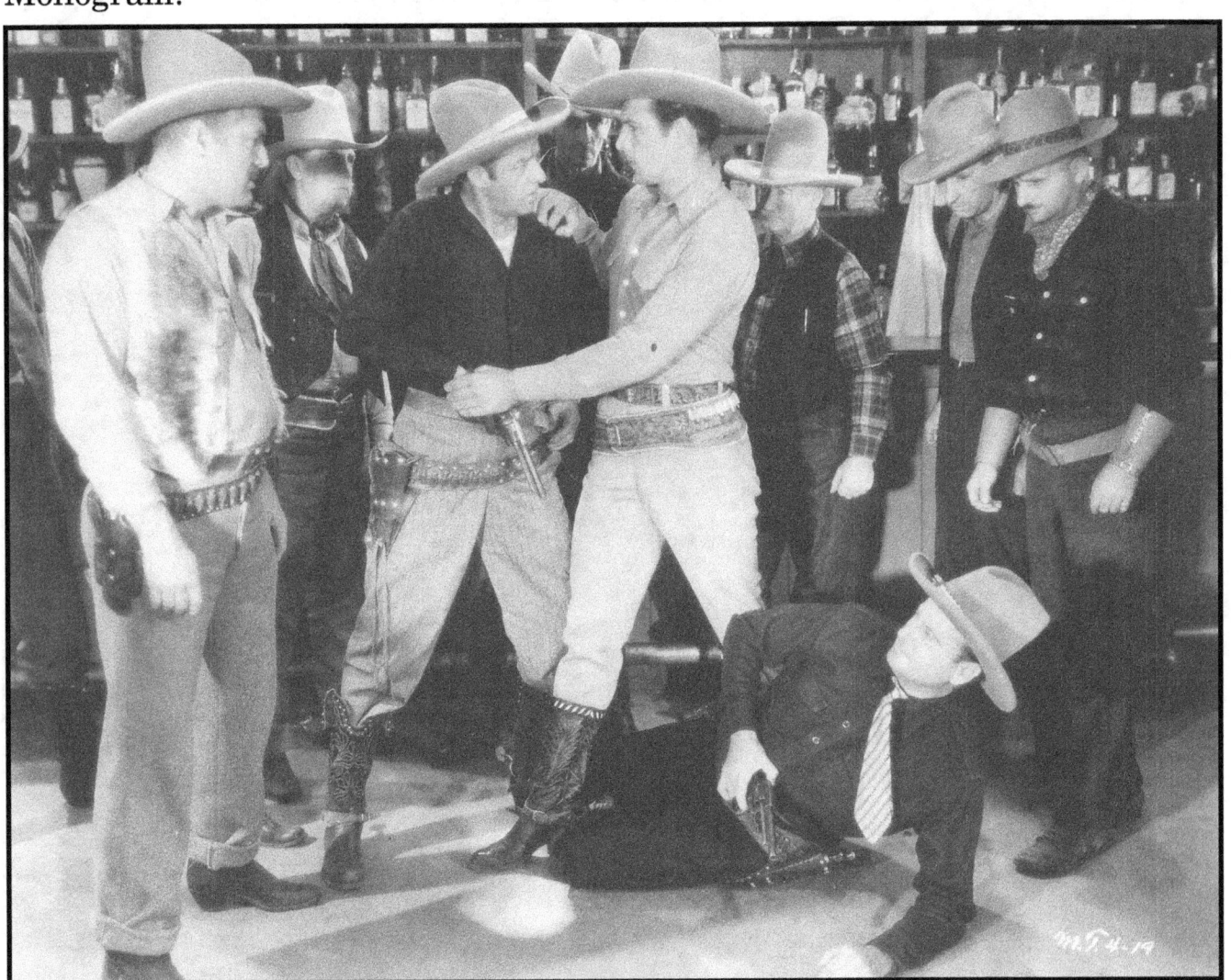

Something's about to happen in this scene from "Galloping Through," between Tyler and a frequent adversary Al Bridge. (author's collection

In 1931, Johnston and Carr re-organized the Syndicate operation to become Monogram, a company that lasted until 1953, when it re-branded itself as Allied Artists. The third film the company released was Tyler's "Partners of the Trail."

In an ad dated April 24, 1931, in the Film Daily, the new company announced a schedule of "16 action westerns and 12 action melodramas." Eight of those westerns starred Tyler.

The anonymous critic writing for the Motion Picture Daily (Aug. 28, 1931) said, "Tom Tyler turns bad in his latest 'Partners of the Trail.' He is seen as the murderer of another man's wife in Boston and then goes West to rob whatever he can lay hands on., Durant, who has been accused of his wife's death, escapes from a Boston jail to get the real killer. Both meet, unknown to each other, and fall in love with the same girl, a burlesque dancer acting as a waitress to get money enough to return home, until Tyler reveals his identity. Instead of killing him, Durant lets him off after Tyler confessed to the sheriff. Durant is absolved of the crime and gets the girl. Betty Mack plays the

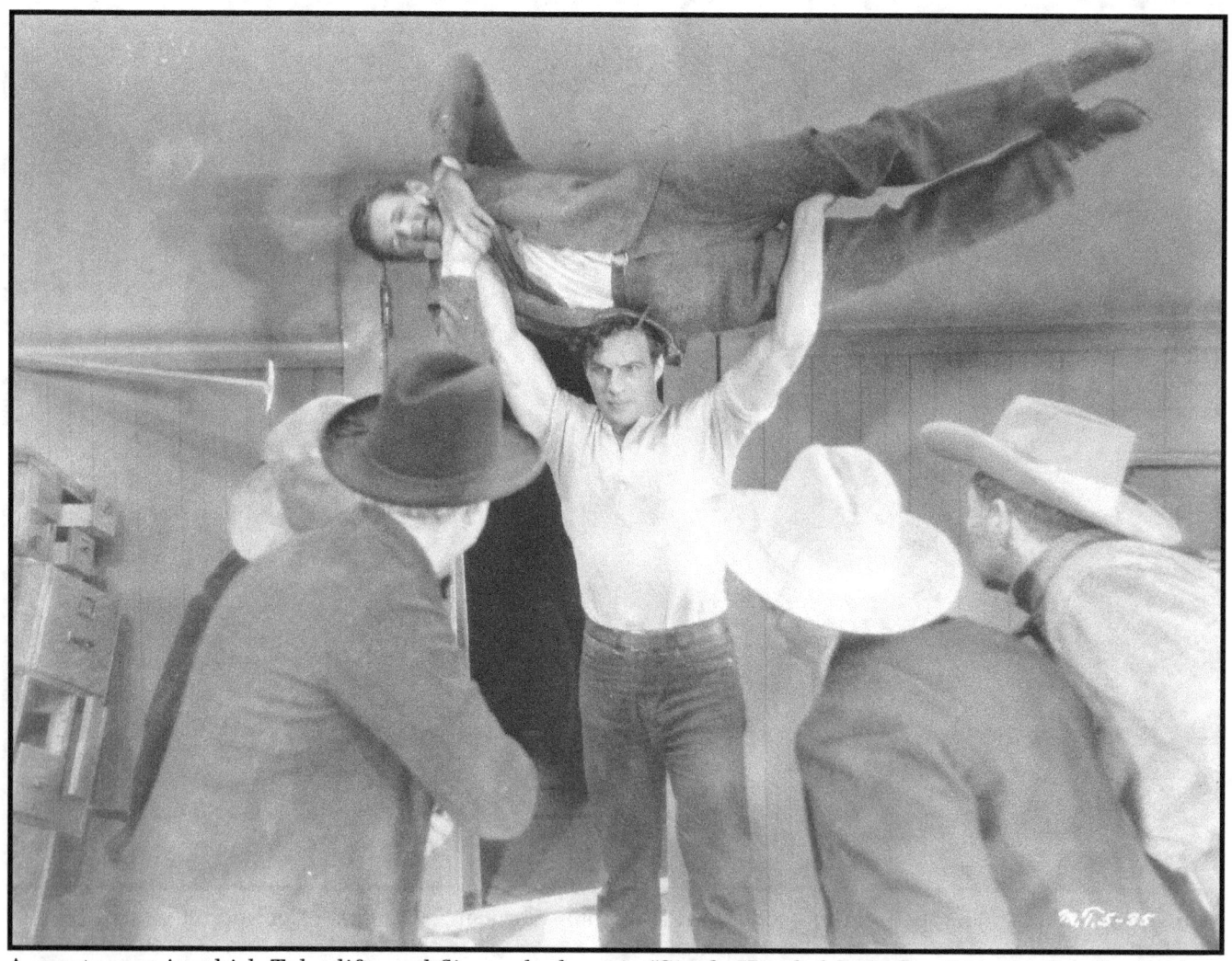

A great scene in which Tyler lifts and flings a bad guy in "Single Handed Saunders." (author's collection)

heroine. Audience reaction at Leow's New York was lukewarm."

That was a little confusing. Durant, by the way, was played by Reginald Sheffield.

Let's try what Les Adams wrote for IMBD; "Prison escapee Larry Condon [Tyler] is on the trail of a man who, he believes, railroaded him. Eluding the sheriff and his posse and posing as an outlaw he joins an outlaw gang and becomes friends with John Durant. They both fall in love with dancer Ruby Gerard, working as a waitress to earn money to return home back east. Larry later learns that Durant is the man he is trailing but, because of a bond established between the two, Larry decides to rescue Durant from a life of crime. The gang isn't having any of that but Durant saves Larry's life at the cost of his own and, before he dies, exonerates Larry from the crime he was jailed on."

On Nov. 18, 1931, the reviewer for the Bioscope, a British film publication, wrote, "It is pleasing to meet with a 'Western' in which the interest is sustained by quite good acting and a story with some semblance of originality." The Film Daily (Aug. 30, 1931) declared the film was "pretty weak and illogical motivations throughout."

The director of this film was Wallace Fox, another B film director who toiled at Monogram for years primarily on westerns and occasionally films such as "The Corpse Vanishes" with Bela Lugosi and "Bowery Blitzkrieg" with the East Side Kids. He would direct Tyler again several years in the future in "Powdersmoke Range."

Unfortunately, this is one of the Monograms that is not available at this time as is

"The Man from Death Valley" that was next from the studio.

Movie Age reported, (Oct. 6, 1931) "A pleasing action story with some thrilling gun play and fast rising. The story concerns a sheriff in league with a pair of bandits to hold up a cattleman's bank. Tom Tyler, hiding his identity as a Unites States marshal sent out to break up the gang, furnishes the suspense. He overhears the plot to rob the bank at a certain hour and beats the robbers' time by making the haul himself. He is caught by the sheriff who also discovers the hiding place of the gold, going back for it later to double-cross the bandits. Tyler is on the verge of being lynched when he makes his escape from the jail through the aid of his sweetheart and all ends well with the thieves falling out and killing themselves off."

Betty Mack who plays the love interest appeared with Tyler in five pictures.

Lloyd Nosler directed four films, three of which were with Tyler at Monoram.

Trade ad for Tyler's Monogram series.

However, he had a very long career as an editor working on the silent version of "Ben Hur," as well as the Greta Garbo and John Gilbert vehicle "Flesh and the Devil." His career concluded by editing a number of television series in the late 1950s.

"Two Fisted Justice" was reviewed by The Women's University Club which was the Los Angeles branch of the American Association of University Women in November of 1931. The anonymous reviewer did not like the picture.

"The action of this story is supposed to take place during the days of the Civil War when a self-appointed group of rough riders were stationed at a frontier town in Kentucky to establish law and order, While many so-called 'westerns' lack the smoothness of direction, acting and supervision of other films, they are often accepted, especially by juvenile audiences, because of the romantically heroic characters and vivid actions. But this one does not entertain, The story is inconsistent and complicated, the action violent and the ethics are confused. It is recommended for no one," the reviewer concluded.

The National Board of Review (December,1931) noted differently, "Tom Tyler defending the frontier for Lincoln when the army was needed to fight for the Union. Though lacking somewhat in the polish of more expensive productions it is interesting, well done and has considerable historical value."

This was the only feature film directed by George Arthur Durlam, who worked primarily as a writer. He also wrote the film.

Because Abraham Lincoln is a character in the film, The New York Exhibitor (Jan. 10, 1932) advised theater owners to book the film in honor of Lincoln's birthday.

Although I have a lobby card showing Tyler and Yakima Canutt meeting Lincoln, the president does not appear in the version sold by Sinister Cinema. It's quite possible that print had been altered well before the company acquired it.

The problem with the film is its overly ambitious plot. Tyler's character Kentucky Carson is secretly the leader of a group of vigilantes who wear concealing ponchos. He carries a letter from Abrahm Lincoln that allows him to appoint a federal marshal. The masked riders are seemingly the opposition of the corrupt administration that runs the town.

The father of the postmistress – who is in love with Tyler – has been opening mail to determine if there is something valuable enough to steal from the stage. The boss of the town and the bartender who serves as the judge are his confederates.

Tyler has also adopted a child whose parents were killed by Native Americans. That scene has an alarming image of a native scalping someone and then standing up holding a huge amount of hair, quite graphic for its time.

THE FILMS AND LIFE OF TOM TYLER

HOW WOULD YOU LIKE TWELVE SUCCESSIVE WEEKS OF TYPICAL 'TARZAN' BUSINESS?

The 12 Episodes of
JUNGLE MYSTERY
Will do the trick!

Wild animals that will drive you wild with thrills!
Unexpected shocks that will give you a real wallop!
Every episode ending with bring-'em-back suspense!
Action piled on action piled on action piled on action!

Featuring
TOM TYLER

Based on "Ivory Trail" by **TALBOT MUNDY**. Directed by Ray Taylor and with a cast including Noah Beery, Jr., William Desmond, Cecelia Parker, Philo McCullough and Carmelita Geraghty, it offers 12 chapters of sensational, thrilling jungle adventures. An ADVENTURE SERIAL.

ACTION • EXCITEMENT • THRILLS • WILD ANIMALS
AND ONLY ENOUGH DIALOGUE TO CARRY THE THEME!

"Jungle Mystery" is the only Tyler Universal serial that is not available for screening, although the serial has been restored and has been shown publicly'.

The boy is a witness to a murder and the leader of the town named Slavin – who comes across as a villainous W.C. Fields – threatens to kill the boy's dog to find out who committed the killing.

The film is an over-complicated mess.

So how much did a western star make at Monogram in its early years? I don't have access to Tyler's contract but Bob Steele's 1932 contract with Monogram is part of author Bob Nareau's book, "The 'Real' Bob Steele and a Man called 'Brad'." I'm willing to bet Tyler was making a similar amount. According to the contract, Steele was making $26,000 for completing eight westerns with the stipulation all of the films would be completed within a year and that Steele would receive $500 a week until the sum of $26,000 was reached.

Five hundred dollars a week in the depths of the Great Depression is the equivalent today of $10,808.39.

Universal was known for its product that was aimed at neighborhood houses and small-town theaters and in the early 1930s was, along with Nat Levine, the leaders in serial production. Starting with "Battling with Buffalo Bill" in 1931 Universal would star Tyler in three more chapterplays: "Jungle Mystery," "Clancy of the Mounted" and "Phantom of the Air."

"Battling with Buffalo Bill" is on DVD as is a restored version of "Phantom of the Air." Only about half of "Clancy of the Mounted" seems to exist (it's on YouTube). "Jungle Mystery" was preserved in 2016 (along with the edited 1935 feature version which ran only 75 minutes) and officially re-premiered at the Cinecon Classic Film Festival in Hollywood, CA in 2016.

Let's look at his first Universal production, "Battling with Buffalo Bill." According to serial historian Jerry Blake, Universal had intended for Tim McCoy to take the part. McCoy had done Universal's first sound serial. McCoy, though, left to work at Columbia and Universal cast Tyler.

Originally though, Universal announced that John Wayne was going to play the second male lead and Johnny Mack Brown was playing Buffalo Bill, according to the Motion Picture Herald on June 13, 1931. The same article stated the studio was aiming its serial productions to juveniles.

"Battling with Buffalo Bills" was supposedly inspired by the life of William F. Cody, although there's little evidence that any of the narrative is fact-based. Its plot is fairly standard for a western: the bad white guy creates tension with Native Americans in order to steal the gold-rich land being mined by white settlers.

It's what I call a "chase" serial. There are innumerable scenes of the hero riding hard to save someone or to speak with the Native Americans and then riding back.

In this day and age, the serial certainly crosses the line of political correctness as native people are described as "red devils." The opening scene of the first chapter has two white guys awaiting to be burned at the stake by one native tribe. They talk about the action that is to come and the last short shows the flames dancing higher towards their feet. By the way, this is the "good" tribe. Considering what is about to happen they are remarkably nonchalant. The serial emphasizes the fact that is a sound production by having an actor playing a cowboy opening each chapter with a performed narration instead of a printed title card recalling the action of the last chapter.

Director John Ford's brother Francis plays bad guy Jim Rodney with little subtlety in the Snidely Whiplash style. The heroine and love interest Lucile Browne gets second billing, while the second male lead is Rex Bell, the future husband of Clara Bow and lieutenant governor of Nevada after his screen career ended.

The film is at times technically crude for its time with bouncy camera truck scenes. Some of the fight scenes appear to be under-cranked to speed up the action. Perhaps the production's worst offense is all the stock footage used for it. Universal had produced many, many westerns in the silent era and this footage is easy to spot. There are too many scenes in which Tyler is pointing off to the distance and we cut to a stock footage of indeterminate age. Often times the stock footage creates a difficulty to determine if the audience is seeing the Blackfeet allied with the bad guy or the Cheyenne who are more or less cooperating with the white settlers.

If the goal of casting Tyler is to have a good-looking hero, the company achieved that. Tyler looks great but is not allowed to have much opportunity to actually craft a character. This Buffalo Bill is like a superhero who appears almost out of nowhere to right the wrong caused by the villain. Most of Buffalo Bill's lines are shouted commands.

One interesting note is the fact the celebrated Olympic and professional athlete Jim Thorpe had a small part in the film. Thorpe, a Native American, had recently ended his professional sports career and according to publicity put out by Universal, was discovered as a construction worker. He had been in one film previous to the serial, 1931's "Touchdown," and after "Battling with Buffalo Bill, he appeared in many films until 1950 in both credited and uncredited performances.

The Motion Picture Herald (Oct. 1, 1931) reviewer wrote, "Universal offers something spectacular and something very exciting for the youngster viewpoint in this new serial, which has much to do with the life of William F. ('Buffalo Bill') Cody. However, adults have probably seen it all before in the early Indian pictures with the redskins attacking the white settlers, and the soldiers rising hard to the rescue with Buffalo Bill as their scout."

The Film Daily declared in its review (Oct. 4, 1931) the production "will no doubt exercise a strong appeal for youngsters, But for adults it is weak for it is filled with too much repetition."

"Galloping Thru" received a very positive review from the Film Daily (Feb. 7, 1932) calling it "fast action western thriller packed with dare-devil stunts and hair-breadth escapes.

"The Forty-Niners" is essentially a Pre-code western that relies on stock footage. (Author's collection)

THE FILMS AND LIFE OF TOM TYLER

"Fans who are strong for westerns will find plenty to cheer about in this melodrama which carries a strong story and enough citron to fill two ordinary features of this kind. Tom Tyler set out to avenge the murder of his father, In his search for the culprits Tom has to wade through the guns of every badman in town. On one of the sequences Tom drives the stage coach as it dashes madly down a steep mountain road. The stage crashes and fall over the precipice but Tom hangs on to reins and carries on with the harnessed horses down the steep grade. Other stunts as equally thrilling follow in quick succession. There is a neat romance and much suspense in the story. It's a rip-snortin' meller that doesn't rub the wrong way."

Harrison's Reviews (March 12, 1932) was more reserved in its reaction. "A fair western. The story is not particularly novel but there is enough human interest and action to hold the spectator's interest. There is much suspense towards the end when the hero and villain meet to shoot it out. The hero wins the spectator's sympathy because of his upright character and loyalty to his friend."

There seemed to have been a trend in the handful of Tyler's Monogram features that are still available today. There was a clear increase in budget over the Syndicate offerings and an effort in scripting to do something a little bit different.

In "Single Handed Saunders," (1932) Tyler plays Matt, a blacksmith in a town divided into two camps: homesteaders growing crops and cattlemen who want no barriers to where their herds can graze. The town's judge understands the cattlemen are wrong but is murdered in hopes the cattlemen can take possession of the town. Matt's brother, Phillip, has returned from law school and is easily corrupted by the duplicitous Senator Graham. Phillip joins into a plan to place all of the property in town under the Senator's control. Matt leads the homesteaders in a successful revolt, although Phillip dies in the process realizing the error he made.

And, of course, there is a plotline involving a romance.

Tyler does well with the role of the blacksmith, who is a low-key, but beloved member of the community. One highpoint of the film is a fight with Tyler lifting the actor playing Phillip over his head and throwing him towards a group of bad guys.

The only regrettable part of the film is the supposed comic relief by black actor Fred Toones who was billed as "Snowflake," Matt's assistant at the blacksmith shop. Toones was one of several actors who were trying to copy Stepin Fetchit, the most successful black actor in motion pictures at the time earning $1 million.

Fetchit was supposed to be playing "the laziest man in the word," but to both modern and contemporary audiences he summed up every negative stereotype to be associated with black people.

Variety reported the film had a 12-day shooting schedule and was completed in January.

"The Man from New Mexico" is one of the Monograms that is lost at this point, so it is difficult to reassess it. The director was the ubiquitous J. P. McGowan. Reviews at the time, emphasize the use of standard western tropes. Motion Picture Reviews (1932) assessed "The Man from New Mexico" as a formula western. "Children will enjoy direct action and uncomplicated motives. A beautiful heroine, a brave hero and a wicked villain plus skillful riding and hard fighting, where right triumphs make good entertainment for junior matinees. 'The Man from New Mexico' is made according to the formula above and is unimportant to all but the younger members of the family."

Photoplay (July 1932) was not as charitable. "Tom Tyler takes a flock of cattle rustlers for a ride and saves a blushing wild rose and her old pappy from the infamous clutches of the dastardly villain who practically gurgles, 'Ah-h-h – me proud beauty,' as he slithers toward the girl. Then came the yawn."

"Vanishing Men" (1932) is a cattle-rustling film, according to the summary on IMBD, which is also not available at this time. In the Motion Picture Herald (June 4, 1932), Rita C. McGoldrick wrote, "The Western theme is speeded up to intrigue us into the problem that confronts the clever rider, Tom Tyler." "Honor of the Mounted" (1932) has Tyler as a member of the Canadian Royal Mounted Police named Tom Halliday who is pursuing the man who has murdered a local trapper. Halliday was in the trapper's cabin when he was stabbed but he was in another room. He only has a voice to identify the killer. Trailing the man who be believes is the killer, he comes to the United States and comes to a small border town where the local merchant is in the business of buying furs from trappers.

Halliday lays a trap to reveal the killer which kicks off an action filled conclusion. Tyler and Stanley Blystone, who plays the villain, have a great knock-down fight in which Tyler falls down a staircase in spectacular fashion. That's followed by a chase on horseback, then running and finally Blystone attempts to escape by jumping in a canoe. Tyler swims after him and eventually catches up with him.

Director Harry Fraser, also wrote the screenplay, had a long career writing and directing B westerns, although he was involved in other film projects as well, such as writing the teen exploitation film "I Accuse my Parents" and being one of the writers on Republic's "Captain America" serial. He also directed the infamous film "Chained for Life" starring the Hilton sisters who were famous conjoined twins. Westerns, though, seemed to have been his specialty.

Tyler's love interest was played by newcomer and 19-year-old Celia Ryland who had just five months experience as an extra before being chosen for the role, according to a story in a column dated May 14, 1932, in the Hollywood Filmograph. She appeared in two other films before leaving acting.

In The Film Daily (July 8, 1933) there was double-truck trade ad announcing the Monogram's 1933-1934 season, the studio not only bragged about its increased production budgets but also the nature of its new films. There are no mentions of any westerns on the schedule instead they offer their version of "Jane Eyre," "Beggars in Ermine" starring Lionel Atwill, and "Derby Day," set at a country fair.

It's clear that Monogram wanted to position itself as a studio that did more than produce program westerns.

In 1933, Tom's series was replaced by a series of westerns produced by Paul Malvern's Lone Star Productions for release through Monogram. Film Daily announced on June 24, 1933, that John Wayne would be starring in the series.

Once the Monogram series concluded, Tom was in demand once more at Universal for his next serial, "Jungle Mystery" (1932). The Hollywood Filmograph announced on May 21, 1932, that Tyler had been hired to star in "Jungle Mystery."

The serial was based upon a story by Talbot Mundy and Ray Taylor, the director of "Battling with Buffalo Bill" helmed the production. Taylor specialized in serials and B westerns and had a long association with Universal. He is perhaps best known for his work on the three "Flash Gordon" serials. He also directed Tyler's other two Universal serials. In the mid-1940s, he would again direct Tyler in "Boss of Boomtown."

The critics at Motion Picture Review (August 1932) always having a juvenile audience in mind wrote, "An exciting series of adventures in Africa in which a hidden hoard of ivory and a lost son (brother of the heroine) are the inspirations for the action. In some respects, the plot is better than many serials for the modern gangster with his low intrigues is absent. Here the setting is the jungle and war-like natives and wild animals provide the thrills. It is obviously an imitation of Tarzan but its producers do not seem to realize that the appeal of 'Tarzan' lay in its greater simplicity and in a closer adherence, if not reality, at least to probability. These are lacking the 'Jungle Mystery' and the whole is overcharged with exaggerated thrills. It is not recommended for junior matinees because of the younger children who are in attendance."

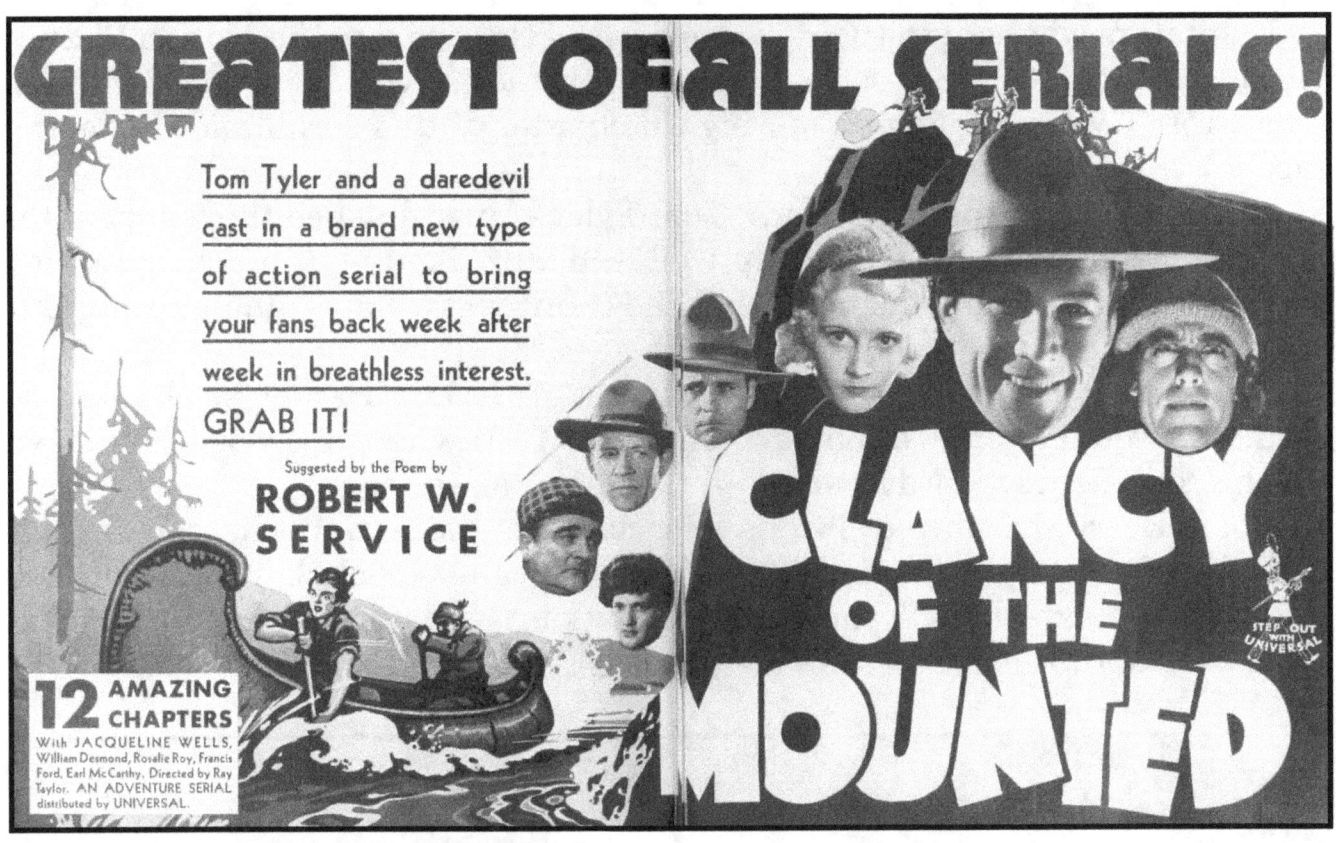

In 1933, Tyler was the serial king of Universal.

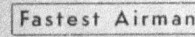

Exhibitors who sent in their own reviews of the serial to the Motion Picture Herald (March 18, 1933) seemed to think the serial was a success for them. One wrote, "We are going on our eighth chapter of this serial and it is going nicely."

Another theater manager said, "Tom Tyler – Just finished the last chapter of this splendid serial., It held up well and was liked very much. You may think serials a little old fashioned but the chances are you could increase your patronage by playing a good one. I did."

Universal publicized heavily the casting of Cecelia Parker as the female lead. She would later be a contract player at MGM where she was best known for the role of Andy Hardy's sister in that popular series.

Noah Berry Jr. played Tyler's associate on the serial. His career that stretched from 1920 when he appeared as a seven-year-old boy in an uncredited role to 1986 when TV audiences knew him as James Garner's father in "The "Rockford Files."

There is a lull in the action in this scene from "Clancy of the Mounted."

In 2016 a restored print of the serial was shown at Cinecon in Los Angeles. After that screening there were reports that VCI would release a Blu-ray of it, but of this writing that hasn't happened as yet. I asked members of the B Movies & Serials group on Facebook if anyone had seen it and one member shared this reaction from Nitrateville.com. Camille Scaysbrook (aka "Brooksie") wrote, "To some, this long-unseen Universal serial is an eloquent essay on montage theory. Exactly how many times can the same piece of stock footage be used? How many different stories can it tell? Why does that same herd of elephants head for the hills at the drop of a hat, every single time? To others - and I fell into this camp – it was a surprisingly entertaining piece of campery. "The story, such as it is, tells of two rival groups seeking a legendary cache of ivory in deepest darkest Africa. Another family is searching for their lost son, and his girlfriend (Cecilia Parker) spends a lot of time wandering into the jungle, getting lost, and being attacked by animals. Then, there's the Jungle Mystery himself, a sort of half-man, half-ape who turns up at various points, bellowing his signature "EOOOUCH!" The dialogue is dreadful, the ethnic stereotypes are as broad as you'd imagine, and though the performances range from the wooden to the uninspired, 'The Jungle Mystery' never commits the worst of low-budget sins – that of merely being boring.

There were a hardcore group of fans who watched every episode, but for others, the gong that ended each chapter was a signal that it was now safe to enter the theatre. I would happily watch it again, though I admit that the 75-minute feature cutdown might be a bridge too far."

Freuler Film Associates was founded by John Freuler, a man with experience owning theaters and exchanges. He was known in the industry for signing Charlie Chaplin to an early contract in the silent era. In 1932 he started producing low-budget films under two brands: Freuler Film Associates and Monarch Film Corporation. For Monarch, the movies were described as melodramas in the trade press. With his two brands, 13 films were released and four of them were Tom Tyler westerns.

Freuler's operation was primarily active in 1932, and 1933 with two films in 1932 and one in 1935.

The Film Daily announced Sept. 1, 1932, that Freuler had signed Tyler to a contract for six films, "The Forty-Niners," "War of the Range," "Remember the Alamo," "Red Man's Country," "When a Man Rides Alone and "Deadwood Pass." Only four were completed and released. The westerns were part of a very ambitious schedule announced by Freuler that included 12 melodramas, and six thrillers.

Tyler underscored his ability to play a modern-day hero – without the benefit of a horse – in "Phantom of the Air." (author's collection)

Freuler was not able to fulfill his production schedule though and failed. The film industry at that time was populated with independent producers with big hopes.

Want to know how fast these films were made and released? That Film Daily story noted "The Forty-Niners" would start production the following week. It was then ready for The Film Daily to review in a little more than three months – that included production, the making of prints, the delivery of those prints to the states rights exchanges, and the creation of the publicity materials.

The quicker these films were in theaters the more financially secure these low-budget independents would be.

The Film Daily declared (Dec. 14, 1932) that "The Forty-Niners" has "plenty of action in frontier meller with wagon train, Indians and everything."

The review continued, "They crammed all the good old western ingredients into this one and with the work of Tom Tyler this horse opera no doubt will appeal to the kid. The film gets moving too slow for the first half but after that picks up with plenty of action centering around the adventures of the covert wagon train attacked by Indians and a stampede of buffaloes for good measure. Hero Tom accompanies the train, being interested in the girl who is traveling with her father to claim a mine location in California. Tyler has got a line on the chap who has been hired to lead the wagon train and learned that he is playing into the hands of the hostile Indians, having sacrificed two other trains of pioneers before this one. Works up to a good snappy climax with the Indian attack, the rescue of U.S. Cavalry, the death of the villain at the hands of the Indian girl he betrayed and the heroine realizing that Tom was her true pal all the time and not the horrid villain."

The film was directed by J.P. McCarthy and reunites Tyler with a man he bested in several films, Al Bridge. Bridge was effective as the snarling amoral bad guy. He had a long career in westerns but also was a busy character actor who was a regular in Preston Sturges comedies.

"The Forty-Niners" is a truly amazing Pre-Code B-western. The film takes it time to set up the story. A father and daughter are part of a wagon train waiting to make its trip to California. Our heroine Virginia (Betty Mack) has a drunk for a father. He has a map denoting where his rich gold claim would be and naturally shows it to O'Hara (Al Bridge). He is more than your standard bad guy. As a scout he has led two other wagon trains west, but what he has done is to lead them off the trail and into a trap where a native tribe slaughters them and then splits the settlers' belongings.

He is essentially a serial killer.

O'Hara also lives without the benefit of marriage with a young native woman who he physically mistreats.

Tyler plays Tennessee Matthews, a guide who talks about his cabin near Yellowstone. He instantly falls in love with our heroine. Naturally O'Hara also has his eyes on this woman. He eventually saves the day and O'Hara is killed by his one-time native lover.

"Phantom of the Air" is a truly enjoyable serial. (author's collection)

Matthews and Virginia ride off at the film's conclusion to his cabin. Interestingly enough they are not married.

All of the elements that are mentioned in The Film Daily review are stock footage: the angry tribes, the buffalo stampede, the cavalry to the rescue. It's clear the film was built around what stock footage is available and it's also clear that F. McGrew Willis wanted to give the standard characters of a western a different edge.

I can only assume the intended audience of youngsters wouldn't notice the stock footage or at least that's what The Film Daily hoped.

In "When a Man Rides Alone" (1933), Tyler plays the son of the man who was murdered by his partner named Montana Slade. The two men had a gold mining operation and following the murder Slade took it over, ignoring the stakeholder who had invested his money into the mine.

Now Tyler assumes the identity of The Llano Kid, the road agent who is stealing only the gold from that mine and then using the proceeds to pay back his father's investors.

The local sheriff suspects that Tyler is the Llano Kid but can't catch him. Adele Lacy plays the very spirited heroine; the daughter of the miner Tyler is trying to help in his war against Slade. She had appeared with Tyler in his Monogram production, "Vanishing Men."

This film is several notches above the other Tyler westerns McGowan had directed. Perhaps his editor understood the need to keep the story moving forward.

"Deadwood Pass" (1933) benefited from a slight variation in the usual plot with Tyler playing a postal inspector who is trying to locate a group of securities that were stolen by a mysterious criminal known as The Hawk. Tyler assumes the role and acquires a distinctive tattoo to work his way into a gang who are controlling the Deadwood Pass which is where the stolen securities are believed to be buried.

Written by Tyler's friend the prolific Oliver Drake and directed by J.P. Mc-Gowan, the film is at the level of his Syndicate talkies. It's competent.

The film also benefits from having Wally Wales as a co-star. He was a fixture in many westerns as a star in the late 1920s and early 1930s. An actual cowboy from Montana, Wales realized by the mid-1930s that stardom was not going to be his path so he switched to character parts under the name of Hal Taliaferro – Taliaferro was his middle name. He appeared in about 200 films as a character actor.

Film Daily, June 6, 1933, noted in its review, "Snappy western has plenty of stirring action and excitement in which Tom Tyler scores. This one gets back to the good old formula of a series of fast writing gunplay and fistfights. Tom Tyler at first appears to the audience as a notorious bad man, The Hawk, who has just been released from doing a stretch for a big robbery in which the loot was cached and the authorities never found it. Later it develops that Tom is a government agent and has been sent in to pose as the hawk in order to learn from the gang just where the loot is hidden. Things get tough for our hero when the real Hawk suddenly appears on the scene and Tyler has to do some fast action to get himself out of the jam. The climax is a stirring pitched battle between the hero and the gang with the sheriff's posse coming along just in the nick of time. Meanwhile Tom has learned that the secret tattoo mark of the hawk which he has duplicated on his body contains the secret to the hideout of the loot. Has all the elements that makes for a satisfactory action western."

As anyone who watches B westerns realizes all too often the title of the film really doesn't convey the actual story of the film. "War of the Range" really is about a range war.

Tyler plays the son of a cattleman who is planning to seal up a trail used by other ranchers to move herds to market. Tyler opposes his father's move especially when he has worked out a solution with the homesteaders who have control of part of the property.

I'll give credit to the production for actually having real cattle herds for the film as opposed to using stock footage.

Again, it was a production featuring Oliver Drake's screenplay and J.P. McGowan's direction.

The review of "War of the Range" the Film Daily (Nov. 22, 1933) said, "Routine western with crudely developed plot has only action to recommend it. Here is a rather crude sample of the western that follows the threadbare formula to the last and injects nothing new or novel. Tom Tyler works overtime in his part but there is a good supply of action and thrills but they cannot disguise the lack of logic in many of the situations that simply don't make any sense …Tyler works at odds with his own father and running down a bunch of cattle rustlers. The old man has fenced off his land which the cattlemen used to run their cattle through to grazing land and water. This gives opportunity to the bad man and his gang to start trouble. It takes Tyler's father a long time to see the error of his methods and then the hero's dad and his ranch hands and the sheriff's posse all go into action for a Grand Slam finish. Direction week photography OK"

And with that, Tyler was done with his association with Frueler, whose lack of production and distribution success sent him back to being a theater owner.

Universal starred Tyler in two serials in 1933, "Clancy of the Mounted" followed by "Phantom of the Air."

Starring in Universal serials gave Tyler another avenue to build an audience and to work on a production with better production values than what Monogram or Frueler could offer. There was also a pitfall: typecasting.

In his book, "I Was That Masked Man," Clayton Moore wrote, "I couldn't help but wonder if they [serials] were a sort of dead end. Few real movie stares started out in serials – John Wayne was a notable exception, It was almost as though once the industry pegged you as serial actor, they couldn't see you in any other light."

Leonard J. Kohl, in his book "Sinister Serials of Boris Karloff, Bela Lugosi and Lon Chaney, Jr." was told by Three Stooges director Ed Bernds "At

Columbia Studios there was only one rung lower than [two-reel comedies] – that was serials."

For Tyler, the issue with all working actors not under a contract was remaining employed and the Universal serial provided a paycheck. Luckily for him his hard work in redefining himself – which will come shortly – will pay off in non-western, non-serial gigs.

It's interesting to note that in all five of Tyler's serials in the early 1930s, William Desmond plays a key supporting role. He started his film career in 1915 after appearing in vaudeville and the stage and developed into a star of both dramas and westerns. He also became a serial hero. He was almost 50 with the coming of sound and he took on many character and supporting roles. He was one of the ranch owners in "The Phantom of the West," a leader of the mining town in "Battling with Buffalo Bill," the father of the heroine in "Jungle Mystery," an Irish frontiersman in "Clancy of the Mounted," and the inventor in "Phantom of the Air."

Desmond was part of group of actors that turned up in westerns time and time again. If you watch enough B westerns you see performers such as Desmond, along with Tom London – who could either be a friend to the hero or a villain – and heavies (or sheriffs) such as Bud Osborne. Osborne was seen in more than 500 films.

Only the first six chapters of the Universal's 12-chapter "Clancy of the Mounted" (1932) serial can be seen today so it's difficult to judge it, however what does exist shows Universal wanted to try the relatively exotic location of Canada and the Royal Mounted Police in its new production.

However, it is essentially a tried-and-true western tale with a villain trying to jump the claim of a murdered prospector whose daughter has come to be with him.

Tyler looks striking in his red Mountie uniform and although the serial is set in forest instead of the plains, it presents a number of familiar western story elements. Universal claimed the serial was based on "the world-famous poem of the same name by Robert W. Service.

There are several dramatic scenes set on a river and the bad guy is another in a string of white guys of some local prominence who have teamed up with local evil native – naturally called a "half-breed." The French-Canadian accents are unconvincing in this one.

The Universal Weekly, (Dec. 10, 1932) the house news publication for the studio noted that Tyler and his female lead Jacqueline Wells had both been the victims of the flu and production was temporarily halted.

The publication reported (Feb. 25, 1933) the studio showed the serial to a group of representatives of women's organizations and the production received positive comments as suitable and exciting for both adults and children.

Universal supplied theaters with badges, photos and membership card to gives to kids. The cards would be punched once a week to encourage the young audiences seeing the entire serial.

According to the studio, exhibitors loved the serial. "If you play serials don't miss this one. Splendid story holds attention. Wonderful photography. The best chapter play for many moons. It fills my show two days a week with real people, too," wrote Ned Pedigo of the Deluxe Theater in Garber, OK (April 22, 1933).

Hollywood Movies, a fan magazine wrote (February 1933), wrote, "Tom Tyler, who slightly resembles Ricardo Cortez, and blonde Jacqueline Well have the leading roles in this latest Universal film epic which is based on the famous poem by that Canadian writer, Robert W. Service. The picture is a serial, chuck full of interest and presents plausible adventures of the Dominion's red-coated police. Good."

In its review section featuring comments from theater owners, the Motion Picture Herald (Aug. 12, 1933) shared the following: "On the fourth episode. Do the kids like it Raised our Saturday matinee from about 40 children average to 120 average. This is good for a town of 1,000 population. The grownups like it too. – A.B. Jefferies, Piedmont, MO."

Another review from a theater manager called the serial "fair entertainment" but complained about "too much repetition."

The next and final chapterplay for Universal is the best one, at least for me. "Phantom of the Air" is a science fiction aviation story that – while it does use stock footage – has plenty of original footage of take-off, landing, crashes and planes in the air.

Reliable William Desmond is inventor Thomas Edmonds this time. He has made a device that counters the effects of gravity and can provide its operator the ability to remotely control a plane.

Tyler plays captain Bob Raymond of the Border Patrol. Raymond flies border missions to hunt down smugglers. He competes in air races and meets Edmonds through a race. Edmonds is impressed and is looking for pilot to test-fly his invention.

Edmonds's daughter Mary, played by Gloria Shea, has been seeing another pilot socially, Mortimer Crome (LeRoy Mason). What she doesn't know is that Crome is the head of a smuggling group and he wants the invention to sell to the highest bidder.

The serial is a battle between Edmonds and Raymond and Crome and his henchmen, including a skinny and positively evil Walter Brennan in the role of "Skid."

While I enjoyed this serial I must admit one reason was that I could see it as it was originally intended to be seen. The production was released in restored form by VCI on Blu-ray and is gorgeous.

Gloria Shea has much more to do in this serial than some other heroines. Her character is a competent flier as well and she isn't easily intimidated by bad guys. That's refreshing.

For Tyler, this was another chance to portray a character outside of the western.

LeRoy Mason makes an appropriately oily smuggler. Mason was another actor who tried to switch roles. Although he often appeared as bad guys, he also played heroic figures in a series of Frankie Darro action films from the mid-1930s.

It shows once again that Tyler wasn't just a cowboy hero but made a fine all-purpose heroic figure.

Tyler, though, was destined for more western roles with his next contract with a new Poverty Row studio.

C. MICHAEL DOBBS

Chapter Four

Reliable proves somewhat reliable

With his time at both Universal and Freuler done, Tyler starred in 18 westerns for a newly formed independent, Reliable Pictures. Reliable tuned out to be aptly named for Tyler's career as it gave him some career stability his shorter stints at previous production companies didn't.

Reliable Pictures was the brain child of two film vets, Bernard B. Ray and Harry S. Webb.

Ray was born in Moscow, Russia, in 1895 and immigrated to the United States. According to a short biographic piece in the 1937 Film Daily product guide and director's annual, "Probably the youngest pioneer in pictures, and he's still in his 30s. Broke into the industry a quarter of a century ago with the American Biograph Company in its laboratory. Then west with David W. Griffith to the Mutual Film Corporation. Was with Triangle – remember? – as cameraman. Later, in charge of an independent laboratory in Hollywood. Subsequently with Capitol Film Corp.. with Educational and in partnership with Ferdinand P. Earle. Directed his first picture in 1920 and since has been directing and producing. Organized Reliable Pictures in 1933 and produced and directed 49 pictures during the last three years. For relaxation, plays a great game of chess, a music lover, attends all symphonies. Stands five feet six inches. Tips the scales at 150."

If he was indeed born in 1895, as noted by IMBD, he was actually 42 in 1937.

Ray's career as a producer, director and writer continued until 1960 with his last film being "Spring Affair." Ray is an interesting guy as he experimented in a variety of genres, not just westerns and many of his films received positive notices from the trades. They range from the sex exploitation film, "It's All in the Mind," which the Legion of Decency condemned but several reviewers thought was inventive, to a 1942 comedy he made at PRC with Harry Langdon called "House of Errors."

Film Daily's critic wrote of "House of Errors," "the direction is excellent ... his production on a limited budget amazing."

In 1940, Ray produced and directed "Broken Strings," a film aimed at the black audience starring Clarence Muse as a classical concert violinist.

Webb had worked at Universal in the silent era as well with serial producer Nat Levine. Jack Perrin was the star of a series of westerns that Webb produced in the mid-1920s. He directed early talkie westerns for The Big 4 Corporation.

Webb produced westerns for Syndicate in 1930 and 1931 including working with Tyler in "West of Cheyenne" (1931).

Together their new company lasted four years before it eventually became absorbed into the newly re-organized Monogram in 1937. The two men parted ways with Ray eventually going to PRC and Webb to the newly reorganized Monogram where Webb's career ended in 1940.

In the true fashion of the low-budget states rights filmmaking, Webb directed several films but under a different name – his was "Henri Samuels."

Reliable had several action stars besides Tyler. They included famed stuntman Richard Talmadge, Western star Jack Perrin and Rin-Tin-Tin Jr. Webb was well known to Tyler for writing, producing and directing some of his Syndicate/Monogram films. He had a long career in the low-budget field.

Ads for some of Tyler's considerable work at Reliable Pictures. (author's collection).

The world of the low budget/states rights studios was a world of hope and hype. There was a short story that was in the Film Daily on Aug. 11, 1936, that read, "B.B. Ray and Harry Webb of Reliable Pictures announced they will make a series of six westerns starring the 'Santa Fe Kid,' a new star. The company will also make four action stunt melodramas and 4 James Oliver Curwood outdoor adventure picture. In addition to these, Reliable will produce two exploitation pictures the first being an all-Yiddish talker."

While Reliable stars Bob Custer and Rin Tin Tin Jr. did star (separately) in five films based on Curwood stories, Custer only starred in one film that featured the "Santa Fe Kid" in "Santa Fe Rides," which was also his last film before retiring from the screen. Although there were certainly Yiddish films produced in the United States in the 1930s I could not find any produced by Ray.

I can't help but admire producers such as Ray and Webb. If they get knocked down, they get back up, adopt a new studio name and get back into the business.

There was an ad in The Film Daily (Aug. 17, 1936), that read "It is untrue that Reliable Picture Corp. is being liquidated and that BB Ray will join another organization." Instead, the ad noted there will be six Bob Custer, three James Oliver Curwood stories starring Rin Tin Tin Jr. and "four special exploitation pictures" for the 1936 to 1937 season. Clearly the Tom Tyler westerns were completed by this time. However. this schedule was not fulfilled.

Webb announced a slate of 12 features to be produced by a new entity called Metropolitan Pictures (Film Daily, April 14, 1938). A 1939 trade ad announced 16 films. Ray was reputed to be involved in this company as well although it is Webb that received the attention. Metropolitan stayed in business until 1940 when Webb made the move to Monogram, producing more westerns through the 1940 season.

A trade ad announcing the Reliable 1934-35 season would include six "action, thriller feature westerns" with the first release being "Ridin' Through" on March 15, 1934, with a new film every six weeks.

Variety published a story on May 15, 1934, that pointed out an increase in the production of B westerns. The headline read, "Another of those spasmodic cowboy revivals on; market soon glutted."

"Sudden boom and horse opera production has started and there are now 14 companies making or about to make Hollywood's oldest type of product.

"This surprising interest in Mesquiteers is almost sure to flood the market and already some New York laboratories and states right exchanges, which picked up the negative, had begun turning them back to producers.

"Western producers are answering a demand by exhibs, particularly in the South and middle west, made three months ago when there was a season shortage. Only two in the group are majors, rest are indies and most are of the shoestring caliber. Among the 14 are Sol Lesser and John Zanft who are dickering with Fox for a release on the series starring George O'Brien. "Mascot is a newcomer preparing a series with Ken Maynard. Universal has a Buck Jones starting in August on a series and Monogram has John Wayne.

"Other producers and their stars are Supreme pictures (Sam Katzman) starting May 15 on a string with Bob Steele; Marion Cohen and Al Mannon, starring Rex Bell; Willis Kent, due in from New York, to do some with Lane Chandler.

"J.P. McGowan director has started a western for Master Arts exchange here it stars Frank Gilmore, a newcomer, who mortgaged his Van Nuys ranch where the film is being shot to angel the picture.

"Bob Holt is doing a string with Ed Cobb; Benny Ray alternates Tom Tyler and Jack Perrin for William Steiner in New York [this was the Reliable series]; Bob Horner has Bill Cody; Herman Fowler turned out 'Four Bad Men' with Noah Berry Jr.; Denver Dixon begins a Buddy Roosevelt opera this week and Bob Tansy has finished six three-wheelers for William Pizor release and starts a mess of Northwest Mounties shortly."

Like other low budget westerns, the Reliable films were without the benefit of a musical score. They used a theme song on the Tyler films, but no music that would heighten the action or suspense. By this time A films had scores, but I'm sure producers such as Ray and Webb saw that as unnecessary expense. They did have several of Tyler's films with a rough and ready cowboy band at the campfire performing a public domain western tune.

It should be noted that aside from Buck Jones, all of the major western stars in the 1930s had times in which they were hired by low budget producers. This was not a badge of failure or necessarily diminishing box office appeal, but instead a reality of the industry at that time. There was a demand for westerns and the major studios didn't always fulfill it.

Before looking at Tyler's Reliable films, I'd like to emphasize that making these low-budget films were a lot of physical work. Shooting on outdoor locations with fast schedules, B westerns may have been quick but not easy.

The key to understanding how B westerns – or any other B film – is a viable economic model. Make the film as cheaply as one could – knowing that cutting corners too much could result in poor bookings – increased the potential for profits. And the profits for the B-western producers did not come from box-office results. It came from the satisfaction of the territorial distributors who bought the rights to the film in order to rent them to theater owners.

If a company's films were seen as affordable and turned a profit for the theater owners because of their popularity with the audiences, the model worked. In his autobiography, "Tim Coy Rembers the West," McCoy, a contemporary of Tyler's, recalls working for Puritan Pictures in the mid-1930s. "Puritan was not one of the most prestigious production companies and the quality of the films I made for them, which were sometimes completed after only three-or-four-days' shooting, left much to be desired." This is from a man whose initial Western stardom was at MGM.

Two scenes from "Ridin' Thru." One of Tyler's changing roster of sidekicks is seen here: Ben Corbett. (author's collection)

Ridin' Thru 1934
Director: Harry S. Webb as Henri Samuels

The Film Daily Feb 24, 1934, offered a good synopsis, "Fair western built around dude ranch and stallion used as lure by horse rustlers. Fairly novel story developed with a pleasant romantic interest and the usual number of conflicts this one should satisfy kid audiences in particular. Difficulties center around a ranch which has been thrown open to the dudes because the owner has become hard up through thefts of horses from his herds the rancher has summoned Tyler to help find the thieves. It is shown that a white stallion has been luring away the mares and that then the equines were driven into a concealed valley. The foreman of the ranch is the leader of the crooks. Tom gets a job at the ranch and then proceeds to corral the crooks blocked every step of the way by foreman and his cohorts to a fighting finish. The development of Tom's affair with the rancher's niece is carried right through the story to a clinch at the end. Ruth Hiatt plays that heroine."

The Philadelphia Exhibitor March 2, 1934, "Horses are being stolen and Tom Tyler makes up his mind to find out. He does and wins the girl. Western is up to the usual standard."

The most prominent co-star of this film is the white horse who is the leader of the wild horses in the area. Amazingly enough it's not all stock footage. The horse is more interesting than sidekick Ben Corbett, whose employment in movies still confounds me. His efforts at comedy are far from satisfactory.

"Ridin' Thru" is one of those westerns apparently set in the 1930s, so there are automobiles on the range – something that as a kid always confused me. I wondered if people actually rode horses when there were cars?

The dude ranch setting allowed the film makers to have several shots of women walking around in bathing suits, adding a little appeal for older male audiences. The party scene – complete with a band – has more extras than usually in a Reliable production.

Tyler's horse is pretty impressive as he can untie knots, saving Tyler from the bad guys.

Co-star Ruth Hiatt was also in an uncredited part in "Her Man" as was Tyler.

Mystery Ranch 1934
Director: B.B. Ray

Film Daily (May 26, 1934) "'Mystery Ranch' is a corking western that mixes history and novelty with fast moving action. Much removed from the usual western and having a story that mingles humor, romance and novelty with

Ad slick for "Mystery Ranch. (author's collection)

almost continuous action this one will make the thrill fans happy. Tyler, a native westerner, who has been writing blood and thunder stories for magazines accepts an invitation to visit mystery ranch where he is assured things happen that will make his stories seem pallid. The invite is a gag to lure a trade to mystery ranch on Tyler's fame so they stage a lynching, a shooting and a hold up to provide the atmosphere Tyler quickly discerns the play acting so that when he witnesses a real hold up he just looks on. The hold up men come to the ranch with their loot. Tyler induces his secretary to act as a hold up man take the loot and the girl and flee thinking this to show he is not being duped. From this point on the action is fast and furious with Tom the bandits and the sheriff off hastening to recover the loot and the girl."

The cast included three familiar names to western fans: Charles King, Tom London and George Cheseboro.

The review also noted that the direction was good and that the photography was good.

The Philadelphia Exhibitor in its July 1, 1934, edition, "Action-packed western that will please the thrill hunting fans anywhere. Picture has more plot than usual has plenty of opportunity for the usual thriller stunts. Western advocates will be satisfied. Estimate: moves right along."

This is one of my favorite Tyler films as it tries and succeeds in coming up with a new story angle. The introduction has Tyler spoofing himself and the conventions of the western, including very florid dialogue. "My Oriental blood is boiling! I thirst for revenge," said the villain into the comic opening.

Tyler's comedy relief sidekick is his secretary Percival played by Frank Hall Crane who is as about as effective a comic sidekick as Ben Corbett.

The ranchers stage various cliched western scenes, including a hanging, to impress the writer and there is a neat sequence involving a runaway carriage. Tyler – and his stunt man – stops the carriage and when the heroine questions how the writer managed to do this, Tyler attributes it to his exercising at the YMCA!

The climactic fistfight between Tyler and three – count 'em – bad guys could have been quite dramatic if there had been a stunt coordinator like Yakima Canutt planning the brawl and if director B.B. Ray had actually moved his camera and included different angles and shots. In a film in which there were no apparent sound effects added, during this fight there is one suspicious crack with a punch thrown by Tyler to Tom London. It really sounds like Tyler definitely connected.

Eventually Reliable would add a sound effect or two during a fight to underscore the actions.

A behind-the scenes photo the set of "Mystery Ranch" featuring Tyler, dressed smartly in a suit, with Roberta Gale next to him and producer and director B.B. Ray, next to her. Courtesy of the late film historian Richard Bojarski.

The film's director is B. B. Ray himself and he seems a little more competent than some of the directors Tyler had to endure, but the fight scene betrays the speed of the production.

Fightin' Hero 1934
Director: Harry S. Webb

Tyler plays Tom Hall, a wanted outlaw with a price on his head. He is pursued by two men who he successfully evades.

Riding into town, Hall gets a beer where he overhears the owner of the saloon, Bert Hawley (Edward Hear) is cheating a young man in cards, he decides to intervene. He figures out the cheat and reveals him.

Hall leaves the saloon but the saloon owner has him followed. He overhears a trial in progress. A young Mexican woman, Conchita (Renee Borden) is accused of murdering a man who she explains was assaulting her. Hall volunteers to be the woman's attorney and gets a recess. While recreating the girl's version of events, Hall notices that Hawley is taking aim at him, shoots the gun from Hawley's hand and escapes out of a window, riding out of town with her.

Conchita declares her love for Hall, something that makes him uncomfortable. He directs her to stop thinking about love and instead how they are going to get her out of the charges that she killed someone. After he drops her off to Conchita's aunt's house, Hall is chased by the sheriff and his deputy, who are out looking for him.

A thief, named Morales (J.P. McGowan), posing as a miner, plans to hold up the stage carrying a $50,000 payload. Hall becomes part of the plan.

Hawley visits Conchita and shows her Hall's wanted poster. He wants her cooperation in capturing Hall, distracting him so she can disarm him. He manages to escape although Conchita discovers he is actually an express agent on the correct side of the law. Hawley decides to use this information so the Morales mob can get rid of him.

Hall tells the sheriff who he is, but the sheriff is dubious. Hall heads off to confront and stop the Morales gang.

After a chase and a fight, Hall emerges victorious and engaged.

This film gave Tyler a couple of scenes in which his mood changes from affable to angry. While he doesn't over-act, it would appear that he welcomed the opportunity.

While Webb was consistently a better director than his partner Ray and the ubiquitous J.P. McGowan, There are long and medium shots, a clear indication of a rule in low-budget filmmaking that holds true to this day: set-ups mean money.

McGowan seems to be a more effective actor than director.

Borden makes an effective heroine, despite a pretty awful Mexican accent. She had a very short career in film.

Variety noted, "Enough excitement and plot in this chase to keep them interested throughout the 53 minutes. As usual Tom Tyler has most of his personality wrapped up in that whimsical smile but the lad's knack for hard riding and putting on the assemblance of a good fist fight provides a neat selling point for 'Fighting Hero.'"

Film Daily (July 17, 1934) "Lively western carries lots of action from start to finish. Plenty of action carried along on a plot that sustains interest makes this one red meat for the thrill fans"

Motion Picture Daily Oct. 3,1934 "The main thought to be found with this Tom Tyler vehicle is that it plays fast and loose with the truth. Some of its instances are so far-fetched that they are certain to be greeted with snickers even from an audience of western fans. That is exactly what happened at a neighborhood showing of the film. Tyler's name is the only one in the cast that means anything. 'The Fighting Hero' it's one of those westerns in which the hero, representative of the forces of law-and-order, poses as a bad man in order to track down a gang of outlaws. In this case, Tyler is an operative for an express company out to solve the hold up of some gold shipments. After being chased hither and yon by the sheriff and others who really believe him to be a bandit Tyler reveals his true identity and receives as his biggest reward the love of a Spanish senorita. The picture creates plenty of noise, is packed with action and is best suited for juveniles. Harry S. Webb directed."

Several trade papers printed reviews from theater managers and "Fighting Hero" received two. The following were published in the Motion Picture Herald on Dec. 29, 1934:

"'Fighting Hero. Tom Tyler – average western plenty of action. Pleased. Business slightly below average on the count of cold weather. Avon Park, FL. "'Fighting Hero. Tom Tyler – A good western better than usual for Tyler. Lots of action. fair business." Henderson, NC

Terror on the Plains 1934
Director: Harry S. Webb

Predating the singing cowboy trend, the film opens with Tom Lansing (Tyler) in his cattle herding camp listening to a decidedly unpolished singer. A letter about his father causes him to resign from the outfit immediately. His father has been framed for a murder by outlaw Butcher Wells.

The canyon used in Deadwood Pass makes another appearance. It's the gateway to a ghost town where Wells (William Gould) and his gang are hiding. Wells is holding a young woman named Bess (Roberta Gale) he found stranded in the desert and has decided to marry her.

Tyler poses as an outlaw to meet Wells and enter the hideout. Wells is suspicious since Tyler had tried to allow Bess's escape.

Wells tells Lansing, "We share everything except our women." This is definitely a Pre-Code movie.

Naturally, the two men fight for Bess and Webb handles the lengthy fight scene fairly well. Lansing wins and is forced to marry Bess – yes, there is a parson as part of the gang.

Lansing then must participate in a hold-up as a test. Luckily his sidekick, the former camp cook, has been waiting for him, enabling Lansing to be in position to prevent the robbery.

The parson turns out is the only witness to clear Tyler's father.

When the gang suspects Lansing after his sidekick has been captured, a gun fight ensues. Webb is less successful here in building suspense as the fight is mostly shot in long shots. Tyler's horse runs out of the camp, a signal for the sheriff and his posse to move in. The fact the sheriff was waiting was not a plot point this viewer expected as there was no indication to the plan. Wells escapes on horseback and Lansing follows, naturally catching up with him and beating him again in a fistfight.

The film ends with Lansing back with his cattle outfit and officially in love with Bess.

Webb used close-ups effectively in his film, unlike his partner B.B. Ray. He also took advantage of some higher ground for some panoramic shots. This is a remake of "West of Cheyenne" with Tyler that Webb directed several years before.

Unconquered Bandit 1934
Director: Harry S. Webb

The film opens on two rustlers about to change a brand when they are spotted. A Mexican rancher Gasparo (Joe De La Cruz) comes by and realizes what they are doing. Tom Morgan (Tyler) rides up with his father Mr. Morgan (John Elliot). They are both in Spanish style outfits. They have a ranch below in the border and Tom is half-Mexican.

Gasparo tells the men that Cleyborn (the always evil William Gould) wants to drive him off his property and back to Mexico (even though as Gasparo noted they are all American citizens) because there has been a gold strike on his land.

At a party at the Morgan ranch – complete with a mariachi band and dancing extras – a traveler, Helen Cleyborn, Cleyborn's niece, (Lillian Gilmore) seeks directions. Tom invites her in.

He doesn't know that his father and Gasparo are being attacked by Cleyborn's men. Tom and his men drive away Clayborn's men but not before his father is killed. He swears revenge on Clayborn and says he will assume the persona of a notorious thief The Nighthawk (Slim Whitaker with a phony Mexican accent) and rob Cleyborn. He also wants to seduce the niece and break her heart.

He raids Clayborn's ranch successfully, but his conscience bothers him as he has actually fallen in love with Helen. He tells her his plan and she approves of it.

The real Nighthawk betrays Morgan after Morgan tells him he is going to bow out of their arrangement. Morgan is captured by Clayborn and his men and sent to jail.

Helen goes to her uncle and confesses her love with Morgan and her uncle's efforts to remove the settlers. Clayborn even admits that his efforts indirectly caused the death of Tom's father.

Cleyborn sets things up that Morgan would be released from jail so he can identify the Nighthawk, not knowing that the real Nighthawk, who had tipped off Cleyborn leading to Morgan's arrest, would be there to collect a reward.

The Nighthawk, sensing a trap, kills Cleyborn, but Morgan captures him. The settlers are returned to their homes and Morgan and Helen are headed to marriage.

This film varies the format a bit with the Mexican angle and Tyler looks great in the Mexican suit. This is another effort in which Reliable seems to be wanting to break out of the usual cowboy fare. There is an element of social justice here as well as respect for Mexican settlers.

The logic of the script is a little wonky: why would Tyler's character actually trust The Nighthawk? Would Helen instantly forgive him for his deception? And the change in Cleyborn's character? That was completely unexpected but again the change was welcomed.

Film Daily, Jan. 8, 1935, noted, "Good western with better story material than usually found in this type of picture. Greater pains were taken and building a picture around a story in this case and although not as spectacular as some blood and thunder films, the movement carries through well to the finish without revealing just what is going to happen. This is a good idea to keep the kids puzzled and guessing. Tom Tyler cast as half English and half Spanish loses his father at the hands of the Cleyborn gang and he swears vengeance. He meets Cleyborn's niece on route to her uncle for a visit and decides to decoy her thus striking Cleyborn with a subtle weapon. While making false affection to her Tyler actually falls in love and confesses his deception. She forgives him but Nighthawk with whom Tyler has plotted against Cleyborn double crosses him and the posse is about to hang Tyler when he escapes and exposes the real nighthawk, thus clearing himself and winning the heroine. Plenty of lusty fist fighting. Direction fair, photography OK."

Coyote Trails 1935
Director: Harry S. Webb

Ray and Webb were clearly in the remake mode with this production revisiting the plot of "Ridin' Thru." Tom Riley (Tyler) and Windy (Ben Corbett) are heading to a ranch for jobs. The ranch has been the subject of horse stealing with rival ranchers rustling horses and blaming it on a wild white stallion luring the mares. In reality The Phantom does lead the herd away from the rustlers as well and, as in the first film, uses a tunnel in the mountains to get away.

Although Ray and Webb change some of the plot from the first film, it has been built around the footage of the white stallion from the earlier film. The principal difference is in this film, the stallion is caught in a trap – in an effort to capture him for a reward set by rancher Lafe McKee – and Riley releases him.

The heroine, rising on her horse, encounters the stallion who leads her horse in an out-of-control gallop. Riley rescues her and makes her a bet he will capture and break the horse.

Character actor Richard Alexander is the bad guy of the story and he brings a true sense of physical menace to this role.

Of the two films using the same basic plot, I'd give the edge to "Coyote Trails."

The Philadelphia Exhibitor (March 2, 1935) said, "A gang of rustlers have conspired with an apparently respectable rancher to steal horses from the ranch of the heroine's father. Blame as placed on phantom, a wild horse, can't be conquered. Tom comes into the picture, not only saves the life of the horse, rides it, but finds out where the rustlers have been taking the stolen cattle. He saves the day exposes the gang and wins the girl. Estimate: standard Tyler."

An exhibitor from Flomaton, AL, wrote, "Good western. Better than average Tyler. If he could put over a better exhibition of fighting he would go over better here. Ben Corbett's always good." (Motion Picture Herald Oct. 26, 1935)

Tracy Rides 1935
Director: Harry S. Webb

Tom Tracy (Tyler)is a sheriff who has to arrest his future brother-on-law Ned (Eddie Cobb) for the murder of a sheep rancher. Ned escapes, but Tracy captures him but not after getting shot in the shoulder by him. The two men hide from Ned's father who is intent on saving his son from a trial.

Tracy's fiancée (Virginia Brown Faire) tries to convince Tracy that for the sake of their love he should let her brother go, but Tyler sticks to his duty. Ned manages to escape and the cattlemen decide to capture him. Tyler escapes but is seriously wounded. He returns to his fiancée's house in a daze.

The film concludes with a stand-off between the sheep and cattlemen that is broken through Tracy's help and Ned's accidental shooting. Before he dies, Ned expresses remorse.

Tyler's character and situation gave him more to work with in this film. He seems truly conflicted between the cattlemen who elected him to sheriff, love for his fiancée and doing his duty to arrest the murderer.

The film does use some stock footage, but actually stages believable cattle stampeded at one point. While there are a couple of brawls, the violence here is largely emotional and the direction of the film emphasizes the human emotions in the situation.

I think this one of Tyler's best Reliable films.

Film Daily (May 5, 1935) "Snappy western with Tyler getting over punch stuff in nice action plot. A very pleasing western in which there is something doing right through to the last frame. Tom Tyler as a sheriff has a tough assignment in trying to apprehend the brother of his sweetheart for murder. The young lad, during a drunken spree, had shot a sheep herder and the sheriff hero is out to arrest him the cattleman headed by the boy's father stormed the cabin in which Tom is holding his prisoner and succeeded in freeing him. Then starts the beginning of what looks like a pitched battle between the cattlemen and the sheep herders. The latter wants the murder of their group arrested and punished while the cattlemen want to drive through the sheep-

Tyler looks after an injured Eddie Cobb in "Tracy Rides." Cobb was an amazingly ubiquitous presence in American motion pictures as a star, a supporting player and an extra. IMBd lists 669 credits! (author's collection)

herder's territory in order to reach water for their cattle. Works up to a good tense climax with a surprise solution for the problem of the murderer."

The heroine is played by Virginia Brown Faire and Film Daily said the "direction was fast, the photographer was OK."

A theater manager in Henderson, NC, wrote about the film, "This western was not as good as usual. We didn't have any comments good or bad, follow this up with a good short and it will pass."

Born to Battle 1935
Director: Harry S. Webb

After spooking a carriage, Tyler playing a wandering cowboy, Tom Saunders, stops the runaway team and apologizes. He has a wild reputation and has the nickname of "Cyclone Tom."

He and his pals ride into town with their guns being fired in the air. He then tears a Chinese laundry apart looking for his shirt, an action that leads to his arrest and a visit to a judge.

Charles King steps up and pays Tyler's fine and has the judge parole Saunders to him. He wants Saunders to manage a ranch and keep rustlers and nesters off of the ranch's property.

Saunders must inform the current manager he is being replaced. Along the trail he picks up two new friends – and when they come into the town he accidentally meets the man he is supposed to replace.

William Desmond plays the old superintendent and, unknown to him he is talking to his replacement, he hires Saunders to take care of the rustlers and nesters before the new superintendent arrives. Saunders remains quiet about who he is.

His two pals get hired to protect the nesters. When Saunders discovers the nesters are the father and daughter whose team he had spooked, he becomes suspicious they are being used as scapegoats.

Saunders is framed for a shooting death and sent off to the sheriff. The nesters have been imprisoned by the real rustlers who are ranch hands.
Chases back and forth ensue in this plot-heavy film until Saunders catches rustler Richard Alexander and predictably proposes to the heroine.
There is a famous western trope of the good bad man or the bad guy who is reformed. This movie is a variety of that and shows what I call the "immature a-hole who is reformed." The film's treatment of Chinese characters shows Saunders's character as a racist as well.

His character is not very likable at first, which in a way is refreshing when compared to the typical western hero

Jean Carmen, who played the heroine, is not the Jeanne Carmen, who was active in movies in the 1950s and '60s as a blonde sex symbol. This Jean Carmen appeared in other westerns as well as roles with the comedy teams of Wheeler and Woolsey and the Three Stooges. She has a most definite Jean Harlow look in this film.

There is decided effort for comedy in this film with the courtroom scene as well as the two actors playing Tyler's pals – both recognizable faces in westerns – Nelson McDowell as "Blinky" and Julian Rivero as "Pablo."

The Philadelphia Exhibitor (June 1, 1935) wrote, "Stronger than usual on comedy photographed well 'Born to Battle' should satisfy.

Silent Valley 1935
Director: B.B. Ray

The film opens with a cattle rustling followed by Sheriff Tom Hall (Tyler) tracking the stolen cattle with the legitimate owner, who admits to Hall he and other ranchers haven't been impressed with him as sheriff.

Hall discovers a disguised way to the rustlers' hideout and one of his deputies is shot. He trails one of the rustlers to the home of his friend Fred, (Wally

This still has almost every character in "Born to Battle!" Tyler is fighting Richard Alexander – a frequent adversary – while William Desmond has a gun pulled just in case. (author's collection)

Wales). Fred is nervous about talking with Hall, which fuels Hall's suspicions. The boss of the gang, Farley, (Al Bridge) manages to replace Hall's deputy with one of his men, Pete (Slim Whitaker). Fred, though, is having cold feet and wants out. He is forced to stay in the gang as he owes money to Farley. One of the gang, Harry (Charles King) is revealed to be the man who shot Hall's deputy. During the apprehension, Harry gives up, but Pete kills him in cold blood. Hall beats Pete in a fight and then takes his deputy's badge.

Fred wants out of the gang, but Farley will not allow that.

Despite laying a trap, Farley is caught and Fred's confession prevents him from going to prison.

Once again, a Tyler western benefits from Wally Wales's involvement. In this film he was the young man who had gambling problems and was now forced to engage in criminal activity. Wales had a long career as a character actor after his time as a star was over, working until 1952 when he retired. For me, he presented a sense of authenticity as he was raised on a ranch in Montana, where he became known for his horsemanship.

Philadelphia Exhibitor (July 15, 1935), wrote, "Usual western plot has the hero, the sheriff, but entanglements arise when the heroine's brother gets mixed up with the gang. 'Silent Valley' runs true to form also keeps to pattern when he saves the brother, rounds up the gang, wins the girl. Tyler keeps to his usual standard."

The Silver Bullet 1935
Director: B.B. Ray

A gang of three no-goods come into town, guns blazing in order to scare the residents into submission. Two of them head to the general store to buy more ammunition – that is to take more ammunition – when Tom Henderson (Tyler) interrupts and throws them out. He's a prospector working a claim.

The trio of bad guys ambush Henderson out of town and while they don't hurt him they stop his burro and steal his supplies.

They are working for the town's banker, (Charles King) who secretly is the head of an outlaw gang, which is terrorizing the community. Henderson has made an impression on the townspeople and is appointed sheriff by a group of residents.

The ubiquitous character actor Lafe McKee plays the blind newspaper publisher and owner of the town's general store. McKee practices his marksmanship by having his assistant tap the tin can targets with a long stick.

McKee is searching for the man who blinded him and believes he can recognize the guy by the sound of his voice. He was blinded by a man who killed his wife in an effort to jump his claim.

Henderson is supposed to release the bad guy he arrested to the county marshal but in reality the "marshal" is another gang member who frames Henderson. The gang robs the bank, as well.

Charlie King casts doubt among the townspeople who won't go along with Henderson in pursuit but the real county marshal sets out to help Tyler.

Henderson tracks down the gang and runs out of bullets in the firefight. He takes the bullet off of a necklace given to him by his girlfriend and uses it to stop the remaining gang member.

Naturally King is exposed as the leader and caught.

Wally Wales makes another appearance in a Tyler film as his deputy. Ray actually uses an effective moving shot on one scene, something his films generally don't have. There is also a group of close-ups in one sequence. Perhaps he was learning from his partner Harry Webb.

Motion Picture Daily (Oct. 27, 1935), wrote, "A Tom Tyler western has little to excite audiences past the childhood stage. It is quite routine in every department. That old standby of the western picture, the Jekyll/Hyde town banker is called upon again to provide the villainy. Tyler in becoming the town's new sheriff inherits a nice chunk of trouble. The fellow who runs the bank is using his position of trust to cover up his activities as the head of a gang of outlaws when, through a ruse, they get Tyler to free one of their number. The brand-new sheriff has a lot of explaining to do to clear himself of the suspicion of being one of the outfit. He sallies fourth alone to battle the gang. When his bullets failed to go off, he saves himself from being shot by one of the gang by using a silver bullet given to him by his sweetheart."

The Laramie Kid 1935
Director: Harry Webb

This is one of the most interesting Reliable films with Tyler given a more challenging role of a young man, Tom Talbot, with a gambling problem. He tells his girlfriend, Peggy, (Alberta Vaughn) that he has lost his entire savings of $2,000 betting in a horse race.

Peggy's father needs $1,000 to save his ranch. The banker Jim Morley (Al Ferguson) is sweet on Peggy. Talbot is intent on getting the $1,000 to save the ranch and win over her father.

He accidentally falls in with a group of bank robbers and although he had nothing to do with the robbery he is now a wanted man.

Captured by Peggy's father, Tyler pleads guilty to ensure that he gets the $1,000 reward saving his ranch. Peggy is determined to prove Talbot's innocence.

Talbot must serve his time on the prison road crew.

Peggy discovers the bag from the robbery and it's filled with blank pieces of paper instead of money.

On the road gang, Talbot discovers his pal Shorty (Snub Pollard) who tells him one of the bank robbery gang revealed that Morley engineered the robbery to hide a shortfall of cash.

Talbot escapes from the road gang – although he did not intend to – and clears his name.

The casting of this film should be noted. Alberta Vaughn was a studio mate of Tyler's working at FBO at the same time as he was under contract. At FBO, she was in comedies and with her curly hair, round face and bee-stung lips she looked a lot like Betty Boop! She made the transition to talkies and starred in a number of short comedies with Al Cook. She made her last two films for Reliable – this one and Richard Talmadge's "The Live Wire" also in 1935. She retired from the screen but occasionally made the headlines for a string of incidences with alcohol.

Vaughn has much more to do as the heroine in this film than many other of the female leads in the Tyler Reliable films and turns in a good performance. Snub Pollard was a prominent silent comic with a trademark droopy mustache who remained working in films long past his days of stardom in two-reelers. He supported Harold Lloyd and Charley Chase and worked for Mack Sennet and Hal Roach. During the sound era he kept working in a wide variety of films in bit parts or as an uncredited extra. He was Tex Ritter's sidekick Pee-Wee in series of films in the late 1930s for Grand National. He worked steadily in television right up until his death in 1962.

Philadelphia Exhibitor (Nov. 15, 1935) wrote, "Typical Tyler certain to satisfy. This sees him going to jail falsely in order that the $1,000 reward may be used to help pay a debt owed by the heroine's father. Tom is convicted on an alleged bank robbery charge but later it develops that the town's banker is short, arrange the robbery to cover up. Before it is all over Tyler has cleared. The banker gang rounded up. Satisfying."

Rio Rattler 1935

Director: Franklyn Shamray (IMBD lists this as a name used by B.B. Ray)

Tom Denton (Tyler) and his pal Soapy (Eddie Gribbon) stop at a saloon and Soapy is desperate for a drink despite Tyler reminding him their new job requires him to stay sober. The bartender cheats Soapy and a fight ensues when Tyler comes in. A cowboy named Bob (Tom London) at the bar helps the two escape from the angry crowd.

Bob rides along with them but takes another road. Shortly after they leave one another Bob is shot. Before he passes, he tells Denton and Soapy that he is an undercover ranger heading to the border town of Rio to force out a dangerous gang. Denton assumes the identity of the murdered lawman.

Of course, the leader of the gang is the bank owner Mason (William Gould) and his chief thug is the Rattler played by Slim Whitaker.

Things get complicated when the murdered ranger's sister comes to town. Mason learned Denton is not really the ranger and hatches a plan to expose him by using the ranger's sister.

Tyler comes up with a plan to expose the ranger's murderer and reveal the leader of the gang.

In a rare move for a Reliable film, Soapy the sidekick is killed. Eddie Gribbon's career in films started in 1917 and continued until 1958. Gribbon was featured in silent comedies as well as dramas and worked in all genres of films.

There's a cute gag involving three of the bar room thugs – who are singers – with long beards called the Smith Brothers, a reference to the mascots of the cough drop. They later turn up as allies.

The film also features a cowboy band performing in the town's saloon – music, other than the tinny record used for the opening, is a rarity in a Reliable production.

Philadelphia Exhibitor (Dec. 15, 1935) wrote, "Up to standard Tyler. This shows him cleaning up a town in which a gang headed by the Rio Rattler has been holding sway. Even though the murdered ranger's sister mistakes him for the man who killed her brother, though his pal is shot, hero Tom never fails, brings the gang to justice, reveals a leading citizen as another gang member, wins the girl. Western fans won't have any complaints."

Trigger Tom 1935
Director: Harry Webb

Tom Hunter (Tyler) is a cattle rancher who hires Stub (Al St. John) to help him in a cattle deal in the Blue Mountains, notorious for outlaws. As they attempt to get to the ranch where they want to buy cattle, someone shoots at them. Hunter captures the assailant but releases him into the custody of someone who identifies himself as a marshal. This is the venerable William Gould playing Mose Jekyll, who we all know is the bad guy in charge.

Hunter had received a letter from a cattle rancher in the Blue Mountains that he wants to sell his herd. What Hunter and Stub don't realize is the community there is a bunch of men wanted by the law who exists under the protection of Jekyll, who sells their cattle and takes percentage. The leaders of the community don't want the sale to go through as it would mean a cattle drive along the secretive trails that would reveal the existence of the small town.

Hunter persists and finds the rancher who had contacted him. Jekyll's afraid that if the sale goes through his control of the ranchers ends.

Jorgenson, (John Elliot) wants to get his niece out of the community but needs money but Jekyll is determined to stop the sale.

Jorgenson agrees to make the sale to Hunter and a young rancher in the town, Sam (Wally Wales) agrees to sell his cattle as well.

In an unusual duel, Jorgenson wins a duel against Slater, (Lloyd Ingraham) the leader of the community and wins the right to use the pass to get the cattle out of the mountains. Jekyll has other ideas and intends to blow the pass up as the cattle pass through it. Hunter rushes to stop them and is successful.

Reliable apparently spent more time and care on this film. The cattle drive is largely stock footage but the budget actually allowed for some cattle on set. The pass is the one used in "Deadwood Pass" and other films where Webb actually staged an explosion.

St. John plays the role of sidekick straight with only a pratfall in the character's introduction. Other than that, he plays the role straight. Well-known for his slapstick origins in silent films – he was Roscoe "Fatty" Arbuckle's cousin – St. John added westerns to his credits in 1930. Best known as Al "Fuzzy St. John, his best-known credits are as the sidekick and co-star of the Buster Crabbe westerns made in the 1940s at PRC.

Philadelphia Exhibitor reported, "Up to the high Tyler standard. Good stuff for the western lovers. This has a little different plot will satisfy."

Fast Bullets 1935
Director: Harry S. Webb billed as Henri Samuels

The film opens with Ranger Tom Milton (Tyler) interrogating someone about the Travis gang that killed several rangers. His Commander Drummond (William Gould in a rare, good guy role) gives him and his partner the order to try to stop the gang.

Milton discovers three members of the gang and manages to beat two of them, taking them to justice. Milton stays in the field to try to capture more gang members and comes across the third, Jimmy, (Rex Lease) who was cooking bacon. Milton tries to convince him to give him information about Travis as opposed to going to prison. He gives Jimmy all the reasons why he should stay free and Jimmy agrees to help him.

Jimmy reluctantly agrees to take Milton to the gang boss Travis in order for Milton to capture him. They meet Travis (Al Bridge) and Milton saves his life and asks Travis to join his gang. Milton also meets the saloon's dancing girl Joan (Margaret Nearing) who happens to be Jimmy's sister. She wants her brother to go straight.

Travis doesn't say "yes" immediately and Milton goes out on the range to see what he can find and sees a suspicious cabin. Later that night, he discovers boxes of explosives and drilling equipment in the cabin. Milton narrowly escaped.

One of the captured gang members has escaped and tells Travis who Milton is. Milton is captured and Jimmy is told to shoot him. Travis learns the rangers are on their way and decides to use Milton as a decoy before the slaughter.

Jimmy brings the note to ranger commander and declares his allegiance to Milton. Using dummies on horseback, the rangers outwitted the gang. Milton beats Travis and saves Joan from the carriage loaded with explosives with runaway horses.

Again, this Reliable production seems a step up from many of the others in the series. It has a different theme song and introduces the cast members with clips of them from the movie. The dialogue is above the Reliable average and Tyler seems more comfortable with it.

The film also has a pretty lengthy song and dance number in the saloon featuring the heroine played by Nearing, a vaudeville and circus star who had a short career in films.

There is a well-planned and edited chase sequence in the first third of the film that shows greater care than in other films. The climactic runaway carriage sequence is also well shot and edited for a low budget western.

Rex Lease had a long career in Hollywood as a lead in low budget films and character parts in bigger films. As the Variety review below indicates Lease was considered a western star at this point in his career. His character is supposed to be younger than Tyler's but Lease was born in the same year as Tyler was.

Variety said, "Producer of this thriller hit upon the bright idea of using two western stars instead of the customary single hero unlike some attempts to bolster films strength by this artifice. Bernard B. Ray absolutely has heightened the appeal. Rex Lease, that bronco rider, was tossed in with Tom Tyler when the latter generally is viewed as sufficient. Has not dimmed Tyler's luster and affords lease plenty of opportunities.

"'Fast Bullets' is a fast-moving tale of Texas Rangers fight to route a band of contraband runners. Tom Tyler, of course, is the leading figure in the ranger operations with Rex Lease introduced as his friend who finally wins his spurs as a full-fledged officer. Standard formula is followed for the most part with early encounters with brigands and then the customary daring rescue of the girl's sweetheart; run-away a wagon filled with ammunition and capture of bandits through a novel ruse. A spark of originality is introduced when dummies on horseback are employed to decoy the outlaws while the real rangers do a rear-guard attack."

Ridin' on 1936
Director: Ira Webb

Tom Rork (Tyler) is a cowboy riding to Wolf Creek when he is shot at by an unknown assailant. His horse gets spooked by a carriage driven by Doc Onderdunk (Robert McKenzie), who is also the area's deputy sheriff, dentist and undertaker.

The Rorks and the O'Neils, competing ranchers, are in a fight over the rights of property on the range.

Tom and Onderduck go their separate ways until Tom stops at a cabin to ask directions he finds a murdered man slumped over his dinner table. As he leaves the cabin, Onderdunk pulls up and explains to Tom the murdered man was in the middle of a range war between the two families. Tom represents his father who owns land in the region.

On his way to his ranch, Tom encounters a woman, Gloria O'Neil (Joan Barclay) who is being chased and then lassoed by Mike Gonzado (Slim Whitaker). Tom disarms him and they escape. The two are then shot at and followed by another group of riders. It turns out the woman belongs to the opposing family to Tom's and is wanted for murder.

Gloria's brother Danny comes to rescue them and Tom isn't happy when he realizes Danny had switched horses to throw the posse off his trail. To add to Tom's suspicions, the brother Danny (Rex Lease) and his father (Earl Dwire) are very threatening to him.

Tyler's character is a detective in his film as he collects shells that are evidence to show a link between murders and the attempted shooting.

Because he helped Gloria, his father kicks him out of the family. Tom meets with Gloria the next morning and explained his theory about the murder. Danny turns up and hears the explanation and forms an alliance.

The problem is revealed: the Rork foreman is rustling cattle from both families causing the range war.

This Reliable production seems to be another upgrade in budget, with a larger cast and the use of a different western town set, a welcomed visual element. The shoot-out at the end of the film is actually impressive for a Reliable.

The film gives Barclay something more to do than the average Reliable heroine and gives Rex Lease another co-starring role, again as someone juvenile to Tyler's character. McKenzie who plays Onderduck adds some comedy but his character has the gravitas of a solid sidekick.

Director Ira Webb was Harry Webb's brother and his credit pops up on several Tyler Reliable productions. An occasional director, he also was an associate producer for Ron Ormand's westerns released in the late 1940s through Robert Lippert's organization. These include the five westerns featuring James Ellison and Russell Hayden that Ormand made that also co-starred Tyler.

It should be noted how often the careers of performers, producers/directors and crew crisscross one another in the B movie field is pretty remarkable. Ira Webb's career arc is pretty astounding: working on low budget westerns to start and to end but in the middle, he was nominated for three Academy Awards for Art Direction and won the Oscar for "Phantom of the Opera" in 1943.

The Philadelphia Exhibitor (Aug. 1, 1936) "Hero Tom comes back to his homeland finds his father battling the rival clan because of homesteading rights he falls in love with the heroin, the opposing leader's daughter. Eventually, it is proved that the party responsible for all the trouble is the father's foreman, who has been double crossing as well as murdering. With plentiful shooting, hard riding, not much dialogue, but lots of action, this holds to the usual Tyler standard."

Variety (June 14, 1937) called it a "routine western … It's a Tom Tyler picture and he is supported by the familiar faces."

Roamin' Wild 1936
Director: B.B. Ray

The film opens with Marshal Tom Barton (Tyler) and his posse successfully chasing down bank robbers. He learns he is being promoted and his younger brother Reed (John Elliot) will take his place, something that evokes his reservations. He tells him, "Living by the gun; someday we'll miss. We all do."

The brother is assigned to Placerville, a gold mining community, which Tom says is dangerous as the last marshal there was shot in the back. A gang, pulling an illegal "tax" scam on the miners, kills the son of a miner in cold blood in front of him. Tom goes there to check on his brother who has stopped making reports. The brother is presumed to have been murdered.

Meanwhile a new stage company has been started for the region but in its initial run, the owner has been murdered, clearly a deal between the stage line manager Clark (Al Ferguson) and the fake marshal (Charles Whittaker) in town. They try to force the owner's daughter Mary (Carol Wyndham) to sell the line to them. Tom advises her to resist the sale until he can help her more. Tom is riding into Placerville, when he stops for a drink of water and is confronted by a miner, Dad Sommers (Fred Parker). He tells Tom his water has been poisoned and he fills him in on the tax scam. They both head into town.

They run into a traveling peddler Abe (Max Davidson) being harassing by the tax scam gang. Tom dispatches them handily. All of them head into town.

An encounter with Chinese miners – Tom scared the gang members away who were trying to rob them – results in Tom finding his brother in still alive. After his assault Reed was found by the miners who have been taking care of him.

Clark and his gang learned that Tom is with the miners and assault the cabin. Tom escapes through a tunnel under the cabin and leads the gang away from it.

In the climax, the plan Tom has devised is discovered by the gang but Mary tries to put it in action by driving the wagon with the mail and gold in it with the stagecoach as the decoy.

All turns out the way it should, naturally

A more elaborate story is staged surprisingly well by director Ray. There are more variety of shots and the editing is tighter.

The script is by Robert Emmett Tansey, a figure long associated with making B westerns. It has more going on than in the typical Reliable.

The supporting cast is a veritable who's who of the Reliable rep company with Lafe McKee, Slim Whittaker, Bud Osborne, Wally West, Earl Dwire, Al Ferguson, and George Chesebro all on screen. Adding "comedy" is Max Davidson, a long-time film vet perhaps best known for his two-reel comedies at Hal Roach. Davidson did ethnic Jewish characters, which eventually ended his career as he faced increasing criticism for perpetuating stereotypes. Those stereotypes persist in moments in this production.

What isn't stereotyped are the Chinese miners. They are played by Chinese actors and they are treated without any of the typical racial treatments of the day. Usually a white actor in "yellow face" would be the one delivering the lines, but in this film a Chinese actor speaks. Unfortunately, there is no record about who he was.

The concluding chase and fight point out just how dirty and dangerous making a B western can be. Tyler and Ferguson fight in the rear of the wagon. It's clearly Tyler for at least half of the wagon scenes and not a stunt man.

When Ferguson's character is thrown out of the wagon – undoubtedly a stunt performer, I hope – the wagon is still being driven at break neck speed by Wyndham. Tyler stands behind the seat, grabs the reins and stops the wagon. He then jumps down and grabs the horses to calm them. I could imagine that Tyler and his castmates really wanted this scene to be accomplished in one take. It was dangerous and dusty, but typical for the low budget B movie-making experience.

Film Daily, (April 29, 1936), wrote, "Lively, interesting western makes satisfactory fare for outdoor picture fans. Situations plentiful for the houses playing westerns. Everything happens out of doors and the photography shows the natural backgrounds off beautifully. The story has enough material to hold one interested and with the chases and gunplay, the action moves along well. Tom Tyler is a handsome western hero and members of the cast acquit themselves well. A gang of outlaws is shaking down gold prospectors and staging holdups. Tom Tyler, as a marshal, is sent in to clean things up. He finds Carol Wyndham's father has been killed in a stagecoach robbery and the gang is trying to prevent Carol from operating the stage line so that they can get it from her. Tom is wise to their plans and arranges things so that the stage does get through and in so doing is able to clean up the outfit. At the same time, he stays on to become the girl's partner in the stagecoach line as well as her partner for life. Direction good, photography fine."

Pinto Rustlers 1936
Director: Harry S. Webb as Henri Samuels

Tom Dawson's (Tyler) father is shot and he swears revenge on the Pinto Rustlers, the gang that did it. Tom gets sworn into law enforcement. Dawson is given Mac (Al St. John) as his partner.

The leader of the gang Bud Waldon (Earl Dwire) learns his brother Ed (Murdock MacQuarrie) is moving his herd of horses and alerts the gang to intercept them. They kidnap the brother in order to get the combination for his safe.

Seeing members of the gang approaching, Dawson fakes passing out while in handcuffs and clutching a fake wanted poster. They take him back to their camp. Al watches from afar.

They accept Tom and he goes with Bud who instructs him to inquire at a nearby ranch for work. The ranch's is his brother's and the man's daughter, Ann (Marie Burton also known as Catherine Cotter) hires Dawson.

Dawson is able to get Mac to be accepted as a safecracker after kidnapping the man the gang is expecting. – luckily Mac has experience.

When the real safecracker escapes, Dawson and Mac have to form a new plan.

With several other plot twist and turns, Dawson is able to bring in Nick alive in order to find out who killed his father and where the father of the heroine is located.

The second film written by Robert Emmet Tansey is much more routine than his previous effort with the theme of the good guy impersonating a criminal and working his way into the gang.

Veteran actor – his first credit was "Birth of a Nation" – George Walsh plays the muscle of the criminal gang "Nick" with a very heavy accent. Is it supposed to be Mexican or Italian? I'm assuming Mexican.

Once again St. John plays a sidekick role straight and without a beard!

Variety's "Barn" reviewed the film writing, "More shooting than usual in this western but otherwise it's of the usual formula even to the boy meets girl moment which involves the femme being saved in a runaway. Will mostly have to take its chances as the week half of a dual or for the weekends where the kids will be free to dime the box offices. Opening on the pic would awaken almost any audience however since there's more gun racket than in a war film."

Santa Fe Bound 1936

Director: Harry Webb as Henri Samuels with Jeanne Martel in their first film

Tom Crenshaw is on the trail to Sante Fe where he sees an older man bushwhacked. Crenshaw kills the man (an outlaw named Tex French) who shot the older man. The older man asks Crenshaw to deliver his wallet to a woman named "Molly" in Sante Fe but dies before he can say the last name.

Upon arriving in Sante Fe, Crenshaw runs into One Shot Morgan (Slim Whitaker) who has just run two men out of town without their guns and in their long underwear. He says he would do the same to Crenshaw but Crenshaw turns the tables on One Shot who winds up pants-less and in a full rain barrel.

Crenshaw also meets Molly Bates (Jeanne Martel) and get a job at her ranch. She says she has had a difficult time getting people to work there because of One Shot.

Once we see Richard Cramer (playing Stanton) as part of the cast you know he is the brains behind the operation. He wants the ranch.

Stanton sends a man out to watch Crenshaw and he sees that Crenshaw has the wallet from the murdered man and that he has hidden it in the bunkhouse.

Experienced western fans will know what will happen next. Stanton shows up at the ranch with the sheriff and they arrest Crenshaw for the murder of

Molly's father and the theft of the money. Stanton convinces the sheriff to bring Crenshaw to the county seat for trial that night. Naturally Stanton incites a lynching party.

The lynching party actually is the means by which Crenshaw escapes. The note he took from Tex French identifies Crenshaw as the notorious outlaw whom Stanton wants on his payroll.
Crenshaw, under the cover of darkness and using a pretty fake Mexican accent, manages to get the $5,000 stolen from the murdered man. He gets the money to Molly.

When a pal of Tex French turns up, (Denton played by Charles King) at Stanton's ranch, Crenshaw is on a tough place. He manages to escape but pursued by the rest of the gang and is slightly wounded.

Stanton and his gang follow Crenshaw to Molly's ranch but they don't find him. Molly suggests getting the help of other ranchers and attack Stanton. Stanton and Denton are turned over to the sheriff.

The script lacks logic at key moments and recycles many worn out ideas. As usual, Tyler does his best and Martel plays the plucky heroine well. The script didn't do them any favor.

Once again Variety's reviewer with the pen name "Barn" had the chore of reviewing another Tom Tyler production from Reliable. In this case his last Reliable film "Santa Fe Bound."

"Getting away with a bushwhacking start which nets a couple of killings. 'Santa Fe bound doesn't let down at any time in its short hour and as entertainment provision in enough quantities to satisfy Tom Tyler who is starred in it gets a break in femme leads. Jeanne Martel handling the calf eyed assignment nicely. Although most of the stuff is in serious vain Tyler and Whittaker work out one good comedy sequence which calls for the latter to shed his pants and be doused in a rain barrel. The Martel girl is attractive has no trouble remembering her lines and has a nice chassis. For no reason that is apparent Kramer is trying to get the gal and the ranch going to the links of having her father plot pelted from the roadside brush. He was towing a gun he was touting a gob of money just loaned him by the bank which Tyler gets to bring back to his daughter. His having the dough is misconstrued and he's compelled to don the clothes of an outlaw. But to the girl the wolf's clothes never fool her – she knows he has a heart of gold all the time."

What is the legacy of the Reliable series? It gave Tyler a starring series which he definitely needed. It was very uneven in quality, though. This was not uncommon for the western pictures at the time.

The Dixie Company started in 1930 to put various illustrations on the cardboard lid of its ice cream treats in a cardboard cup. It eventually started putting movie stars on the lids, which kids collected. In 1934, the company started putting cowboy stars on the lids – Ken Maynard was the first. They also produced these 8 by 10 full color photos for kids with information about the star on the back. Here is Tyler's from his Reliable days. (author's collection)

Ray and Webb's films suffer from the over-use of the same locations, a lack of music and a complete confusion about whether or not Tyler should have a sidekick and who that would be. Should he be supported by a straight sidekick such as Al St. John – ironically – or a comic one such as Eddie Gribbon and Ben Corbett?

It's fascinating to me that Reliable hadn't understood Tyler's success at FBO, which was due in part by having Frankie Darro as a recurring cast member frequently as an aide to Tyler's characters.

When some care was taken, Reliable was able to produce perfectly acceptable low budget westerns. The truth is the Reliable series are the westerns from which Tyler acquired much of his reputation as a cowboy performer for contemporary audiences. The Reliable series was sold to television stations as early as 1948 when the Motion Picture Herald noted WPIX from New York City had gained the rights to 36 low budget films, including Tyler's films.

The Reliable films were also available for non-theatrical showings by rentals from several companies.

Tyler, along with other veteran performers such as Col. Tim McCoy, Hoot Gibson and Ken Maynard, among others, was gaining new fans through television. As Buster Crabbe told me in a 1972 interview, "I never considered myself a movie star. One of the reasons for that is that I never had a top-grade triple-A script and a top-grade triple-A director and producer. I never had the chance to work with a real big director in the business. The result is that I made action pictures, which turned out to be fortunate for me. The Billy the Kid westerns [his PRC series], all the westerns I did for Paramount, the serials I made, and the other things stood me in good stead and when television came along they sort of resurrected me."

Today, it is the Reliable films and Tyler's Victory series that are the easiest of his western films to see. I always got the sense of no matter how routine the story, Tyler gives it his all. He obviously shines, though, when there is a variation in the standard hero character such as 'The Laramie Kid," in which his character has a gambling problem.

Was Tyler hired for a new film series after his Reliable series ended in 1936? A trade ad in the Motion Picture Herald on July 25, 1936, would indicate so, but in the tradition of low-budget filmmaking in the 1930s it was apparently just wishful thinking.

The ad touted the experience of producer C.C. Burr who headed up B.J.S. Productions, and read in part, "The Lone Prairie, based on a famous American classic read by millions by James Fenimore Cooper, author of 'The Last of the Mohicans" and 'The Deer Slayer' etc. Blazing action against backgrounds of classic and scenic beauty, fast writing, modern production with a vast ready-made audience. The cast will costar George Eldredge and Queenie Smith, famous youthful stars of opera, musical comedy and legitimate stage and more recently in pictures and radio augmented by such stars as Harry Carey, Tom Tyler, Lloyd Hughes and a nationally known band.

"There will be five other special outdoor musical attractions each with a special cast. They can't miss. They will make you a factor in your field. You'll have something everybody will want – a good show, that grand and glorious feeling. Well-backed by resources and manpower these quality productions will be made and delivered according to schedule. Significant cast, sparkling stories, you know we make real pictures. Why not for you?"

As far as I could tell none of these musical westerns ever were produced. Burr did produce three films in 1936, none of them were westerns and were released through Puritan Pictures, another states rights outfit. He did make several musical westerns with singer Fred Scott released in 1939 and 1940. However Tyler soon had an offer, which he accepted. The Motion Picture Herald on Sept. 5, 1936, reported Sam Katzman of Victory Pictures had signed Tyler to a series of eight films. Until he was under contract at Republic in a few years in the future, this was his last series of films.

It should be noted that even though movies were considered by some as ephemeral, the re-release business was a strong one in the industry. Several organizations made deals with the original studios that made a movie to re-release it several years after its initial release.

While there were studios that regularly re-released some of their biggest hits – such as RKO re-releasing "King Kong" to new acclaim and box office receipts or MGM re-releasing "Gone with the Wind – there were companies that brought independently produced B films back to theaters. The most prominent as Astor Pictures, the most successful of these businesses.

As Michael R. Pitts wrote in his excellent book, "Astor Pictures: A Filmography and History of the Reissue King 1933-1965," the company's slogan was "where all the big major company releases go for reissue."

Pitts explained, "The re-release of movies both by parent companies and later purchasers was nothing new to the film industry when [Robert M.] Savini started Astor but he took the process to a new level, chiefly operating as a distributor of movies made by others and through adroit planning and showmanship making a profit that eventually led to him becoming a millionaire." It should be noted that Astor just didn't re-release B films, but also big budget films such as "Hell's Angels," as well as films considered classics such as William. S. Hart's epic silent western "Tumbleweeds." Film like these played in theaters in big cities

Pitts noted that Astor also occasionally made its own movies, as well. In Tyler's case, his sound Syndicate and Monogram films as well as at least one of his Reliable productions were all made available for re-release in 1937 and 1938 for neighborhood and rural theaters who needed affordable product.

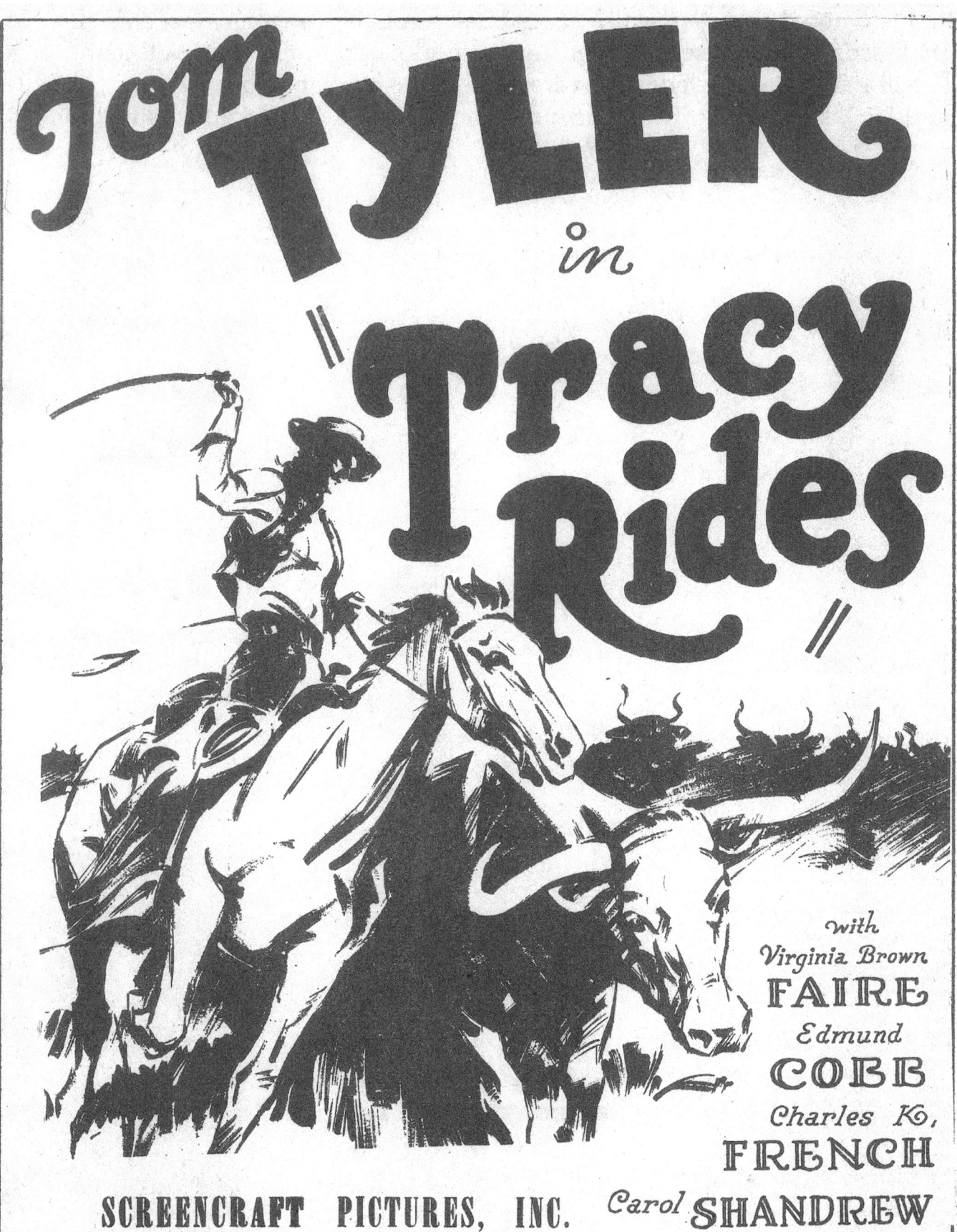

TOM TYLER in "TRACY RIDES"

THE CAST

Tom Tracy	TOM TYLER
Molly	Virginia Brown Faire
Ned	Edmund Cobb
Hampton	Charles K. French
Judy	Carol Shandrew
Green	Lafe McKee

Directed by HARRY S. WEBB

Story by	Norman Hughes
Continuity	Rose Gordon
Dialogue	Betty Burbridge
Photography	J. Henry Kruse—IATSE
Editing	Fred Bain
Assistant Director	Bobby Ray
Recording	J. S. Westmoreland
Sound	Freeman Lang

One-Col. Mat "E"

Tyler's "Boy" Is Film's Big Thrill

Horse Understands Actor's Every Command

Fellow daredevils are Tom Tyler and his wonder horse, "Boy," and inseparable companions as well.

Both Tom and "Boy" are to be seen this week at the ....theatre in "Tracy Rides," their latest contribution to the ever popular western type of picture story.

The title tells the tale. Tom and Boy are the whole picture—although, in fairness we must admit that the rest of the cast of splendid players do admirable work in a thoroughly entertaining film. But Tom Tyler is our favorite thrill actor and Boy gets better as he goes along. He really does everything—and does it in the best manner of the most veteran Hollywood trouper. In other words, Boy understands.

Tyler says that Boy is eleven-tenths human. Says that when he starts on a particularly hazardous tear down a mountain, rolling, sliding and pitching, Boy gives him a look before the command to "shoot," a look straight-in-the-eye, Tom says, which plainly indicates that he's with him to the last—sink or swim! Boy has never made the slightest effort to evade any stunt. In fact, he has never shown trepidation where other good horses refuse, point-blank, to go on. His trust in Tyler is unfailing—and as long as they're a team Boy may be depended upon.

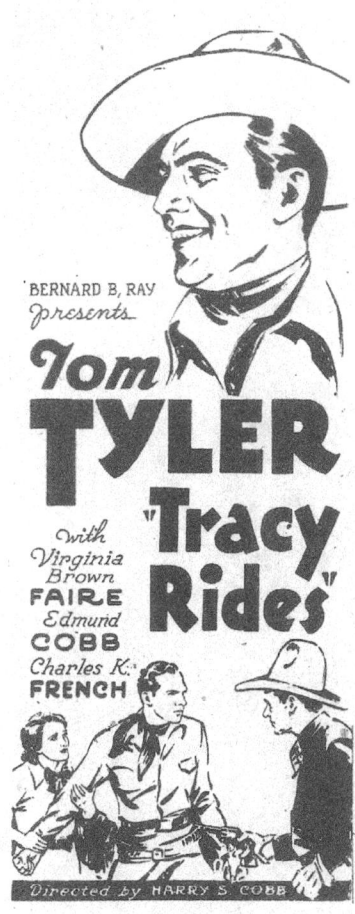

One-Col. Mat "G"

One-Col. Mat "B"

THE FILMS AND LIFE OF TOM TYLER

One-Col. Mat "D"

22 x 28

Two-Column Mat "C"

Two-Column Mat "F"

CATCHLINES

See Tom Tyler, the single-handed two-gun daredevil of the range in his latest western thriller, "Tracy Rides."

* * *

Ridin' to win or die, Tom Tyler, king of the plains, performs heroic feats of riding and fighting in "Tracy Rides," his latest horse opera.

* * *

"Tracy Rides" to fame and fortune, Tom Tyler meets up with an evil gang of horse thieves but, with his brand of two-fisted fighting and two-gun shooting, he soon puts them in their place.

* * *

You can't miss this great action picture, "Tracy Rides," with Tom Tyler in the saddle.

* * *

'Unconquered Bandit' Spells Action

Lillian Gilmore Dainty Heroine

Is Tom Tyler's Sweetheart In New Western

Harry S. Webb, who directed the new Steiner Western, "Unconquered Bandit", starring Tom Tyler, which comes to the Theatre on , took particular pains to surround Mr. Tyler with a strong cast for this production. Casting a Western is usually easy enough, for, as a general rule the types are not varied, inasmuch as many of the open air adventure picture plots follow a somewhat familiar trail. This, however, has never been quite the case with the Tyler films, for the star himself, is nothing if not insistent upon using only stories with an original slant.

As regards the "Unconquered Bandit", both star and director realized that they had a story registering many uncommon angles, and exploiting several unusual characters, each of which required deft portrayal by a talented player. After considerable thought and trouble Mr. Webb succeeded in filling the different roles to his satisfaction, but finding a feminine lead for the part of Helen Cleyburn proved a task of difficulty, until he was fortunate enough to secure the services of Lillian Gilmore.

A DIFFICULT ROLE

Miss Gilmore fulfilled all the physical requirements, being a dainty type of beauty, and what was of signal importance, an actress of superior quality. In the story both Helen and Tom are favorably impressed with each other at their initial meeting. But it is not until after Tom's dad has been killed by bandits, instigated by a San Diego politician and, incidentally a chief of cattle-rustlers, known as Cleyburn, that the hero begins to make love to the girl. His real motives are not, however, affectionate, as Helen is Cleyburn's niece, and it is Tom's intention to win her, and use the girl as a pawn on the chess-board of the revenge he intends to take on the uncle. But he really falls in love with Helen, and she with him.

The plot pivots on this incident and it is in portraying the varied moods of the girl placed in such an extraordinary situation that Lillian Gilmore thoroughly justifies the director's judgment in choosing her for the role. Charles Whitaker was selected as the sinister Night Hawk, the outlaw whose identity Tom Tyler borrows temporarily as a disguise.

An Echo from the Old West

Tom Tyler's new starring vehicle, "Unconquered Bandit" carries an echo on the wings of the Past from bygone Western days when outlaws rode the Mexican Border trails. Watch for the gay, enthralling scenes of the great Fiesta held at the Morgan Hacienda in this thrilling, romantic picture, which will be the leading attraction at the Theatre on , with your favorite star in his finest, most exciting role, and a superb lineup of selected players in the supporting cast.

1-Col. Ad. Cut or Mat No. 80

A WESTERN WITH A UNIQUE PLOT

In the old Western days, when the notorious outlaws, Murietta and Ringo, were still terrorizing the inhabitants of the border-lands of California, Gasparo De Gama, leader of a group of Mexican settlers who are now United States citizens, surprises a band of cattle-rustlers. Gasparo boldly attacks the thieves, but is outmaneuvered by them, and has to fight for his life. At this juncture Tom Morgan, accompanied by his father and pal, Pedro Gonzales, ride to the rescue. They beat off the rustlers and save Gasparo.

Tom learns from Gasparo that the defeated rustlers belong to a gang headed by Cleyburn. The latter is a sort of political king in San Diego. Apart from his political activities, he is a noted land-shark, and receiver of stolen cattle. Gasparo has recently discovered gold on his homestead, and as a result of this, Cleyburn is employing every foul means at his command to take their lands away from the settlers.

Tom Morgan, with his father and Pedro, ride to the settlement. The elder Morgan decides to remain there temporarily, for the purpose of examining the mine, in which he is inclined to purchase a half interest. Tom and Pedro continue their journey toward the Morgan hacienda below the border.

That night there is a fiesta held at the Morgan hacienda. While the merrymakers are enjoying themselves, a coach with outriders drives up and halts. The driver has lost his way and enquires the road to San Diego. Tom catches sight of a pretty girl in the coach and invites her to take part in the festivities. She accepts the invitation and is made the object of flattering attentions by Tom. As their acquaintance ripens, he learns that she is Helen Cleyburn, niece of the unscrupulous politician and rustler-leader, just arrived, on a surprise visit from the East to her uncle. After partaking of refreshments, she thanks her gallant cavalier and proceeds on her journey.

Meanwhile Tom's father has completed his investigation of the mine's possibilities. He is satisfied with the financial outlook and decides to buy a half interest in the property. Just as they are considering the deal, Cleyburn's henchmen ride up and give the settlers notice to abandon their lands, or be removed by force. The settlers refuse and a fight follows, during which the elder Morgan falls a victim to a bandit bullet. A rider from the settlement gives the alarm to Tom Morgan, and the latter, with Pedro and his vaqueroes gallop furiously to the rescue. But Tom finds his father dead and takes a solemn oath to be revenged on Cleyburn.

His plot of vengeance includes the participation of a celebrated hill-bandit, Jose Porfirio, known far and near as The Night Hawk. Tom confers with Porfirio and they strike a bargain, whereby Tom will assume the role of the Night Hawk, and devote himself to raids upon Cleyburn's properties seizing the latter's gold treasure, his horses and payrolls. All of this loot he intends to turn over to the poor settlers who have been ruined by the ruthless Cleyburn's robbery of their homesteads. He will play the part of a modern Robin Hood in the disguise of the notorious bandit.

He further proposes to use Helen Cleyburn as a means to help his revenge. His one chance meeting with the girl has revealed to him that she is inclined to like him. By making love to her, proposing marriage and being accepted, he will turn her over to the genuine Night Hawk, who will wed her and force Cleyburn to pay out his last cent in order to have the marriage annulled.

Tom carries out his scheme, with one exception, for he actually falls in love with Helen, the girl he intended to deceive. This complicates matters, for he confesses everthing to her. However, as Helen returns his affection, she forgives her impetuous lover. They determine to notify her uncle of their engagement and marry, without revealing Tom's prior intentions. But Tom has not reckoned on the crooked dealing of the real Night Hawk, who doublecrosses him and sets a trap in which Tom lands, whereby he is arrested as a bandit and imprisoned. Finally, Tom, through his own ingenuity, escapes from jail, saves Helen, brings the arch-outlaw to justice, and the lovers have a happy future together.

TOM TYLER

1-Col. Cut or Mat No. 50

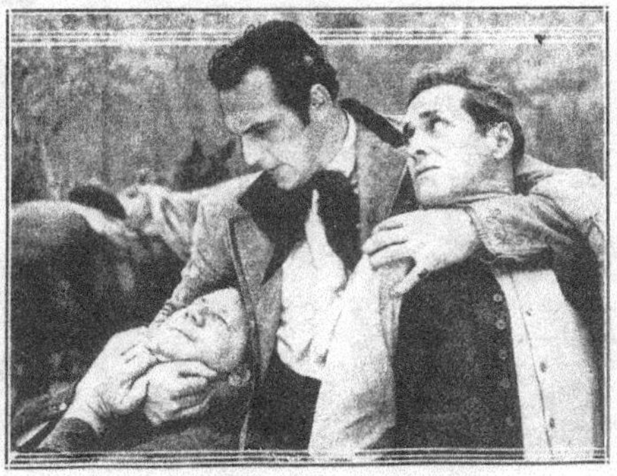

2-Column Scene Cut or Mat No. 81

Tom Tyler is Horseman and Weight-Lifting Champ

BORN NEW YORKER—TYPIFIES WEST

Born at Port Henry, New York, about twenty-two years ago, Tom Tyler, Steiner star appearing currently on the local screens in "Unconquerable Bandit", has attained prominence in several fields of endeavour, and found himself internationally famous in the world of athletics ere he reached full manhood.

When a member of the Los Angeles Athletic Club, the now celebrated film star created a new world's amateur record in the right hand clean and jerk lift of 213 pounds, thereby breaking the former record held by Noah Young, also a member of the club, and until then undefeated.

Tyler is a perfect specimen of the all-around athlete. He scales at 197 pounds and is remarkably fast on his feet. He can perform an extraordinary variety of acrobatic tricks, thrilling stunts on the horizontal bar, and, among his other accomplishments, is a horseman par excellence. His first theatrical experience was as a stage extra, and through other following engagements he developed the love of the Thespian art which was destined later to lead him to film stardom. In the interval he was ever a man of action, the quiet life never appealed to him, and during his wanderlust period he was at times an exhibitional strong man, a crack amateur boxer, a rough-and-ready lumberjack of the Michigan woods, besides putting in a spell, while a mere lad, as a schooner sailor. And today fans the wide world over hail him as the champion rider, dead-shot gunman and fistic battler of the screen!

Elliott Cast As Tom Tyler's Dad

John Elliott furnishes an excellent bit of character work in the role of Tom Tyler's dad, who is killed by rustlers and leaves a heritage of revenge to his son in "Unconquered Bandit", the new Tyler Western, now on view at the Theatre. Mr. Elliott is an oldtime favorite with the fans. He has had thirty-five years experience in all branches of show business. He went to the Coast in 1919 with Marjorie Rambeau, entered the screen field, and has since appeared in picture after picture, being much in demand by directors on account of his availability for parts demanding unusual versatility and smart action.

1-Col. Ad. Cut or Mat No. 82

Program Shorts

• • •

Tom Tyler is riding the range again, giving you innumerable thrills in his new Western, "Unconquered Bandit". This is a Western that will keep you jumping in your seat from sheer excitement, as Tom adopts the identity of a ferocious bandit in order to trap the men who murdered his father, and battles with fists and gun for the sake of the girl he loves. Romance, flying bullets, galloping steeds, an adventure picture brimful of action from start to finish!

• • •

You get the very cream of Western adventure in "Unconquered Bandit", Tom Tyler's new thriller, fast, furious action, gunplay galore, and above all—Tom himself in some of the most daring stunts ever filmed. It's the real thing in romantic melodrama, a feature with universal appeal, it will hit the adults as hard as the juveniles, and incidentally, make the young one fairly yell with enthusiasm.

• • •

A whirlwind drama of love, laughter and slaughter in the fiery days when outlaws still stole, fought and died along the Mexican Border, a land where men took the law in their own hands, when necessary—that's "Unconquered Bandit", most sensational and finest of the Tom Tyler pictures. Romance in the saddle, thrilling conflicts of wits, fists, knives and guns, the beau ideal of open-air adventure entertainment, with a punch in every minute of action.

• • •

Tom Tyler in "Unconquered Bandit", his latest Western! Don't miss this fast-moving film which tells a vivid, novel story of old Border days, when men who were quick on the trigger shot to kill at the slightest pretence, when the Old West was in its virile fighting prime! Hitting the high spots of adventure, thrills and romance from the start, this picture speeds without a lingering pause into an amazing cyclonic finish!

The Law Didn't Assist Tyler

So Acting By Western Code He Helped Himself

In Old Western days the range-riders had no patience with the laws' delays. If a man was wronged, and there didn't seem to be any chance of getting his rights quickly, he went out and righted matters with his gun. That's why Tom Tyler, in his new Western thriller "Unconquered Bandit", which comes to the Theatre on , takes the law into his own hands, when his father is slain by border ruffians, and goes on the warpath, as relentless as an Indian brave of the Frontier, looking for vengeance.

But Tom takes a step altogether out of the ordinary, for he assumes the identity of a notorious outlaw of the hills, and disguised as the Night Hawk, proceeds to exact a toll of revenge from a man so powerful politically and wealthy, that he can't reach him by any other means. His plan even involves making love to Helen Cleyburn, played by Lillian Gilmore, as she is the niece of his arch-enemy who is responsible for his dad's death. But his plan is thrown out of gear by an unlooked for contingency, for his lovemaking turns from duplicity to earnest, because Helen proves too fascinating to resist.

It's this odd twist to the plot that takes "Unconquerable Bandit" altogether out of the usual Western formula, and gives the film a power of human interest appeal seldom found in Westerns. Yet, entirely apart from its romantic urge, the picture fairly surges with furious action. Tom Tyler shoots and battles his way out of more tight corners than ever before, his horsemanship stunts are amazing, and the spectators aren't likely to forget in a hurry the exciting sequence in which he escapes from jail, saves the girl he loves from the bandit confederate who tries to doublecross him, and solves the vexing problem of eliminating the bad men who have been terrorizing the whole Mexican border.

Tom Tyler Lively Western Star

"Unconquered Bandit" Makes Palpable Hit With Strand Theatre Patrons

Tom Tyler and Clever Cast Score Brilliantly in Thrilling Western

(REVIEW)

It was a highly pleased audience that left the Strand Theatre last night after witnessing the initial screen showing of "Unconquerable Bandit", the new Steiner Western, and latest starring vehicle of that ever popular son of mountain, plain and border—Tom Tyler. The actor in question holds a long, unbroken record of success in his particular line, and it is safe to assert that this present offering of mad adventure and romance under "the wide and starry sky" can be ranked among the best of his pictures.

Perhaps it may even be listed as superior to anything he has yet sponsored in films, if one is to judge by the congratulatory remarks dropped by the outgoing audience, many of whom undoubtedly were tried and true Tyler fans and had no hesitancy in declaring for everyone to hear, that their favorite had surpassed himself in his latest role. Certainly the writer's reaction to the feature was that of immense satisfaction, not unmingled with surprise, for one is usually prepared to find Western entertainment somewhat handicapped by lack of plot originality.

Such was not the case with "Unconquered Bandit". The device of having the hero masquerade as a notorious outlaw is, of course, ancient enough. But the point is that everything turns out quite different from what you expect, and a singularly effective twist is given the plot by the shattering of the hero's plans for revenge on the man who killed his father, when he falls desperately in love with the girl whom he designs to use as a tool in digging a pitfall for his enemy. Here's where real human interest steps in and makes the picture stand out in bold relief as a surefire drawing card.

It would not be fair to prospective patrons to reveal the inner workings and splendid climax of the story. But suffice it to say that for whirlwind action, shock-

CASH IN WITH WESTERNS

thrills and sustained suspense, "Unconquered Bandit" will prove an unmeasured delight to all in search of peppy amusement, and a genuine box office gift for the exhibitor. Too much praise cannot be awarded Mr. Tyler's performance, as well as that of his leading lady, Lillian Gilmore; and the fine work of an excellent supporting cast, among whom are Charles Whitaker, William Gould, John Elliott, Earl Dwire, Joe De La Cruz, George Chesebro, Lew Meehan, Dick Alexander and George Hazel.

BERNARD B. RAY
Presents
TOM TYLER
in
"UNCONQUERED BANDIT"

CAST

Tom Morgan	Tom Tyler
Helen Cleyburn	Lillian Gilmore
The Night Hawk	Charles Whitaker
Cleyburn	William Gould
Senor Morgan	John Elliott
Pedro	Earl Dwire
Gasparo	Joe De La Cruz
Dick	George Chesebro
George	Lew Meehan
Pat	Dick Alexander
Alonzo	George Hazel

Directed by
HARRY S. WEBB

Story	Carl Krusada
Continuity	Rose Gordon
Dialogue	Lou C. Borden
Photography	J. Henry Kruse, I.A.T.S.E.
Editing	Fred Bain
Assistant Director	William Nolte
Sound	J. S. Westmoreland
Art Technician	Charles Stevens

DISTRIBUTED BY WILLIAM STEINER
Passed by National Board of Review   Copyrighted MCMXXIV

Cattle Rustling A Major Crime

Raids by cattle rustlers, or "stock-thieves" were common occurrences in old Western days, and form an important part of the plot of "Unconquered Bandit", the new Tom Tyler film, now playing at the Theatre. It was a crime held in particular detestation by the ranchmen, as well might be the case, seeing that their principal investments were in stock, and short shrift was given the raiders caught red-handed by the indignant range-riders. As a matter of fact, a horse-thief had less chance than a murderer of escaping with his life, if rounded up.

Tom Tyler's escapade in masquerading as Night Hawk, the master-thief of "Unconquered Bandit", is therefore an experiment deeply fraught with peril of no ordinary kind. How he eludes his pursuers, plans and executes his vengeance on the ruffians who murdered his father, and persuades the girl he loves of his innocence, provides one of the most wildly exciting plots ever filmed. The star is surrounded by an unusually talented cast. Pretty Lillian Gilmore appears as Helen Cleyburn, Tom's sweetheart, and plays the role with a piquant dash and allure which has won her golden tributes from the newspaper critics.

Director Harry Webb Discusses Accurate Trend of Western Plots

Finds Films True To Life In Most Cases

Harry S. Webb, who directed the new Steiner Western, "Unconquered Bandit", now playing at the Theatre, flouts the idea frequently advanced by film critics to the effect that there is an absurd amount of exaggeration in plots dealing with outdoor adventure pictures. During the making of "Unconquered Bandit", a newspaper man paying a friendly visit asked Mr. Webb if it was not straining probabilities too far, when Tom Tyler is shown deliberately assuming the identity of Night Hawk, a notorious outlaw, in order to further a scheme of revenge on the men who killed his father.

"Not at all", responded the director. "No doubt you are under the impression that such a thing couldn't happen in real life. I'll grant you that. In the modern underworld nobody would be likely to pass himself off as Al Capone, for instance. But remember, we're dealing with an entirely different era of American life, and that the bandits of the Old West were not men who operated within the comparatively limited area of a city. They had the mountain ranges and far-flung trails of the wide plains for their hunting grounds in search of loot. A big-shot outlaw of those days might be known to thousands of folks by reputation, not one of whom ever set eyes on him.

"Curiously enough, I can quote you an instance, which, in some respects may be said to be a historical precedent for Tom Tyler's masquerade as the Night Hawk. In 1850, before railroads spanned the Western country, there was a bandit known as Black Bart who was a darb at the stage-holdup game. Though there was a large reward for his capture, dead or alive, he fooled all his pursuers until one day two deputy sheriffs who were trailing a horse thief, found two men, one fatally wounded, the other dead, lying in a canyon. The chap still alive acknowledged that he was Black Bart. He knew he was dying and had nothing to conceal.

"His story was an odd reflection on human vanity, as shown by the inordinate pride of some ruffians in their professional exploits. It seems that the dead man had, for several months past, been poaching, so to speak, on Black Bart's preserves. In other words, he had adopted Bart's moniker while sticking up stages, and on one occasion raided a ranch single-handed, and pouched the payroll intended for the employees.

"On each occasion he introduced himself to his victim as Black Bart, judging that the terror of the name would simplify things for him a whole lot, which, as a matter of fact it did. But the real Black Bart finally heard about his imitator's duplicity, and resenting not only the substitute's success, but his audacity in trading on the genuine terror's reputation, set out to eliminate him. When they met and blazed away at each other, the real Black Bart got his man, but the impersonator gave him such a battle that it resulted ultimately in the arch-villain's death. So far as honest citizens were concerned, there were two rogues the less in the world, and everything was okay.

"You can read the whole story in the yellowed pages of old newspaper files in any large California public library. It merely goes to show that 'truth is stranger than fiction', and that Westerns run a lot closer to real life than most folks imagine."

CATCH LINES

Through smoke and bullets, six-shooter blazing, gallops the screen's daredevil Tom Tyler, in his latest Steiner Western, "Unconquered Bandit". You've seen him ride and fight before, but you've never experienced such thrills as he gives you in this red-hot action story of the mountains and plains!

• • •

Would YOU take the chance of getting a rope 'round your neck just for a pretty girl's sake? Tom Tyler does that, and more, in his new rip-roaring yarn of the West, "Unconquered Bandit", a film that rattles with machine-gun speed from its lightning start right up to its crashing finish!

• • •

Imagine having to pass for a hunted outlaw, with honest folks just crazy to lynch you, or shoot you down from abush! Tom Tyler leads exactly that sort of a double life in his latest Western, "Unconquered Bandit", firstly, because he wants to avenge a father's murder, secondly because it's the only way he can win the girl he loves. A picture with a punch in every foot of film!

• • •

You know what is likely to happen when Tom Tyler spurs hell-for-leather over a Western trail, all set for trouble! And there's plenty happens when the fast-riding, hard fighting ace of the screen strikes out for love and revenge in his new Steiner picture, "Unconquered Bandit"!

• • •

The law couldn't help Tom Tyler when ruffians shot down his beloved father. So he follows the Western code and takes the law into his own capable hands in "Unconquered Bandit", his latest and best melodrama of the open, a film crammed with irresistible appeal for young and old.

• • •

Tom Tyler is in the saddle again, the shooting, fighting terror of "Unconquered Bandit", his latest Steiner Western. Flying fists and hissing bullets, thundering hoof-beats, romance and thrills galore, one exciting event crowding so fast on the heels of the next that you'll find yourself breathing only in gasps—a whirlwind of action!

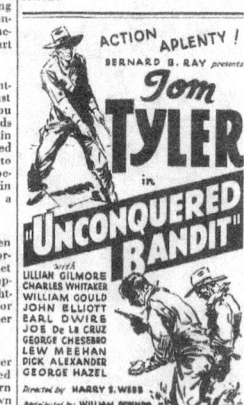

POSTER AND LOBBY DIS

11 x 14

11 x 14

11 x 14

22 x 28

11 x 14

SIX-SHEET

ACCESSORIES
EXCHANGES NOTE
Order accessories below
directly from
HAROLD J. FLAVIN
Inc.
250 West 54th Street
New York, N. Y.

8—11x14 lobby photos
2—22x28 lobby photos
1—14x36 insert card
20— 8x10 stills

COLORED SLIDES
ONE SHEETS
THREE SHEETS
SIX SHEETS

PLAYS IN FULL COLOR!

11 x 14

11 x 14

11 x 14

22 x 28 and SLIDE

TITLE CARD

ONE-SHEET

THREE-SHEET

This Space Reserved For Illustration of Insert Card Not Yet Ready At Time of Going to Press

YOU CAN'T GET ALONG WITHOUT
WESTERNS

BOOK
TOM TYLER
FOR PROFITS

THE CURRENT SERIES
...

"RIDIN' THRU"
"TRACY RIDES"
"MYSTERY RANCH"
"FIGHTING HERO"
"THE SILVER BULLET"
"TERROR OF THE PLAINS"

THE NEW SERIES
...

"UNCONQUERED BANDIT"
"BORN TO BATTLE"
"COYOTE TRAILS"
"SILENT VALLEY"
"LARAMIE KID"
"RIO RATTLER"

NATIONALLY DISTRIBUTED BY
WILLIAM STEINER
PARAMOUNT BUILDING, NEW YORK, N. Y.

Exclusive Distributors for Latin America
TRANS-OCEANIC FILM EXPORT CO.
723 Seventh Avenue, New York
Cable Address: TRANSFILM

Tom Tyler—Dare-Devil of Westerns

"THE LARAMIE KID" THRILLS AND FASCINATES PATRONS IN DEBUT AT STRAND THEATRE

Tom Tyler a Dashing Figure as Battling Hero of New Steiner Western

"The Laramie Kid", a new Steiner Western, starring Tom Tyler, made its debut at the Strand Theatre last night, and earned a place on official records as probably the best of a brilliant series of films dealing with the great outdoors, which has won the unqualified approval of movie fans the whole country over. These Tyler pictures are every whit as exciting and fast of pace as a blood-and-thunder serial, but unlike the serial, a concise, coherent plot distinguishes each feature, and there is always a logical climax.

In the case of "The Laramie Kid", the story is even more alluring than those of its predecessors in the series, because it is intensely human, and shows its hero in a self-sacrifice act that wins him instant sympathy from the average person, although doubtless there may be hardboiled onlookers who will not agree with this view.

For Tom deliberately surrenders himself as prisoner to the father of Peggy Bland, the girl he loves, assuming the guilt of a bank holdup, so that old Bland may profit by the reward offered for the arrest of any one of the bandits. Banker Morley holds a mortgage on Bland's ranch. He would also like to have a mortgage on Peggy, in a matrimonial sense. If Peggy is willing to accept the wily banker, all will be well with the Bland homestead. Otherwise—it will be just too bad for the ranch owner!

A BREAK FOR LIBERTY

Tom's action clears Peggy and her dad of their money troubles. She knows he is guiltless of complicity in the bank-raid. He pays a heavy price for his self-sacrifice, as he is sentenced to five years in prison. Investigations by Peggy convince the girl that Morley sent the sheriff, who pursued the outlaws, on a false trail. Meanwhile a fellow prisoner to whom Tom renders a service, tells him that Morley staged the bank-robbery to cover up a cash shortage, and is really hand-in-glove with the gang. Tom regains his liberty in an unexpected prison break and hides in Bland's barn. Dad discovers him, but sends the sheriff the wrong way when he comes searching for the escaped prisoner, as the old man knows what a great service Tom rendered him. But hearing that Peggy has ridden up Blackrock Canyon, Tom is filled with apprehension for her safety, as he is aware that the bandit gang has its headquarters there. He follows her trail, but before leaving he asks Dad to send the posse after them, for he fears the worst.

A train robbery has just taken place in which Ed Larkin, a former acquaintance of Tom's who has gone wrong, is badly wounded. Fearful of revealing their hideaway, Larkin's comrades refuse to procure a physician for him. His lung is perforated by a bullet and he is slowly bleeding to death, when Peggy discovers him in the empty shack where he is lying, and cares for him as well as she can. Larkin is grateful, and before dying gives her all details regarding the gang's operations and Morley's connection with it.

Tom's arrival, via the roof, which he crashes through in time to save Peggy from Morley, the coming of the sheriff's posse and clearing of the hero's good name, brings the film to a satisfactory conclusion. As thrilling as it is fascinating, this latest Tyler offering is a splendid box office asset.

Two-Column Ad. Cut or Mat No. 30

Reliable Pictures Corporation
BERNARD B. RAY presents
TOM TYLER
in
"THE LARAMIE KID"

The Players	Their Roles
TOM TYLER	TOM TALBOT
Alberta Vaughn	Peggy
Al Ferguson	Jim Morley
Murdock MacQuarrie	Dad Bland
George Chesebro	Ed Larkin
Snub Pollard	Shorty
Steve Clark	Sheriff

Author	*Cameraman*
C. C. CHURCH	J. HENRY CRUSE
Editor	*Recorder*
FRED BAIN	J. S. WESTMORLAND
Assistant Director	*Art Technician*
WILLIAM NOLTE	JERRY KUMLER
Director	*Distributor*
HARRY S. WEBB	WILLIAM STEINER

Passed by National Board of Review   Copyrighted MCMXXXV

Peggy's Dad Is A Veteran Trouper

Murdock MacQuarrie, appearing as the father of Peggy Bland, heroine of the new Tom Tyler Western now playing at the .... Theatre, is a veteran of stage and screen. He was born in San Francisco, and is remembered in "legitimate" circles for his fine work in "Lights O' London", with Henry Miller, and other notable footlight dramas. He entered pictures in 1902 with the old Biograph Company. Later he directed and acted for Universal, Goldwyn, First National and other major companies.

Closing Notice

This evening will be your last opportunity to see "The Laramie Kid", Tom Tyler's latest starring vehicle, which ends its engagement to-night, after a prosperous run at the .... Theatre. Press and public agree that this remarkable Western outdoes all its predecessors in point of fast, sustained action, breathless suspense and decisive shock-thrills. It is one of the most faithful and yet sensational pictures of outdoor adventure life ever filmed, directed by Harry S. Webb, and presented with a fine supporting cast of noted players.

EXPLOITATION

"THE LARAMIE KID" BALLYHOO

Tom Tyler's horsemanship, his fighting ability, his magnetic personality as a dashing Western hero, are qualities you can play-up to the limit in advertising this feature. His name is known wherever the fans await the showing of a Western, and they are never weary of hearing his praises sounded. If you use handbills, point out that Tyler is surrounded by a cast that numbers some of the West's best riders. Also dwell on the plot's romantic interest, and don't let your customers lose sight of the fact that the heroine role is filled by Alberta Vaughn, one of the screen's prettiest and most talented artists. The children will especially look forward to the coming of Tom Tyler, their great favorite. You can safely go after the juvenile trade strong. The youngsters are crazy about this star, and he has no equal as a magnet for drawing them into your house.

METAL SHERIFF'S BADGE

Makes an ideal novelty to exhibit this picture and is something that every kid will be proud to wear. Is made of metal, with a slip pin on the back. Badges comes to you fastened upon a card measuring 4x6 inches, with appropriate wording on star and picture. Particularly effective with Tom Tyler Wild West Clubs, or for general give-away purposes.

Prices of badges attached to card, with your theatre name and playdates.

1000—$15.00; 500—$8.00; 250—$4.50

ECONOMY NOVELTY AND PRINTING COMPANY
239 West 39th Street   New York, N. Y.

PROGRAM SHORTS

As the hero of his latest and most thrilling Western, "The Laramie Kid", Tom Tyler undergoes more than the ordinary amount of troubles that usually fall to the common lot. He takes the blame of a bank-holdup on his shoulders is sentenced, escapes, and finally proves his innocence in a climax that brings the story to a spectacular conclusion. A film that's an eye-opener for everyone, all the hard riding, savage battling and romance that could be concentrated in a single feature.

* * *

"The Laramie Kid", the finest Western of the noted Tom Tyler series that has taken the screen by storm! Don't miss this one! Of all adventure yarns of the wide open spaces, it registers as the most virile and melodramatic. With just enough comedy and sentiment to balance its whirlwind action. Something here for every member of the family, with never-failing appeal for both kiddies and adults.

* * *

Winds of mad, wild adventure will sweep through red-blood scenes of sensational delight in "The Laramie Kid", Tom Tyler's new Western. For the screen's ace battler and rider is riding the range again, galloping over dangerous trails, evading ambushes laid by lurking enemies, coming to hand-grips with those that dare meet him in the open, fighting with fists and gun for his honor and the sake of a girl who loves him!

* * *

The great Western of the season! That's "The Laramie Kid", the new Steiner feature, starring Tom Tyler. When the guns begin to roar and wild hoofs thunder through mountain defiles, on plain and in valley, you may be sure Tom Tyler has gone into action. Fights that will make the blood leap in your veins, romance that will win the sympathy of all feminine patrons, a picture that will send you home a more enthusiastic Tyler fan than ever!

* * *

Vivid, nerve-shaking, gripping. Colorful thrills and romantic glamor; a seasoning of comedy and a bit of pathos! That's the makeup of "The Laramie Kid", starring Tom Tyler, a genuine Western in point of rousing melodrama, but different from, and superior to all contemporary Westerns, because its plot strikes across a fresh trail, and keeps its audiences tense with expectation from whirling start to crashing climax!

* * *

A ripping, speed-mad Western in which Tom Tyler takes you over rough trails among outlaws who die with their boots on, taking desperate chances for life and love! But the plotters who try to down a fighting hombre get nothing but trouble and sudden death at the hands of "The Laramie Kid". A film with action rapid as the swift rat-tat-tat of a machine gun!

* * *

After you've sat through the colorful scenes and cyclonic action of "The Laramie Kid", the latest Tom Tyler production, all other Westerns will seem tame in comparison. Here's gunplay galore, lots of human interest, a strong dash of romance, terror, tragedy and triumphant love under the starry skies. Wait till you see Tom Tyler riding hell-for-leather, scrapping, shooting, taking deadly risks and liking 'em.

A Cast De Luxe

Harry S. Webb, who directed the new Tom Tyler Western, "The Laramie Kid", now playing at the .... Theatre took particular pains toward the providing of a cast that would be worthy of both story and principal. Besides Alberta Vaughn, as the lovely heroine; the following well-known players appear in support of Mr. Tyler: Al Ferguson, as Jim Morley; Murdock MacQuarrie, as Dad Bland; George Chesebro, as Ed Larkin; Snub Pollard, as Shorty; and Steve Clark, as the fast-shooting sheriff. The film is produced from an original screen play by C. C. Church.

Two-Column Ad. Cut or Mat No. 29

1-Col. Ad. Cut or Mat No. 31

POSTER AND LOBBY DI

G. MICHAEL DOBBS

11 x 14

11 x 14

11 x 14

22 x 28

11 x 14

SIX-SHEET

ACCESSORIES
EXCHANGES NOTE
Order accessories below
directly from
HAROLD J. FLAVIN
Inc.
250 West 54th Street
New York, N. Y.

8—11x14 lobby photos
2—22x28 lobby photos
1—14x36 insert card
20— 8x10 stills
COLORED SLIDES
ONE SHEETS
THREE SHEETS
SIX SHEETS

161

SPLAYS IN FULL COLOR!

11 x 14

11 x 14

11 x 14

22 x 28 and SLIDE

TITLE CARD

ONE-SHEET

THREE-SHEET

This Space Reserved For Illustration of Insert Card Not Yet Ready At Time of Going to Press

Tom Tyler Rings Popularity Bell

Western Thriller Proves Popular With Patrons Of Strand Theatre

Tom Tyler Provides Lively Action

Pretty Roberta Gale Pleasing Heroine

Patrons of the Strand Theatre this week have been vociferous in their applause when "Mystery Ranch," Tom Tyler's latest starring western appears on the silver sheet. The Strand, known as a "cold" house in show business, is certainly belying its reputation at the present time, as the patrons stamp, whistle and applaud the numerous stunts which Tyler has devised for their entertainment in his newest picture.

With the aid of an excellent supporting cast, plus Tom's almost human horse, "Boy," the western star gives us in this picture an entirely new idea in western plot structure plus a number of dangerous stunts as only Tyler can perform them.

So, drop your evening paper or leave the dishes undried tonight, and hustle down to the Strand before the playing time of "Mystery Ranch" is finished or else, after hearing the accounts of the picture from your neighbors, you will be kicking yourself for not having taken our advice.

In addition to the particular brand of fighting, shooting and riding stunts ordinarily expected of Tyler, you will see the cowboy star in an entirely new role, playing the part of an author of western stories instead of the person authors usually write about. Further, you will see a new screen star in the small person of Roberta Gale, who has her first big part in pictures in "Mystery Ranch."

So drop what you are doing and get the car out of the garage and hurry down to the Strand before it is too late.

Woop-Te-Do Kids Tom Tyler Comin!

Here comes Tom Tyler—everybody's hero—he's ridin' like sixty—and who cares about prosperity!

Pshaw, we clean forgot to tell you that he's headin' for the ...... Theatre where he'll arrive tomorrow, and no mistake about it —and the name of the picture is "Mystery Ranch." Didja say it sounds excitin'—gosh, it is excitin' and you'll be sittin' on the edge of your seat and prayin', swearin' and cheerin' for Tyler who 'bout makes everything hum—all by himself!!

Did you say excitin'—well!!!

It has a swell cast of red-blooded, hard-ridin' hombres and a good looking girl who causes a whole lot of trouble—and Boy, Tyler's horse, well, Boy gives the grandest performance of his career.

You won't be wantin' to stay home, will ya? So better plan now to see "Mystery Ranch."

Two-Column Mat No. 54

EXPLOITATION

"Mystery Ranch,, Ballyhoo

Hire a boy and build a dummy horse around him and have him walk through the theatre section holding the reins of the "horse" which will bob up and down as he walks. This can be built of oil cloth much in the same manner as a circus clown often "rides" a dummy horse. Let him stand still and crack a whip over his head at intervals, making a cracking noise—and being careful not to touch passersby. When he has caused a great deal of attention he can give out handbills announcing "Mystery Ranch" at your theatre with the playdates.

Metal Sheriff's Badge

Makes an ideal novelty to exhibit this Tom Tyler picture, and is something that every kid will be proud to wear.

Is made of metal, with a slip pin on back. Badges come to you fastened onto a card measuring 4 x 6 inches, with appropriate wording on star and picture. Particularly effective in connection with Tom Tyler Wild West Clubs, or for general give-away purposes.

Prices of badges attached to card, with your theatre name and playdates:
1000 — $15.00   500 — $8.00   250 — $4.50

ECONOMY NOVELTY AND PRINTING COMPANY
239 West 39th Street, New York City

Program Shorts

Ride with two-fisted, hard-shootin' Tom Tyler, king of the western stars, as he pushes down the trail to romance and fame in "Mystery Ranch," latest and best of the Tyler thrillers.

Don't fail to see the latest shoot-'em-up western starring Tom Tyler, king of the western stars, the hardest fightin' two-fisted cow puncher who ever swung a lariat.

A fight and a romantic clinch is guaranteed in every scene of the latest Tom Tyler western, "Mystery Ranch." What a daredevil this lad is. And can he shoot straight—and sure. When you want action, see T-ler.

"Boy" Does Daring Act In Tyler Film

Horse Understands Actor's Mere Wish

Tom and Boy are an inseparable team of daredevils!

We refer to Tom Tyler and his trick horse Boy—both of whom may be seen this week at the .... Theatre in the Steiner production "Mystery Ranch."

The title tells the tale. Tom and Boy are the whole picture—although, in fairness we must admit that the rest of the cast of splendid players do admirable work in a thoroughly entertaining film. But Tom Tyler is our favorite thrill actor and Boy gets better as he goes along. He really does everything—and does it in the best manner of the most veteran Hollywood trouper. In other words, Boy understands.

Tyler says that Boy is eleven-tenths human. Says that when he starts on a particularly hazardous tear down a mountain, rolling, sliding and pitching, Boy gives him a look before the command to "shoot," a look, straight-in-the-eye, Tom says which plainly indicates that he's with him to the last—sink—or swim! Boy has never made the slightest effort to evade any stunt. In fact, he has never shown trepidation where other good horses refuse, point-blank, to go on. His trust in Tyler is unfailing—and as long as they're a team Boy may be depended upon!

One-Col. Mat No. 56

Tyler's Popularity Is Growing With Each Succeeding Picture

Action Picture Fans Look Forward to New Pictures

Who said the western pictures are dying out because of lost faces with the public? Someone made that statement about two years ago with the result that the production of western pictures was curtailed for over a year, without the public being given a real opportunity to voice its sentiment regarding this type of entertainment.

Practically alone among the producers of western pictures, the sponsors of the Tom Tyler starring productions continued to turn out just as many new pictures per season as had been their wont when the so-called "western" was among the most popular types of pictures.

And the Tyler sponsors have not gone broke because of their determination to proceed with their program despite the warnings of other producers. Today, the sponsors of these pictures are well in the forefront of the Hollywood production executives.

As a matter of cold fact, based upon a recent analysis, the "western" instead of losing its popularity of recent years, has actually gained many many new devotees, and we are not speaking of the children who, naturally, want nothing but western pictures. No, the new audience comprises hundreds of thousands of picture-goers who have grown sick and tired of sex, musical comedy and long drawn out smart aleck types of drawing-room pictures, in which the cast sits or stands about indulging in so-called smart talk but which is commonly known as wise cracks.

Rich and poor, educated and uneducated, cultured and uncultured people, all want the sort of picture that entertains and amuses without demanding too great concentration. They are tired after their day's activities and require relaxation. But they cannot get what they want if they must continually strain to hear the smart dialogue, nor if they must suffer the bedlam of sound which usually accompanies the musical picture. Those pictures have a definite place in the amusement schedule but they should not comprise the major portion of the public's film fare.

True, there is noise and rapid action in the western picture, but it is the kind of noise and action that does not require analysis by the grown-ups. The true western picture must contain lots of sound and action in order to please its most critical audience, the child.

Tom Tyler is a clean, upstanding young fellow, not born on the western plains but, having lived there for many years, has absorbed the true spirit of the dauntless men who originally settled the west. His pictures are built around stories that are clean in every respect. They are built for family consumption so that the youngsters, as well as the grown-ups can find in them lots of good clean fun.

Don't let anybody tell you that the western picture has lost its popularity.

BERNARD B. RAY
Presents
TOM TYLER
in
"MYSTERY RANCH"

Cast

Tom Morris	TOM TYLER
Mary Henderson	Roberta Gale
Mrs. Henderson	Louise Gabo
George Andrews	Jack Gable
Percy Jenkins	Frank Hall Crane
Sam	Charles King
Blake	Tom London
Kern	George Chesebro

Directed by
RAY BERNARD

Story	J. K. Henry
Continuity	Rose Gordon
Dialogue	Carl Krusada
Photography	J. Henry Kruse, I. A. T. S. E.
Editing	Fred Bain
Assistant Director	B. Raymond
Sound	J. S. Westmoreland
Distributed by	William Steiner
Associate Producer	Harry S. Webb

Passed by National Board of Review, Copyrighted MCMXXXIV

THE FILMS AND LIFE OF **TOM TYLER**

YOU CAN'T GET ALONG WITHOUT WESTERNS

BOOK

TOM TYLER

FOR PROFITS

•

THE NEW SERIES

"RIDIN' THRU"

"TRACY RIDES"

"MYSTERY RANCH"

"FIGHTING HERO"

"TERROR OF THE PLAINS"

"THE SILVER BULLET"

•

DISTRIBUTED BY

WILLIAM STEINER

Exclusive Distributors for Latin America

TRANS-OCEANIC FILM EXPORT CO.

723 Seventh Avenue, New York

Cable Address: TRANSFILM

Printed in U. S. A.   JOFREY PTG. CORP., New York

Tom Tyler Rings Popularity Bell

Western Thriller Proves Popular With Patrons Of Strand Theatre

Tom Tyler Provides Lively Action

Pretty Roberta Gale Pleasing Heroine

Patrons of the Strand Theatre this week have been vociferous in their applause when "Mystery Ranch," Tom Tyler's latest starring western appears on the silver sheet. The Strand, known as a "cold" house in show business, is certainly belying its reputation at the present time, as the patrons stamp, whistle and applaud the numerous stunts which Tyler has devised for their entertainment in his newest picture.

With the aid of an excellent supporting cast, plus Tom's almost-human horse, "Boy," the western star gives us in this picture an entirely new idea in western plot structure plus a number of dangerous stunts as only Tyler can perform them.

So, drop your evening paper or leave the dishes undried tonight, and hustle down to the Strand before the playing time of "Mystery Ranch" is finished or else, after hearing the accounts of the picture from your neighbors, you will be kicking yourself for not having taken our advice.

In addition to the particular brand of fighting, shooting and riding stunts ordinarily expected of Tyler, you will see the cowboy star in an entirely new role, playing the part of an author of western stories instead of the person authors usually write about. Further, you will see a new screen star in the small person of Roberta Gale, who has her first big part in pictures in "Mystery Ranch."

So drop what you are doing and get the car out of the garage and hurry down to the Strand before it is too late.

Woop-Te-Do Kids Tom Tyler Comin'!

Here comes Tom Tyler—everybody's hero—he's ridin' like sixty—and who cares about prosperity?

Pshaw, we clean forgot to tell you that he's headin' for the ...... Theatre where he'll arrive tomorrow, and no mistake about it —and the name of the picture is "Mystery Ranch." Didja say it sounds excitin—gosh, it is excitin' and you'll be sittin' on the edge of your seat and prayin', swearin' and cheerin' for Tyler who 'bout makes everything hum—all by himself!.

Did you say excitin'—well!!!

It has a swell cast of red-blooded, hard-ridin' hombres and a good looking girl who causes a whole lot of trouble—and Boy, Tyler's horse, well, Boy gives the grandest performance of his career.

You won't be wantin' to stay home, will ya? So better plan now to see "Mystery Ranch."

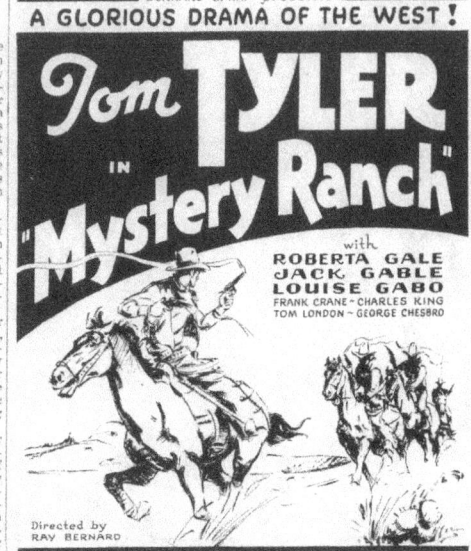

A GLORIOUS DRAMA OF THE WEST!
BERNARD B. RAY presents
Tom TYLER in "MYSTERY RANCH"
with ROBERTA GALE JACK GABLE LOUISE GABO
FRANK CRANE — CHARLES KING
TOM LONDON — GEORGE CHESBRO
Directed by RAY BERNARD

Two-Column Mat No. 54

EXPLOITATION

"Mystery Ranch" Ballyhoo

Hire a boy and build a dummy horse around him and have him walk through the theatre section holding the reins of the "horse" which will bob up and down as he walks. This can be built of oil cloth much in the same manner as a circus clown often "rides" a dummy horse. Let him stand still and crack a whip over his head at intervals, making a cracking noise—and being careful not to touch passersby. When he has caused a great deal of attention he can give out handbills announcing "Mystery Ranch" at your theatre with the playdates.

Metal Sheriff's Badge

Makes an ideal novelty to exhibit this Tom Tyler picture, and is something that every kid will be proud to wear.

Is made of metal, with a slip pin on back. Badges come to you fastened onto a card measuring 4 x 6 inches, with appropriate wording on star and picture. Particularly effective in connection with Tom Tyler Wild West Clubs, or for general give-away purposes.

Prices of badges attached to card, with your theatre name and playdates:

1000 — $15.00   500 — $8.00   250 — $4.50

ECONOMY NOVELTY AND PRINTING COMPANY
239 West 39th Street, New York City

Program Shorts

Ride along with two-fisted, hard-shootin' Tom Tyler, king of the western stars, as he pushes down the trail to romance and fame in "Mystery Ranch," latest and best of the Tyler thrillers.

Don't fail to see the latest shoot-'em-up western starring Tom Tyler, king of the western stars, the hardest fightin' two-fisted cow puncher who ever swung a lariat.

A fight and a romantic clinch is guaranteed in every scene of the latest Tom Tyler western, "Mystery Ranch." What a daredevil this lad is. And can he shoot straight—and sure. When you want action, see Tyler.

"Boy" Does Daring Act In Tyler Film

Horse Understands Actor's Mere Wish

Tom and Boy are an inseparable team of daredevils!

We refer to Tom Tyler and his trick horse Boy—both of whom may be seen this week at the .... Theatre in the Steiner production "Mystery Ranch."

The title tells the tale. Tom and Boy are the whole picture—although, in fairness we must admit that the rest of the cast of splendid players do admirable work in a thoroughly entertaining film. But Tom Tyler is our favorite thrill actor and Boy gets better as he goes along. He really does everything—and does it in the best manner of the most veteran Hollywood trouper. In other words, Boy understands.

Tyler says that Boy is eleven-tenths human. Says that when he starts on a particularly hazardous tear down a mountain, rolling, sliding and pitching, Boy gives him a look before the command to "shoot," a look, straight-in-the-eye, Tom says which plainly indicates that he's with him to the last—sink—or swim! Boy has never made the slightest effort to evade any stunt. In fact, he has never shown trepidation where other good horses refuse, point-blank, to go on. His trust in Tyler is unfailing—and as long as they're a team Boy may be depended upon!

Romance and Adventure in a Western Setting!
BERNARD B. RAY presents
Tom TYLER in "MYSTERY RANCH"
with Roberta GALE Jack GABLE Louise GABO
FRANK CRANE CHARLES KING TOM LONDON GEORGE CHESBRO
Directed by RAY BERNARD

One-Col. Mat No. 56

Tyler's Popularity Is Growing With Each Succeeding Picture

Action Picture Fans Look Forward to New Pictures

Who said the western pictures are dying out because of lack of interest with the public? Someone made that statement about two years ago with the result that the production of western pictures was curtailed for over a year, without the public being given a real opportunity to voice its sentiment regarding this type of entertainment.

Practically alone among the producers of western pictures, the sponsors of the Tom Tyler starring productions continued to turn out just as many new pictures per season as had been their wont when the so-called "western" was among the most popular types of pictures.

And the Tyler sponsors have not gone broke because of their determination to proceed with their program despite the warnings of other producers. Today, the sponsors of these pictures are well in the forefront of the Hollywood production executives.

As a matter of cold fact, based upon a recent analysis, the "western" instead of losing its popularity of recent years, has actually gained many new devotees, and we are not speaking of the children who, naturally, want nothing but western pictures. No, the new audience comprises hundreds of thousands of picture-goers who have grown sick and tired of sex, musical comedy and long drawn out smart aleck types of drawing-room pictures, in which the cast sits or stands about indulging in so-called smart talk but which is commonly known as wise-cracks.

Rich and poor, educated and uneducated, cultured and uncultured people, all want the sort of picture that entertains and amuses without demanding too great concentration. They are tired after their day's activities and require relaxation. But they cannot get what they want if they must continually strain to hear the smart dialogue, nor if they must suffer the bedlam of sound which usually accompanies the musical picture. Those pictures have a definite place in the amusement schedule but they should not comprise the major portion of the public's film fare.

True, there is noise and rapid action in the western picture, but it is the kind of noise and action that does not require analysis by the grown-ups. The true western picture must contain lots of sound and action in order to please its most critical audience, the child.

Tom Tyler is a clean, upstanding young fellow, not born on the western plains but, having lived there for many years, has absorbed the true spirit of the dauntless men who originally settled the west. His pictures are built around stories that are clean in every respect. They are built for family consumption so that the youngsters, as well as the grown-ups can find in them lots of good clean fun.

Don't let anybody tell you that the western picture has lost its popularity.

BERNARD B. RAY
Presents
TOM TYLER
in
"MYSTERY RANCH"

Cast

Tom Morris	TOM TYLER
Mary Henderson	Roberta Gale
Mrs. Henderson	Louise Gabo
George Andrews	Jack Gable
Percy Jenkins	Frank Hall Crane
Sam	Charles King
Blake	Tom London
Kern	George Chesbro

Directed by
RAY BERNARD

Story	J. K. Henry
Continuity	Rose Gordon
Dialogue	Carl Krusada
Photography	J. Henry Kruse, I.A.T.S.E.
Editing	Fred Bain
Assistant Director	B. Raymond
Sound	J. S. Westmoreland
Distributed by	William Steiner
Associate Producer	Harry S. Webb

Passed by National Board of Review. Copyrighted MCMXXXIV

ACTION ADVERTISING THAT CORRALS CROWDS!

TITLE CARD

THIS SPACE RESERVED FOR ILLUSTRATION OF INSERT CARD NOT YET READY AT TIME OF GOING TO PRESS.

ONE-SHEET

THREE-SHEET

ACCESSORIES EXCHANGES NOTE
Order accessories below directly from
HAROLD J. FLAVIN Inc.
1600 Broadway
New York City
8—11 x 14 lobby photos
2—22 x 28 lobby photos
1—14 x 36 insert card
20—8 x 10 stills
ONE SHEETS
THREE SHEETS
SIX SHEETS

SIX-SHEET

"Mystery Ranch" Box Office Winner

Tyler Stars In Lively Western

Western Hero Seen in New Role

An absolutely new idea in western stories is presented in the latest Tom Tyler starring vehicle, "Mystery Ranch," which will be the major feature on the bill at the .... Theatre on ....

Instead of opening the story showing Tom as a dyed-in-the-wool cowboy, fighting to avenge the wrongs of cattlemen, the star this time plays the role of a writer of western stories which, to his stern parent, are so wild-eyed as to be unbelievable. Tom's position in the controversy is that his stories are too tame and that he needs a visit to the west in order to obtain first hand material.

Tom gets permission of his father to make the trip. His father secretly writes the owner of the ranch which Tom will visit, explaining his son's mission and urging the owner to put on an act which will have his son gasping at the wildness of life in the west.

Tom and his secretary arrive at the ranch and are greeted with real old western enthusiasm (the six-gun variety), but Tom now goes into his real character and pulls some stunts that leave the ranch boys gasping for breath.

"Mystery Ranch" is an unusual western story, with many unique angles, capable of interesting even the most jaded picture fan.

Aiding and abetting the cowboy star in this picture are Roberta Gale, Louise Gabo, Jack Gable, Frank Hall Crane, Charles King, Tom London and George Chesebro. The story was written by J. K. Henry and the picture was directed by Ray Bernard.

Crowd Surprised At Tyler In 'Civies'

The residents of one of the outlying suburbs of Hollywood were greatly surprised recently at the sight of a western cowboy in civilian clothes when Tom Tyler and his company visited the suburbs to make several scenes for his newest western production, "Mystery Ranch," now playing to capacity audiences at the .... Theatre.

Tom had visited the suburb before on location trips for previous pictures but, as the stories called for purely western characterizations, he always appeared in his famous cowboy outfit. But the producers of Tom's pictures had found an entirely new type of story for Tom to do, and part of the action called for Tom to appear dressed in street clothes. So the surprise of the natives was pardonable when the usually rugged appearing western star showed up looking like a drug store cowboy.

"Mystery Ranch" is a different type of western story in that its main character, as represented by Tyler, is a writer of western stories. His plots are so tame that his father suggests a visit to the west in order to obtain some first hand material. The author goes west, and the men of the ranch he visits determine to have some fun with what they consider a tenderfoot. But Tyler turns the tables and, when he leaves the ranch, he leaves a wiser but sorrier bunch of cattlemen.

Roberta Gale, Louise Gabo, Jack Gable, Frank Hall Crane, George Chesebro and many others, familiar to western picture fans, appear with Tyler in "Mystery Ranch." Ray Bernard directed the story, which was written by J. K. Henry.

One-Col. Mat No. 50

A DIFFERENT WESTERN STORY

Tom Morris, a successful writer of Western novels, is being criticised by his father for writing about the West in the lurid way he does. Tom tells his father that the reading public want the lurid stuff and pays him good money for giving them what they want. But the father still thinks it is all wrong. Finally Tom shows him a letter received from a Western ranch owner who says that the West Tom pictures in his books is not nearly strong enough. If Tom would but visit Mystery Ranch the owner would show him Western men that would make his novel characters look like sissies. The father says the woman, the owner of Mystery Ranch, who had sent the letter, must be nuts. But Tom thinks there might be material for a new novel in it and decides to go and to take along his secretary Percy Jenkins.

The two arrive at the way station and are greeted by Mrs. Henderson, her daughter and a lot of yipping, shooting cowboys. On the way to the ranch several things happen; a lynching, a runaway and so forth. In other words, Mrs. Henderson and her ranch hands are "putting it on" for Tom's benefit. But Tom soon finds out their intentions and decides to go them one better each time. He does and the ranch people are worried they will have a hard time to startle this writer who takes things so easy.

Arrived at the ranch the fun continues. There is a fake feud where two men shoot it out to the death,

One-Col. Mat No. 51

then a chase after horse thieves, where Tom inadvertently gets hold of the culprits and slaps the tar out of them, again "topping" the ranch people at their own game.

Tom and Mary have a scene where he complains that things at the ranch are far too tame for him, it seems nothing exciting ever happens. Mrs. Henderson claims that she has a couple of more stunts up her sleeve and if they don't click she will give up.

However, two crooks, Blake and Kern, come to the ranch and explain their car broke down and ask for a tow to bring it in. They leave a very heavy bag in the ranch living room. When they have gone with the aid of the ranch flivver to bring in their disabled car, Tom and Percy look into the heavy bag and find it is filled with gold bullion. Tom has an idea.

He will change the bullion and put old iron scraps and horseshoes in its place, then Percy will disguise himself as a holdup man and rob the bag and take Mary along. Then later Tom will ride to the rescue and bring back the girl and the bag and give all of them the big laugh.

But Sam, the top-hand overhears this and while Tom and Percy are outside he quickly re-changes the gold for the scrap iron, then waits. Percy pretends to be a bandit and gets the bag and Mary to come with him. But along the trail he in turn is held up by Sam who takes the bag and the girl along with him, telling the girl he is in on the plot and she and he will in turn fool Tom and his partner.

When Tom is ready to ride out and make the grand stand play, the sheriff bursts in with some deputies and says the holdup was real. He wants Blake and Kern, and where is the bullion. Tom says it is in a gunny sack under the sofa, gets it out, but finds to his consternation the gunny sack contains only scrap iron. The sheriff now suspects Tom and tries to hold him, but Tom escapes to look for Mary and the bag with the real gold.

Meantime the two crooks, Blake and Kern, also escape and ride to get the gold back. They fail because Tom gets there in time and after a terrific fight makes them prisoners.

Tyler Has Good Player Support

While Tom Tyler is the bright particular star of "Mystery Ranch," his newest production now playing at the Strand Theatre, there are actors and actresses in the cast who rate feature billing in any picture.

In his latest picture, Tom has the able support of such well known players as Roberta Gale, one of the prettiest and most talented girls in Hollywood, Louise Gabo, a character actress of great talent, George Chesebro who can transform himself into the most hated type of villain, Jack Gable, Frank Hall Crane, Charles King and Tom London, all capable players in wide demand for pictures.

"Mystery Ranch," Tom's current western, has an unusual type of story, showing Tom in the earlier sequences in the role of an author of western stories who goes west to get first hand material for new novels. His appearance at the ranch is the signal for a lot of western high jinks staged by the cowboys and designed to give Tom an erroneous impression of the west. Tom is not fooled and turns the tables on the western kibitzers by starting some funny business of his own.

But the good natured fun winds up in a serious fight and Tom has his troubles for a time extricating himself from a nasty mess.

Tom Tyler Is Horseman and Weight-Lifting Champ

BORN NEW YORKER — TYPIFIES WEST

Born at Port Henry, New York, about twenty-one years ago, Tom Tyler, Steiner star appearing currently on the local screens in "Mystery Ranch," has attained prominence in several fields of endeavor and has achieved a remarkable following on his attainment to manhood.

Tyler, a member of the Los Angeles Athletic Club, created a new world's amateur record in the right hand clean and jerk lift of 213 pounds, breaking the former record of 212 pounds held by Noah Young, also a member of the same club—and which record remained for eight years.

Tyler is a perfect example of all-around athlete. He weighs 197 pounds and is remarkably fast on his feet. He can perform an outstanding variety of acrobatic tricks, stunts on the horizontal bars and among his other accomplishments he is a brilliant horseman.

He first started in amateur theatricals as an extra—and to add to his other accomplishments he has been, at one time or another, a crack football player, strong man and amateur boxer, lumberjack and even a stevedore when he shipped, as a young lad, on a lumber schooner!

CATCH LINES

See Tom Tyler, the single-handed two-gun daredevil of the range in his latest western thriller "Mystery Ranch."

* * *

Ridin' to win or die, Tom Tyler, king of the plains, performs heroic feats of riding and fighting in "Mystery Ranch," his latest horse opera.

* * *

"In Mystery Ranch" Tom Tyler meets up with an evil gang of horse thieves but, with his brand of two-fisted fighting and two-gun shooting, he soon puts them in their place.

* * *

You can't miss this great action picture, "Mystery Ranch," with Tom Tyler in the saddle.

* * *

Seein's believin', but you can't believe the fighting and shooting ability of Tom Tyler, star of "Mystery Ranch," until you see the picture.

Dangerous Stunts Are Tyler's Meat

Some really dangerous stunts—leaving synthetic thrills far behind—are featured in the new Steiner production "Mystery Ranch," which is the current attraction at the .... Theatre.

Tom Tyler, who is the star, can certainly be set down as one of the world's greatest daredevils as the result of the stunts he performs in this picture. He does everything ever done before by other daredevils and adds some new stunts.

From riding under his horse, actually hanging on although the animal's hoofs click dangerously near his head at every step, then standing in the saddle and catching hold of a tree branch while the horse is full of gallop, to outdistancing all manner of pursuit, he runs the full gamut of daring horsemanship.

In addition to the popular Tyler, "Mystery Ranch" also boasts the presence of beautiful Roberta Gale, Louise Gabo, Jack Gable, Frank Crane Hall, Charles King, Tom London and George Chesebro.

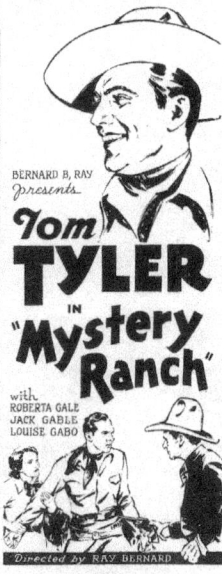

One-Col. Mat No. 53

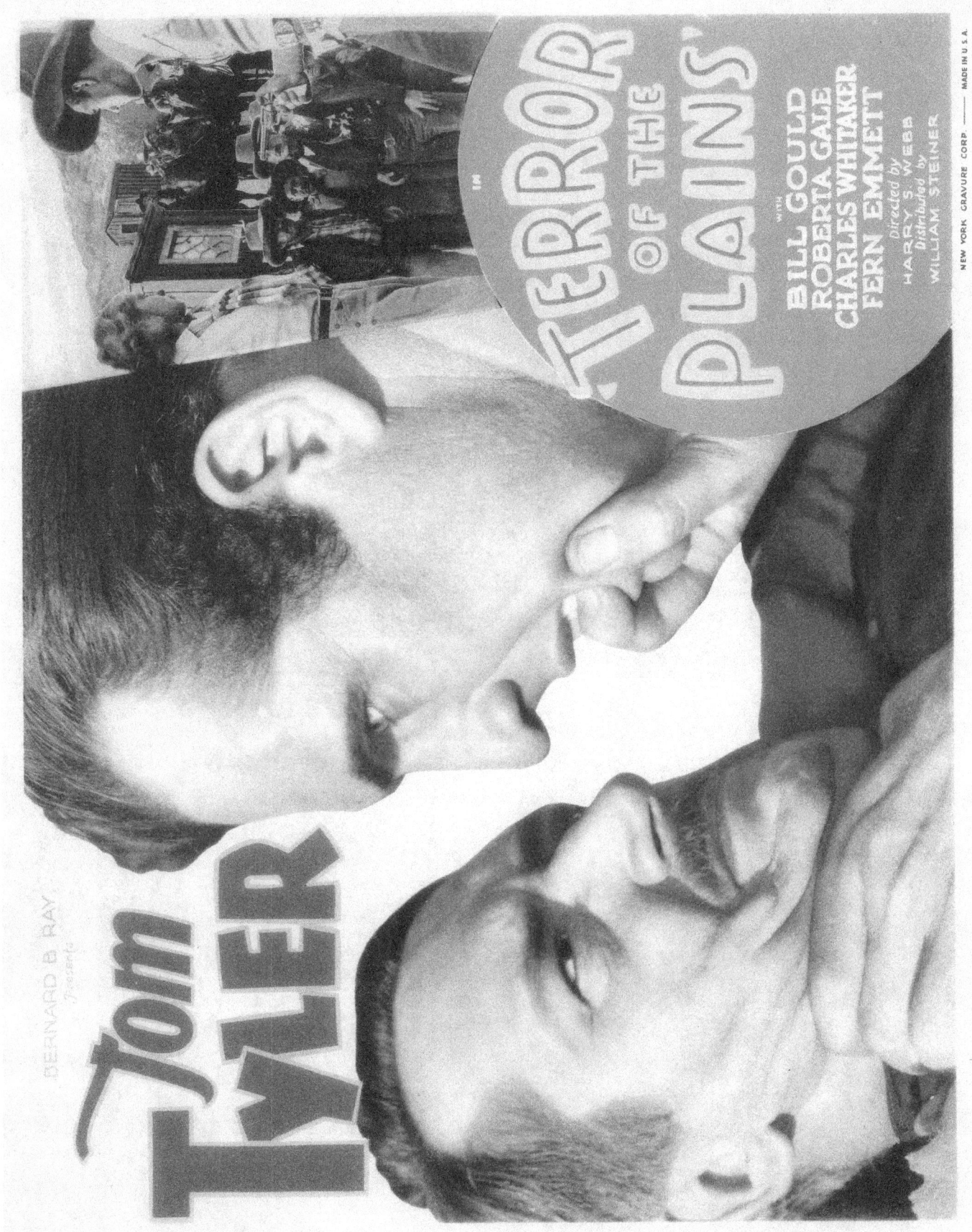

Chapter Five

What should have been the big break: Powdersmoke Range and The Last Outlaw

It could be argued that these two productions were in many ways the most significant in Tyler's career to date because it allowed him to break out of the cowboy hero mode into something different: an outright villain. It was a radical enough move that one reviewer feared this performance would hurt Tyler with the core audience of his westerns.

Instead, what the films did was to showcase Tyler's deep interest in stretching his wings as an actor. Granted the role of the repentant bad guy was not new to westerns as in "Powdersmoke Range," but what was new is the fact that a western star of program pictures was willing to do it – make that shift from being a good guy to a bad guy.

Tyler got some of the best reviews of his career to date by doing so.

The Film Daily's columnist Phil M. Daly wrote on Sept. 30, 1935, "Why doesn't some smart producer get on to the fact that one of the most impressive colorful and dynamic heavies the films has ever developed is available? Referring to Tom Tyler, whose work in RKO Radio's 'Powdersmoke Range' is simply magnificent but why waste him on westerns? He's big caliber for big films."

Tyler's role along with Harry Carey's formed the true core of the story. Bob Steele's character was essentially a reformed juvenile delinquent and his backstory provided context for how Carey's character treated Sundown Saunders.

The fact the film was produced and released by a major studio was also the kind of affirmation that should have helped Tyler's career.

The reality is that Tyler would not see different kinds of roles until he was through with his association with Reliable and then Sam Katzman's Victory productions several years later.

The movie was based on the novels written by William Colt McDonald and the first film based on the story was "The Law of the 45's," which was then adapted into the film of the same name in 1935. The film, released by First Division Pictures, starred Guinn "Big Boy" Williams as Tucson Smith and Al. St. John as Stoney Martin. There was not a third member of the team.

"Powdersmoke Range" tells a tried-and-true western story. Three saddle pals (Tucson Smith/Harry Carey, Lullaby Joslin/Guinn Williams and Stony Brooke/Hoot Gibson) are heading to a ranch that their friend and reformed bandit Jeff Ferguson (Bob Steele) has bought with money they have loaned him. Instead of finding the ranch deal settled and closed, the three friends discover the community's strong man Big Steve Ogden (Sam Hardy) and his crooked deputy Brose Glasgow (Adrian Morris) are holding Ferguson allegedly for the death of the owner of the ranch they were to buy.

Tucson, who is clearly the leader of the threesome, takes steps to legally claim the property, which infuriates Ogden so much he sends for notorious gun for hire Sundown Saunders (Tom Tyler) to murder Tucson. Tucson instead wins the duel, deliberately wounding Saunders rather than killing him. Tucson wants to try to rehabilitate Saunders, who has shown he has his own sense of justice.

Ogden's men attempt a range war at the ranch to force the threesome and their allies to leave, but the attempt fails. Saunders joins Tucson in the fight and takes a bullet intended for him and dies.

There is a woman in the cast, Boot Mallory, whose role is quite small, providing a minimal love interest for Steele.

The tone of this film is different than the great Three Mesquiteers series started a few years later at Republic. At 57, Carey's age made him the leader of the group with Gibson and Williams generally fussing and bickering between themselves. Carey's age and acting ability lent the film a real gravitas. His Tucson was a fair, reasonable man who would not tolerate any sort of injustice.

Tyler's Sundown Saunders was a finely crafted portrayal of a gunslinger with rules. His character made clear he would just as well shoot the man who hired him than Smith. His redemption seems real and is satisfying.

The scenes between Carey and Tyler showed two well-known, but in my book, under-rated actors enjoying moments on screen that were more challenging than what they had been in program westerns.

It's interesting to note how director Wallace Fox's career was spun by the RKO publicity department. In one trade mention, he is characterized as one of the "young" directors to which RKO is giving a break. He was a production manager at the studio who was now getting the chance to direct.

In reality, Fox's first directing job was in 1929 and he had directed Tyler in "Partners of the Trail" for Monogram in 1931.

According to trade reports, RKO was so impressed with the reception for "Powdersmoke Range," Fox had a follow-up assignment at the studio for the Richard Dix western "Yellow Dust." However, after one more assignment at

"Powdersmoke Range" had casting gimmick, but it also had a solid story of redemption between Harry Carey and Tyler.

the studio, "Racing Lady," Fox was back laboring on B-westerns, this time for Monogram. Aside from a stint at Universal in the mid-1940s, Fox was firmly entrenched in the B-western world until his retirement in 1954.

The trade papers began buzzing about the film in the summer of 1935. Film Daily noted on July 1, 1935, that Harry Carey, Tom Keene, Bob Steele, and Big Boy Williams had been, signed to "important roles" in the film. Keene did not appear in the film.
On July 6, Film Daily reported the film was one of 10 RKO movies starting

production. On July 12, The Film Daily announced the cast on the front page, "Major company trend to put unusually strong casts in westerns appears to have hit a peak at RKO, whose 'Powdersmoke Range' has a lineup of stellar western personalities."

The movie was the subject of an editorial in the Motion Picture Herald, July 20, 1935, "Mr. Arthur L. Mayer, that dynamic exhibitor who insistently demands the action, drama, now vacationing somewhere afar while the Rialto [the famed New York City theater] is being rebuilt, should be cheered up by a cable revealing the new movement in Hollywood to take the making of westerns really seriously.

"Those who would like to see a picture start somewhere and go thence to the conclusion, hell for leather all the while and with shooting in it will be pleased when the boards announce RKO's 'Powdersmoke Range' which has a cast of no less than 10 count 'em players of star rank including such exciting figures as Hoot Gibson, Harry Carey, Tom Tyler, Buffalo Bill Jr., Wally Wales, Francis Ford, Art Mix, Franklyn Farnham and others. It does seem too bad there wasn't a spot somewhere for William S Hart, too.

"The western did great things for the movies –there's a debt to repay to an old and honored art form."

It would appear that someone at RKO wanted to combine the star power and built-in audience of B westerns into a larger budgeted "adult" western. It was novel approach that in this case succeeded. No one had done a film like this one before. There were films, such as the several Tyler made with Rex Lease, that might team up several performers but generally there would be the star of the movie and then a lesser-known actor.

The result was a western the critics seemed to actually like. The Philadelphia Exhibitor (Sept. 1, 1935) reported, "Apparently 'The Grand Hotel' of westerns, this includes practically all leading open-air names, should be highly exploitable for houses playing such fair. Even Sam Hardy is present as the crooked element, ultimately routed by the cowboys. Romantic angle is slight, but sufficient for needs. Same applies to the story, but for what the audiences will go for is present in the many western names. Show could have stood more hard driving but the western heroes will make up for any deficiency."

In a departure from its usual dismissive stance on westerns, Variety's "Scho" (March 11, 1935) actually liked the film. Note: Variety critics write under pen names.

"RKO has a bang-up western release in 'Powdersmoke Range' period film entailing a top-notch cast and judging from Hollywood's recent horse opera output an exceptionally good story. Will do moderately well on its own in some spots and has sufficient name strength to count for something else in the dualers.

"Cliff Reed associate producer garnered a swell cast top lined them with two western fan faves, Hoot Gibson and Harry Carey and then turned them over to Wallace Fox for a corking directorial job. Adele Buffington's script provides all of the action and good dialogue necessary to hold the Mustang fans. "The manner in which the gunplay is handled goes back to old time. There being one good street duel, a mass shooting spree and the finale fight to the death in a saloon. Sounds like another World War but the canonnerring is well enough spaced and timed to make everything plausible. Story itself departs from the usual western musical comedy stuff and at times is believable." The Film Daily (Sept. 25, 1935) also really liked the picture. "Bang up western starring five big western names will wow them in every theatre. This is the last word in westerns with a swell action story that gets away from the routine formula stuff a mile and gives you an hour's footage of suspense-thrills built cunningly with clever characterization and twisting plot that weaves in and out of punchy situations to a smash climax. And the lineup of big names will simply have the action fans – young and old – rooting their heads off. Harry Carey, Hoot Gibson, Bob Steele, Tom Tyler, Guinn Williams and for good measure Sam Hardy, Boots Mallory, Buzz Barton, Wally Wales, Art Mix, Buffalo Bill Junior, Buddy Roosevelt, Franklyn and William Farnum. How can it miss?

"The action centers around Carey, Gibson and Williams as the three pals who come into the tough mining town in the early days and clean out the crooked mayor of the border town and his henchman after some tough sledding against heavy odds. Tom Tyler given an impressive performance as the bad gunfighter who later sides with the boys and helps them clean up in the final pitch battle, which is a corker. Direction fine; photography the best."

Screenland's review of the film was positive (December 1935). "Horse opera deluxe. Whether or not you're a western fan, here's action, fun, and excitement. The cast, a regular roundup of some of the film's greatest western stars, includes Harry Carey, Hoot Gibson, Bob Steele, Tom Tyler and many more Boots Mallory is the pretty girl whose ranch is being raided by rustlers. Plenty of gunplay, and a pistol duel between Carey and Tyler that's a thriller a swell western."

The film was a hit. For instance, in San Francisco at the Embassy Theater, it played a week at 15 cents, 25 cents and 35 cents tickets range and grossed $3,800. The theater's average weekly gross was $3,600.
Motion Picture Herald (Dec. 7, 1935) noted, "Instead of selling 'Powdersmoke

Range' as another western, Lew Bray, of the Vernon Theatre in Vernon, TX, played it up as the greatest galaxy of western stars ever to appear in one picture. This was stressed in ads and heralds. Lou also promoted a showcase in which to display western relics including branding irons, powder horns, steer heads, spurs et cetera and dressed as doorman in cowboy regalia promoted from a local rancher."

Theater managers liked the film. In the Motion Picture Herald Oct. 26, 1935, the manager of a theater in Cairo, MI, noted, "a very good western that certainly pleased our Saturday- Sunday crowd business, above average you can't miss on this one."

"A western that has all the western stars and the picture is of the best that we have run for some time period Good Friday and Saturday program. Will satisfy most all the customers." Royal Theater, Kimball SD, (Motion Picture Herald July 18, 1936.)

Obviously, RKO was impressed.

"The Last Outlaw" made a positive impression on many critics.

The Last Outlaw 1936

According to the Motion Picture Herald, the success of "Powdersmoke Range" spurred RKO to develop another non-traditional western, "The Last Outlaw," known in development as "Last of the Bad Men." The official name change was made in April of 1936 as noted by the Film Daily.

The production reunited Carey, Gibson and Tyler and added a venerable acting name and Carey's contemporary Henry B. Walthall to the cast.

The director was Christy Cabanne, who in 1936 was a contract director at RKO. He had a very long career in Hollywood with 167 directing credits according to IMBD from 1912 to 1948. He worked on mostly low to medium-budgeted films. A freelancer, he did have an extended time at RKO, where he directed "The Last Outlaw," as well as a period in the 1940s at Universal where he would direct Tyler again in "The Mummy's Hand."

In Hollywood Spectator, June 20, 1936, editor Welford Beaton provided a bit of history about the production as well as analysis, "There was one story which John Ford for a long time wanted to direct but studios did not think it was important enough to take the time of such an important director. Jack's idea was to do something, obviously such a wise thing to do that one wonders why it did not occur to somebody before. It was to it was to tell a story, almost anyone would do it as long as it was not a variant of the standard western story, against a Wild West background. Giving up hope of doing it himself he developed the idea and sold it to RKO. Robert Sisk's associate producer rose to it as a hungry trout does to a fly. Assigned to John Twist and Jack Townley the task of writing it into a screenplay, which was handed to Christy Cabanne to direct and it came to the screen as 'The Last Outlaw.' Paul Jacobs reviewed it in the Spectator of May 23. I viewed it last week. It interested me tremendously by virtue of the possibilities it suggests. It is quite an ordinary crook drama lifted from city streets and set down in the boundless West, one of eastern crooks seeking refuge in western plains and running afoul of an old-time outlaw and an old-time sheriff. Hollywood is given too much to shooting against walls and telling its stories. It would be wiser to shoot against the horizon. The screen is primarily a pictorial art, and no picture can equal those provided by the great outdoors. Producers faced the dreary prospect of telling the old stories over again or shutting up shop. An easy way to make old situations look new would be to transplant them in western scenery and inject a dash of cowboy in them. Bob Sisk has shown how to do it. Even the most sophisticated stories would gain strength and flavor from the wisp of a western breeze."

The Literary Digest raved about the film saying, "The first new idea in western picture-making in 20 years, Will be screened in the largest theaters in the largest cities."

Motion Picture Herald May 30, 1936, noted, "Here's a show with surprises for audiences and exhibitors. It holds a lot of entertainment for any kind of theatergoer. It has a potential showmanship quality which intelligently applied should be instrumental in creating considerably more interest with all kinds of patrons than is usually the case with outdoor action attractions. Basically, a western, the picture actually is an engaging and forceful human-interest drama. As such its field should not be limited to western followers.

"Intelligently prepared and directed and acted in an atmosphere of convincing realism the picture while retaining plenty of thrill action is anything but formula. This departure is attained in the manner in which human interest drama is developed, the way in which just the right amount of heroic of interest is worked in, and the way in which comedy, some of which boldly kids the musical trend in recent westerns, is incorporated. Dominating all other phases, however, are the situations in which an ex-convict outlaw strives to conceal his identity from his daughter until the finale. In these, as in all other occasions when he is on the screen, Harry Carey gives a heart moving performance.

"Released from jail, Payton [Carey] returns to the locale where he was convicted of crime to meet Deputy Sheriff Yates, [Walthall], the old two-gun frontier officer who originally arrested him. He holds no bitterness and the action becomes sincerely convincing when Payton discovers that the girl Sally [Margaret Callahan] whom Yates is caring for is his daughter. While this is going on, the cocky and modern idea worshiping sheriff, Billings [Russell Hopkins], is making a play for Sally and also trying to show up Yates as an outdated old timer. Simultaneously there is an atmosphere of romantic conflict involving Billings Sally and cowboy Wilson [Hoot Gibson].

"A gang of tough Chicago mobsters landed in town and looted the same bank which years before Payton had taken apart. They escaped Billings' scientific traps and the citizens demand action. To save his own reputation Billings accuses Payton of the crime. Yates however flushes the bandits and they make a getaway using Sally as a shield. Payton, Wilson and Yates take up the trail into the badlands which the old timers know like a book. The gang was cornered and then in a thrill action climax Payton saves Sally. As Billings' sheriff methods are discounted, Yates is reelected sheriff and the romantic fade out gives Sally two happinesses – knowledge of who her father is and romance with Wilson.

"A long step forward in the making of modern westerns, this picture should be properly introduced with the campaign sufficiently strong and intelligent to convince any kind of patron, those who are not ordinarily interested in westerns as well as the thrill action fans. The materials and personalities acting performances story content and production values are at hand."

The Film Daily (June 3, 1936) said, "Swell western done with classy touches and new technique tied to a bang-up story."

Screenland magazine in a letter to the editor John Ebert of Burlington IA wrote, "Hats off to RKO for the Best Western since 'The Covered Wagon. I mean 'Powdersmoke Range. All the stars were fine but especially Hoot Gibson come on RKO and give us some more all-star westerns."

Variety's "Chic" was in form when it comes to westerns (May 17, 1936) and wrote, "Chances here for a good story but uninspired script job, lack of love interest and delayed suspense proved pretty much of a clog. Three heroes of the mustang melodramas in a single cast, which gives Hoot Gibson the romantic lead with a comedy slant. Gibson's age makes him more of a cradle robber than a Romeo and he fails to hold the interest up from that angle. Story was gagged rather than written in the apparent belief that the sure fires would walk on their own feet. Result is that the attenuated story and labored dialogue cramp the production, while there is too much stalling in the forefront of the story. The result is that a competent cast is thrown away on a forlorn hope."

He added, "Tom Tyler as a gangster is so-so."

Independent Exhibitors Film Bulletin (June 1, 1936) Roland Barton wrote, "Dramatic western set in western locale but really human-interest drama with homespun characters should not be classed as typical western. Rates three stars for rural and action spots title and cast both outwardly stamped this as another horse opera but is principally a human-interest drama the writing and fighting are there but subordinated to a tale about a paroled bad man who returns to his home town to go straight and protect his now grown-up daughter. Harry Carey proves he is still a first-rate trouper in the top roll. Old Henry B Walthall shines too as the sheriff who sent Carry to prison years before and is now befriended by him. Tom Tyler is seen in the strange role of one of the gangsters and he risks audience sympathy by playing the part for all its worth. The romance between Hoot Gibson and Margaret Callahan is off key throughout. It was bad casting to give Hoot a romantic role. A liberal sprinkling of comedy and several cowboy ditties rendered in tongue in cheek manner by Fred Scott provide pleasant relief. Despite its aim to be suitable fare for general audiences, 'Last Outlaw 'will have little chance outside the action houses where it should do above average."

A fan magazine, Movie Mirror, wrote, "A western that should make the usual epic go away and hide. Usual names, yes. But the story is so much better than we have come to expect from western fare that it will be enjoyed by audiences everywhere. Even if you've long since tired of the plot they always use, we advise you to see this one. Twenty years before the story opens, Sheriff Henry B. Walthall sends outlaw Harry Carey to prison for bank robbery. In the meantime, and not knowing her identity, Walthall has been bringing up Carey's daughter. As the story opens, Carey is out of prison and returns to the old stamping ground. A young sheriff with newfangled ideas is in office and Hoot Gibson is in love with the girl. Now comes a tough band of gangsters who blow the safe, the same safe that sent Carey to prison and, with the girl as a shield, they flee to the hills. How the three old timers gang up on the gangsters and take them into custody as they thrill with plenty of sly humor. Walthall and Carey shared top acting honors and it was indeed a welcome sight to see these old timers strut their stuff. Gibson was another one that we hadn't seen for a long time. Plenty of comedy, too, by that vaudeville team of Mayer and Jans and Fred Scott sings a take-off on the recent cowboy successes for a round of applause. Your reviewer says a swell western that should suit everyone."

Motion Picture Reviews (June 1936) noted, "Western should have human appeal and good ones ring the bell for movie audiences. This one does. Harry Carey plays the role of a man who returns to his home town as an ex-convict who wishes to go straight. A bank robbery places him under immediate suspicion of the police. One official trusts him and his knowledge of criminal psychology and probable hideouts comes in handy. It is highly dramatic, fast action and immensely funny at times with none of the brutal cruelty so common to the general run of modern westerns."

"The Last Outlaw" benefits from another nuanced performance from Harry Carey, as the outlaw who has spent the last 25 years of his life in prison. His Dean Payton is a stranger in a strange land. Despite his understandable confusion, he is a gentle man who has learned much about himself.

I can easily understand why so many critics loved this film. It successfully takes western stereotypes and uses them in a fresh new way.

Hoot Gibson may have been miscast in the film as the romantic lead. Gibson, who was a genuine B western superstar and a rodeo champion, was 43 when this film was made, quite a bit older than Margaret Callahan, who at the shooting time was 25 years old. Under contract at RKO, this was her last film.

Still Gibson, who made humor a key part of his western persona – he was known for carrying his gun in his boot – clearly did his best. What helps is that he and Carey were old friends and co-stars. There is an easiness between them in their scenes together.

Walthall started in films, after a successful stage career, in 1909 and is best known, perhaps, for his working relationship with director D. W. Griffith. He appeared in a major role in "Birth of a Nation" (1915). By the time of the shooting of this film, Walthall had re-invented himself into a busy character actor. He completed two more films after this one and died in 1936.

I love the scene in which Gibson, Carey, Walthall and Callahan all go to a western film. Looking at the posters, Gibson says disgustedly, Movie cowboy!" His reactions when the film begins – it is a musical western – are equally dismissive. The ironic part of that scene is that Fred Scott – a real singing cowboy for a short time – performs.

Tyler is an unredeemable hoodlum in this film and shows a real edge in his performance. He shoots the doctor in cold blood who has removed a bullet from one of the gang members.

What is significant about Tyler's two RKO features is that they provided him a showcase to exhibit that he had actual skill as an actor and that he was willing to take roles other than the cowboy hero. It's my guess these two roles served him well when the Victory series was finished and for the first time in years he was not the star of his own series, but a freelance actor.

Rather than simply give up on acting he persevered and showed he could be as mean a villain as he was the stalwart hero. It would take Tyler several more years to get that variety of parts as a freelancer.

Although both films – from a major studio – were critically and commercially a success, all of the cowboy stars featured in them received no immediate change in their careers. They all went back to making low budget program westerns.

C. MICHAEL DOBBS

Chapter Six

Victory?

The Film Daily noted on Sept. 19, 1936, that, in typical fashion, Katzman had wasted no time. He had completed his first film with Tyler and had started work on the second.

Boxoffice noted on May 1, 1937, that "Mystery Range," the second to last Victory feature, was in production.

Katzman, by the time he formed Victory, was a seasoned veteran in the low-budget states rights field. He was also known for his tight budgets and fast schedules.

Victory had been started by the legendary producer in 1935. His operation lasted until 1940 when he went to Monogram and partnered with producer Jack Dietz and formed Banner Productions. While at Monogram he received an offer to produce serials at Columbia, but soon enough he was producing musical comedies there as well.

In an interview published in Starlog magazine producer Charles Schneer – known for his collaborations with animator Ray Harryhausen – said Katzman, "knew everything there was to know about making a movie. He was a very enterprising fellow and was enormously intuitive. But he was a very tough taskmaster and a real skinflint. I managed to get along well with Sam, because I knew what he was and respected what he did. Unfortunately, all his input was negative. He never contributed anything positive. I would suggest an idea, and he would knock it down. I would argue with him, but I never got very far. He wouldn't say: 'Do this instead of that.' He would only say: 'Don't do this' – and I didn't. I certainly learned the value of a dollar from Sam."

Regardless of his known reputation for low budgets, of all of the states rights guys operating in the 1930s, Katzman was undoubtedly the one with the longest and most successful career, producing a variety of genres until 1972 and working with Columbia, 20th Century Fox and even MGM. He died in 1973.

Here is what Katzman thought of his own productions. Frederick C. Othman of the United Press, released this following story on Oct. 20, 1943:

John Carradine, the man with a face like a worn razor blade, announced yesterday that with luck he was working in his final movie; henceforth he hopes to devote himself to Shakespeare. His cinema swan song was a dilly. Carradine, a Shakespearean actor of note, who earns better than $3,000 a week in pictures and still doesn't like them, was playing a half-wit in a horror movie called "The Voodoo Man." This concerns a gruesome threesome consisting of Carradine, Bela Lugosi and George Zucco, who carved the souls out of beautiful ladies and in so doing turned them into zombie. Then Carradine puts his blonde zombies into coolers and makes love to them through plate glass windows. That sort of movie.

"I call this a moron picture," said producer Sam Katzman with more frankness than most of his fellows. "I have made a number of these films and I claim there must be something wrong with anybody who goes to see them." Katzman went on at length in this vein while his assistant Barney Sarecky tried to shush him and the $3,000 per week half-wit practiced voodoo rhythm on Monogram studio's idea of a Haitian drum.

For the last couple of weeks, Carradine has been a half-wit by day on the sound stages and a Hamlet by night at the Community Playhouse in Pasadena. He has organized a Shakespearean repertory company which opens Sunday for two weeks in San Francisco, moves on to Seattle and eventually reaches the East Coast. It may even play Hollywood.

"Only I don't want it to," he said. "This is not a show town. Anybody brings a play here usually loses his shirt. The only profit he gets is showing off in front of the movie actors. So, I'm not bringing Shakespeare to Hollywood unless the booking situation forces me into it."

"That's the big trouble getting theaters when you want to play in them. My advanced ticket sales and San Francisco has been excellent but I have every hope of never coming back to the movies. I never did like them, (although he liked all was the weekly $3,000.) Occasionally I got to play in a good one but mostly I have been in pictures that never got anywhere and never settled anything; that only caused the patrons to waste an hour and a half of their valuable time.

"Of course, if I don't succeed with Shakespeare I'll be back to make some more pictures (a man has got to eat even when he's built like a carving knife). After all I do appreciate all the money Hollywood's paid me"

So much for Carradine and Hamlet and good luck to them both. The man we can't get off our mind is Katzman, the only strictly honest producer we ever met. Some of the others have said about the same thing but have promised to knife us if we quoted them in print. Katzman says the movie business is phony and he doesn't care who knows he thinks so

"Just look at me," he said, "making all this money and with a fancy house and swimming pool. Do I deserve it? For making moron movies?"

Assistant Sarecky by now was urging him to quit talking and telling him that if he didn't stop every last word he said would be in print.

"But it's true," Katzman said, "This is a cockeyed business we dream up these hokey stories and we hire some actors and then find directors like Bill Beaudine. Then the money flows in as if we were great geniuses. We're not. We're just lucky to be sitting in the right seats."

Sarecky sadly shook his head. The prop man dusted off some skulls to decorate the set. The misses Claire James, Terry Walker, Louise Currie, Wanda McKay and Ellen Hall walked in to have their souls removed. Carradine gave them one of his best leers and Katzman went out to have a cup of coffee. He said he needed it.

Of course, not all of Katzman's films over a very long career were as bad as "Voodoo Man" – a film that does have its supporters, like many of his horror productions – but this interview does say something important and honest about Katzman. He was making low budget films that had the potential on paper to turn a profit and in reality they did.

During his Victory years, Katzman had the services of some solid performers. Besides Tyler, several productions featured Herman Brix, the Olympic champion who later re-named himself Bruce Bennett; Ralph Byrd, best known as playing Dick Tracy in a series of serials at Republic; and horror star Bela Lugosi.

All of the Victory films starring Tyler can be seen on DVD through oldies.com or on YouTube or the Tubi streaming service.

Rip Roarin' Buckeroo
Director: Robert F. Hill

The film opens with a boxing match – stock footage of two different fights – and then to new footage of Scotty McQuade (Tyler) fighting in the ring and not doing well. Scotty complains to his corner man that he can't see well and he's knocked out. It's been a fix and his cornerman was in on the deception. He is brought back to the locker room and eventually comes around, thanks in part to Alexander, his dog, who pulled his robe off of him. Looking in the hall he sees the three men who conspired against him drop a bottle into the trash. It's what they used on him. He beats the three and in the next scene we see him in a suit walking with his dog in the rough mountainous territory.

An old car sputters to a stop nearby. The driver, Frozen Face Cohen (Sammy

Cohen), asks Scotty if he could drive such a wreck, Scotty says yes and Frozen tells him he works at a nearby ranch, The Double Y, where Scotty could probably get a job.

Scotty declares he is through with fighting as it's a rotten business and vows never to box again. On the way back Scotty "meets cute" with the female lead Betty Rose Hayden (played by Beth Marion).

His new boss Col. Hayden (John Elliot) hires him. Scotty denies he is the boxer that the colonel knows who also expressed his belief Scotty threw his last fight.

Scotty is put to the test of breaking a bronco that threw the foreman Bones Kennedy (Charles King). He, too, is thrown but gets back on a second time and breaks the horse successfully.

The crooked fight performer, Lou Slater (Forrest Taylor) turns up at the ranch, which he is using as headquarters for boxing events he's staging at a nearby cattlemen convention. Slater makes two bets with the colonel about the upcoming horse race and boxing march.

Scotty knocks out Bones, who attacked him for embarrassing him over the horse Scotty broke. Scotty confronts Slater, not knowing the colonel has bet almost everything he has over a fight Slater has fixed. Slater has lied to the colonel about Scotty and the colonel fires him. Scotty wanders into the mountains and has his dog (!) lead his horse back to the ranch with a note apologizing to Betty.

Betty asks him to reconsider riding for her father in the big race and Scotty initially declines but then turns up just in time. Slater instructs one of his crooked boxers to go out the bend in the race and shoot Scotty, something that Frozen Face prevents.

Slater then manages to convince the sheriff to jail Scotty. He is saved by Frozen Face appearing in drag at the jail. Scotty then battles Slater's boxer in the ring and wins.

Tyler seems to have had fun playing a fighter turned cow puncher, however improbable that combination might be.

Sammy Cohen seems to be an odd choice for a western. While he avoids the Jewish cliches, he just seems out of place in a western and would have been better used in an urban drama. He's effective as a sidekick, though, in that he actually helps the hero.

Director Robert Hill put the film together in a seemingly far more proficient manner than Tyler's previous directors. There's a variety of set-ups and the brief but effective use of rear projection. There is canned music during the big race scene. The photography is solid as well.

It's too bad there are just too many moments in the screenplay that are cringe-worthy from the dog walking the horse back to the ranch to Scotty just hanging out in the rocks singing to himself – Tyler didn't have a terrible singing voice, by the way. The climactic boxing scene, if staged by a good fight coordinator, would have been better.

Hill started his work as a director in 1916 in shorts. Among his sound credits are "Tarzan the Fearless" with Buster Crabbe and numerous westerns with Bill Cody. He was one of three directors on "Flash Gordon's Trip to Mars."

He did a fair amount of work for Katzman during the Victory period including the serial "Shadow of Chinatown" with Bela Lugosi and "Flying Fists" with Herman Brix, later known as Bruce Bennett.

This film, despite its script flaws, looks better than the Reliable series and seems to have been budgeted higher than those films.

Phantom of the Range
Director: Robert F. Hill

Ominous canned music introduces this film with two cowboys being scared off in a day for night scene by a rider dressed all in white – the implication is literally a ghost rider. The rider spreads the word to several teams digging in the desert to return to base.

There an unidentified older man (John Elliot) and Brandon (Forrest Taylor) talk about what they are doing: trying to find the hidden treasure left by the late miner Hiram Moore. They agree that at the impending auction they will buy the property.

Jeanne Moore (Beth Marion) is wandering in the desert yelling out for water, hoping to meet someone to help her. Jerry Lane (Tyler) hears her. He thinks the water is for her, but she uses most of his canteen for her car.

Lane rides into town. He's interested into buying a ranch but when he learns there is an auction of the Moore place he goes there to see what the property is like. Director Hill plays the auctioneer.

The auction starts with Moore's belongings and Elliot is interested in an oil painting. He thinks the secret of the treasure may be contained in the paining. The bidding is between Elliot and Jeanne until Lane comes in and buys the painting.

Lane buys the property for $2,000 and gives the painting to Jeanne, who naturally, resents the present.

Lane is now helped by Eddie Parsons, an out-of-work British gentleman's gentleman (Sammy Cohen returning with an English accent), Lane hires

Jeanne as his secretary and hires a housekeeper as well – who turns out to be a spy for the bad guys.

Back at the ranch, Parsons has found a map to the buried treasure in the frame of the painting. He stuffs it in his pocket when he hears Lane and Jeanne return and looks at the painting themselves to attempt to find a clue. The housekeeper advocates for the ghost theory, which doesn't impress Lane. The housekeeper subsequently signal the ghost rider to ride through the property so Lane and Jeanne can see the "ghost." While they are distracted the housekeeper takes the painting and delivers it to Brandon.

Eddie admits he had found the map and gives it to Lane. The housekeeper overhears.

Tex, the ghost rider, wants more money to keep his mouth shut and is shot down in front of Lane by henchman Graydo (Charles King). Lane is then framed for the shooting and arrested. He takes off though as he says that if he remains free he can prove his innocence.

Eddie has the map; a fact the housekeeper tells Brandon. The sheriff has left a deputy but Brandon and his thugs knock out the deputy and make their way into the house.

Lane returns to the ranch and helps the deputy who goes to get the sheriff. Lane has the men cornered until the housekeeper breaks a vase over his head. He escapes with the bag guys in pursuit.

He strings up a rope to trip the horses (ancient stock footage) and the sheriff finds most of the mob. Lane goes after Graydo who confesses to the murder of Tex in front of the sheriff.

The film ends as it should with Lane and Jeanne finding the treasure and each other.

There are some odd choices in this film such as a fight scene which was shot without sound and then crowd noises edited in. I wonder if the actual sound was missing or damaged?

Once again music is employed several points in the film – canned music but a score none-the-less. Cohen stops the narrative with a song at one point. In fact, Cohen's character as an arbitrary English servant is rather inexplicable. He is certainly not a sidekick.

The location work is also superior to the Reliable films.

Cheyenne Rides Again
Director: Robert F. Hill

"Cheyenne" Tom Wade (Tyler) is being pursued by a gang but manages to ditch them long enough to change his clothes and his horse. He then happens upon the people chasing him and joins them. It's a posse chasing a stagecoach bandit and he takes off with them.

One of the posse members Girard (Creighton Chaney better known as Lon Chaney, Jr.) is not convinced that Cheyenne wasn't involved in the robbery.

The film now introduces the sidekick and comic relief, Dopey (Jimmie Fox), who is at Cheyenne's ranch singing a truly terrible and unfunny song. The horse Cheyenne was riding at the hold-up comes running rider-less into the barn at the ranch and Dopey washes a large white spot off the horse that had been used to disguise it.

The posse rides to Cheyenne's ranch and they search the barn where Girard discovers the bucket of water and sponge Dopey used to wash the horse.

The sheriff tells Cheyenne the robber only took a bag of money from a cattleman and ignored the strong box, mail and the passengers' money.

Girard, of course, wants to take the money for himself and his pals. Cheyenne is obviously some sort of law man and tells Dopey the case is not over as yet. Cheyenne hides the money just in time as Girard and his gang comes into his ranch house.

The gang finds out Cheyenne is a cattle detective and forces him to give them the money. Cheyenne pulls a fast one taking on the gang in a fight and then escapes, crashing through a window.

Cheyenne and Dopey lose the gang and head to town, while Girard heads back to the ranch house to search it thoroughly.

At the local saloon, Dopey gets a beer with a message for Cheyenne. Cheyenne reveals his identity to the sheriff (Slim Whittaker) and explain he is trying to get the rustlers who are operating in the area.

Rollins, a rancher, (Ted Lorch) is the brains behind the rustling, and has been under surveillance by Sally (Lucile Brown) who works with Cheyenne.

Cheyenne breaks into the Rollins ranch house – making sure that Mary is all right – and works out the terms of giving the stolen money to Rollins. Meanwhile Girard has figured out that Cheyenne is the law and rides out to the ranch to confront him. Dopey follows him.

Girard arrives to identify him and in another big fight throws his gun at Cheyenne, knocking him out. They tie him up and lock him in a bedroom.

Dopey rescues Cheyenne and escapes with Mary while Cheyenne tackles the gang. They all ride off with the gang behind them.

There is a climatic fight, the arrival of the sheriff and the apprehension of the bad guys. Naturally a marriage proposal is offered as expected.

Hill shows once again he had a better idea of what he was doing than Tyler's previous directors in the states right format. The fight scenes with the gang are dynamically staged and edited. He once again adds quick close-ups to aid in presenting the action. The director also performs a bit part as the bartender at the saloon where Dopey is supposed to be getting information.

There is some stock footage and definitely some padding with the repetition of the song for which Dopey is apparently well known. Despite those lapses, the film is generally better than many of Tyler's Reliable series. Lucille Browne was a busy heroine in westerns and action films until her retirement from the screen in the late 1930s to help raise her family. She returned to acting in a few years, doing bit roles and one of her later films also included Tyler – in an uncredited role – "Ladies of Washington" in 1944. Chaney was still struggling to make his mark in Hollywood and several years away from his star turns in "Of Mice and Men (1939)" and "The Wolf Man (1941)."

The film was shot on the famed Iverson movie ranch.

This 1938 herald came from a theater in North Carolina and it shows how they used "Cheyenne Rides Again." It was for a Saturday matinee for kids and was supported by cartoons, a two-reel comedy and a serial chapter. (author's collection)

Feud of the Trail

Director: Robert F. Hill

This is the second film in which Tyler plays Tom Wade, cattle detective, who is called away from his leave to investigate and apprehend some rustlers. He is accompanied by another officer, Jerry (Milburn Morante).

An older man driving a car is held up when Wade and Jerry come across him. They pursue the three robbers.

One of the robbers is a dead ringer for Wade – Tyler in a dual role. Wade finds the three men as they divide up the loot and chases them. Jerry manages to shoot the Wade look-alike.

The bandit dies and Wade wears his clothes to get up close to the two other robbers, who he captures.

At the office, Wade's superior tells him to go to the ranch that was the home to his look-a-like. There is supposedly the presence of gold on the ranch and a crime family headed up by Ma Holcomb (Vane Calvert) is attempting to seize the ranch, first by a proposal of marriage and then with an offer to buy the ranch.

Lance Holcomb manages to buy the ranch from John Granger (Lafe McKee) and John heads off to the bank to deposit the money. Lance sees Granger riding, shoots him and then steals the money.

Wade comes upon the wounded man but does not tell him who he is. He brings him back to his ranch.

Wade decides not to tell either Granger's father or sister (Harley Wood) even though he clearly is uncomfortable and often clueless. Lance Holcomb is sent to the ranch by his mother to capture Wade/Granger for the reward on Granger's head.

Wade heads over to the Holcomb ranch to retrieve the deed, gets into a fight and is rescued by Jerry who lets the Holcombs believe that he has arrested Wade.

The Holcombs head back to the Granger ranch. With several twists and turns – and an explosion in a gold mine – the law wins out and the Grangers hang onto their ranch and their gold mine.

One of the main interests in this film's plot is the "Ma Barker" style villain, the matriarch of the Holcomb family. Hill allows Calvert to truly play the character as quite nasty, bullying her son and her ranch hands. I like how she was prepared to save herself as her son took the rap.

The female lead was played by Harley or Harlene Wood – she had several other names as well – who labored in B-films for her brief movie career in the 1930s. Her most significant credit was that of "Blondie" in the 1936 exploitation film "Marihuana" produced by master of the road show Dwain Esper. She also appeared in several Three Stooges shorts. In the mid-1950s, she and her husband started writing songs, their most prominent was "Let There be Peace on Earth."

In this film, the director played the head of the cattlemen's association. The film also has another opportunity for Tyler to sing. This time he is clearly making fun of the singing cowboy. There is another musical number in the saloon with an unidentified cowboy band.

The sidekick Jerry played by Morante is a blatant impersonation of Gabby Hayes. His boasting is supposed to be comic relief but I found him to be fairly obnoxious.

Here is the interesting thing about this movie: while it is more competently made from a technical viewpoint, it has, like other entries in this series, an odd element or two. In this film, Tyler was made the look-alike brother of the heroine. After he reveals the truth to her and her father, the heroine develops a crush on him. Although there isn't the usual hug and kiss at the conclusion it was quite creepy to have this character fall in love with someone who looked exactly like her brother.

"Good program western for small house," was the verdict published by the Check-up on Nov. 15, 1938.

Mystery Range
Director: Robert F. Hill

The film opens with a note being written by an unseen person. It reads: "The bearer, is Luke Bardes, the man I told you of. He is unknown in your part of the country but has complete knowledge of safe trails across the border. M.K." The note is passed from one anonymous person to another.

Director Hill makes his usual cameo and this time he plays Tyler's boss. Once again, Tyler is playing as an agent of the Cattleman's Protective Association. His assignment is to arrest the fugitive Bardes who is expected to cross the border.

Tyler follows his man to a ranch where Jed Travis (Lafe McKee) signals Luke Bardes (Richard Alexander), whom Tyler subsequently ropes and captures. Tyler's sidekick and fellow agent Jim Dolan (Milburn Morante) brings him to town and Tyler heads to the nearby ranch. Tyler finds the note and presents it to McKee and assumes the identity of Bardes.

McKee reveals he is the uncle and guardian of Jennifer (Jerry Bergh) who in five days will become the owner of the ranch. McKee and his men have been sabotaging the ranch so she will willingly sell it to the anonymous man who had sent Bardes to the ranch to assist in the scheme.

Tyler's job is to distract her while McKee's men run her herds across the border.

Jennifer has contacted the Cattleman's Protective Association for help but doesn't realize who Tyler is until he carefully tells her the truth.

Tyler's sidekick (alleged comic relief) discovers why Jed Travis and his confederates wants his niece's ranch – a railroad is planned to go through it.

After the brains villain Kurt Morgan (Roger Williams) has been exposed and captured, Tyler rides back to the ranch to tell Jennifer what is happening. Meanwhile Bardes has escaped from jail and ambushes the sidekick rescuing his boss.

Bardes and Morgan make it to the ranch before Tyler and attempt to threaten Jenny into signing the sales papers.

Naturally, Tyler cleans up the various outlaws.

It should be noted this film has a score through a fair amount of its running time. Library music for sure, but it's clear Katzman saw the need to upgrade his movies. The film stops dead in its tracks for an unnecessary musical number in which Dolan sings "Home on the Range" in a saloon, bringing all the hardened cowboys to sing along as tears roll down their cheeks.

Once again, Hill puts in more effort in his direction than as seen in many of Tyler's Reliable films. He has more closeups and better scene compositions. Bergh only made one other film – a western with Tex Ritter – and then no longer worked as an actor in Hollywood. She – and the film – received the following notice by The Film Daily's anonymous columnist Phil M. Daily in the June 25, 1937, edition, "Were we surprised and intrigued when we learned all about a film gal's yen for perfume as we read an article in the press book on Victory's 'Mystery Range' with Tom Tyler. Jerry Bergh is the leading lady with Tom who has the perfume habit. She has 82 different kinds of a different perfume for every mood sometimes, as the storybook informs us, 'she goes a little berserk and daubs on a whole collection of scents.' Gosh, not all 82 scents at once, we hope."

It's a better-made film than some of the Reliable films but it didn't have the production finesse that Republic product was already showing.

After directing this film, Hill worked on the Herman Brix/Bruce Bennett production of "Million Dollar Racket" in 1937. For the remaining films in the Tyler series, Katzman took over as director and Hill went to Monogram and Universal. Whether there was a falling out, I'm yet to discover but Hill did work for Katzman again on "East Side Kids" at Monogram.

Katzman directed only five films in his long career. Three Tyler films and two Herman Brix/Bruce Bennett vehicles, "Sky Rocket" and "Amateur Crook."

It's interesting to compare the Tyler series versus the Brix series of films. The productions values are superior as the Brix films were contemporary adventure stories or dramas. Westerns with their outdoors locations were cheaper to stage and by watching the Tyler series back-to-back it's clear that Katzman didn't spend much money on the few interior sets used in the westerns.

Neither the defection of a director or a studio fire was insurmountable to Katzman. Boxoffice reported on June 12, 1937, "The $25,000 fire which gutted the Victory Picture studio in Culver City early this week has not affected production on that company's current picture, spokesman for the studio said. The fire, which is thought to have started in the property room, spread through the wooden structure and consumed one of the sound stages, inflicting heavy damages on the remainder of the property. Sam Katzman, Victory producer, put the Tom Tyler western 'Mystery Range,' back into work the following day, the cameras and office equipment having been carried to safety."

Orphan of the Pecos
Director: Sam Katzman

Hank Gelbert (Lafe McKee) fires his foreman Jess Brand (Forrest Taylor) who kills him and then robs him.

Meanwhile cowboy-in-search -of-work Tom Rayburn (Tom Tyler) has run into a medicine show quack and ventriloquist Professor Jeremiah Mathews (Ted Lorch) while on the road.

Out riding, Jess runs into Ann (Jeanne Martel) the daughter of the man he killed and professes his love for her. She rejects him again, saying all he wants is the ranch.

Ann and Jess find Rayburn in the house near the body. Naturally, he is accused of the murder and Jess plants the money he took from the safe on Rayburn.

Rayburn escapes as the sheriff approaches.

Promising Ann he would come back, Rayburn produces the letter from her late father offering him Jess's job. Ann believes he is not the murderer and Rayburn offers the theory that Jess would have more to gain with her father's murder.

Jess realizes the medicine show doctor could sign an affidavit to show Rayburn was the murderer and takes the performer to a shack to sign the document. Rayburn has followed the group to the shack, crashes through the roof allowing the professor and him to escape.

Jess comes to Ann's ranch, where Rayburn is hiding. Ann gives Jess his last wage but Jess is suspicious. Rayburn gets the drop on him and the professor provides Rayburn with his alibi.

Meanwhile with Jess's gang approaching, the professor uses his ventriloquism skills to trick Jess into a confession. The professor and Ann escape as Rayburn takes on the gang.

After a chase and a fight, Rayburn is in control of the gang just in time for the sheriff to pullup.

Katzman's direction is pedestrian at best. I've seen far worse. He minimizes set-ups as much as possible. Lorch's character adds a little variety in comedy relief. There are several energetic fights with Tyler that are shot without Hill's imagination as a director.

The moment that stretches believability, which I now expect in a Victory western, happens when the professor uses his vocal powers to precisely imitate the dead Lafe McKee (naturally they use McKee's actual voice). The imitation is so dead-on that Jess panics. How would the professor know what the murdered man sounds like?

Variety (Sept. 28, 1938) thought the following of the film, "The success of Bergen and McCarthy has brought a cycle of ventriloquism to the westerns. Now it isn't only possible to catch outlaws in the open spaces with a horse, a sheriff, or radio but by throwing curves with the vocal cords. 'Orphan' comes as the third western series to use a voice juggler and his dummy, The Three Mesquiteers and the Jack Luden opuses have preceded. Tom Tyler uses Ted Lorch, the vent, to ghost a murderer into spilling as the climax of this one.

"'Orphan' gives the idea in title that there are kids mixed up in this but the orphan turns out to be Jeanne Martel who is old enough to be an eye catcher. Lake McKee, her father, gets the goods on his foreman, Forest Taylor, fires him and gets potted for doing it. Safe is looted and when found, Tom Tyler, who has been sent for by the old man, was bending over the body. In a hole, he scours the country trying to find the guilty man. Getting an idea who it is he follows through by having Lorch carry out his threat and the case pops. It's a family affair, Jeanne Martel being Mrs. Tyler in real life …Tyler shows off in several scraps which do a great deal of damage to the furniture and the chases are up to par, tempo is a little too slow. There's not a whole lot of talking in the screenplay. Basil Dickey evidently figuring audiences are so familiar with the basic western story it only takes action because the western follower knows the right words to put in the right places. As biz goes it will average so so."

"Satisfactory, though routine, western," reported the Check-up on Dec. 7, 1938

Brothers of the West
Director: Sam Katzman

Tyler is back as his recurring character, Tom Wade of the Cattlemen's Protective Association, and he is off to New York City on vacation. Just as he is about to leave, he gets a telegram saying that his brother Ed (Bob Terry) has been accused of murder and has disappeared.

Annie Wade (Dororthy Short), the wife of the accused man, tells the sheriff (Lafe McKee) she has no idea where her husband might be. Wade turns up in time to talk with the sheriff.

Meanwhile, Wade spots an unknown woman seen lurking outside of the house and listening. Wade takes off after her.

The woman, Celia, (Lois Wilde) is the daughter of the murdered man, a bank president to whom Ed owned money.

Crooked lawyer Jeff Tracey (Roger Williams) is the leader of the gang that shot the bank president. They now hold Wade's brother prisoner trying to get him to reveal where he hid the payroll he was guarding for the banker.

Tracey thinks he has killed Wade, but our hero fakes his death and gathers evidence, including the bullet that Tracey shot at him as well as examining the tracks left by Tracey's car.

Wade comes to the sheriff with his evidence. He needs a deputy though to help him and Jake the Hobo (Jack "Tiny" Lipson) agrees to help Wade as long as his time in the jail is lengthened. He likes it there with its secure place to sleep and free meals.

Jake is assigned to see if he can find the car with the unique tire tracks, which he does, but is chased away and didn't get the license plate.

Tracey and Celia visit Wade and his sister-in-law and Wade tells them a little of what he has learned. Tracey is noticeably nervous.

Tracey lures Wade into a trap and captures him. Meanwhile Celia has found the cabin where Ed is being held captive thanks to Ed starting a fire. Ed tells her that Tracy is the leader of the gang and how her father was murdered.

Tracey brings in Tom Wade bound up in ropes and threatens Ed that unless he tells them where the bank money is hidden he will kill his brother. Ed agrees to show them where he hid the money.

Once again there is a chase or two, a big fight (complete with close-ups) and hugs.

So, just when was this western supposed to take place? Tyler's snappy 1937 suit would indicate the story is contemporary but is it?

The Katzman moment of this film is when Tyler's horse lets out a neigh and Tyler said, "That's my horse. He always tips me off."

Lois Wilde helps Tyler out with the ropes in "Brothers of the West." (author's collection)

Comic/sidekick support of sorts comes from Jack "Tiny" Lipson, who made quite a few appearances in westerns during the 1930s. He appeared in many two-reel comedies, including some Three Stooges offerings. Perhaps his best-known role was that of King Vultan in chapters five through 13 of the first "Flash Gordon" serial. He also appeared in the famous cabin scene in "Night at the Opera" with the Marx Brothers.

"Okay kid grind western," opined the Check-up on Nov 15, 1938.

Lost Ranch
Director: Sam Katzman
The last of Tyler series produced by Sam Katzman, this entry continues the series concept of Tyler playing an on-going character. Film Daily noted in its Nov. 22, 1937, edition that exteriors were being shot for the movie that week.

Two young women are driving through the country Rita (Jeanne Martel) and Minnie (Marjorie Beebe). They are traveling to meet Rita's father. They are spotted by a cowboy who reports to lead henchman Terry (Roger Williams) who goes out to intercept the women.

Our hero Tom Wade (Tyler) is introduced in a scene in which he and his sidekick Happy (Howard Bryant) are riding. Wade is singing and Happy is making gestures in response. He dislikes Wade's choice of a love song and both men launch into a version of "Home on the Range."

The bad guys do meet the two women and start escort them. The women put on the speed to escape and the resulting gun fire attracts Wade's attention.

Stopping the car by shooting out a tire there is a resulting gun fight which drives the bad guys away.

Rita's father John Carroll, (Lafe McKee, who else?) is being held by Carson (Forrest Taylor). Rita has instructions from her father to stay in town until she hears from him. Carson delivers a fake message to her. He tries to convince her that Wade and his sidekick are the bad guys and the whole incident was staged.

Wade visits the sheriff and explains that he was asked to look into a deal that involves Carroll.

Wade manages to have a talk with Rita to try to find out what she knows. Apparently her father owned a ranch in the area and now wants to sell it but there is some sort of "government secret."

Carson and his men grab Rita and knock out Wade.

Carroll explained to his daughter that Carlson and his gang are smugglers and wanted his ranch as it was close to the border. He did not sell to them and they took him prisoner. They intend to use the daughter as leverage in getting the ranch.

Rita is able to write a coded letter to Wade which directs him to follow a trail of beads off of her purse.

After a chase and a big fight, Wade emerges triumphant.

Katzman evidently felt the need to add a western song to the film and the result is totally unconvincing as the dubbing job is poor. The scene just takes up time.

Martel has more screen time than the usual B-western heroine in a Victory production and she puts in a serviceable performance. Her character has both courage and brains.

Forrest Taylor had a long career as a character actor and he was especially good as a weaselly villain. There is always something satisfying in seeing him beat up.

As far as sidekicks go, Happy is close to bottom of the barrel.

The Philadelphia Exhibitor noted on June 1, 1938. "a grind male audience was apathetic. Estimate: routine grind Western."

Film Daily, May 6, 1937, Tyler completed his last two movies for Victory, "Feud of the Trail" and "Mystery Range." The Film Daily reported July 20, 1937, that Tyler had been signed for an 18-week tour with the Wallace Brothers Circus taking the place of Hoot Gibson.

The Motion Picture Herald printed a letter in its Aug. 21, 1937, edition urging exhibitors to take action when Tyler was in town with the Wallace Bros. Circus. "When the Wallace Brothers circus was in Decatur [Il] Mr. and Mrs. Morrow and their daughter Betty, met the western picture star Tom Tyler, who is the feature attraction with the circus. We found him to be a most gracious, charming host. I think every exhibitor should take advantage of the opportunity to meet this popular star when Wallace Brothers are within visiting distance. Ask for Mr. West, the publicity agent with the circus and he will arrange for an interview. Everyone in attendance at the circus went for Tyler in a big way. He was fairly mobbed by autograph seekers after the performance had concluded. When my next Tyler feature is shown next week I shall have a special Tyler matinee and admit autograph holders free. I can't understand why the major companies have passed up this star. Thirty years in show business tells me that he is of major caliber. Cliff E. Morrow, Morrow's theater in Decatur IL."

After Tyler's tenure, Katzman apparently shut down production. Boxoffice noted he had been in a "long hiatus." Katzman was clearly in need of additional westerns and on Sept. 6, 1938, announced to the Film Daily that he had signed Col. Tim McCoy to a series of eight westerns. The first film, in typical Katzman fashion, was announced as being ready for release on Oct. 10, 1938.

The Rise of Republic and what it meant to B filmmaking
I need to interrupt the timeline of Tyler's films with a note about the impact of Republic Pictures' formation in 1935. The simple truth is that Republic led a new era in B film production that would have a major impact on the motion picture industry.

As detailed in Jack Mathis' essential book, "Republic Confidential," coming from advertising, Herbet J. Yates had entered the world of film laboratory, processing film stock and producing prints. By 1927, he had formed Consolidated Film Industries, which did a lot of businesses with independent producers to whom he extended credit.

Yates wanted his own studio and set about a series of acquisitions that would give him his objective. He wanted Monogram because it had film exchanges, eliminating the need for the states right distribution model. He wanted Nat Levine's Mascot because that company had its own studio, the former Mack Sennett studio.

Yates, according to Mathis, approached Monogram first, which welcomed the idea of a merger. Yates also wanted Mascot, Chesterfield, Majestic and Liberty studios as well. Writing about his initial interest in Monogram, Mathis said, "But saddled with the same cash flow problems that were plaguing their poverty row neighbors, Monogram's president Way Ray Johnston and production head Trem Carr were amenable to Yates's proposal seeing in it as salvation from daily financial hassles as well as a means to secure more money for bigger productions. For Yates, it was an opportunity to acquire and establish production company and network of exchanges through which to distribute the films as a base for future expansion. And Yates, whose broad business background and savvy entrepreneurial spirit put him at an advantage over most showmen he dealt with, realized the union was all but risk free since an amalgamation at his instigation meant that he controlled the managerial strings."

In 1935, Yates' new studio, Republic, released its first film, the John Wayne program western "Westward Ho!" By the end of 1935, Mathis noted the company had released 11 features and six westerns.

The marriage of all these filmmakers were short lived, though. By August of 1936, W. Ray Johnston was out, re-forming Monogram, which in some ways would attempt to be Republic's biggest competition. Levine was out in February 1937, eventually going to MGM for a short stint. The fact that both Republic and Monogram had their own exchanges meant they had a leg-up on the producers such as B.B. Ray and Sam Katzman.

Republic quickly showed great technical proficiency in their films. Every major studio made program films and their films simply looked better than those of the independents. As director Nick Grinde noted in his essay, a B unit at a major had many resources; anything that had been created for an A film – sets, costumes, music – was theirs to be used. B.B. Ray and Katzman did not have the depths of those resources.

Music was an element of motion picture-making that was missing from independent product. Music could be used to heighten excitement, suspense or romance, but very seldom in independent B program films.

I believe it was simply an issue of budget. Ray and Katzman apparently didn't see it as the worth the effort. The trouble was that as soon as Republic started making its films, the difference was noticeable. The early John Wayne films at Republic had better direction and photography than many other B westerns of the time.

Mathis explained that Yates increased the budgets for the program westerns because "better class theaters were now booking these once-shunned stepchildren." Better films meant better bookings, which had the potential for greater profit.

Chapter Seven

Freelancing

Tyler's freelancing career shows several things. First, he held his own against star actors. Tyler was clearly seen as a solid and respected performer. Tyler appeared opposite people such as Cary Grant, Ronald Coleman, Jean Arthur – who had appeared with him at FBO – Lucille Ball, John Wayne, Randolph Scott, Robert Mitchem, Robert Ryan, Gary Cooper and Errol Flynn, among others.

There were producers and directors who clearly supported him, the most important of those being director John Ford. Producer Harry Sherman cast him in three of his films at Paramount. He appeared in three of Tim Holt's post-WW II westerns. Producer Ron Ormond certainly liked him by including him in nine of his western productions at the end of Tyler's career.

There has been the allegation made that Tyler was a "stiff" performer. I strongly disagree. If you look at his films, you see a growth of an actor. He was in films directed by George Marshall, Victor Fleming, Samuel Fuller, Cecil B. DeMille, Allan Dwan, William Wyler, George Stevens, Robert Wise, Howard Hawks and Raoul Walsh. All of these directors had access to literally hundreds of performers for casting. They wouldn't have picked someone who couldn't deliver what they wanted.

Not to be redundant, but it's important to emphasize that Tyler's career after cowboy stardom did not follow the path of many other of his sagebrush colleagues. If you look at popular performers such as Hoot Gibson, Wild Bill Elliot, Ken Maynard, Col. Tim McCoy, Charles Starrett and Johnny Mack Brown, for instance, once they were done with being a cowboy star, there was very little additional career activity in film. Only Harry Carey and Bob Steele came close to what Tyler pursued in his career.

In his last years in Hollywood when he was clearly ill, Tyler also benefited from his positive reputation in the industry, appearing on four episodes of "The Cisco Kid," two episodes of "The Roy Rogers Show," two episodes of "Adventures of Wild Bill Hickok," and four episodes of "The Gene Autry Show." He had built up considerable good will through his reputation as a professional with whom it was easy to work. People knew he was ill and having hard times and helped him.

I've made every effort to note where readers can see these films. Several are simply not on streaming services or on DVD/Blu-ray.

1938

King of Alcatraz
Director: Robert Florey

Can be seen at https://archive.org/details/king-of-alcatraz-1938

This is a great example of B moviemaking at a major studio, in this case Paramount. Director Robert Florey put together a suspenseful film that incorporates two buddies (Lloyd Nolan and Robert Preston) who fight over women storyline with a crime kingpin (J. Carroll Naish) assembling a gang to get him out of prison and the country by hijacking a ship.

Tyler plays a member of the gang, Gus Banshek. His RKO co-star, Harry Carey plays the captain of the ship.

The film was featured in a huge trade ad in Motion Picture Daily July 18, 1938, featuring Paramount pictures with the emphasis that these will make money for theater owners. It was described in the ad as "a powerful story of what happens after the government puts the finger on the racket kings. The plot is novel, fresh up-to-the-minute! Some of the highlights are the capture of a passenger ship by escaping gangsters, an emergency operation on shipboard directed by radio instructions from a doctor hundreds of miles away plus a romance that's true and tender."

The Motion Picture Daily's review (Oct. 3, 1938) noted, "'King of Alcatraz' hews to the line of straight melodrama. Although a large cast participates, the theme is carried almost exclusively by Lloyd Nolan, J. Carroll Naish, Robert Preston and Gail Patrick. Produced by William C. Thomas, the film is based on an exciting screenplay written by Irving Reis. Robert Florey's direction stresses the excitement content of all the story phases.

"Escaped from Alcatraz, Carroll Nash, disguised as an old woman and surrounded by his mobsters, boards a freighter. Operators Nolan and Preston, romantic rivals, preside over the radio room. Miss Patrick's loved by both, is the ship's nurse. In Chinese pirate style Naish and his minions take control of the boat. Ensues a welter of exciting goings on with Nash and Preston alternately resisting and surrendering to Naish's orders. Comes a coup in which Nolan is seriously wounded and Preston only slightly so. To save Nolan's life Miss Patrick operates on him receiving instructions as to procedure from doctor aboard another vessel via radio. The climax has Nolan and Miss Patrick settling down on a chicken ranch, where accommodations have been reserved for Preston. Audiences are left to guess Naish's fate. Running time 55 minutes. A."

Tyler doesn't have a lot to do in the film, but in my outlook he has managed to shed the image of the cowboy hero, which will assist him in his career.

1939 turned out to be an auspicious year for Tyler and his career.

Stagecoach
Directed by John Ford
Can be seen on several different streaming services as well as on DVD
Previewed Feb. 11, 1939

This is the film in which John Ford revived the adult western, showing it to still be a genre that could tell insightful stories about interesting characters. It is also the film that established John Wayne as capable of carrying an A film and allowing him to rise out of the B film stage of his career.

Tyler plays the pivotal role of Luke Plummer, the man responsible for wrongly putting John Wayne's character of Ringo into prison. Tyler uses his

"Stagecoach" was one of the most important films in Tyler's career. (author's collection)

knowledge of silent screen acting to establish his character since he has little dialogue. He had to convey both the depth of Plummer's evil as well as his fear of facing Ringo in the climactic ending. Tyler gives a great performance.

"Stagecoach" was an acclaimed hit for Ford and certainly added to Tyler's resume.

Newsweek March 6, 1939, noted, "This United Artists release was produced by Walter Wanger on a modest budget without the box office insurance of important name players. For all that, it will probably rank among the first 10 in 1939's film poll. Against the pictorial thrilling Arizona background, the action of 'Stagecoach' builds from its initial suspense into a steady crescendo of excitement. The acting is uniformly excellent. But the film success is more fully explained by names of its adapter and director – Dudley Nichols and John Ford. This team has brought to a western some of the rare quality that made 'The Informer' a screen masterpiece."

Commonweal magazine wrote in its March 10, 1939, edition, "It is an engrossing drama. Its excitement comes from the skillful characterizations of each member of this group, for those who like their westerns fast and exciting there is plenty of action. But there is something bigger here a gripping drama, superbly told, embellished by excellent with splendid performance and direction."

"The Night Riders" marked Tyler's first work with Republic. His time there is covered in the next chapter.

Frontier Marshall
Directed by Allan Dwan
Can be seen on YouTube

Tyler played an uncredited role of "Buck Newtown" in this re-telling of the Wyatt Earp and Doc Halliday story with Randolph Scott and Cesar Romero in the respective roles.

Tyler's character is part of the gang of thugs employed by the crooked gambler played by John Carradine. The gang also includes Lon Chaney, Richard Alexander and Joe Sawyer. Tyler's character gets dispatched during the fight at the O.K. Corral, the conclusion of the picture.

Motion Picture Herald July 29, 1939. "This is a film for the 'Stagecoach' and 'Dodge City' trade, a roaring melodrama with guns blazing lethally from start to finish and the story of tombstone Arizona and its untempered youth, told in terms of a personal story well worth the telling brought to the screen without benefit of bombastic ballyhoo, it stacks up with anything in kind recently released."

Drums Along the Mohawk
Directed by John Ford

Can be seen at the Internet Archives

Tyler plays a militia man towards the end of the picture repeatedly asking the defeated and captured natives "Where's Caldwell?" Caldwell is a villainous white man played by John Carradine.

The film was a major Technicolor release for the studio and received favorable reviews. Today the story of white settlers during the time of the Revolution fighting near inhuman natives is a bit hard to take. It's definitely a product of its times.

In its December 2, 1939, edition, Boxoffice declared the film the recipient of its "November Blue Ribbon Award," and stated, "'Drums along the Mohawk,' 20th Century-Fox's vivid Technicolor film of Indian warfare has been selected by the National Screen Council as the outstanding November release, and winner of the Boxoffice blue ribbon award for that month ... 'Drums along the Mohawk' portrays early America in the days when pioneers were building new frontiers in the wilderness and fighting against the onslaught of the savage Iroquois, the women fighting side by side with their men folk. The story opens with a city-bred bride beginning her married life as a pioneer in Mohawk Valley and adjusting herself to a life of hardship and privation. She and her husband find their fortunes progressing only to have tomahawks swooped down and destroy all that they have built."

Gone With the Wind
Directed by Victor Fleming (with assistance from Sam Wood)

Can be seen on several paid streaming services and Blu-Ray

What many people thought of as the greatest movie ever made (and for years was the highest grossing film in the history of cinema) has been problematic since its release in 1939. Its insistence on painting the secession of the South states as "romantic" in order so that a great culture would be saved – complete with slavery – is not well received today and deservedly so.

Tyler appears in the scene of Atlanta residents fleeing the city as Gen. Sherman approaches. He played a mounted Confederate colonel (with a full beard) urging people to leave.

1940

The Grapes of Wrath
Directed by John Ford

It can be seen on Prime, Apple TV and other paid streaming services, as well as DVD

The controversial novel about the Dustbowl and the Great Depression by John Steinbeck gave birth to what became a controversial movie and an instant classic. It has proven to be one of Ford's best films featuring great performances and striking photography. Tyler plays a state trooper who breaks up an encampment of displaced people trying to get to California from the Midwest for a new life.

This is Tyler's third film with Ford.

Columnist Sidney Skolsky wrote in 1939, "Offhand, I can think of no picture that will influence picture making as much. I am excepting those pictures which brought about technical changes such as the 'Birth of a Nation,' the first talking picture 'The Jazz Singer' and the first genuine Technicolor picture. 'The Grapes of Wrath' without any innovation in the technical department, will alter the style of pictures to be produced."

"The Light of Western Stars" gave Tyler another good villainous role, this time with Victor Jory as the hero. (author's collection)

The Light of Western Stars
Directed by Lesley Selander
Can be watched on Tubi

This is the first time Tyler was to work for producer Harry Sherman, who is best known for producing the Hopalong Cassidy series for Paramount. An adaptation of a Zane Grey novel, The Movies and the People who Make Them 1940 described it as "western screen classic redone with lavish pictorial background which helps to tell Zane Grey's somewhat dated story of the aristocratic eastern belle who weds and finally reforms an irresponsible ranch foreman."

Tyler plays a crooked sheriff in the pocket of the villain. It's a solid performance that includes one hell of a fight between his character and the hero, played by Victor Jory. Jory, usually cast in villain roles, gets not only to play the hero but an interesting hero with almost too much back story. If I have a criticism of the film, it's that it has almost too many plot elements for its running time.

Tyler can be seen in the finale of the film as one of the cowboys who come to the aid of Ralph Bellemy. You can see Tyler standing behind a police officer holding Bellemy. (author's collection)

Brother Orchid

Directed by Lloyd Bacon

Can be seen on YouTube (paid), Prime and Apple TV

This Edward G. Robinson film helped re-define the gangster image that had stuck with the acclaimed actor. He plays Little John Sarto, a mobster, whose authority has been usurped by his former number two Jack Buck (Humphry Bogart). On the lam, Sarto is taken in to a monastery where he learned a different life. He comes back into the world to make sure his former girlfriend is safe with her new boyfriend, a cowboy (Ralph Bellamy). Tyler plays a friend of Bellamy's who helps him out in the climactic fight at the end of the film. The movie was a hit and it holds up very well, in my opinion.

Showman Trade Review wrote June 1, 1940, "This is an extremely funny comedy and the part is just made to order for Robinson. He is entirely at home as a gangster. Although to some it may be a little unbelievable, the picture is entertaining and should do better than average. Ann Southern as the only other big part and she grows more capable with each new role. Robinson, whether as the gangster or the monk, is tops in his role and one cannot imagine any one possibly doing the job as well. The direction of Lloyd Bacon is speedy and he smoothly describes the laughs to mingle with the drama and the action."

The Westerner
Directed by William Wyler
Can be seen on Plex streaming service

Telling a story inspired by western historical figure "Judge" Roy Bean, this is a big-budgeted adult western starring Gary Cooper as a cowboy who becomes involved in a range war between cattlemen and homesteaders. This film made a character star out of Walter Brennan, who appeared with Tyler as a thug in "Phantom of the Air." Brennan plays the self-appointed judge and bartender of a Texas cattle community and is clearly a psychopath.

Tyler plays King Evans and has a solid featured character performance in the first 30 minutes of the film.

The reviewer for the Chicago Daily Times said, "As exciting as tossing a lighted match at a string for firecrackers and good fun, too."

The Mummy's Hand
Directed by Christy Cabanne
Can be seen at https://archive.org/details/the-mummys-hand and DVD

Without a doubt this movie, along with his roles as Captain Marvel and The Phantom has kept Tyler's name alive with contemporary fans perhaps more than any individual westerns he made.

Universal B unit producer Ben Pivar (who would cast Tyler again in the western "Boss of Boomtown"), made the film, which kicked off a successful series of subsequent Mummy films starring Lon Chaney.

Author Thomas Reeder relates in his excellent book about Pivar ("Stop Yellin' Ben Pivar and the Horror, Mystery and Action-Adventure Films of his Universal Unit") shooting commenced in June 1940 and the film was released in September of that year. The budget for the film was $80,000 and Reeder explained the film's look benefitted from footage used from Boris Karloff's "The Mummy" (1932) as well as sets that had been made for James Whale's legendary flop "Green Hell."

It was thought that Tyler looked like Karloff in long shots of original footage. Personally, I don't see a great resemblance, but Tyler clearly gave the role all he had.

Part of the film that resonated with audiences was the makeup for Kharis the mummy. Jack Pierce, the same make-up artist who created classic makeups for Boris Karloff and Bela Lugosi in the classic Universal horror films, essentially recreated the style of mummy make-up for this film that he initially developed in 1932.

The makeup applied to Tyler's face was for close-ups, Reeder wrote, the old-fashioned style of make-up that had to be re-made take-after-take. As a story in September 1940 in the New York Times noted of Pierce's make-up designs, "Dressing room Number 5 has been a manufactory for monsters because all of Pierce's hobgoblin makeups are secret routines and therefore never are applied in the open makeup department. The room has no furniture beyond two wooden kitchen chairs, a barber's chair for makeup purposes, a wardrobe and an iron cot where the historic monsters have rested after the haunt.

"Here for 30 mornings during the mummy's hand starting at 4 a.m. and ending at 10 a.m., ex-cowboy Tom Tyler sat in a bathing suit while Pierce turned his face into cracked skin by applications of cotton and collodion and swabbed him in 1,500 yards of mummy bandages which were pre-rotted by acid.

"Although 'The Mummy's Hand' sets were to the right of number 5, Pierce and Tyler turned to the left when going on duty and reached the camera by a roundabout route. In this they observed a superstition established by Boris Karloff who turned left to reach the set on his first morning as the Frankenstein monster and then and ever after that hit turned left no matter where the sets of a subsequent film might be located. No dweller in Number 5 today would dare to flout that tradition."

Pierce used a mask for other shots and for ease of the make-up process. The latter series used a mask exclusively for the Chaney films.

One of the most effective parts of the films was the decision to matte out Tyler's eyes when there is a close-up of Kharis. This is incredibly creepy.

Plot-wise the only thing that survives from the Karloff film is the concept of love and duty being preserved through thousands of years. This mummy is at the mercy of whomever has tanna leaves, the thing that can keep him alive as he guards the tomb of the dead princess. Unlike the Karloff version, this mummy does not have the ability to speak. Once again, Tyler clearly uses his experience as a silent film actor to bring some level of characterization to the role.

The film benefits from a talented cast – George Zucco, Dick Foran, Wallace Ford, Cecil Kellaway and Peggy Moran – with Ford and Kellaway providing alleged comic relief.

Cabanne had directed Tyler in "The Last Outlaw." A busy low budget specialist, he staged some nicely creepy moments. I wonder if the eye-less look is something he contributed?

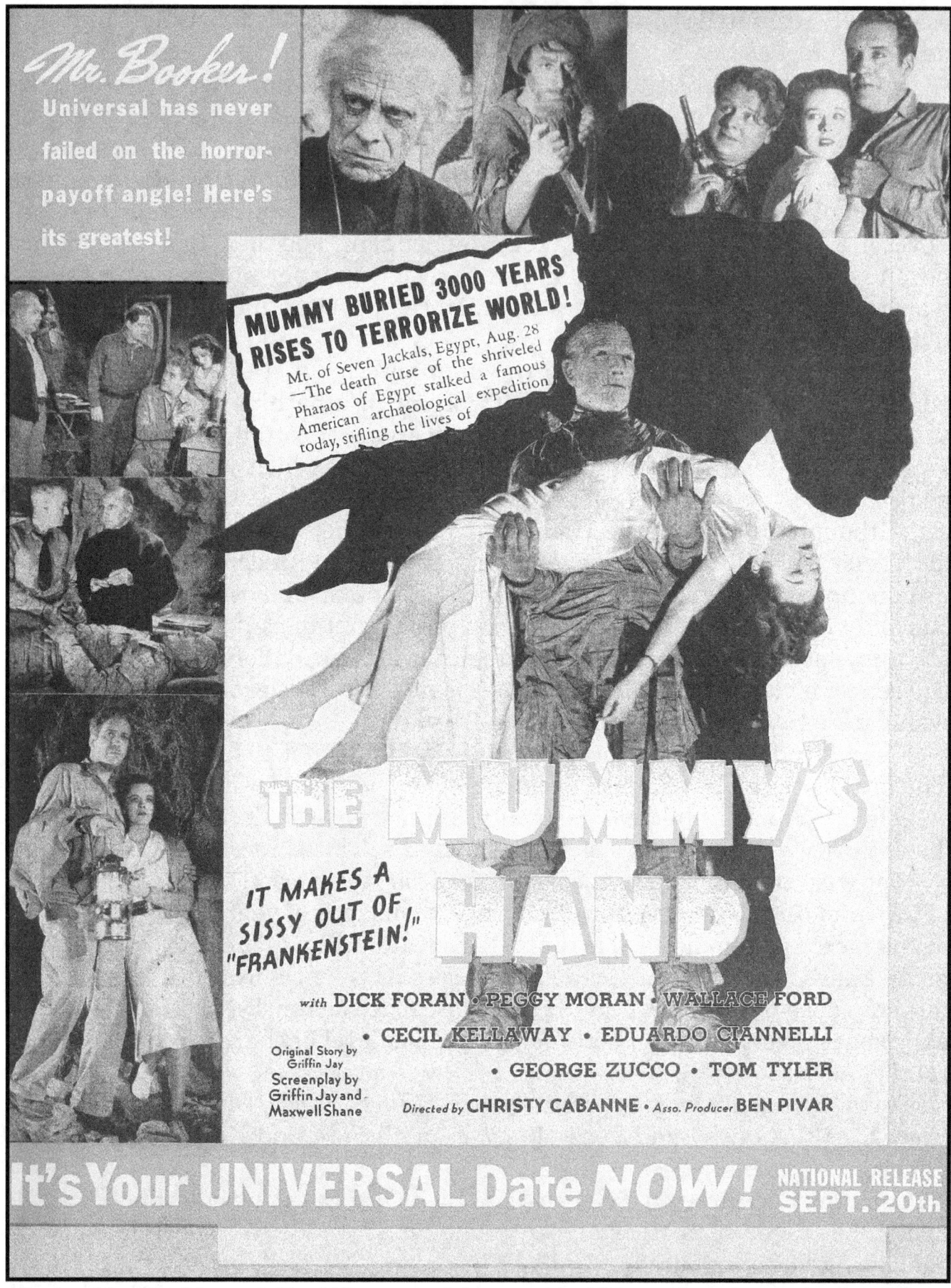

A trade ad for "The Mummy's Hand." Its success led to a series of "Mummy" movies starring Lon Chaney. Notice that in the ad, Tyler's eyes have been blacked out which is how they appeared in the movie.

It's a fast-moving B movie with some corny comedy and a really effective monster. Clearly, there wasn't a thought of a sequel or series as Kharis is dispatched by being set on fire, but the studio execs must have seen that the success of the film warranted more mummy movies.

The Movies and the People who Make Them 1940 wrote, "Neighborhood types should enjoy all this and even sophisticated audiences may be spooked into a few guffaws. On the whole it's pretty casual. A Karloff clutch or a good Lugosi leer would have helped no end. Dick Foran and Wallace Ford played the archaeologists Eduardo Cianelli enacts the role of the high priest and cowboy Tom Tyler prowls as the mummy. Peggy Moran also slips in for a few screams."

Variety didn't like the film very much. "Hobe" wrote in its Sept. 25,1940 edition, "With at least a nod at its Boris Karloff picture of seven years ago 'The Mummy,' Universal has whipped up another little pseudo chiller for the same trade. It's calling this one 'The Mummy's Hand' and it's transparently just a road company edition. This time the embalmed menace is played by Tom Tyler. It's all strictly for the lesser duals.

"Picture is muddled in the writing and clumsy in the production story jumps around without apparent reason with flashbacks to ancient Egypt and floundering between slapstick and eerie melodrama box. And apparently with the idea of throwing the creeps into the audience the sequence is taking place in the excavations into early Egypt. Remains are shown in green tinted film. Actual yarn about a couple of Rover Boy archaeologists who team up with a trooping magician from Brooklyn with the latter's daughter as the heart interest is formula stuff.

"Direction and photography are bush league. Acting varies from a violent mugging to smooth under-playing with Cecil Kellaway as the sleight of hand performer and Wallace Ford as the subordinate archaeologist; the only ones achieving conviction. Ford gives the tip off on the picture when the jackals howling in the soundtrack, the revived mummy stumbling around in the background and various assorted villains creeping through the scenery he mutters, 'There are a lot of strange things around here that need explaining.' He is so right."

The make-up process was also the subject of this story:
News scribe told how to be a mummy
by Frederick C. Othman, United Press
"We shook hands today with the mummy. He was a mummified cowboy to be exact and we don't guess we will ever have another experience like that. Neither will the mummy. It happened at Universal Studios, home of the horror

picture. In production was a number entitled 'The Mummy's Hand.' It was the story of Prince Kharis buried alive in a pyramid 3,000 years ago and kept living through the centuries by mysterious fluid which the high priests of Karnac injected into his veins once each night during the cycle of the full moon – so according to the plot though.

"Celebrated archaeologists Dick Foran, Peggy Moran and Wallace Ford went to Egypt and they started rummaging around in the tomb. That made the mummy mad and he ripped his shrouds, climbed from his sarcophagus and murdered a few scientists. But the mummy turned out to our utter amazement to be that rootin'–tootin' shooting cowboy of at least 150 horse operas. Tom Tyler in person.

"How he came to be playing a mummy? He said was something that even he didn't quite understand. It takes six hours every morning for makeup man Jack Pierce to turn Tyler into a mummy. When the job is through Tyler is so uncomfortable that he can work only three hours before the cameras. Then he returns to the makeup department, where Pierce and an assistant spent another hour and a half peeling 3,000 centuries of disintegration from him. This is a ticklish job. If they are not careful they also peel away part of Mr. Tyler.

"When we arrived at the makeup room it was 11 a.m. The mummy had been sitting in Pierce's barber chair since 5 a.m. And he was ready for work. It was enough to turn your stomach to look at him. Pierce, who created the Frankenstein monster for the screen and who has had a successful career turning men into monsters ever since, he said he got the inspiration for the mummy from watching a hippopotamus at the zoo. He said he believed that the skin of an Egyptian mummy ought to be about the texture and color of a hippo's, only more wrinkled.

"So, I covered all of Mr. Tyler's face, neck, and hands with thin slivers of cotton," Pierce said, "then I saturated it with spirit gum and when it dries it wrinkles like his own skin only the wrinkles are bigger and deeper. Then I paint him all over with a nice grey paint and when the job's done, I fleck him with particles of clay. They rub off when he touches his face and that's good to show how his flesh is disintegrating."

"So far so good said we but what about Tyler's hair, which looked like no hair before or since. That was simple, Pierce said, "I just rubbed in a mixture of glue and clay and let it dry. The mummy gulped and asked for a cigarette. He said his head itched and it would be alright for him to scratch it? Pierce said it wouldn't. The mummy compromised on a smoke.

"To remove the makeup, Pierce said he saturated head, face and hands with acetone. "It hurts like the devil," the mummy said. "It just stings a little, that is all, "Pierce said, "It cuts into the makeup. When I stop, I cover all over

Jack Pierce's make-up was impressive as it had been for the opening scene of "The Mummy" with Boris Karloff in 1932. (author's collection

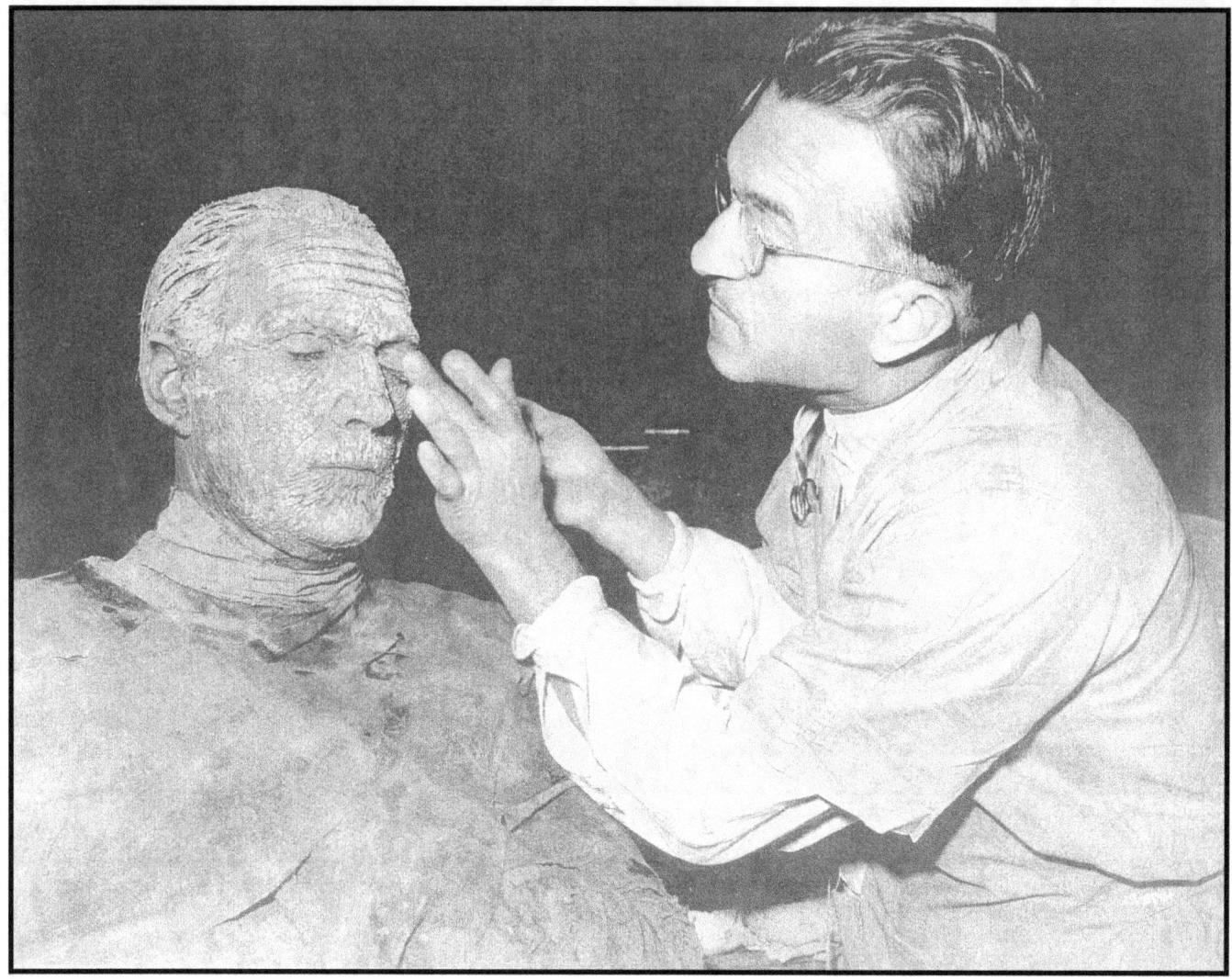

Pierce's make-up had to be built from scratch every day.

with the hot oil and rub. I've got to be particularly careful of the ears. If one of those little hairs doesn't get unstuck before a pull there's liable to be some damage.

"Pierce said his mummy went to the studio commissary for a private lunch. They eat ahead of the other actors and technicians because the latter have weak stomachs. They can't enjoy their meals with a mummy in their midst."

Cherokee Strip
Directed by Lesley Selander
    Unavailable

Produced by Harry Sherman for Paramount, this is the second time the producer used Tyler.

Showman's Trade Review Oct. 5, 1940, wrote, "This is the first big special production from the maker of top outdoor pictures, Harry Sherman. That it will enjoy a wide success at the box office, is a foregone conclusion. Here's quality entertainment for the western addicts, perfect in every detail, and good enough to rate top billing from the big cities to the small Hamlets. Any audience will enjoy its action and color and rave about the performances of the hand-picked stellar cast particularly Richard Dix who matches his outstanding work in Cimarron. The above average supporting cast includes Florence Rice, Victor Jory, Andy Clyde, George E. Stone and Morris Ankrum, each scores a personal hit with their portrayals. It is by far director Leslie Selander's best effort to date and Russell Harlan's photography is a big asset to the excellence of the finished product. The top flight Sherman production values are evident in every foot of the film."

Texas Rangers Ride Again

Directed by James Hogan

Can be seen on Internet Archive

Set contemporarily, this drama is a Western crime procedure with a 1940 twist. The Texas Rangers care called in to investigate a large-scale cattle-rustling operation. It's a solidly made interesting western. Watch for Robert Ryan in a bit part as well as a bevy of classic character actors.

Tyler plays Ranger Gilpin and is uncredited in this film.

James Pierce was also in the cast, played a ranch owner. Pierce was in the 1924 production of "Leatherstocking."

Showman's Trade Review Nov. 4, 1940, wrote, "Good action, a better than usual cast and well-chosen locations make this picture for any house which has a following for action stories and these combine to offset a plot as standard and transparent as a freshly washed window. Acting honors fall to May Robson as the stout-hearted old ranch owner, Howard as a regulation western hero and Quinn, who does well as a sub villain. Few law enforcement bodies are more widely known than the Texas Rangers which can be capitalized on for school essay cooperation library and bookstore tie-ups and spot radio announcements following the twice weekly national broadcast of the musical group billed as Texas Rangers. A modern police car with special trailer for horses such as the Rangers are seen using in this picture will make an interesting arousing St. ballyhoo."

1941

In 1941, there were plans that PRC needed to produce a series with relative newcomer Lee Powell teamed with Tyler. Powell who had played the

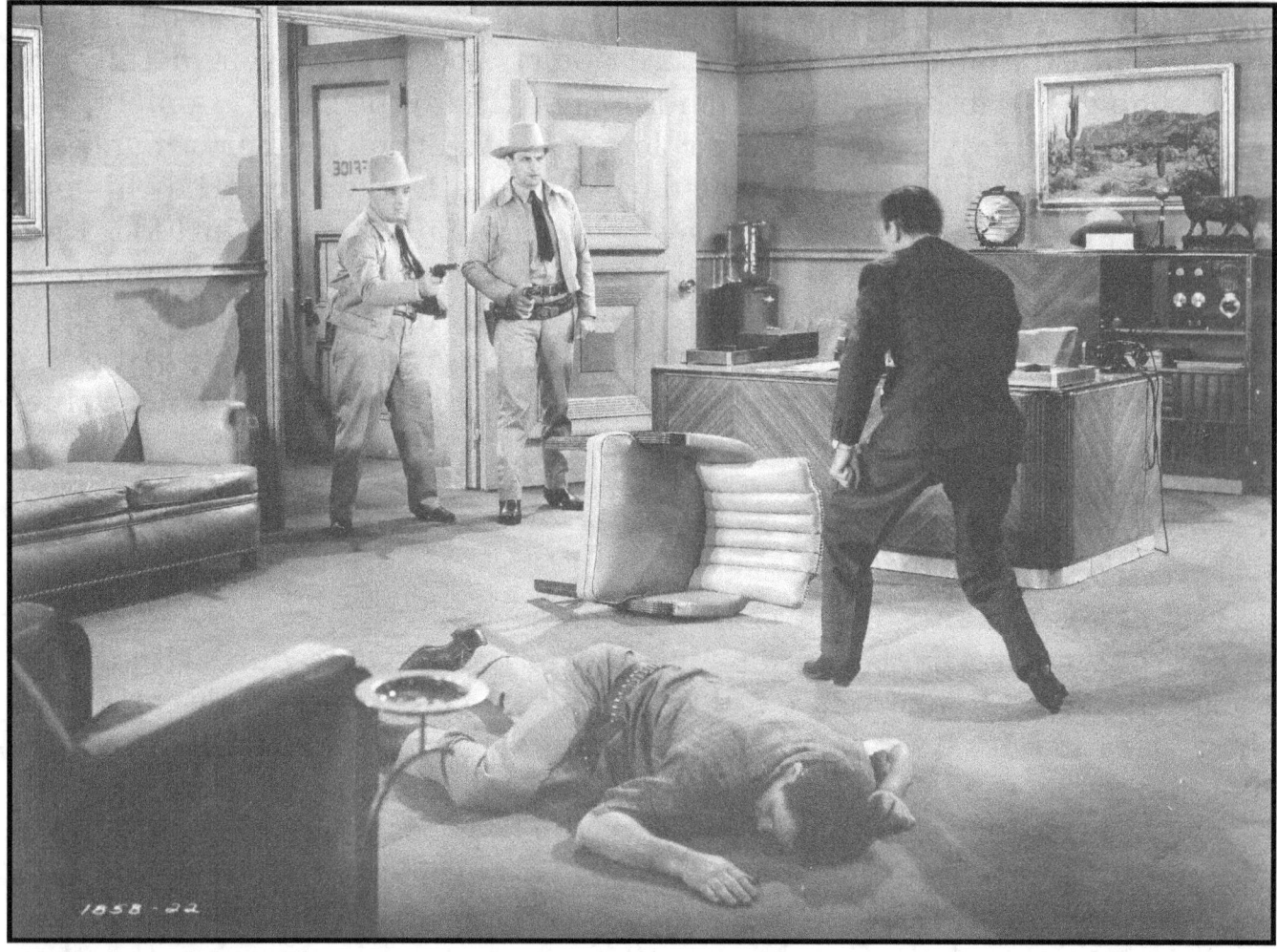
Tyler appeared in an uncredited role in "Texas Rangers Ride Again."

Lone Ranger in the first Republic serial, had made a handful of films after that success. Tyler would be the lead in the series as his name was far more recognizable to fans.

On May 28, 1941, Variety reported, "Producers Releasing Corp. signed Tom Tyler as top rider in a series of buckaroo pictures with the general title of 'Frontier Marshal' for the 1941-42 program. O. Henry Briggs, president of the company, also signed Lee Powell as the male lead and is looking for a comic." Something happened, though. According to B-western.com, "Tyler signed with Republic Pictures and his term player's contract(s) ran from July 8, 1941, through July 7, 1943. His initial salary was $150 per week with a raise to $200 weekly for year two."

To give some perspective the buying power of $150 in 1941 is $3,280 in 2025 dollars.

In the June 23 and June 25, 1941, editions of Motion Picture Daily, "Republic has signed Tom Tyler to replace Bob Livingston in the 'Three Mesquiteers' series of westerns.' and "... Tom Tyler today obtained his release from a co-starring contract with Lee Powell in six 'Frontier Marshal' westerns on the Producers Releasing Corp. schedule. PRC is seeking a player to replace Tyler."

It should be noted that Tyler was a known commodity to Republic having appeared in "The Night Riders" in 1939.

In the June 30, 1941, edition of The Film Daily, it was reported, "Tom Tyler, who was scheduled to co-star with Lee Powell in PRC's 'Frontier Marshal' series, has been given a contract release. Sigmund Neufeld, producer in charge of PRC's three western units, is looking for a 'name' western star to replace Tyler, but Powell will play the part originally slated for him."

Of the two companies, Republic, of course, had the more superior cinematic resources and The Three Mesquiteers were among the top western series in the industry.

Powell wound up co-starring in a series of six westerns at PRC with Bill "Cowboy Rambler" Boyd – not to be mistaken for the Hopalong Cassidy star – and Art Davis. Boyd was a popular Western singer with The Cowboy Ramblers. Davis was also an established musician. The general consensus of the films was negative.

Hedda Hopper's Hollywood
Episode 2

Can be seen on YouTube

The renowned and highly influential movie gossip columnist Hedda Hopper was a hit in newspapers, made a successful transition to radio and in 1941 Paramount hired her to make six one-reel (seven to 10 minutes) short subjects featuring the off-screen life of movie stars.

Tyler is seen at the trendy nightclub Mocambo with his apparent friend Desi Arnez – at least that's what Hopper has presented. Lucille Ball is mentioned but is off dancing with someone. Tyler waves to someone and the camera cuts to dancing star 18-year-old Ann Miller, who had started in show business age 13.

Tyler is out on the town with Desi Arnez and "flirts" with Ann Miller in a short that was common to a number of studios allegedly showing stars in their "real" lives.

Most of what is presented seems carefully staged as opposed to off-the-cuff behind the scenes footage.

Motion Picture Daily (Dec. 17, 1941) said of the short, "This is average inside Hollywood fare. As in the reel's predecessor, a good deal of attention is focused upon Miss Hopper, who is first seen entertaining a few screen players and veteran William Farnum at her home. Subsequently it shifts to the Milwaukee premiere of Miss Hopper's first Hedda Hopper's Hollywood, then to the groundbreaking ceremonies of what is to be the Motion Picture Relief Fund Home, and finally to the Mocambo, a Hollywood night spot."

Buck Privates
Directed by Arthur Lubin
Can be seen on The Internet Archive.
In the film that made Bud Abbott and Lou Costello comedy movie superstars, Tyler plays (uncredited) a referee in the boxing sequence.

Border Vigilantes
Directed by Derwin Abrahams
Can be seen on Tubi
Producer Harry Sherman

Tyler isn't playing any favorites as the ref in "Buck Privates."

Once again cast Tyler into one of his productions. By this stage of the Hopalong Cassidy series, it was thought as being among the very best B western productions.

Victor Jory is the mastermind behind an effort to terrorize local miners into selling their mines. The miners ask Hopalong Cassidy to help them figure out why the gang behind the campaign is always ahead of every effort to rout them out. Of course, Jory is not just the brains villain, he is also part of the miner association.

Tyler plays Jim Yager, the lead thug for Jory and again does very well in the role.

Showman's Trade Review April 5, 1941, "Another exciting epic in the life of Hopalong Cassidy and like its predecessors, a swell western with fine performances, direction and production. The picture is top flight fare for the outdoor addicts and should please any others looking for real entertainment. It's one of the best of this fine series, with plenty of hard writing, gunfights and red-blooded action. William Boyd and his sidekicks Russell Hayden and Andy Clyde again deliver their usual fine performances aided by a better than average group of supporting players. Derwin Abrahams, making his directorial bow rates a big hand for his work. Harry Sherman's production values, which include photography, musical score and art direction are perfectly blended into the finished product; An excellent all-around job of picture making."

Bad Men of Missouri
Directed by Ray Enright
Unavailable

Tyler appears in an uncredited role as a deputy in this Warner Bros. production of the story of the Younger brothers outlaw gang. The film starred Dennis Morgan, Wayne Morris and Arthur Kennedy in the title roles with Jane Wyman as the female lead. The bad guy was played by Victor Jory. The Motion Picture Herald (Aug. 2, 1941) noted, "Terrific tempo marks bad men of Missouri a rootin'–tootin' outdoor action picture which purports to tell the story of the Younger Brothers, Midwest terrors who are treated in the film as Robin Hoods."

Riders of the Timberline
Directed by Lesley Selander
Can be seen on Tubi

Hopalong Cassidy is called by an old friend Jim Kerrigan (J. Farrell MacDonald) to high timber country to help him get his logs out to market. Kerrigan's efforts are being thwarted through a series of accidents by the operatives of a rival lumberman, one of whom, Bill Slade, (Tyler) is on Kerrigan's payroll. If the contract can't be met, the rival can take over the operation. Slade is telling his fellow lumberjacks the camp is jinxed and encouraging them to quit.

Victor Jory is again part of the cast – clearly producer Harry Sherman liked both Jory and Tyler – and this time plays a good guy; a French-Canadian lumberjack allied with Kerrigan. Jory clearly is having a ball playing a rather broad character – with an even broader accent – and he and Tyler once again get into a very satisfying brawl. Tyler is solid in his villainy.

I really enjoyed this B western for its clear insistence of presenting a typical western story in a very non-typical locale.

Showman's Trade Review (Sept. 27, 1941) said, "With the lumber country as its locale this one is quite different from the ordinary western, though Hopalong has few chances to use his gun as he rides about although occasionally he is seen in action aboard a hand car or atop a log on a cable railway. The scenery is beautiful, as is usual with pictures in this series, and photographer Russell Harlan has included some beautiful shots in the picture. This one has the benefit of J. Farrell MacDonald and Victor Jory in its cast, two additional names to feature. Also, this picture marks the return to the screen of Anna Q. Nillsen, star of the silent days."

1942

Valley of the Sun

Directed by George Marshall

Can be seen on paid YouTube, as well as Apple TV and Prime

This western combines a lot of different elements, as the review below noted. Romance, humor, and social commentary are all part of the package. Although the film actually used many Native American actors, Tyler was cast as Geronimo, a prominent role in the film. While he is not credited on the poster, he was featured by name in the film's trailer.

Again, Tyler is cast by a major director in a well-marketed release, this time from RKO.

I found it as sort of an odd combination, but reviewers seemed to like the film, although one noted it was not as good as Marshall's "Destry Rides Again." Motion Picture Herald, Jan. 10, 1942, wrote, "From the skilled hands of Clarence Buddington Kelland who is given to the screen such fine film fare as 'Mr. Deeds Goes to Town' and 'Arizona' comes 'Valley of the Sun' a story about Indians and the West which ran as a serial in the Saturday Evening Post. It has sufficient adventure, fighting, shooting, Indians on the march, dance and warpath, to meet the requirements of the most demanding action fan and enough humor and romance to satisfy those not of this category.

"The background of the picture is Arizona in 1868 where the Indians and the authorities were clashing. James Craig, who portrays an Indian scout attached to the army, is the hero and the one who understands and sympathizes with the Indians, and Dean Jagger plays the Indian agent, who was always breaking his promises to the Indians and cheating them. The two men are in perpetual conflict over the Indians and over Lucille Ball, with Jagger finally losing all, including the girl.

"Among the film's most exciting moments are a good fist fight between the hero and villain, a struggle for supremacy in a tug of war on horses, in arrow shooting and hatchet throwing between Craig and Geronimo played by Tom Tyler ... Particularly humorous are the attempts made by Craig and his cronies to prevent the fair Lucille from marrying Jagger, one of which consisted of dropping red ants from the ceiling on the bridegroom during the ceremony. "Good histrionic performances are very much in evidence. Lucille Ball, who is more a product of the 20th century, nevertheless makes a spirited and attractive western heroine, and James Craig and Dean Jagger are good in their respective roles. Honorable mention must go to Sir Cedric Hardwicke as friendly Lord Warwick and Peter Whitney as a brute with a kind heart. Billy Gilbert is humorous as usual as a justice of the peace, and old timers may be interested in seeing Antonio Marino once again playing an Apache chief.

Tyler was included in the trade ads for this dramedy western.

"Graham Baker has produced the picture with care and with real Indians and George Marshall who has directed such pictures as 'Destry Rides Again' and 'Texas' has kept the picture moving and interesting throughout… The exhibitor need not be afraid to meet the customers on their way out."

Photoplay (April 1942) noted in its review, "Craig's fight for Jagger's life with the Indian Geronimo played by Tom Tyler is terrifically suspenseful. Lusty and gusty, 'Valley of the Sun' is an escapist piece of entertainment."

Talk of the Town

Directed by George Stevens
Can be seen on Tubi
Tyler was in "Talk of the Town," one of the most acclaimed films of 1942 and one of his best roles. The film was nominated for seven Oscars, including Outstanding Motion Picture.

Tyler's name was featured in magazine advertising.

Stevens is considered a great director who today is unfortunately overlooked. Among his films include "Woman of the Year," 'I Remember Mama," "Shane" and "The Diary of Anne Frank."

Set in a small factory town Cary Grant plays a factory worker advocating for better treatment and conditions. When the woolen mill burns down and allegedly kills the foreman Clyde Bracken (Tyler), Grant is the suspect the whole town is seeking, but he is hiding out in a cottage owned by Jean Arthur's character rented out to Ronald Colman's law professor.

The film, which in part, centers on the transformation of a law professor from a dry academic to a man who sees how the law benefits people, had its premiere in Washington D.C. Colman's character is successfully nominated for the Supreme Court and the screening in the capitol was attended by the sitting members of the Supreme Court, according to a report in Showman's Trade Review in its Oct. 24. 1942 edition.

The film was booked into Radio City Music Hall in New York City, always a sign of prestige.

The Exhibitor, July 29, 1942, wrote, "This is one of the better productions of the season, one which through casting, story, direction, and production will reach the higher grosses. It has a different type of story and the players are aces in their roles. Chalk it up as one of the top-notchers from Columbia."

The Film Daily" wrote (July 27, 1942), "Ace script, cast and production earmark this as a smash box office hit. 'The Talk of the Town' should prove just that.

One of the most prestigious films in Tyler's career and proved that he could hold his own with the likes of Cary Grant and Ronald Colman. He was featured in ads for the film. (author's collection)

Tyler's character is seen mostly at the conclusion of the film. Here he takes a punch from Grant and is the center of the courtroom scene. (author's collection

It is smashing entertainment with all of the qualities that make for popular acclaim. The money-making possibilities of the film are illimitable. Excelling in every department, brimming with humanity, choked with delicious humor, this picture stacks up as one of the finest, definitely one of the most diverting of the year. It is a fascinating supremely absorbing, often exciting film exhibit prickly with social implications."

1943

The Phantom

Directed by B. Reeves Eason
Can see seen on YouTube, DVD and on Prime

Based on the famed comic strip of the same name, this serial was a cut above the usual chapterplay produced by Columbia and Tyler was perfectly cast as the jungle hero.

Created by writer Lee Falk in 1936, The Phantom was a costumed and masked hero before the advent of superheroes in comic books. The comic strip is still being produced and is read around the world.

Falk's concept, The Phantom, who is also known as The Ghost Who Walks, appears immortal to the people he protects, but is actually part of a long line of heroes – the first Phantom was in 1536 – who has passed the responsibility from father to son, making his existence appear seamless.

He has no super powers, but rather physical strength and fighting prowess. He carries two pistols and is an excellent shot.

The Showman's Trade Review reported the serial went into production at the Darmour Studio in its Nov. 13, 1943, edition.

In the first chapter of the serial, the current Phantom is poisoned and called for his son Godfrey Prescot (Tyler). Prescott is already in Africa assisting a professor on his search for a lost African civilization. Not only is there a crooked trader who is also attempting to find the civilization, there is also a Nazi who is attempting to build a landing strip in the jungle.

The serial was unseen for many years as the rights had reverted to King Features, the owner of the comic strip. VCI had released the serial on VHS but achieved more attention with its DVD transfer in 2001.

A well-known story among serial fans is that producer Sam Katzman, who had taken over the serial production for Columbia, decided to produce a remake using the footage from the previous serial and had shot much of it – relying on footage from the original film – when it was discovered Columbia no longer had the rights to the character. Katzman eventually decided to film

"The Adventures of Captain Africa" in 1955 with actor John Hart playing the tile character in a costume that allowed the use of footage of Tyler. The production has become notorious as one of the most inept and unsatisfactory serials ever made.

I think Tyler made an excellent comic strip hero. The Phantom in the strip has a level of both reserve and dignity, qualities Tyler brings to the role. Tyler does well as the newest Phantom still finding his way.

My only criticism is the fact that "African" natives all look like white people masquerading as some sort of (maybe) Southeast Asians or South American natives, but it is a serial, after all!

Trade ad for "The Phantom."

Showman's Trade review, (Jan. 1, 1944) wrote, "The film has production values with plenty of extras and first-rate sets. The action has been directed so it appears more plausible than most serials, yet the element of mystery is there to attract the kids and give the proper amount of excitement. For your information, the first episode, "The Sign of the Skull," is 28 minutes long; the others will run about 15. Columbia has prepared a good line of accessories, including a different one sheet for each episode with sufficient sniping space." "Sniping space" means the posters for each chapter were identical except for an area that could have a different printed message, such as the title of the chapter. In the case of a window card – these were cardboard posters deigned to be propped up in a window of allied business in exchange for free tickets – there was a snipping space that allowed the theater manager to write in details of that movie's showing.

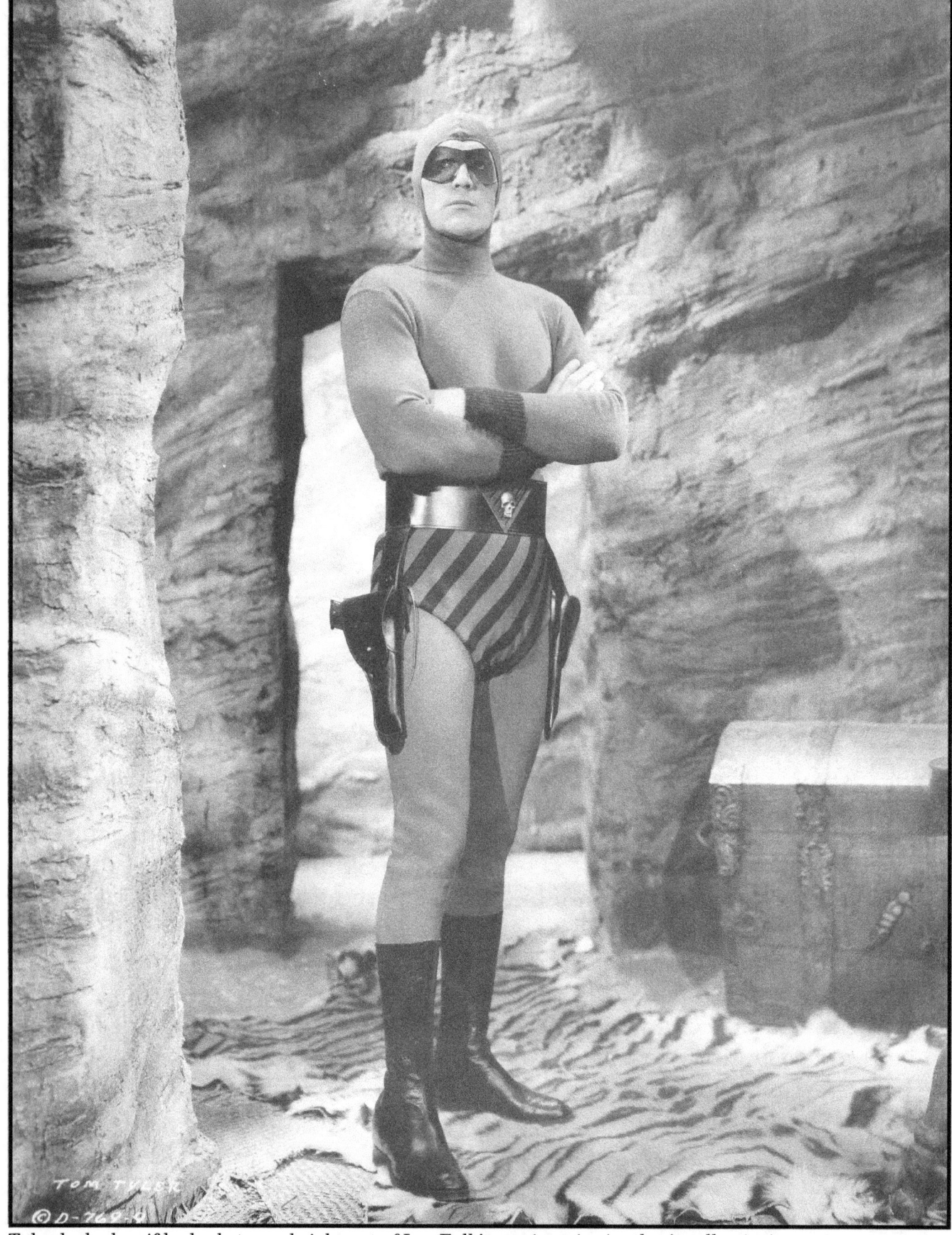
Tyler looked as if he had stepped right out of Lee Falk's comic strip. (author's collection)

Like the comic strip, the serials details the passing of the mantle of the Phantom from father to son. (author's collection)

Unlike many other Columbia serials, this one had solid production values. (author's collection)

1944

Gun to Gun
Directed by D. Ross Lederman
Unavailable

Tyler is seen in this two-reel western in an uncredited role as the town's sheriff. The film stars Robert Shayne and Lupita Tovar.

Showman's Trade Review, (Feb. 17, 1944) wrote, "While this short will stir up some action for the western fans it misses the boat for average audiences due to the overworked plot upon which it is forced to rely. Directed by D. Ross Lederman and starring Robert Shane, Lupita Tovar, Pedro de Cordova, Harry Woods and Anita Carmago. The film deals with crooked officials who have imposed exorbitant taxes upon the original land grant holders in Southern California."

The Navy Way
Directed by William Berke
Can be seen on Tubi and YouTube

A product of its time, this film tells the stories of several young men who enter Navy boot camp and prepare for service. Much of the film was filmed at Great Lakes Naval Station. One of these young men is Tom Keene who plays a Wyoming rancher. Tyler is one of his ranch hands who gives him the telegram that tells him his brother has been lost at sea in a battle, therefore propelling his entry into the Navy. Although he has dialogue, his role in not credited.

Motion Picture Herald noted in its Feb. 26, 1944, edition, "Stepping forth in the direction of bigger and better things, producers William Pine and William Thomas present here an armed service picture which is not a melodrama as most of their pictures have been, but accounts for its 74 minutes of running time with more entertainment than the companies 65-minute enterprises have averaged. The film introduces Robert Lowry as a star whose performance stacks up with the best and surrounds him with dependables who round out a smoothly functioning cast."

Boss of Boomtown
Directed by Ray Taylor
Could be watched on DVD from VCI Entertainment but is now out-of-print. Amazon still has copies for sale.

Tyler found himself employed at Universal and the Ben Pivar unit once more, but this time for a western starring Rod Cameron. The film's associate producer was Tyler's old friend Oliver Drake.

Thomas Reeder reported in his book, "Stop Yellin' Ben Pivar and the Horror, Mystery, and Action-Adventure Films of his Universal B-Unit," this was first of a series of westerns starring the new Universal hire, Cameron, who replaced Johnny Mack Brown who left for Monogram. All but this one co-starred singer Eddie Dew, but this film did have "comic" Fuzzy Knight, an inheritance from the Brown series. Knight was ubiquitous in B westerns for reasons that confound this writer. I just don't find him funny.

While this film starred Cameron, it co-starred Tyler and the plot centers around the fighting friends premise. Cameron and Tyler were well cast in their roles and Universal missed an opportunity to team them up in other productions.

Other than Knight, the film is enjoyable and well-made. It's a shame the DVD is out of print.

The Exhibitor (June 28, 1944) said, "This is the usual western, given a

"Boss of Boomtown" missed an opportunity of teaming Tyler (left) up with Rod Cameron as they worked well together on film. (author's collection)

trifle better production. Comedy relief is so-so musical numbers heard are 'Texas,' '99 Days,' 'Cowboys Lament,' and 'My Proud Beauty,' the latter sung by [Vivian]Austin."

Ladies of Washington

Directed by Louis King

Tyler again has an uncredited role, this time as a federal agent.

"The Independent (May 27, 1944) reviewed the film and said, "This is an inconsequential little film with a weak and implausible story and a hurried air about it. The production is strictly double-feature stuff.

"The material for a good drama offers itself in 'Ladies of Washington' but it has been put to the most obvious use, making it impossible for a person to work up more than a mild interest in what transpires in the film. The Washington background and the promise held out by the title are the chief means of attracting the attention. The picture is a not very successful attempt to show how a group of young women lives in wartime Washington. Actually, it is the story of one of them, a girl who in her determination to get revenge against a married government official for romantic reasons, becomes involved in an enemy plot. Her punishment is commission to an institution for the psychopathic. A picture for those who don't care too much."

The Princess and the Pirate

Directed by David Butler

Can be seen on YouTube

A flashy Technicolor pirate comedy produced by Samuel Goldwyn in which Bob Hope plays a cowardly actor – what else? – who gets mixed up with a real pirate (Victor McLaglen), an incognito princess (Virgina Mayo) and various corrupt government officials on a Caribbean island.

It's a pretty typical Hope vehicle, with comedy that breaks the fourth wall and the use of various anachronisms to appeal to 1940s audiences, such as a joke about Bing Crosby.

Tyler plays an aide to the island's governor (Walter Slezak) who escorts him to the tavern where Hope and Mayo are performing. He looks great in a swashbuckling wardrobe.

An existing pay document shows that Tyler made a rate of $100 a day for the film.

There are trade story after story about how audiences embraced the film, making it a hit. The Exhibitor wrote, "Packed with loads of laughs, good material, swell performances, and Hope this will bring in high returns. It compares with the better zany comedies and Hope still proves he is tops as a comedian. Direction by David Butler is good as is the entire production. One song is heard, 'Kiss Me in the Moonlight.'"

1945

Sing Me a Song of Texas
Directed by Vernon Keays
Can be seen through grey market DVD dealers

Tyler is the male lead in this musical western that crams as many musical acts as it can in its running time. The cast includes Hal McIntyre and his Orchestra, the Hoosier Hotshots, comedian Pinky Tomlin and Foy Willing and his Riders of the Purple Sage. Additional comic relief is offered by Noah Berry Sr and Slim Summerville. Tyler's co-star from "Powdersmoke Range" "Guinn "Big Boy" Williams, is also featured.

Today, when we think of a movie musical we generally associate big budget film events. Through the 1940s, studios such as Republic, Columbia and Universal regularly featured low-budget musicals.

Tyler did well in this light as air romantic musical.

Noah Berry plays an old ranch owner who decides to set up a contest between his two grandnieces he hasn't seen in many years to determine who is to get his ranch in his will. He pretends to be dead to facilitate his decision. Tyler plays the ranch foreman who assists Berry in his efforts and does well with the light – and at times, awfully stupid – material.

Showman's Trade review (July 14, 1945) wrote, "Routine outdoor musical that has the specialties of such entertainers as the Riders of the Purple Sage, Hoosier Hot Shots, Pinky Tomlin and Hal McIntyre's Orchestra to pep it up and give it something besides the off-repleted plot to amuse the regular theatergoers. It's satisfactory material for the western spot for it has action in addition to the above-mentioned variety of entertainers. Rosemary Lane and Carol Matthews are good as the nieces of Noah Berry, the old rancher who starts all the trouble. Tom Tyler is very satisfactory as the romantic lead for Rosemary Lane and Guinn Williams and Slim Somerville do well among the others in the cast."

They Were Expendable

Directed by John Ford and Robert Montgomery

Can be seen on YouTube, Prime, Apple TV and Google

Director John Ford was in the war effort working in the Navy Field Photographic Unit, commissioned as a captain in the Naval Reserve, when he made this film. Based on a 1942 novel by William Lindsay White, the book is based on real people and events.

Starring Robert Montgomery and John Wayne, the film tells the story of P.T. Boats and the role they played in the Pacific Theater. The film is almost like a documentary at times. Ford was shooting real events for the Navy.

According to War History Online, Montgomery certainly had first-hand knowledge of Naval warfare, "Rising to the rank of lieutenant commander, he saw action in both the European and Pacific Theaters. He was aboard the destroyer USS Barton (DD-722) during the Allied landings at Normandy, being among the first to set foot in Cherbourg Harbor, and participated in action at the likes of Guadalcanal, Espiritu Santo, New Georgia and Noumea."

The film is under-stated and gritty and has been hailed as one of the best films made about WWII. Tyler has a small uncredited part as a captain who is checking other military personnel onto a flight.

The Showman's Trade Review wrote (Nov. 17, 1945), "A picture of many powerful and gripping scenes and one that depicts a heroic chapter of the war in the Pacific. It is a war picture and for all of its grand acting and superlative direction there is limited audience appeal. The acting of Montgomery, Wayne, Donna Reed and others and excellent. Could become a must attraction if the first run reaction is such as to build up the interest the picture deserves as a brilliant piece of screen drama wrought from actual war."

San Antonio

Directed by David Bulter

Can be seen on Max, Hulu premium services and free on ClassicwesternsandTelevision.com

I don't know if Errol Flynn actually made a believable western star, but Warners Bros. certainly attempted it several times. Flynn is charming and every inch a movie star in this story of a Texas cattleman named Clay Hardin who comes back from self-imposed exile in Mexico to get justice from the mastermind who stole his cattle and tried to kill him.

Tyler plays bad guy Lafe McWilliams, who is supposed to stop Flynn's character from reaching the big boss. Tyler's role is prominent and he shows once again that his villain roles were just as watchable as his heroes.

The film was nominated for an Oscar for Best Song and best Art Direction and was a hit with audiences.

Harrison's Report (Nov. 24, 1945) noted, "In spite of the fact that it offers nothing startling in the way of novelty of plot or of action this glorified western photographed in Technicolor is a good entertainment of its type. It should go over fairly well with an average audience, for it blends fast and exciting action with romance and comedy. Errol Flynn's popularity will undoubtedly mean much at the box office."

Motion Picture Herald (Nov. 9, 1946) reported in its "What the Picture Did for Me," "Old-timer Tom Tyler had a small but very good role in this [San Antonio]. Would like to see him more often. S.T. Jackson, Jackson Theatre, Flomaton, Alabama."

1946

Badman's Territory

Directed by Tim Whelen

Can be seen on DVD from the Warner Archive and online for a fee on YouTube, Google and Apple TV.

A Randolph Scott western in which he plays a lawman in pursuit of the James Brothers (Lawrence Tierney as Jesse and Tyler as Frank) who have taken their wounded brothers into the panhandle of Oklahoma where the law cannot reach them.

I like the fact the screenwriters actually used a historic fact that through a series of political moves the panhandle of Oklahoma was not initially affiliated with any state and the settlers there were self-governed. Unlike the movie, which purports that legendary outlaws took advantage of the fact to use the panhandle as a hiding-in-plain-sight location, the actual residents disapproved of the appearance of being lawless, according to the Oklahoma Historical Society.

A number of B western players such as Gabby Hayes, Morgan Conway, Chief Thundercloud, Steve Brodie and George Chesebro are among the cast. Hayes plays a pretty lawless version of his patented geezer characterization, making his character of Coyote an alcoholic.

Tierney and Tyler certainly keep the attention of the viewer every time they are on the screen, although the script doesn't do much with the characters.

The promotion for this movie emphasized the fact that the legendary outlaws James Brothers, Belle Starr and the Daltons were all characters in the film. The approach was not unlike the 1940s Universal horror movies that would feature multiple monsters.

Tyler, Randoph Scott and Lawrence Tierney in a scene for "Badman's Territory." Tyler was also featured in ads for the movie. This is the first time Tyler played Frank James. (author's collection)

The Film Bulletin (May 13, 1946) made the film its "Exploitation Picture of the Issue" with a two-page spread about the film. "This rip-roaring outdoor melodrama makes little hardly any compromise with those story elements that too often debilitate westerns. The emphasis in bad man's territory is on Action and note the capital A. The showman has a powerful exploitation angle in the assemblage greatest ever of famous outlaws who motivate the two-gun career of sheriff Randolph Scott. Give this show both guns, boys!"

Never Say Goodbye

Directed by James Kern

Can be seen on YouTube, Google and AppleTV among other paid streamers

This romantic comedy is about a divorced couple who are brought back together by their daughter hatching a plot to make her father jealous.

Tyler is once again in an Errol Flynn vehicle but this time in an uncredited role as a police officer.

The Showman's Trade Review (Oct. 26, 1946) wrote "Errol Flynn departs from his usual customary role and gives a satisfactory account of himself in this farce-comedy which will entertain his followers and also many others. For the women there is a surprise in store when they get a glimpse of Forrest Tucker. The swoon-agers will find he has plenty of what it takes to 'send' them."

I have to admit that I've never seen Tucker described as a sex symbol.

1947

Cheyenne

Directed by Raoul Walsh

Can be seen on the Internet Archive

Tyler gets to work with another prominent director, Raoul Walsh, in this big budget Warner Bros. western.

Dennis Morgan plays a gambler, James Wylie, who is forced by Wells Fargo agents to undertake an effort to capture "The Poet Bandit," a thief who has plagued the Wells Fargo stage line, leaving a piece of poetry in empty strongboxes.

While on the stagecoach heading to Cheyenne, Morgan is stopped by an outlaw gang with Tyler and Bob Steele as two prominent members. They open the strongbox only to see the Poet has already stolen the gold shipment. Tyler is the member of the outlaw gang known as Pecos, who takes control of the stage robbery. While his face is covered by a bandana, Wylie spots a tattoo on his hand, which later in a saloon identifies him. Tyler has a fairly prominent part in the film, with more lines than Steele.

The film has a detective story edge with Morgan posing as the Poet Bandit to fool the outlaw gang of which Pecos is part. That role means he also is playing the husband to Ann Kincaid (Jane Wyman) who actually the wife to the real Poet Bandit, played by Bruce Bennett. Ann doesn't know who her husband really is and that he is cheating on her with a saloon performer played by Janis Paige.

It's a well-made western with a real who-done-it feel.

The Motion Picture Herald (April 26, 1947) wrote, "Don't spare the horses appears to have been the motto of producer Robert Buckner and director Raoul Walsh in making a western which is longer more elaborate, and livelier than run-of-the-mill rawhide opera. Certainly, few westerns come to mind which includes so many and so frequent chase sequences each climaxed by a stagecoach robbery."

To help publicize the film, three of its cast members were featured in an article published by Pasadena Star-News April 20, 1947.

"Gower Gulch's Old Dismay by Patricia Clary

"The cowpokes of western pictures almost went on the shelf 20 years ago when Warners shoved microphones in front of actors and bade them to talk. Three of the famous saddle and sage boys of that tome, Bob Steele, Tom Tyler, and William Desmond, all in Warners 'Cheyenne' recall that the news of talking pictures were received with dismay on Gower Gulch. 'Westerns didn't stop,' Steele said, 'but we were always waiting for the axe to fall. Westerns used titles on the screen and musical scores longer than any other kind of picture.

"Of course, it helped that theaters playing westerns were usually the last to get the new sound equipment in those days. Tyler said Hollywood didn't think it possible for sound and talk to be recorded outdoors. Big stages were being built on all the lots and it was expected that every movie from then on would have to concern subjects that could be squeezed into barns.

"There was consternation all around town Desmond said. It wasn't only the western actors who were excited. There were the producers who had been making money on outdoor pictures. They were the cheapest kind, with the biggest margin of profit. 'When the talkies came in with fixed microphones and vases and open desk drawers it looked like the end.'

"Desmond and his wife sat with Jack L. Warner the night 'The Jazz Singer' was premiered in Hollywood. When Jolson opened his mouth to sing, Desmond opened his in amazement. 'I told Jack he could never afford to put a microphone behind enough bushes to film a chase.'

"And what would a western be without a chase?

"A handsome leading man named Warner Baxter disproved the Hollywood convictions about outdoor pictures. He went with a Fox company on location and they came back with an all talking all outdoor picture, 'In Old Arizona,' good enough to win that year's Academy Award."

1948

The Dude Goes West

Directed by Kurt Neumann

Can be seen on Apple+ and other paid streaming services

Produced by the King Brothers and released through the newly renamed Allied Artists (formerly Monogram), this comedy western stars Eddie Albert and Monogram star Gale Storm.

A well-produced, but somewhat predictable rom com set in the old West, Albert's character is a gunsmith who moves from Brooklyn to Arsenic City, Nevada, where there is much more business in the gun trade.

Albert's character is a stranger in a strange land. He is not an idiot, but an innocent, who uses his eastern book learning to his advantage. Gale Storm plays an easterner as well on route to the same town to meet her father who has told her he has found a gold mine. Binnie Barnes and Gilbert Roland who play the crooks trying to jump the claim for the mine.

Tyler plays Spiggoty, a member of Texas Jack's (Barton McLean) gang. He has a couple of lines and some screen time towards the end of the movie.

Motion Picture Herald (May 1, 1948) wrote, "For 87 minutes of good clean fun liberally sprinkled with shooting, killing, and thieving nobody's audience can do better in this market, nor so well as to sit in on this satire about a Brooklyn gunsmith with a heart of gold who went West in 1875 because guns had gone out of use in Brooklyn, but were still the only law in Arsenic City. As put together by producers Frank and Maurice King who weren't known as satirists heretofore the account of the earnest young easterners' adventures in the far West is the most stimulating amusing surprise package to come off the production line in ready memory…

"From a script by Richard Sale and Mary Louise understandingly directed by Kurt Neumann the producers have evolved a western as replete with plot and action as the biggest of them but set apart from others in that it bids for laughter instead of thrills and gets them. It is in no sense limited to the western type audiences and indeed may very well prosper as well or better at other hands."

Return of the Bad Men

Directed by Ray Enright

Can be seen on paid streaming services

Tyler is cast as Wild Bill Yeager in this western that is sort of a remake of "Badman's Territory." It repeats the concept of having almost every historical Wild West bad guy in conflict with law man Randolph Scott.

Like its predecessor, it's a handsome, well-cast film set at the time of the Oklahoma land rush. The film made its debut in Guthrie, OK, depicted in the film.

Tyler gets some screen time and close-ups as a member of the outlaw gang. That gang also includes former western hero Tom Keene who is almost unrecognizable behind a beard.

Motion Picture Daily (May 21, 1948) wrote, "'Return of the Bad Men' has enough brigands for half a dozen outdoor pictures. The result is an orgy of villainy that will project devotees of violence on the screen into seventh heaven. The display of give and take keeps the footage unrolling at a furious pace from starting gun to finish under Ray Enright's direction. Actually, the film is a fairly routine affair made to seem more important than it is by virtue of a cast with a number of good box office names.

"Topped by Randolph Scott, Robert Ryan, George Gabby Hayes and Ann Jeffries, they have to work hard to put the story over. The prime handicap which they are called upon to overcome is a script with more stereotyped ingredients than might be expected of a western of the pretensions of return of the bad men. It tells the story of a group of cutthroats among them Billy the Kid and the Dalton boys who terrorized the Oklahoma territory at the time of the great land rush.

"Their nemesis is Scott who abandons his ambition to go to California in order to establish law and order Ryan has a routine assignment as one of the bad men. Hayes handles the comedy. Scott's interest is torn between Miss Jeffrey, leader of the baddies who reforms, and Jacqueline White. Ryan's murder of Miss Jeffrey solves Scott's romantic problem."

Red River

Directed by Howard Hawks

Can be seen on Tubi

Tyler is part of the cowhands who work for John Wayne's character in this epic story of a trail drive as well as the relationship between two men, adoptive father and son, played by Montgomery Clift.

Wayne turns in a great performance as the older man who is, frankly, is a control freak psychopath. In many ways, this was Wayne's "Captain Queeg" role, similar to Humphrey Bogart's character in "The Caine Mutiny."

It took two years for the film to come to the screen. The trade papers reported the delay was due to finding a distributor, while director and film historian Peter Bogdanovich asserted in an interview for the Criterion Blu-Ray release of the film the delay was due to interference from Howard Hughes who claimed "Red River" took some story elements from his western "The Outlaw."

Tyler is among many people who toiled in B westerns to be part of the cast. He is not credited but Hawks made sure Tyler was in many scenes. There is a close-up of him and other cast members at the start of the cattle drive and he is prominent as the cowboy who was awakened by a cattle stampede and is riding his horse in his long underwear.

Tyler's big moment comes with Glenn Strange as of one three cowhands who want to quit because of Wayne's abuse of them and the others. His character and the other two are gunned down by Wayne.

Box Office, July 10, 1948, wrote, "A stirring outdoors epic of great sweep and magnitude, Red River compares favorably with the great westerns of all time. It is superbly directed by Howard Hawks and acted to perfection by John Wayne, Walter Brennan, the late Harry Carey and other veterans of cowboy fare as well as by Montgomery Clift, newcomer from the Broadway stage whose portrayal of a stubborn young cattleman places him on the road to stardom Wayne is a strong selling name.

"The picture merits a strong exploitation campaign to acquaint the general public with the wide scope intermission excitement and suspense of its gripping story. Male patrons will revel in the "he-man" plot with its cattle Stampede Indian raids and gunplay and the pulsating climax. While romance enters the scene late, this angle could be stressed to attract women fans. And Cliff's lean and hungry look is certain to appeal to the ladies and create favorable word of mouth for the picture. The picture which was adapted from a widely read Saturday Evening Post story, 'The Old Chisholm Trail,' is made on the grand scale of 'The Covered Wagon,' 'The Iron Horse,' 'Cimarron' and other memorable films laid in the great open spaces of the West. The climax is reminiscent of that in John Ford's 'Stagecoach,' the never-to-be-forgotten western of 1939 which also starred John Wayne. More than 9/10 of the action takes place against the rolling plains and mountain country of Texas and points west and the photography of Russell Harland ASC, creates some breathtakingly beautiful effects.

"Produced and directed by Hawks about two years ago the film has been delayed while distribution terms with the United Artists were straightened out. Its release is scheduled for early September."

The Three Musketeers
Directed by George Sidney
Can be seen on paid streamers such as Apple TV and Prime

This star-studded version of the classic story from MGM boasts of Gene Kelly as D'Artagnan, Lana Turner as Milady de Winter and Vincent Price as Cardinal Richelieu. Tyler appears in a brief scene as a rider arriving at an inn.

Film Daily ran its review on the front page and wrote, "This has the stuff of which movies are made. Or ought to have. At his own peril will anyone take 'The Three Musketeers' seriously? The purpose was to entertain, young and old alike, and that purpose has been met with a whacking commercial distinction which indicates this attraction will be one of the heavy money pictures of the new season. Probably it is required to record that 'The Three Musketeers 'was written by Alexandre Dumas, whose adventure cycle of French royalty in flower was very tall stuff, but never taller than Dumas according to Robert Ardrey who put the script together. 'The Three Musketeers' may be atrocious Dumas but is it is super quality box office."

Blood on the Moon
Directed by Robert Wise
Can be seen on paid streamers such as Prime and Apple TV

Robert Mitchem plays a drifter who is convinced by his pal Tate (Robert Preston) to get involved in a conflict between a cattle owner and homesteaders. In many ways it is a western for its time of the late 1940s with brooding photography, a morally ambiguous hero and, at times, a convoluted plot. In other words, it's a film noir western.

Tyler has a good character role as a henchman, Frank Reardon.

Showman's Trade Review Nov. 13, 1948, wrote, "Although somewhat confusing this odd sort of western has enough action to be a winner. For a good part of the first quarter of the story the audience is in the dark as to what it is all about. The picture is done much more artistically than the usual western drama with subdued conversation shadowy camera angles and the like. In this connection photographer Nick Musuraca's camerawork deserves special mention. Robert Mitchum is Robert Mitchum in the role of the ner'er-do-well-turned hero, which should please his legion of fans and Robert Preston is very good as the villain. Technical departments are handled with thorough care. Mitchum's current popularity plus the action angle should ensure extra grosses in average situations."

1949

This year marks the beginning of Tyler's association with Ron Ormond, the producer/director who picked up Lash LaRue for a series of 11 westerns after his career at PRC ended. Ormond and his wife June had a very colorful career in show business from his being a magician and touring to producing westerns, then exploitation films and finally what could be charitably called Christian scare movies.

Tyler became one of Ormond's regular performers starting with the truly odd western musical "Square Dance Jubilee." In the book "The Exotic Ones," by Jimmy McDonough, screen writer C. Jack Lewis is quoted, "Ron had a cadre of people he used time and time again. He started a lot of people in the business and he helped a lot of old timers who were on their ass mostly because he could hire him cheap like Tom Tyler. He had been a big western star in his day and was a tired sick old man. Hell, Ron kept Tom Tyler eating."
To be clear, Tyler was still in his forties, scarcely an old man, but one who did indeed have serious health problems.,

Ormond struck up a business arrangement with a west coast theater owner named Robert L. Lippert, who was going into the production end of the business with his company Screen Guild. Lippert had an impressive producing career going from being an independent to an affiliation with 20th Century Fox. That distribution deal with Fox led to Lippert's best-known film, "The Fly."

Ormond released many of his films through Lippert, including a series of six westerns starring two actors, James Ellison and Russell Hayden, who had both played sidekicks to William Boyd's Hopalong Cassidy. All of those films featured Tyler as well as Raymond Hatton, Fuzzy Knight and Julie Adams, billed as Betty Ames.

Although Tyler got prominent billing, he was frequently cast as the henchman working for the "brains" boss. They weren't creatively fulfilling roles, but Tyler never walked through them. He added bits of business when he could to give the standard role a bit more interest.

Generally, though, 1949 gave Tyler the opportunity for some solid supporting roles.

I Shot Jesse James
Directed by Samuel Fuller
Can be seen on YouTube

The first film directed by the legendary director, writer and iconoclast, Tyler played Frank James once again to this time Reed Hadley's Jesse James. Tyler had a reunion with Hadley, who played the native chieftain in "Adventures of Captain Marvel."

Fuller convinced producer Robert Lippert to allow him to direct his own screen play and Fuller does an excellent job in telling a story based on historical fact: that Bob Ford who murdered his friend Jesse by shooting him in the back became a pariah instead of a hero.

John Ireland did an outstanding job as the tortured gang member and Fuller weaves fact into his screenplay. Ford did do theatrical re-enactments of how he killed James and he was killed in the silver rush town of Creede, CO, by a man named O'Kelley.

Tyler as Frank James is seen briefly at the beginning of the film but has several substantial scenes at the end when he has hunted Ford down and intends to kill him. Interestingly, he does not kill Ford but instead simply walks off, knowing someone else will do the job. Tyler gives a solid performance.

"Brog" writing in Variety (Feb. 2, 1949) said, "'I Shot Jesse James' as a character study of the man who felled the West's most famous outlaw with a coward's bullet. It's an interesting treatment that doesn't overlook necessary plot and action to give it good grossing possibilities. Physical values are about usual level of Screen Guild releases giving it the dressing for top playing time and houses buying sturdy action product cast members are particularly good. Film fits more in the adult bracket than for kiddie audiences, but title and exploitable angles will give it enough push to attract younger ticket buyers."

The Younger Brothers
Directed by Edwin L. Marin
Available on DVD

Tyler plays "Hatch," a henchman in this western that features a story based on the life and criminal careers of the Younger Brothers.

Harrison Reports, (May 7, 1949), wrote, "Although the photography is in Technicolor and it has a cast of better than average names, this western melodrama is no more than just fair, offering little that would appeal to other than the avid western picture fans. Its best reception should be in theaters that specialize in western fare; in other situations, it probably will serve best as the supporting feature. The story which is a highly fictional account of a period in the lives of the notorious Missouri outlaw brothers, depicts them as men desirous of leading an honest life. Placing notorious bandits on the right side of the law is indeed a fresh twist, but even so the story is only mildly interesting, for it is rambling and never quite credible and several of the central characterizations are grossly exaggerated. Not much can be said for either the direction or the acting. The photography, however, is very good."

Lust for Gold

Directed by S. Sylvan Simon

Can be seen on DVD and YouTube

A well-made story about the fabled Lost Dutchman gold mine, the film opens with an interesting device: a letter from the then governor of Arizona stating the film "represents to the best of our knowledge, the true facts concerning this unusual situation, as substantiated by historical records and legends of the state of Arizona."

The film starts the story with a framing sequence set in 1949 with the grandson of "The Dutchman" seeking the mine. The film jumps back to the 1880s with Jacob Walz (Glenn Ford) and his partner Wiser (Edgar Buchanan) reaching the mine by following another two men and killing them. Walz then kills his partner.

The film is a well-told story of greed and fits quite well into the post-WWII film movie genre of film noir. Ida Lupino plays a scheming femme fatale and Gig Young is her weak husband. Ford does well as the murderous miner.
Tyler plays the owner of the town's saloon, who after listening to Walz for eight hours instructs his bartender to give him a Mickey Finn. It's a nice scene for Tyler.

Motion Picture Daily reviewed the film on May 20, 1949, and wrote, "The picture is a good western airing somewhat in a rather heavy-handed attempt to give its character some depth but on the basis of engaging story developments and attractive names its market groove seems to extend way beyond the usual western outlets. Lust for gold is reminiscent of 'Treasure of Sierra Madre' in theme but lacking in the masterful touches which made the latter production memorable entertainment. Here again is the fabulous gold mine which brings the savage instincts of its seekers to the fore."

She Wore a Yellow Ribbon

Directed by John Ford

Can be seen Blu-Ray, paid streaming sites and Vimeo

One of John Ford's films about the American calvary, this film is bittersweet and contemplative. John Wayne plays an Army officer at the end of his career who is able, with the assistance of a native chief who is his friend, to stop a war before it goes too far.

Wayne gives one of the best performances of his career and Tyler is given a prominent supporting role as Corporal Quayne with a great scene with Wayne and then another with Mildred Natwick. He is an enlisted man who has been wounded in a fight with the natives. Natwick is assisting the doctor as they dig out the bullet and has to match drinks with Tyler to get him to calm down. Tyler even sings!

I think this is one of Ford's best films and it gave Tyler a solid scene. It shows once more he was far more an actor than many of his B westerns would allow him to be.

Motion Picture Daily, in its front-page review (July 27, 1948), predicted the film would earn "big money." It continued, "But how Ford causes it to happen – the values extracted from interesting and unusual detail the thorough authenticity he gives to calvary men and Indian, the mounting conviction that this may be a reliving of an exciting chapter and the development of the far West – is what gives this attraction its distinction. The meticulous and knowing care for which the director is noted extends to the principal performances and once again as become custom with Ford, to pictorial appeal in breathtaking proportions. Photographed in Technicolor at Monument Valley Park on the Utah-Arizona border, the film is incredibly beautiful in its panoramic sweeps... Some of the material is obvious and even corny particularly the broad comedy characterization demanded of Victor McLaglen as Wayne's orderly. But whatever the downbeats may be, they are never loud enough to threaten the general excellence of the film."

Masked Raiders

Directed by Lesley Selander

Available in the "Tim Holt Western Classic Collection Vol. 3" from Warners Bros. Archive

The first of several appearances for Tyler in the Tim Holt series. Holt had been an actor since his youth – the son of star Jack Holt – appearing in a number of different films, including Orson Welles' "The Magnificent Ambersons" and "The Treasure of Sierra Madre."

He made B westerns for RKO before World War II and returned to the studio for many more once he returned from WWII in which he piloted a B-29 in the Pacific Theater.

His co-star was Richard Martin who performed sidekick duty as a half-Mexican/Irish cowpoke.

Director Selander had a very long and prolific career – 1926 to 1968 – with 147 credits in movies and television series episodes. His casts included Tyler on many occasions, including Tyler's last film, "Cow Country."

Tom plays Trig Trevitt, son of a wealthy ranch owner. His brother was played by Clayton Moore.

Showman's Trade Review, Oct. 8, 1949, wrote, "The latest Tim Holt picture is up to par for his western series, being well stocked with the elements – riding, shooting, fighting – to sell it in the regular western action market. This time there's a Robin Hood twist – the masked raiders supposed to be the villains turning out to be ranchers protecting themselves against the supposedly respectable banker and town marshal. Holt and his amusing sidekick Chito Rafferty (played by Richard Martin) are Texas Rangers. The gal who appears oh so feminine when not leading the raiders in mask is very pretty Marjorie Lord. There's a juvenile role, that of her little brother, well brought off by Gary Gray."

Square Dance Jubilee

Directed by Paul Landres

Can be seen on YouTube

Two TV talent scouts, (Don "Red" Berry and Wally Vernon) have been charged to go west and find musical performers for a TV show. This is an American west of 1949 that still looks and behaves like the American west of 1888, but with TV sets and cars. Go figure.

The plot device allows producer Ron Ormond to use the film as a musical revue with a near endless parade of western swing bands and country entertainers. Berry even gets to sing!

The film's "story" involves Berry getting involved in exposing a cattle-rustling ring with Tyler as the "muscle" to the criminal mastermind.

Trade ad for Lippert Productions with "Square Dance Jubilee" at bottom. There are two other films produced by Ron Ormond on the schedule.

Berry had quite a run with Ormond in the early 1950s and this film is labeled as "A Don Barry Production." Berry even sings!

Showman's Trade Review Nov. 19, 1949, wrote, "Satisfactory entertainment for all those who like musical westerns. Loaded with music, entirely of the hillbilly variety, this should please all those who like Spade Cooley and his brand of music. ... A good offering for the small towns where a picture of this type should have a following in the urban areas it will draw best where Spade Cooley and his type of entertainment is known and enjoyed ... Direction by Paul Landres plays up the vaudeville for the sake of entertainment, letting the story come in only when necessary. Production credit goes to Ron Ormond who lined up quite an assortment of artists, to make sure that the film had enough western flavor to satisfy everyone."

Samson and Delilah
Directed by Cecil B. DeMille
Can be seen on YouTube for a rental fee

One of the most acclaimed directors of his time, DeMille is perhaps best known today for "The Ten Commandments," (1956) but he had a very long career and produced movies in many other genres. This Biblically inspired epic was a major hit in 1949, although when watched today it comes across as unintentionally campy.

Victor Mature playing Samson and Hedy LaMarr as Delilah head up a huge cast. Among the character roles one will see George Reeves playing his heart out in a scene with the Philistine king played by George Sanders. In the climactic temple sequence Arthur Q. Bryant plays a Philistine nobleman commenting on Samson in his Elmer Fudd voice.

Tyler played the Philistine in charge of the grist mill. There, Samson, now blinded, was chained to the wheel turning the stone. He had several lines when Samson was calling out for water. Again, it was a minor part but DeMille was known for wanting every detail just right for his productions and he deemed Tyler correct for the role.

Harrison Reports (Oct. 22, 1949) wrote, "Excellent! Cecil B. de Mille, whose name is synonymous with spectacular productions, has produced another major historical extravaganza in 'Samson and Delilah.' Beautifully photographed in Technicolor, it is an impressive and magnificent production that reflects credit on Mr. DeMille and all others concerning in its making. Being a biblical drama, great care was required to avoid either exaggerating or shading down certain scriptural incidents lest offence be given to different racial and religious sects. Mr. DeMille has succeeded, not only in keeping the story authentic, but also in presenting in a highly entertaining way. Its combination of spectacularity and human interests will grip the attention of all moviegoers."

1950

Riders of the Range

Directed by Lesley Selander

Can be seen on Dailymotion

Tim Holt was a believable western star and his post-WWII RKO series were competently made and acted. They come at the end of the B western cycle but they are enjoyable.

Holt and Martin are two cowboys in search of a job and happen upon a ranch owner named Dusty (Jacqueline White) who is need of ranch hands. Dusty's brother, Harry (Robert Clarke) has a gambling problem and owes card shark and local criminal mastermind Clint Burrows (Reed Hadley) $3,000. If Harry can't pay it, the ranch is in danger.

The Ringo Kid (Tyler) believes he is owed the $3,000 by Burrows and steals it from him. That sets the rest of the plot in motion of move and counter move. Tyler does well in the role that is usually subordinate to the "brains" criminal.

Dalton's Women

Directed by Thomas Carr

Can be seen on YouTube

The seventh of a series of Lash LaRue Westerns produced by Ron Ormond, this was the first to be released for the Howco company (in partnership with drive-in theater owners Joy Houck and J. Francis White).

Ormond included Raymond Hatton, Lyle Talbot, Jack Holt and Tom Neal in the cast. LaRue and Al St. John go undercover to stop the Dalton gang. Tyler plays Emmett Dalton.

Ormond's artistic vision for this film is to cram it with many non-story elements, such as numerous musical numbers and a juggler (!). It's not a successful technique and this is a painful film to watch.

Most of Tyler's scenes are at the end of the movie.

Amazingly enough, The Exhibitor (April 1, 1951) thought the film had box office potential. "With an adequate cast and with some other angles arising from a honky tonk chorus and added action from a knock down, hair pulling, clothes ripping brawl of two gals. This shapes up as an OK western with most of the regulation ingredients also present there is some barbershop harmony and production values show up OK."

"The Irish Cowboys Series"

Motion Picture Daily (Feb. 16, 1950) reported that Lippert Productions would release 13 feature films in the next four months, an ambitious schedule, but Lippert was an ambitious producer. Among those would be five of the six films of the series.

Lewis is quoted in the book about Ormond, 'The Exotic Ones," that what he called the "Irish Cowboys" series were shot simultaneously with the same cast, the same costumes and the same sets. Each film, though, used the cast in a different way. Amazingly enough, the films are not bad, thanks to some interesting scripts and the professionalism of the cast. Tyler was part of the ensemble always playing a thug. According to Variety, all of the films were completed in 28 days.

Rather than a traditional western series with the actors playing essentially the same roles, this series treated its cast as a repertory company with the actors performing different roles from film to film. The cast featured James Ellison and Russell Hayden, both of whom had appeared in the Hopalong Cassidy series, among other films. The supporting cast included Raymond Hatton, Fuzzy Knight, Betty Adams – soon to change her name to Julie Adams and have a very long career – and Tyler. Other western actors popped up such as Dennis Moore, George Chesebro, Bud Osborne and George Lewis.

In an interview posted on westernclippings.com, Adams recalled, "I met someone at the Lippert office, talked to them and got the role! I also met Don Berry who was the leading man. We shot it partly at the Iverson Ranch. It only took six days to do it! That picture resulted in my landing the lead in six different pictures at Lippert with James Ellison and Russell Hayden. We had six different scripts – but we shot all the scenes of the stagecoach together, then all of the ranch scenes, whatever – all at the same time. The six movies were done in five weeks. It was economical to do it that way but I never could remember who I was. I had three or four wardrobe changes – a farmhouse dress, a stagecoach dress. I had a difficult time remembering who I was supposed to be. 'Am I the farm girl this time – or the cowgirl?' (Laughs) Not that it made any real difference."

She continued, "These films were the reason I learned to ride. Before I started, I practiced riding for about three weeks in Griffith Park. The horses there were slow and you really had to kick them to get them going. Shooting the actual movie, the director (Tommy Carr) said, 'Action.' When I let into this old horse, he shot away with me and kept on going. We were supposed to ride, see where the badmen were, wheel around and come back. This horse and I would still be flying through the woods had a mountain not broken his stride. (Laughs) Raymond Hatton was in those – such a nice man. He showed me how a horse takes to a scene. He said to take the pony through it – let the horse know how to do it. Rehearse the horse – hit the marks. It was terrific advice! James Ellison – a charming guy; we had a good time. He was so handsome, a very sweet man, as was Russell Hayden."

The series was directed by Thomas Carr, an actor turned director who did a lot of work at Republic on the Sunset Carson series in the late 1940s, as well as some serials at both Republic and Columbia. Among his serial work was splitting the directing duties on "Superman" in 1948.

With the rise of television, he worked on a number of series, most notably the first season of the "Adventures of Superman."

Besides producing the series, Ormond also contributed to the screenplays.

Hostile Country

Motion Picture Daily (May 24, 1950), wrote, "In this first of a new series of Lippert westerns costarring James Ellison and Russell Hayden as Shamrock and his pal Lucky there is plenty what takes place to please the customers in the line of shooting fighting and skullduggery. Throw in as much hard riding in a large capable cast and you have the ingredients for popularity with western fans.

Thomas Carr directed from a script by Maurice Tombragel and producer Ron Ormond.

"A gang of bad men attempts to beat a young lady rancher out of her property by blocking off a pass through which she must get her stock to market by a certain date. To achieve this, they have hidden Shamrock's stepfather who he has never met, and one of them has assumed his identity. Shamrock eliminates

Lippert's films went pretty quickly to the non-theatrical market as this page from the Minot catalog attests.
(author's collection)

the whole gang by dynamiting a barrier at the Canyon Pass and he and Lucky wind up everything to a satisfactory conclusion. The excellent supporting cast includes Raymond Hatton and Fuzzy Knight as well as many others."

Marshal of Helderado

The Exhibitor (Aug. 9, 1950), wrote, "Containing a considerable amount of deft humor, this is above average for the series and is quite entertaining. Ellison and Hayden turn in pleasing performances, ably abetted by Hatton, Knight, and the others.

Crooked River

The Exhibitor Sept. 27, 1950, wrote, "This compares favorably with others in the series as regards the shooting and fighting, which supply enough action to satisfy western fans, but a lengthy flashback prologue detracts somewhat from the pace. Ellison and Hayden turned in routine performances because they carry most of the weight.

Tyler is seen at the left helping to get the drop on star James Ellison. (author's collection)

A nice shot of Tyler from "Marshal of Helderado." (author's collection)

Colorado Ranger

The Exhibiter (June 7, 1950) wrote, "Except for the final scene kiss, which evoked groans from the theater audience, when reviewed, this is a fairly routine item, with adequate fighting and gunplay to satisfy western fans. Ellison, Hatton, Hayden, and Adams turn in standard performances."

West of the Brazos

The Exhibitor (May 10, 1950) wrote, "Ellison and Hayden team nicely in this above par western, which moves at a good clip, and which has ample plot and action to support interest. Capable support is lent by John Cason and Stanley Price."

Fast on the Draw

The Exhibitor, June 21, 1950, wrote, "This is routine, with plenty of stock shots and lots of gunplay. Ellison and Hayden fight and shoot their way through the familiar story, while the romantic angle is minor."

Rio Grande Patrol

Directed by Lesley Selander

Available in the "Tim Holt Western Classic Collection Vol. 3" from Warners Bros. Archive

It's another henchman role for Tyler in this film.

The Exhibitor (Nov. 22, 1950), wrote, "This does not measure up to the general standard of the series. Performances and production values are below par and while there is plenty of shooting and fighting the story tends to drag."

1951

The Great Missouri Raid

Directed by Gordon Douglas

Available on YouTube rental

Another Frank and Jesse James re-telling but this time Tyler is not cast as Frank James. The film is essentially an origin story about what transformed Missouri farmers into outlaws sympathetic to the Confederacy. Tyler is a member of James gang and doesn't receive credit.

Deciding to take advantage of a blanket pardon offered to all who fought on the rebel side, Frank James (Wendall Corey) leads his men into town not knowing the Union major named Trowbridge (Ward Bond) in charge of the district has set a trap for them since several years before members of the James gang had killed his brother when he was torturing Jesse (Macdonald Carey) for information.

It's a sympathetic approach to the legendary criminals.

Paramount promoted this Technicolor release heavily in the trades and it's a shame that Tyler didn't have a bigger part in this film. He is in several scenes of the assembled gang and his character gets killed off rather anonymously.

Film Bulletin (Jan. 1, 1951), wrote, "This Paramount version of an oft-told tale of the notorious James gang is a glorified western outlaw epic, crammed with old fashioned riding, shooting, hell-bent-for-leather action and hewed in eye-filling Technicolor. The box office potentialities of 'The Great Missouri Raid' are very good wherever the big outdoor films click and for exhibitors who fully capitalize upon the exploitation possibilities of the Jesse James story, receipts should even be better in deluxe hours and class situations."

Best of the Badmen
Directed by William D. Russell
Can be seen for a fee on YouTube and on DVD
Another post-Civil War film set in the western states with a group of Quantrill's Raiders making the decision to accept an offer from Union officer Jeff Clanton (Robert Ryan) to go straight. Once again Tyler plays Frank James to Lawrence Tierney's Jesse James, both men part of this group of ex-Confederates.

Robert Preston plays an unethical detective/carpet bagger named Fowler who wants the raiders released to him so he can collect the rewards. Clanton prevents this by administering the oath of allegiance making the group free civilians but in the course one of Fowlers men's rushes in and Clanton shoots him. Since he is now out of the Army he is arrested, tried and sentenced to death.

Naturally, he runs and eventually is rescued by the gang he tried to help and becomes an outlaw with them. He is bitter as he was rail-roaded at the trial orchestrated by Fowler.

Tyler doesn't get as much to do as Frank James in this version of the story. Independent Exhibitors Film Bulletin (May 7, 1951, wrote, "Once again the infamous James and Younger brothers quest for vengeance drags a bloody trail of violence across the screen in RKO's Technicolor entry into an already overcrowded field. Touted as a forgotten story in the violent history in the preface to the film. 'Best of the Bad Men' is just one more addition to the lengthy string of such pictures which must certainly have sated all but the most avid devotees of outlaw westerns. The familiar tale belabored for the umpteenth time by Robert Hardy Andrews and John Twist for this Herman Schlom production, fails to break away from the pack, staggering over the finish line with only some standard gun and fist tussles and a few chase scenes though beautifully photographed to its credit. And the innocuous climax will prove a complete disappointment to all but the most faithful boots and saddle fans. The only situations where appreciable box office receipts can be expected will be the action houses with only moderate returns likely elsewhere as a dualler."

Mysterious Island
Directed by Spencer Gordon Bennet
Can be seen on Tubi
This serial adaptation of the Jules Verne novel was produced by Sam Katzman and Tyler appears in the opening few minutes of the first chapter as a Union Army messenger. He rides into frame, delivers a written message, has a single line and leaves.

1952

Outlaw Women
Directed by Sam Newfield
Can be seen on YouTube

Produced by Ron Ormond, this western does a different kind of angle. The film is primarily set in a town controlled by outlaw women who have, through personal experience, lost any real trust in men, outlaw or not.

Shot in color and starring Marie Windsor – a long forgotten but essential actor in the post WWII film noir movement – the film also includes Jackie Coogan as a gunfighter. It's one of Ormond's most successful productions in my assessment.

Tyler is a gunfighter who is dispatched by Coogan in the first third of the movie.

Harrison's Reports (April 12, 1952) noted, "A fairly good program western melodrama, photographed by the Cinecolor process. The story is somewhat different from the formula stories. The main feature is, of course, the fact that women outlaws control the town and the men outlaws are compelled to take orders from them, which is something the exhibitor should play up in exploiting the picture. There is considerable gunplay, shootings and killings, and stagecoach holdups, and the action holds one's interest throughout. The color is good when one considers that and the color is two-color process. The outdoor scenery is pleasing in that the photography is sharp."

1953

Cow Country
Directed by Lesley Selander
Available on DVD

Exhibitor (May 6, 1953), wrote, "This outdoor opus throws everything into the pot. There is too much story here with plot within plot, murder, and villainy. However, as a western it should please action fans and should do OK as a dualler."

The Independent Film Journal (May2, 1953), opined, "'Cow Country' is an average entry in the western action market. However, its chances of obtaining better than average results are good due to the marquee lure of Edmund O'Brien and all-around good performances by Helen Westcott, Peggy Castle, Bob Lowry, and Barton McLean. Weak link in the film seems to be the writing, with some stilted dialogue slowing the film and spots, plus the presence of some pretty familiar situations. Film lacks action in quite a bit of the footage with the first fist fight and gunshot coming after quite a bit of reelage has unspooled."

IMBD notes that Tyler is credited but his role as "Pete" is cut from the film.

Road Agent

Directed by Lesley Selander

Available in the "Tim Holt Western Classic Collection Vol. 3" from Warners Bros. Archive

Exhibitor (Feb. 13, 1952), wrote, "Regular followers of this Holt-Martin series will be in for a couple of surprises. In the past the boys adhered closely to formula but in this they don capes and masks, become Robin Hoods and break the law. The biggest shocker however is that Holt, who has never even glanced at a girl before, is seen in the final fade out giving the heroine a full-fledged kiss. Despite these changes there is plenty of old-fashioned riding and shooting."

The Lion and the Horse

Directed by Lois King

Can be seen on DVD and on the Internet Archive

Ben, a cowboy, (Steve Cochran) falls in love with a wild stallion, part of a herd he and his friends have rounded up. Although he had his friends promise to hold the horse, it gets sold with the rest of the herd.

Searching for the horse, he travels the rodeo circuit and find the horse. The stallion, who is wilder than ever, has become a big attraction at rodeo with cowboy trying their hand at riding him. His offer to buy the horse was rebuffed and Ben manages to free the horse to escape and Ben mages to rope the stallion, now known as Wildfire. Finding a ranch to take them both on, Ben patiently "breaks" the horse.

All seems well until the rodeo owner turns up, tracing the horse to the ranch. Ben takes off with the horse before the rodeo owner brings the sheriff. When a captive lion escapes from a traveling show, it stalks Ben and Wildfire. The horse leads the lion away from Ben and is attacked by him. The horse stomps the lion to death.

Everything ends well.

A well-directed and acted family drama, the film is essentially the love affair between a cowboy and a horse. Cochran is impressive as Ben, but the horse "playing" Wildfire is even a better performer.

Tyler is reunited with Bob Steele in this film as both are part of the initial group of cowboys who found the stallion and his herd. Tyler gets a few good lines but, due to his illness, is almost unrecognizable.

Theater owners seemed to like the picture. In the Motion Picture Herald (Feb. 7, 1953) a theater manager from Paonia, Colorado, wrote, "A good western with a different story and plenty of action."

What Price Glory
Directed by John Ford
Can be seen on YouTube
John Ford's remake of the successful WWI drama/comedy about two friends/rivals – Capt. Flagg (James Cagney) and Sergeant Quirt (Dan Dailey) – was the last time the director used Tyler. He appears in a scene in which he is an aide to General Cokely (James Gleason). He has no lines but is recognizable. Clearly Ford was helping him out by providing him a payday.

TV Work 1950-1953
The Lone Ranger TV
The Cisco Kid TV four episodes in 1950 and 1951
Adventures of Wild Bill Hickok TV two episodes
The Roy Rogers Show TV two episodes
Sky King TV one episode
Cowboy G - Men TV one episode
Boston Blackie TV two episodes
The Gene Autry Show TV four episodes
The Range Rider TV two episodes

As Boyd Majors wrote on his Western Clippings website, **"Steve Donovan, Western Marshal,"** aired in 1956. The series of 39 episodes was filmed in 1951 but received little distribution until 1955-56 when NBC put it back out for syndication. Tyler appeared in the episode "Commanche Kid."

Crossroads Avenger; the Adventures of the Tucson Kid
Directed by Ed Wood
Can be seen on DVD and on You Tube
This unaired TV pilot was supposed to be a starring vehicle for Tom Keene. A former B western star who had changed his name at one time to try to escape the sagebrush role, he played a frontier insurance investigator, an unusual angle for a western.

Born George Duryea, he switched to Tom Keene in the 1930s and used it until 1944 when he became Richard Powers, a name he used until his retirement from the industry in 1959. Wood was known to be a western fan and Keene accommodated him in this western role by reverting to that name.

Much has been written about Wood and this writer believes his reputation as "the world's worst director" is inaccurate. There are plenty of people who were as or more incompetent as Wood. This was Wood's only production in color.

A separate production company, Tucson Kid Productions, was set up with Lew Dubin as the producer. Dubin was an independent producer who also announced in 1953 (The Exhibitor April 20, 1953) he had teamed with actor Turhan Bey to make a 3-D version of the Lady Godiva story but did nothing else.

This half-hour film does tell a story in a workman-like manner. unlike some of Woods' features. It is nothing significant, though, but it does hang together. Only the most completest Wood, Tom Keene or Tyler fan needs to see this film.

Tyler plays the town's deputy and has considerable screen time. He remained a professional up to the end of his career, doing his best while clearly physically frail and saddled with Wood's awkward dialogue.

That's not all folks!

With the advent of widespread commercial television in 1949, Tyler's films became, like other B-westerns, staples of local television stations. As noted in the previous chapter, many of Tyler's independent films of 1930s were theatrically re-issued by companies such as Astor.

A simple search of his name in the period of 1953-1955 reveals page after page from TV Guide to local newspaper listings that show just how prevalent his Freuler, Reliable and Victory westerns were on television. Republic was also releasing many of its films through its Hollywood Television Service subsidy.

In the March 30,1950, edition of The Independent, it mentioned recently that KTSL had purchased the rights to 300 western films starring Johnny Mack Brown, Tim McCoy, Bob Steele, Tex Ritter, Tom Tyler and Kermit and Ken Maynard. The station paid out $37,500 for the old films.

There was money in these old westerns, and other B movie fare.

Republic started releasing its movies to television through its own subsidiary.

Although he had lived long enough to see this new distribution of his films happen, Tyler did not financially benefit from it. One of his obituaries noted that Tyler wanted to buy the rights for his 1930s westerns.

If Tyler had not been sick, I'm sure he would have still been acting at age 50 and would have seen a resurgence in his career due to his starring films becoming almost ubiquitous on local television station across the nation.

In its Aug. 30, 1954, edition, Broadcasting Telecasting reported Tyler's Mascot serial, "Phantom of the West," was being released to television. It is that television print that can be seen today either online or on DVD.

In the mid-1950s, RKO started re-releasing a number of films featuring Tyler. They included "Valley of the Sun, "Blood on the Mood, and "Badman's Territory."

"Gone With the Wind" and "She Wore A Yellow Ribbon" were both re-re-leased, in 1954.

"The Adventures of Captain Marvel" was re-released by Republic as "The Return of Captain Marvel" on April 15,1954, just about two weeks before his death. The comic book had ceased publication in 1953.

Since television stations continued to show movies daily as part of their local programming, these films were seen into the 1970s when local programmers decided to switch to color productions. Tyler's films from the 1930s, because they are in public domain, benefited from their legal status in the VHS revolution, although bad prints and dubious transfers didn't help.

Because of streaming services, and DVD/Blu-ray releases, much of Tyler's work is, thankfully, still available for re-assessment.

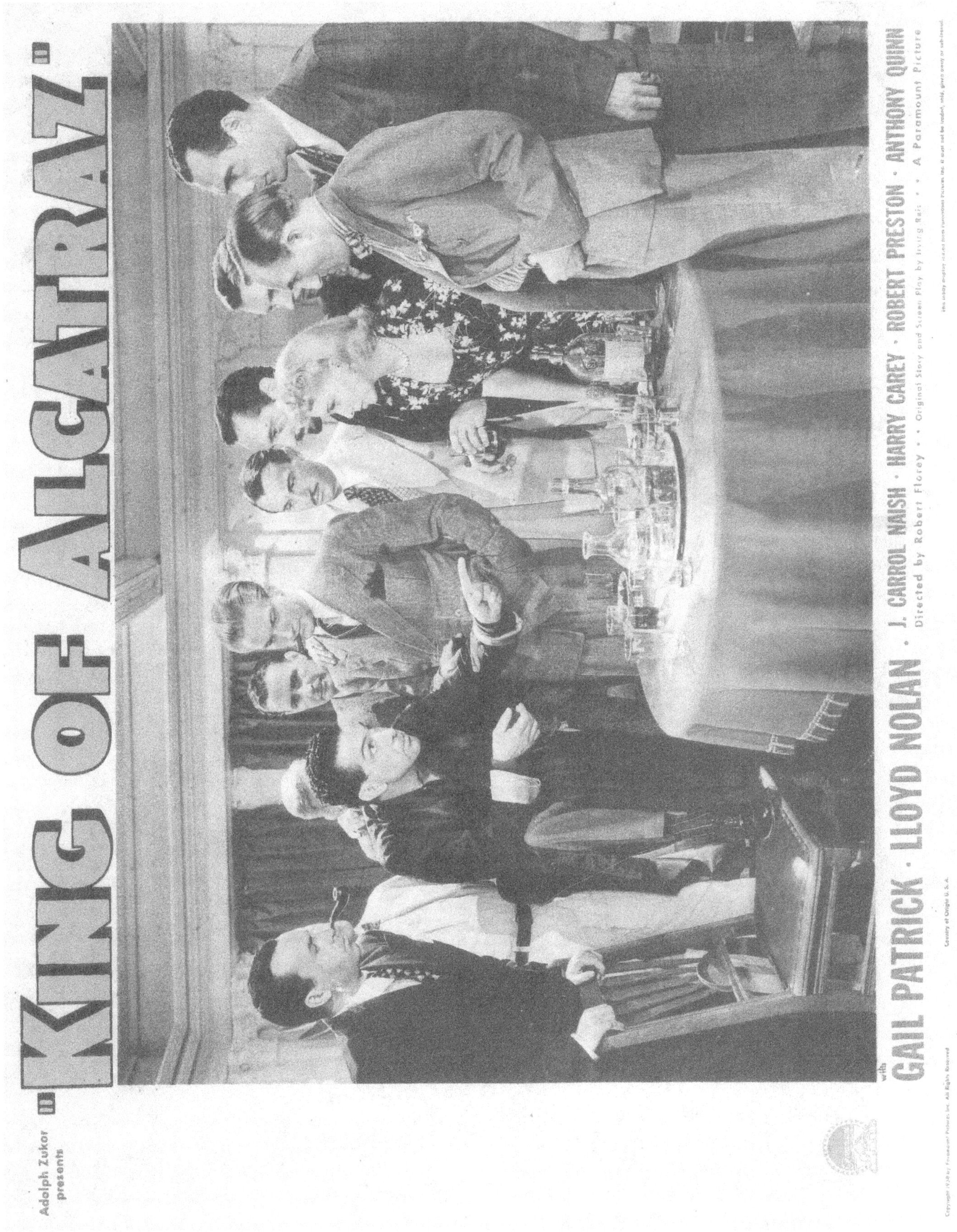
Adolph Zukor presents
"KING OF ALCATRAZ"
with
GAIL PATRICK · LLOYD NOLAN · J. CARROL NAISH · HARRY CAREY · ROBERT PRESTON · ANTHONY QUINN
Directed by Robert Florey · · Original Story and Screen Play by Irving Reis · · A Paramount Picture
Country of Origin U. S. A.

THE FILMS AND LIFE OF TOM TYLER

"Watch out, Tom! That blonde bombshell can explode!"

264

THE FILMS AND LIFE OF *TOM TYLER*

Chapter Eight

The Republic Years

Tyler's association with Republic was a time of career stability. He was finally making series westerns at a studio with real production values and solid distribution.

The Republic films were aimed at smaller theaters that relied on B films or programmers to fill its screen. Although the majors also made B films, both Monogram and Republic were designed for that kind of film.

To be clear, Republic's films did play in larger communities, though, and within the industry there was respect for the smaller studio. Its films had the technical sheen of a major studio, while keeping production costs down and fulfilling the needs of theater owners.

It also produced a handful of A films and worked with directors such as John Ford and Orson Welles, among others.

Although the studio was quick to respond to trends and initially seemed to understand television well – it has a separate division to sell its library to TV stations – it didn't get into television production successfully as it should. TV and management issues spelled Republic's demise.

I've interviewed several people who worked at Republic. One was the legendary character actor Fritz Feld. Initially, I asked him about making "Cat Man of Paris (1946)."

"We called for fun Republic Pictures 'Repulsive Pictures.' Anyway, we played there and Mr. Yates, who was the chief of the studio, which made mostly western pictures, tried a movie called "I've Always Loved You' (1946), a $1,000,000 picture. He attempted to do this picture and a very funny thing happened in it.

"The star of the picture was a musician, a concert pianist [played by Catherine McLeod] who is in a school with different pupils and the teacher walks around correcting them playing the piano saying, 'You have bad fingering.' It was all played by [Arthur] Rubenstein prerecorded and he wasn't told to play badly so he played beautifully.

"So, when the man says 'bad fingering' it is ridiculous. It was the most beautiful music. "Anyway, after the picture is finished I was on the same lot and I had to do the picture you just mentioned."

I also spoke with Dick Wilson, another character actor who hit it big by appearing in many commercials for Charmin toilet paper as "Mr. Whipple" who had a fetish for squeezing the Charmin.

He said, "It was not fun working there. It was one of the smaller studios. I was under contract for the great sum of $75 a week. You were in as many as four movies a day. You would go from one stage to another and they would say, 'You're an Arab, go to wardrobe,' and the next one they'd say, 'You're a seaman, go get a sailor-suit.'

"And they'd give you what to say when you went over there, maybe three or four lines, maybe one, you never knew."

In many interviews with Republic employees, though, there seemed to be a family-like atmosphere at the studio.

In this piece in Film Bulletin, July 12, 1941, writer Jack Harrower explained the Republic philosophy about movie making.

"It was a real educational value to talk to a head of a Hollywood studio whose organization had delivered the entire program announced for 1941 and furthermore delivered it on schedule. We know of no other company that equaled this record. So, we were of course interested in learning from N. J. Siegel, president and operating head of Republic productions, something as to the methods and system that made this possible. Siegel is a quiet spoken modest person and we had to prod him quite a little to make him admit that he had considerable to do with the achievement.

"The system of Republic studio operation boils down to just plain common sense and ordinary business methods which are applied to any other industry in its manufacturing procedure. For instance, they do not have a battalion of players and a division of writers on yearly contract dragging down an average of 40 weeks salary every 12 months whether they are gainfully employed most of that time or not. Certain leading players of course are contracted for by the year or for so many pictures a year. Writers are only hired when there is a definite assignment for them to go to work on. This assignment system puts the writer on his mettle to do his best work so that he will stand a chance of grabbing another assignment when his current scrivening skill stint is completed. At studios where the writers coast along through an entire production season with a steady contract, the human tendency is to slough off a little. A sense of security often tends to develop careless work.

"The contract players make an average of six pictures a year for Republic. Thus, it appears that this studio makes much more use of their people than any other studios. Of a total of 60 players half of them are on a 40-week basis. The other half work the picture-to-picture deals, usually three or four a year.

Another economical procedure at Republic is never to buy a story property until they are practically set to go ahead with production at some definite date. No story material is purchased simply because it has a good basic idea. The story must have at least 60 percent of solid picture values before the studio okays the buy. As Siegel remarked, 'The amount of money thrown away by the industry for stories that are never produced would surprise you.' So, in hiring players and writers on this common-sense basis and only purchasing meaty stories that they are set to produce Republic starts on every picture with a reduced initial overhead that makes it possible to turn out the production at a reasonable cost.

"This economy and operation extends to every operation of actual production. There are no expensive location trips to distant points if there is a spot within a reasonable distance of the studio that will serve the purpose. To the average person in the audience a background of Arizona scenery doesn't look any different than one that is shot in the hills around Hollywood. Because of this economy and efficiency in operation, the Republic people claim that they can put more on the screen for a dollar than can any other Hollywood studio. Therefore, they give the exhibitor more for his dollar, they say.

"Where there has been a general tendency to retrench in production during the past year Republic has pursued a policy of expansion in its studio. In the past year and a half over $1 million has been spent in enlarging the studio. Right now, they are rounding out the buildings with a new mill structure for producing sets, and what is known as a 'scene dock' for storing sets.

"Steady progress has been made in developing Republic players. Gene Autry tops the list as the biggest and steadiest money-getter at the box office. John Wayne was making small westerns when this studio took him over he and he is now developing into an important box office draw. Also, Roy Rogers, now conceded to be one of the top western stars, is building up an impressive following. Judy Canova has hit star rank. Among the younger players are Mary Lee, Lois Ranson, Leni Lynn, Ray Middleton, Lynn Merrick. All of these comers are showing promise.

"In the past four years due to Siegel's management as a moving factor, Republic claims that it has established itself as the leading producer of westerns and serials. The latter comprise 'Dick Tracy,' 'Lone Ranger,' 'Zorro,' 'Captain Marvel,' and 'Jungle Girl.' The westerns are the Autrys, Roy Rogers, The Three Mesquiteers, Don 'Red' Berry.

"Right now, Siegel sees the public trend toward musicals and comedies. Under the war stress, this type of escapist entertainment he thinks will continue to be in demand so that the exhibitor should bear this in mind in his bookings. Republic is planning to put heavy stress on these types of productions for the next quarter period.

"This brings us to a consideration of the policy that was inaugurated by Republic two years ago with their regional sales meetings held quarterly. It has been so successful that the other producers are falling in line and putting less importance, if any at all, on the outmoded annual sales gatherings. Siegel, Yates and Granger have grasped completely the truth that the events are moving so fast in revolutionary war upheavals that it is foolish to try and plan picture production more than a few months ahead. They have divided the selling year into four 13-week periods. Each quarter they gather together the branch managers and the salesman in the meeting for free and frank discussion. Public demands and preferences as the exhibitor sense senses them are noted by the sales force and brought up for discussion. This Republic organization feels that the exhibitors know better than anybody what the public really wants. It is up to them to pass their observations along to these salesmen. Here is one producing outfit that is making a sensible effort to catch the public trends and translate them into the type of entertainment desired. But the main purpose of the quarterly meetings is to furnish a direct check up on what is going over in pictures and what is falling down. This applies to story treatment, players, direction and production values. Yates personally passes the gist of all this along to his studio head Siegel and so the studio tries to function as close to public demand as possible. Common sense is the word for it all. Hollywood can use it."

In another such column, Harrower lauded the campaign with Fawcett to sell the Captain Marvel serial to kids and explained that studio owner Herbert Yates believed in putting smaller ads every week in the trades than the major studios, but Harrower insisted that Republic actually runs more ads than any other studio.

Tyler's first appearance at Republic was in a Three Mesquiteers film, "The Night Riders" playing a villain. Just a few years later he would be one of the series' stars.

The Three Mesquiteers series was very successful for Republic with 51 films made between 1936 to 1943. The films were based on a series of novels by William Colt MacDonald featuring three cowboy pals. One of the books, "Law of the Forty-Fives," was made into a movie of the same name in 1935 with Guinn "Big Boy" Williams and Al St. John. "Powdersmoke Range," also a 1935 production, brought back Willams and teamed him with Hoot Gibson and Harry Carey as the three friends.

As noted in a previous chapter, that film was a hit for RKO, but Republic secured the rights for a series in 1936.

The first film featured Robert Livington as Stoney, Ray "Crash" Corrigan as Tucson and comic actor Syd Saylor as Lullaby. The films center around both the affection the three friends have for one another while also presenting alpha male tension between Stoney and Tucson, especially when it came to romantic interest. The Mesquiteers are three cowboys almost constantly looking for work.

The second film dropped Saylor and replaced with Max Terhune, a comic and ventriloquist who carried his dummy Elmer on the range with him. As unlikely as it reads on paper, somehow it worked.

That line-up maintained until 1938 – in 1937 Ralph Byrd replaced an injured Livingston for one film – when Livingston left and was replaced by John Wayne. Terhune and Wayne stayed until 1939 – that year Wayne's performance in "Stagecoach" brought him to A film roles – and Livingston came back to the role he originated until 1941.

Republic frequently re-released some of its films and later would make more money off of Wayne's Three Mesquiteers entries when he was a big star. Terhune was replaced by screen veteran Raymond Hatton. Short in stature but huge in talent, Hatton could play drama, action and comedy with equal skill in his very long career.

The next shift in cast teamed Livingston and Hatton with Duncan Renaldo, the actor who would be best known as the Cisco Kid in both films and a TV series.

In 1940, Livingston came back and had two new castmates, cowboy vet Bob Steele and comic Rufe Davis.

In 1941, Livingston left the role for good and was replaced by Tyler. Showman's Trade review June 21, 1941, noted "Bob Livingston, one of the original Three Mesquiteers at Republic, ended a five-year contract and checked off the lot. The studio is looking for a replacement to fill out the trio again with Bob Steele and Rufe Davis for the next in the series, 'Empty Saddles,' due to ride July 7 with Lou Gray as an associate producer."

Motion Picture Daily reported Tyler has replaced Livingston June 22, 1941. Tyler's and Steele's careers had many intersections. Both started at FBO and both labored in the low budget independent western field in the 1930s. Both were in "Powdersmoke Range," Both wound up at Republic and both clearly had an interest to act outside of westerns. Steele came to the attention of critics for his portrayal of "Curley" in the acclaimed 1939 version of "Of Mice and Men."

After this series ended Both Tyler and Steele wound up acting together in several more films.

In 1942, Davis was replaced by singer and song writer Jimmie Dodd. Dodd had been looking for a break in films for several years and this role gave him the most exposure until Walt Disney hired him in the 1950s to host "The Mickey Mouse Club."

The last film in the series, "Riders of the Rio Grande" was released in 1943 and the series was discontinued.

To give you an idea of the budget, eight Three Mesquiteers westerns were budgeted at $600,000 according to a story in Boxoffice, March 1, 1941. To put that into perspective, the same article noted the Roy Rogers westerns were at $100,000 each and the standard Gene Autry was at $175,000. The two "Premiere" Autry westerns were at $500,000 each.

Reading reviews in trade papers, the series, despite its many cast changes,

Tyler and his original co-stars when he joined the Three Mesquiteers series. (author's collection)

received solid reviews over its long run. It was also on the top ten list of most popular western series assembled by several trade publications. Showman's Trade Review noted in its Dec 26, 1942, edition, "The Three Mesquiteers, Bob Steele, Tom Tyler and Jimmy Dodd, form a company that has been outstanding among the western series leaders for years. The present members of the group have not been occupying their Mesquiteer roles from the start of the series, but all three have done valiant work maintaining the high standards of the pictures."

Despite the acclaim, the series' days were numbered in 1943. Film Bulletin reported on March 6, 1943, that Jimmie Dodd and Bob Steele had their "options lifted" for more films. Either that meant new cast members or Republic was ending the series.

The studio offered a reason for the series to end in a May 18, 1943, story in Variety, "Republic is working up a new series to take the place of The Three Mesquiteers torn apart by the ravages of war. Bob Steele and Jimmy Dodd are army bound leaving only Tom Tyler, who is over the age limit. Lou Gray, producer of the series, is testing cowboy actors to round up a new outfit not likely to be called for military service. Meanwhile, the Mesquiteers have been shelved, although the studio is clinging to the title rights for future production."

This is simply not correct. According to B-western.com, "After concluding the 1942-43 Mesquiteers releases, Republic decided that the trio had run out of gas and concentrated their efforts on the existing cowboy series of Roy Rogers, Don Barry, Wild Bill Elliott ... and a new star they were grooming named Eddie Dew. Thus, Republic did not exercise the contract renewal options on Tyler and Steele."

According to author Bob Nareau and his book, "The 'Real' Bob Steele and a Man Called 'Brad'," the idea that Steele served in the Army was a fabrication by author Leo A. Miller. He didn't go into the army, but instead he joined Monogram and co-starred with Ken Maynard and Hoot Gibson in their series. Steele would maintain lead status in westerns for several more years and then started accepting character parts in both westerns and non-westerns.
In World War II, Dodd toured the Aleutians and the China-Burma-India area for the USO with his wife Ruth Carrell Dodd as a musical act for the troops. Again, as far as I can tell, he never served in the military either.

Remember, at this time Republic was without its best money-making star, Gene Autry. Autry had enlisted and was a pilot in the Army Air Corps. Without Autry, the studio was making decisions how to replace him during the duration. I think Republic management believed the long-running series needed to be replaced in order to support efforts to build up Roy Rogers in the absence of Autry and establish Bill Elliott as a Republic star, having been closely identified as a Columbia player.

Tyler's time at Republic, though, is best remembered for his role as Captain Marvel in "Adventures of Captain Marvel," perhaps due in part to the fact the serial has been far more available on home video – and to modern audiences – than the Three Mesquiteer films. This is a shame as the Three Mesquiteers films are well made westerns that deserve to be seen. It is also a shame the entire series cannot be easily seen.

The Night Riders
  Directed by George Sherman
  Can be seen on YouTube
  Tyler's second appearance with John Wayne

At this point, the Three Mesquiteers line-up included John Wayne, who replaced Robert Livingston in the role of Stoney Brooke, Ray Corrigan and Max Terhune.

This film was inspired by the true story of James Reavis, a con man who actually convinced people through forged documents that he was the rightful owner of 18,600 acres of Arizona in the mid-1800s. It took years for state and government officials to prove the deceit with Reavis going to prison in 1895.

Director Samuel Fuller made his version of the story – "The Baron of Arizona" – in 1950 so this adaptation was the first for the story.

Sherman keeps the story moving at a fast clip with the Mesquiteers becoming night time vigilantes fighting against the tyranny of the con man who has established himself as the owner of the region.

Tyler is one of his trusted enforcers, exacting tax money from ranchers and farmers as well as seizing their property.

It's a superior B western, as are most of the Mesquiteers films.

Showman's Trade Review, April 3, 1939, noted, "George Douglas, a crooked gambler, is thrown from the Sacramento river boat after being caught cheating at cards. The Mesquiteers are on the boat. Later, Douglas finds refuge with Wills, former engraver of the US mint. Walter Wills has prepared a spurless land grant, supposedly issued by King Philip of Spain to Don Luis Serrano in 1744. It gives de Serrano sole ownership to 13 million acres of fictitious western land. Douglas is induced to assume the role of de Serrano, present the grant to the government and claim the land. He does this, and wanting to control, oppresses the people. The Mesquiteers are driven from their ranch but become masked riders to help the cause of the ranchers. They worked themselves in with Douglas, discover he is an impostor and after a series of anti-climaxes compel him along with Wills to sign a confession. The Mesquiteers have scored again. This trio seems to get the cream of western stories and their latest has been suspensefully and excitingly whipped up. Even Aunt Agatha, who has a positive aversion for outdoor thrillers, will find herself all wrapped up in the situations in this film as securely as little Willy. Wayne, Corrigan, and Terhune are brave, reckless and carefree during their most dangerous moments as any heroes of fiction and they make their performances believable. George Douglas is a suave villain and Doreen McKay and Ruth Rogers furnish ample femininity to the proceedings. Of course, there may be a flower too but whoever dares to make issue of the fact that time marches backwards according to the dates on the newspapers and the note is an old bone picker. If your program requires thrills, action and excitement in a picture with a plot away from the usual western formula, then this should fit the requirements perfectly."

Adventures of Captain Marvel
Directed by William Witney and John English
Can be seen on Tubi, YouTube, Internet Archives and on Blu-ray
Considered by many as the best serial ever made, "Adventures of Captain Marvel" may not be a very good adaptation of the source material in some ways but is indeed worthy of all the accolades it has received since its release. Republic's serial was the first live-action adaptation of a comic book hero, coming along at about the same time as the Fleischer Studio's adaptation of Superman. How it came to Republic is fascinating and it initially had to do with how Republic had handled its first big adaptation of a pop culture phenomenon, the radio show "The Lone Ranger."

As I recounted in my second book about the Max Fleischer animation studios, ('Made of Pen and Ink: The Florida Years"), Republic altered the origin story of the Lone Ranger into a guessing game for audiences and had the character working with other Texas Rangers. The alterations in the story treatment caused friction between the studio and the owner of the Lone Ranger. George Trendle, who owned The Lone Ranger, went to Universal for the serial adaptation of his Green Hornet character to ensure a more authentic adaptation.

Reported in Film Daily April 29, 1940, "Although formal contract had not been signed between Republic Pictures and Superman Inc. calling for the production by the former of a 13-chapter serial based on the comic strip character, 'Superman,' it was learned at the weekend that the deal has been agreed upon in principle.

"Republic, reportedly in competition with Universal and Columbia for the screen rights, will make the Superman serial as part of its 1940-41 lineup. An unusual contractual clause is reported to reserve to Superman, Inc., the right to cancel if, after the release of the first series, it is found that the serial detracts from the popularity of the Superman radio program or the Superman comic strip appearing in Action Comics Monthly and via syndicates.

"Deal was engineered by Paul Kohner, coast agent, and is said to involve one of the highest prices for a comic strip's film rights. A representative of Superman, Inc., is to have the right to be present on the Republic lot and to watch script and production."

Kohner is an important name in cinema. In the silent era, he worked at Universal and was a producer on "The Hunchback of Notre Dame," among others. He founded his agency in 1938 and represented stars such as Ingrid Bergman, Maurice Chevalier, Greta Garbo and directors including Billy Wilder and John Huston. It speaks to the dollar potential of the red-hot character that a powerhouse Hollywood agent would become involved in the deal.

Variety, May 1, 1940, also noted that Superman would be a Republic serial in 15 chapters.

"Hollywood" fan magazine reported in 1940 that Republic was interested in actor Victor McLaglen's son Andrew for the role of Superman. He was 19 years old. After World War II, he started working at Republic in various capacities eventually becoming a director, often working with his father's friend John Wayne.

Motion Picture Herald, June 1, 1940, said that Republic announced its 1940-1941 schedule and noted that "Superman" had its "Super Serial" designation, meaning it would be a 15-episode serial.

But then something happened. Motion Picture Daily Aug. 16, 1940, noted under "Late News Flashes from the Coast" that "Republic today shelved its 'Superman' serial because of restrictions imposed by the copyright owners. 'Dr. Satan' in 15 episodes will be substituted."

Let's go back to one key phrase in the initial announcement story – "A representative of Superman, Inc., is to have the right to be present on the Republic lot and to watch script and production."

The book "Men of Tomorrow: Geeks, Gangsters and the Birth of the Comic Book" by Gerard Jones expertly recounts how Superman came about, but also how the owners of National Periodicals understood how to capitalize on its star property. It can be assumed the production of a live-action version of the character had to be in line with all of the character's origin story and personality. It's not surprising to learn that National Periodicals would have wanted to protect Superman.

In its Sept. 7, 1940, edition The Motion Picture Herald reported that Paramount "had completed negotiations with Harry Donenfeld, president of Superman, Inc., for the production of a series of short subject cartoons which would be produced by the Fleischer Studios, Russell Holman, head of the short subject department, said this week."

Less than a month the deal with Republic failed and Paramount was able to obtain the rights to the comic book hero.

The next month (Oct. 11, 1940) The Motion Picture Herald discussed how Hollywood was raiding radio programs and stars for movies. The story noted Superman and reported, "Paramount is paying a royalty fee of $7,500 to $10,000 a month" for the character.

The story continued, "Manny Reiner, sales manager for shorts for Paramount, estimates that the entire production cost for the 12 shorts will be more than $850,000, which includes the cost of advertising, promotion and exploitation. Thirteen comic book magazines will carry a Paramount ad announcing the release of the short at neighborhood theatres and other promotional items include a national 'Super Boy and Super Girl' contest held through the combined tie-in of radio programs, newspaper strips and motion picture theatres."

Generally, there has been reporting that the Superman shorts were budgeted at about four times the cost of a typical Fleischer black and white short. According to Richard Fleischer, the budget proposed by his father and his uncle was $100,000 per cartoon. This tactic was an effort to avoid doing the series.

Let's put this into some perspective. At Republic Pictures a full-length western in its lowest budget class, called "Jubilee," could cost as much as $50,000, according to the essay by Charles Flynn and Todd McCarthy in the essential book "King of the Bs."

In other words, a 70-80-minute live action film could cost less than a single seven-minute Superman cartoon.

The Fleischers, again according to Richard, agreed to do the series because of their financial obligations to Paramount. Paramount execs okayed the budget.

The Film Daily on Jan. 15, 1941, reported, "Shift of plans to make the series pictures, 'The Adventures of Superman,' in Technicolor instead of the originally planned black and white, has necessitated the postponement of the production's release until the spring, it was learned yesterday from sources close to the situation. Originally, the release was announced for December or the present month.

"The film is currently before the color cameras at the Fleischer Studios in

Miami, Fla., with the staff there concentrating on the initial 'chapter' of which there will be 12 when the entire series of completed.

"Production is based on the comic strip character, 'Superman,' and the first chapter will deal with his advent on Earth from the fictitious planet, Krypton."

Technicolor added greatly to the budget of the films but also added something exhibitors were almost demanding: cartoons in color.

There was growing excitement for the new series as "Phil M. Daly" noted in his column in the Film Daily on May 1, 1941. "Particularly conservative [in a Paramount sales document] was the paragraph about the 12 Superman cartoons in Technicolor. The first of which is completed (all but the scoring) in the Fleischer Studios. These reels will have a huge pre-sold audience value resulting from the sensationally popular comic strip. Here's a celluloid article for Paramount to shout about and outlets to get excited about."

A tease about the new cartoons was in the May 3, 1941, edition of The Showman's Trade Review. Dave Fleischer supposedly sent a memo reading, "After the credit titles dissolve to long shot of the universe, have planets moving about in their orbits and stars twinkling."

The fight between Republic and National Periodicals/Superman, Inc. continued, though.

"Suit for $50,000 damages was filed yesterday in the New York Supreme Court by Republic Productions, Inc., against Detective & Superman, Inc., owner of the comic strip 'Superman.' Republic claims that in April 1940, it made a contract with the defendant which gave it the right to make a film serial based on the 'Superman' cartoon. Subsequently, according to the complaint, the defendant breached the contract and gave the film rights to Fleischer Studios (Film Daily, June 27, 1941)."

The interesting part of this terse report is the fact that Paramount's involvement in securing the rights to Superman was not included in this story nor was any mention of the clause that insured Superman Inc. the right to okay the script.

National Periodicals moved in another direction to try to protect its dominance in the superhero world in light of Republic turning to Fawcett Publications and securing the rights to Captain Marvel for a serial. Motion Picture Daily, Sept. 10, 1941, reported that Republic and Fawcett Publications were named defendants yesterday in a copyright infringement suit filed by Superman, Inc., and Detective Comics, Inc. "The plaintiffs as copyright holder of the action comic strip 'Superman' charges the defendants with creating a character 'Captain Marvel' which is allegedly a copy of the plaintiff's character, Superman."

Tyler as Captain Marvel. (author's collection)

National Periodicals were not about to stop their efforts to maintain the status of its star character, especially in light that Republic turned to Fawcett for its Captain Marvel property.

Boxoffice announced that Republic had put the serial on its production schedule in its Dec. 14, 1940, edition.

Republic started on Dec. 23, 1940, and released the serial on March 28, 1941, according to Republic historian Jack Mathis. Even with a pending lawsuit, Republic forged ahead. It beat the first Superman cartoon to the screen and became the first comic book superhero adaptation in the movies.

The Superman shorts became the second superhero on the big screen. Both productions – the serial and the cartoon series – were groundbreaking This fight about rights to produce a serial also resulted in a lengthy lawsuit that alleged that Captain Marvel was a rip-off of the Man of Steel. That lawsuit was not settled until 1953 when Fawcett decided to drop its line of comic books.

One should realize that according to comic book historians, the Captain Marvel character sold more book than Superman during the 1940s.

As Mathis noted "Adventures of Captain Marvel" was budgeted at $135,553, although the final negative cost was $145,588 (a $10,035, or 7.4%, overspend). It was filmed between Dec. 23, 1940, and Jan.30, 1941, under the working title "Captain Marvel."

The story is an origin story with Billy Batson as the radio operator for an archaeological expedition in Siam – Thailand – in search of relics from the Scorpion Dynasty. Billy was played by child star Frank Coghlan Jr. who started his career in the silents and worked for Cecil B. DeMille. This would be his last acting assignment for years as he would join the Navy afterwards and had a lengthy career in the service before retiring and returning to acting. Billy refuses to enter a sealed room in the tomb they discover. The scientists that enter find themselves trapped and Billy is introduced to the aged wizard Shazam, who explains he is a worthy candidate for his powers that come by simply saying his name.

Billy says, "Shazam!" and in a cloud of smoke becomes Captain Marvel. Marvel must save the world from the effects of the artifact that the scientist found: a set of lenses held in a scorpion statue. Arranged in one way, the lenses can turn anything into gold. Arranged another and it becomes a death ray, capable of melting stone.

The Captain at the entrance of the inner tomb. (author's collection)

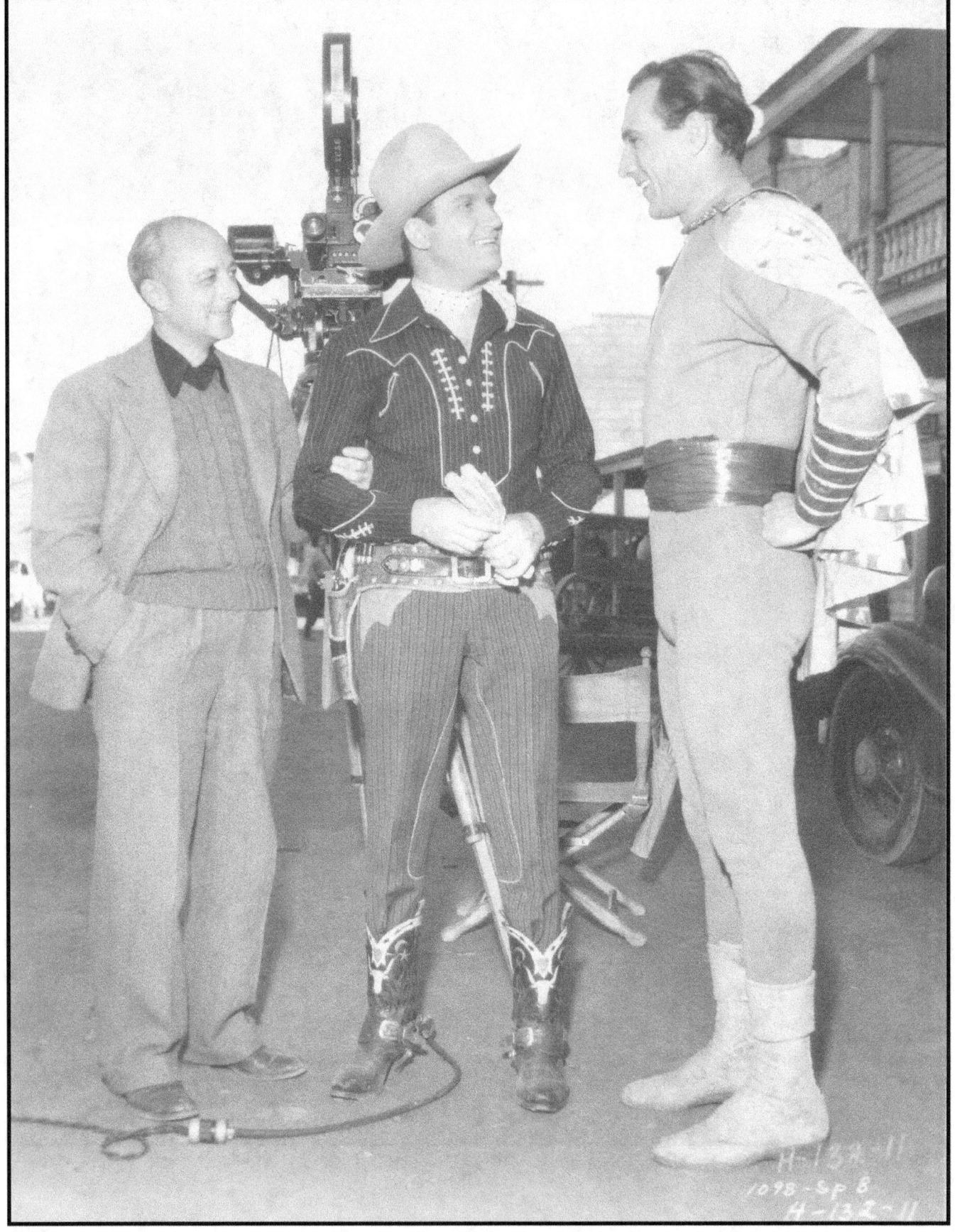
Tyler greets Gene Autry and director Lew Landers on the Republic lot. (author's collection)

One of the members of the expedition is intent on having the artifact for himself and under a shroud become The Scorpion, the villain of the serial. The story's action takes place in the United States and Siam, with the conclusion essentially where the story began.

The serial has a solid cast. William "Billy" Benedict played "Whitey," a friend and associate of Billy's. Louise Currie as the expedition's secretary. B-film regulars Keene Duncan, John Davidson and Robert Strange are also in the cast. Since the identity of the villain is a secret, Gerald Mohr's ominous voice was used to keep audiences guessing.

As other people have written, the fact that Captain Marvel was as invulnerable as Superman posed some writing challenges. How do you create suspense and tension with this sort of hero? Of course, the major difference between the two characters is that Billy is just a young man and he could easily be put into stressful situations. Knock him out or put a gag on him and you've stopped Captain Marvel. There are moments in the serial where Captain Marvel is stunned, such as by electricity.

Smartly, we see that Billy/Captain Marvel is discovering his powers, Tyler gives us expressions of joy and amazement.

The writers, though, stepped up to the challenge and while there are some moments of serial "logic," this is an exciting well written screenplay. One of those moments was the first appearance of the Scorpion. If none of the scientists knew about the artifact, why did he pack his custom-made Scorpion outfit for his trip?

Another issue that fans have noticed is the radical re-writing of the Captain Marvel character. The Marvel comic book character was a gentle sort of hero that lived in a world where there was a genius caterpillar who was a supervillain as well as a talking tiger. There was an element of whimsy that was perfectly integrated into adventure stories.

Kids of the early Forties probably had no clue that "Siam" was not a mountainous region with a volcano and did not have native people who were dressed as some sort of Arab. However, that location matched some Republic stock footage.

Tyler's Marvel, as written, was simply a ruthless superhero who dropped henchmen to their death from buildings, tossed an engine block at another henchman and shot fleeing natives in the back with a machine gun. The moment Marvel has a bad guy in his grip and says, "Talk or I'll…" every kid in the audience knew by that point there was no bluffing with this hero.

This guy simply did not mess around. When Phil Proctor and Peter Bergman

The formidable bad guys with the dangerous scorpion statue. (author's collection)

of the famed comedy troupe The Firesign Theater made their comedy "J Men Forever," they constructed a satirical new story out of Republic serial footage with new dialogue. Captain Marvel was now known as "The Caped Madman" for his violence.

Tyler's performance is striking. He doesn't have a lot of dialogue but that fits with the character. His silent film training meant he could express himself visually. His biggest chunk of dialogue comes at the end of the film and he does very well with it.

The team of William Witney and John English directed the serial and Witney wrote about the experience in his essential book, "In a Door, into a Fight, Out of a Door, into a Chase." Witney details his rise from an editor at Republic to being a director and figuring out, after watching musical director Busby Berkley direct dance sequences, how to better convey action sequences. In terms of action films, he was a seminal figure.

Witney revealed that Tyler was being considered for the role of Superman in the Republic serial and the studio carried over the casting to "Captain Marvel."

He wrote, "Tom Tyler fit the part to a 'T.' If I had to cast the part again, I'd look for his clone."

In the mid-1980s, I had the pleasure of interviewing both Coghlan and Benedict about their careers in film. Naturally I had to ask them about the serial.

I asked, "Although you were very busy during the 1930s, you were probably best known for your role as Billy Batson in the 1940 serial 'Adventures of Captain Marvel." How did that role come about?

"I believe I was handpicked for it as I was one of the best-known young actors available at the time. I kind of looked like the cartoon character Billy Batson. I don't recall competing with a whole bunch of other actors for the part. I think I was pre-selected for it. At the time it just seemed to be another job, but it has now become the classic of the action serials and I guess I'm best remembered for that part even though I made others that I thought were more inducing of stardom than that.

A photo from the sequence shot at the dam with Tyler walking towards the bad guys who are shooting at him. (author's collection)

A lobby card showing Marvel rescuing heroine Louise Curry. (author's collection)

"Tom Tyler and I costarred in it you might say. When I go to conventions it's all Captain Marvel they all seem to remember."

I then asked, "I have to ask you about Tom Tyler. I know though you didn't have much contact with him in the production because you were playing the same person."

"Well, with the exception of when I said 'Shazam' and the puff of smoke would go up Tom would have to step into the same footsteps and repeat the word 'Shazam 'and he was there.

"He would then go about dispensing the villains and I could go off and read but in many cases report to the second unit and continue working on other scenes but yes Tom and I were never in this scene together with the exception of the dissolve of the Shazam."

"Did you get to know him at all?" I asked.

"Tom had been a friend of my family for years. It just so happened that my family, my mother and father, were great friends of another couple and Tom was their best friend. My parents and Tom used to go out to dinners and parties together. I wasn't as buddy-buddy with him as my parents were became he was older. Yes, I had known Tom through the years, admired him. He was an Olympic weightlifter, a very powerful man but with it all he was a modest, mild-mannered gentleman. Of course, we spent 12 weeks on a picture together. We were very friendly. Tom was a good actor. His westerns seemed to be the best known but he played some good important parts."

Benedict has a huge list of credits. He is best known perhaps for his long running involvement in the East Side Kids series at Monogram, later to be followed by the Bowery Boy series.

I asked him, "How did you find yourself at Republic Pictures doing that serial?

"Someone asked for me on that particular show, but the deal was made through an agent. We went to work, Frank doing Billy Batson and I doing Whitey and what fun we had! Believe me! It has become a classic in its own right.

"Those were days we would leave Republic studios at about 5:00 in the morning and take the stretch big sedans – they actually stretched them out – and we would wind our way to Iverson's Ranch, which had been used location-wise for a long time and we would go about our business chasing down whatever we were chasing at the time.

"We put in long hours but we had a lot of fun."

I then asked, "What was the difference between working at Monogram and Republic?"

"At that time, they were pretty much on the same par because they made pictures for a price. In other words, their budgets were low on the totem pole. They were comparable I think in the method they went into making their motion pictures. The big difference between them and larger studios was the amount of money they had to spend and the length of time of the shooting schedule."

My next question was "I know many of your scenes in the Captain Marvel serial were with Frank Coghlan. Did you get to know the star of the film Tom Tyler?

"Oh yes, nice man, quiet, a hard-working individual he took his work very seriously and did a good job, did an excellent job."

A huge part of the success of the film was how Witney and English collaborated with studio's famed special effects team, Theodore and Howard Lydecker, in creating the flying effects. The Lydecker brothers were seen in the film industry as among the elite in special effect involving miniatures and the

Republic serials and action movies were filled with their very effective work. The flying scenes took clever editing to integrate several different elements. There was a flying dummy; the talent of stuntman supreme David Sharpe and Tyler photographed in front of a rear projection screen.

In the serial, you would cut from Tyler to Sharpe doubling him who would leap into the air. There would be a cut to the dummy flying, followed by Tyler seen in front of a rear projection screen flying through clouds. From that shot would be another of Sharpe landing, then a cut back to Tyler. The illusion remains impressive in this era of CGI.

In an interview that was published in Big Reel magazine Sharpe said, "The one who should be really praised is Tom Tyler. He spent many hours strung up in that harness and rigging, while being photographed in front of a process screen, and the pain must have been almost unbearable. He never let out a peep. What a pro."

This Mexican lobby card shows David Sharpe in action as Captain Marvel. (author's collection)

According to the late film historian Val Warren – author of the book, "Lost Lands, Mythical Kingdoms and Unknown Worlds" – Sharpe told him the only time he knew Tyler ever expressed any worries about a stunt was in the sequences in which Captain Marvel is shot at and you could see the "bullets" hitting his chest. Apparently, Tyler was concerned the marksmen would miss his chest and hit his face. I can't say that I blame him!

Jack Mathis explained the origins of the flying dummy came from the effects developed for the flying bat men as seen in the serial "Darkest Africa" (1936). In "Republic Confidential, Volume One," Mathis said, "Redressed from a paper mâché forebear fashioned a year earlier for Republic's ill-fated 'Superman' serial project, the Captain Marvel dummy weighed 15 lbs. and rolled it along a 1/8-inch diameter steel wires so it could soar greater distances than its ancestral bat men from the Republic serial 'Darkest Africa.' The superhero's tight-fitting costume also proved a boon in contending with wind

Louise Curry had very pleasant memories of working on the serial. (author's collection)

resistance over these longer runs, since most of the outfit except for the lightweight jersey and sheer China silk cape was just painted on.

"As with miniature airplanes, gravity was the prime moving force. Ascents were variously achieved by tilting the camera at an opposing angle while the dummy slid downward head first, lashing down the cape and letting it glide backward while the camera was cranked in reverse, or towing it upward by the head on 1/3 wire period to prevent the relatively fragile figure from being damaged at its touchdown point, technicians stood at the ready with a large blanket to encapture it at the end of each flight.

"Unlike most miniatures, which were filmed in post-production on the lot, the seven-foot Captain Marvel dummy accompanied the first unit crew to such exterior locations as Lake Sherwood, downtown Los Angeles, and the Iverson ranch, to heightened realism by integrating its feats with the actors. The fantasy of Captain Marvel floating silently through the air was belied in actuality by a high-pitched whining sound emanating from the four ankle and shoulder wheels as they spun against the twin cables. During one instance at Iverson's the cables were rigged up for a flyby above a tree where two movie horses were tethered. As the dummy sang by one of the horses pricked up its ears, then resumed grazing momentarily before doing a double take at the figure flying overhead. Now thoroughly spooked the unnerved horse bucked reared and broke its bridle requiring the immediate pursuit of wranglers."
This on-location integration of the dummy flying remains impressive to this day. In one chapter the dummy is "flying" above a highway following a truck. It looks amazingly real.

What did the trades think of the new serial?
Motion Picture Herald March 8, 1941, "Based on the Whiz comics magazine cartoon Adventures of Captain Marvel is a serial of the land of fantasy specially designed and produced for juvenile patronage. Starring Tom Tyler as Captain Marvel, who by special power is invincible and able to overcome all dangers and obstacles, the story concerns the expedition to a remote section of Siam seeking knowledge of an ancient Scorpion dynasty. The expedition uncovers a complicated series of lenses which, properly focused, turns any solid object to gold. The lenses are divided among members of the party so that no one of them will have sole possession. A criminal gang sets out to steal the lenses. In the 12th and final chapter, the leader of the gang is uncovered and revealed as one of the expeditionary party. Supporting Tom Tyler are Frank Coghlan, Junior William Benedict, Louise Curry, Robert Strange and Harry Worth. The serial will receive additional publicity and exploitation from Whiz

comics in full page advertisements in the April, May and June issues of the magazine published by Fawcett Publications. The first chapter runs 31 minutes with succeeding episodes two reels each."

Motion Picture Daily, March 4, 1941, "A 12-episode serial based on the character currently appearing in 'Whiz Comic Magazine,' the 'Adventures of Captain Marvel' should prove popular with devotees of the serial adventure story. In addition to the customary excitement attendant unmasked figures and machines for making gold the superman character is still enough of a novelty to add an extra touch.

"When young Billy Batson, (Frank Coghlan Jr.) a member of an expedition into Siam, refuses to violate the tombs of an ancient Scorpion Dynasty, he is rewarded by being given the power to transform himself into Captain Marvel, a Superman, played by Tom Tyler. The hero switches from Coughlan to Tyler as the occasion demands. Excellent effects are obtained for scenes showing Tyler flying through the air. The expedition finds a machine for making gold, but its parts are divided among members of the party. A masked figure attempts to steal the parts."

Showman's Trade Review, March 8, 1941, "Great juvenile fare! What a field day for the kiddies this will be! They'll revel in the fantastic adventures of its superhuman hero and it's likely that many adults will find themselves just as eagerly interested. No one has anything on Captain Marvel. He flies through the air with the greatest of ease (and without the trapeze) picks up men and machine guns throws them around as though he was scattering seed, pushes aside mighty barriers as though they were stacks of kiddies' toy blocks. Few children in their wildest imagination have dreamed of such situations as one sees in this film, for which the combined conjuring's of five scripters were required. If ever a serial could keep them coming back week after week, this must be it. There are many technical details which have been smoothly handled, so that every trick seems to be genuine. William Whitney and John English directed."

And did theater managers like it?

"What the Picture Did for Me, Motion Picture Herald Sept. 13, 1941, 'Adventures of Captain Marvel' – one of the best serials I've played in years. Sammy Jackson, Jackson Theatre, Flomaton, AL.

"Tom Tyler– the best serial we have played in several years all of our young cowboys put up their guns and started wearing capes some of them tried to fly by jumping out of windows – Raymond Paul, Sea Breeze Theater Beaufort, NC."

"What the Picture Did for Me, Motion Picture Herald July 26, 1941, 'We started this serial with an advanced trailer for the week previous and we also had Gene Autry in 'Riding on a Rainbow,' Republic, to start this chapter, and before we knew it we had a packed house. So, between this chapter play and the Gene Autry picture, let each one select the credit they think is due them. As the weather got warm, attendance dropped off, but I believe it held some children followers even during some of the hot Sundays. This serial is well done and followers of the Superman and Captain Marvel cartoons should find this much to their liking. Others may find this on the impossible/ couldn't happen kind. But, on the whole, I am satisfied to have run it and would gladly do so if I had to do it over again. J. E. Stocker, Myrtle Theatre, Detroit, MI.'

A flyer from a theater in Springfield OH, shows the big push they made with "Adventures of Captain Marvel." The show included the first chapter of the serial, plus a cartoon, a two-reel comedy and two feature films. Each child received a Pepsi, a candy bar and the chance to win prizes. All of this for just one thin dime! (author's collection)

Part of the success of the serial was due to the huge collaboration between Republic, theater owners, Fawcett Publishing and local news distributors. The trade papers were filled with examples of theater owners planning with Fawcett and local magazine distributors to give their young audiences copies of the comic book. Many theaters gave out pictures of the serial hero as well.

Part of this campaign was noted in Boxoffice, March 29, 1941, "In line with tie in arrangements made between Republic and Fawcett, publisher of Whiz comics, whose character Captain Marvel, Republic adapted to the screen in its current serial, 'Adventures of Captain Marvel,' Fawcett field men worked with Irving Hillman, manager of the Capital in Danbury CT, on his campaign. "Special banners were placed on news company trucks. One sheet posters and window carts were distributed to various stores and new stands throughout the city. A large new store devoted window to a display.

"On the day prior to the opening Whiz comic books were given were given every boy and girl attending the matinee. A sticker on the cover of each book told the children that Captain Marvel would be seen in the serial at the theater. On the opening day itself 7 by 10-inch color photos of Captain Marvel were given to all attending the matinee.

"Fawcett field men throughout the country are working with theatres in connection with the showing of the serial and Fawcett has announced special cash prizes to the field and distributors for the best promotion campaign."

The serial was re-released to theaters in 1953 with the deceiving title, "The Return of Captain Marvel." In 1966, the serial was re-released again to theaters at the height of the nostalgia/camp craze. It was presented in one sitting, not unlike Columbia's re-release of the 1943 Batman serial at about the same time.

There were several 8mm cut-down reels of the serial sold for home viewing. That's how I first saw parts of this accomplished production.

The aforementioned "J Men Forever," was released in 1979. Because the

The Scorpion thinks he is going to learn the secret of Billy Batson turning into Captain Marvel, but he has a surprise coming! (author's collection)

Captain Marvel throws the scorpion device into the lava of a volcano and Billy loses his powers. Although not canon for the comic books, none-the-less it was a satisfying ending to one of the best serials ever made. (author's collection)

The Spanish language trade paper Cine-mundial (April 1942) had an article about Republic's serials including Captain Marvel.

film was a cannabis comedy, there was actually a tie-in with a rolling paper company!

Outlaws of Cherokee Trail
Directed by Les Orlebeck
On DVD from VCI

The first film of Tyler's run with the Three Mesquiteers (which in this film were Texas Rangers). They are chasing bandits who are holed up outside of their jurisdiction in the Cherokee Strip, a remarkably durable western trope.

They dress as Native Americans at one point to get into the native territory. This is Davis's big comedy moment as he plays poker with native people. An obvious little person is cast as a native baby(!) who is sending signals to the chief during the game about Davis's hand. It's not particularly funny, I'm afraid. It only slows the film down.

I should mention that throughout this series villainy of the rough and tumble kind was often supplied by Republic contract player Roy Barcroft. Whether in a western or a serial, Barcroft could be counted on to be the meanest guy in a

Here is the cast of "Outlaws of Cherokee Trail." (author's collection)

production and western fans loved him for it.

Also, this is the first of many appearances in the series of actress Lois Collier, who often played the female lead. Collier would later go from her roles at Republic to a contract at Universal where she was cast in other B films and serials. She also appeared with the Marx Brothers in "A Night in Casablanca." She ended her career doing television work and retired from acting in the late 1950s.

Watch out for Iron Eyes Cody in a minor role. The actor had a very long career portraying native people, although it was revealed before his death in 1996 that he was actually a second-generation Italian American named Espera Oscar de Corti.

The concluding rescue scene is a wild fight in a bar complete with a very upset horse!

Film Daily, Sept. 19, 1941, "A slam bang western one of the most exciting to gallop off the Republic lot recently. Action aplenty as The Three Mesquiteers ride with the Texas Rangers. Six-shooters do not get the opportunity to grow cold in this film. Both the law and bad men really sling lead and the number of casualties as a result of the gangs lawlessness probably reaches a new high it all points to red blooded entertainment.

"Director Les Orlebeck unerringly followed the formula with good results and gets credit for a snappy megaphone job. Photography and musical scorer blended well with the action. Three Mesquiteers – Bob Steele Tom Tyler and Rufe Davis – act the part of cowboy heroes who proved handy with their fists. Lois Collier supplies the necessary heart throb with Tom Chatterton, Roy Barcroft and Joel Friedkin in satisfactory supporting roles.

"Film has to do with ruthless gang under guidance of Barcroft which takes a jurisdictional advantage by remaining behind the Cherokee border after they have done their dirty work in Texas. The Head of Texas Rangers asked men to observe law and not cross-border line for bandits. In meantime gang leader has planted one of his henchmen with captain of Texas Rangers. Three Mesquiteers get wind of the gangs plot to kidnap the captain's daughter, Miss Collier. In a hard riding and walloping finish, The Three Mesquiteers withstand the gang and help effect their capture."

Gauchos of El Dorado
Directed by Les Orlebeck
On DVD from VCI
The band of bank robbers has some interesting members. Yakima Canutt, the legendary a stuntman and second unit director is among the villains in

this film. His contributions to stunt work are legion, but at the top would be the development (while working with John Wayne) of the way to stage and photograph fight scenes.

Also of note is Duncan Renaldo, who was once a Mesquiteer himself, but is a sympathetic bank robber in this film. He is still a few years off from his starring and best-known role as The Cisco Kid.

Another future cowboy hero is also part of the gang, Eddie Dean, who would achieve starring roles in his work at PRC.

The "Gaucho" of the title is Renaldo's character. Despite the fact that his character is half Irish and half Spanish, Republic writers used the term despite its South American origins.

Steele puts in a good performance as Tucson, who is increasingly nervous about deceiving the mother of the Renaldo character, who believes he is her son.

In the fight scene in a bar, Tyler does a nice stunt by swinging on a lamp halfway across the room. Working in a B western was very physical to say the least.

While the plot of mistaken identity is a little complex, the film is a solid entry

Film Daily, October 24, 1941, "The Three Mesquiteers ride again in a robust and fast moving western. Latest adventure tale of The Three Mesquiteers is an entertaining program film. Customers will go for the fast riding and general display of fistic fireworks in which the trio indulges. Story is one of those formula concoctions which are implausible dramatically but furnish a vehicle for The Three Mesquiteers to ride on to an ultimate triumph. The Mesquiteers come across a Mexican fleeing a gang of robbers. The Mexican is killed but before he dies he asks the Mesquiteers to deliver the money to his mother's ranch.

"The mother who has not seen her son since he was a small boy believes Steele is her son. Not wishing to hurt her feelings Steele remains quiet. Steele and his two friends stay on the ranch and become involved with the local banker who's trying to foreclose so he can get the property which contains a valuable box site deposit. They withstand all efforts to dispose of them and run down the villains.

"Les Orlebeck's direction is concerned more with the action sequences which he reels off smoothly then with the continuity. Three Mesquiteers do it all that is demanded of them. Lois Collier attracts attention by her good looks."

West of Cimarron

Directed by Les Orlebeck

Can be seen on YouTube and on DVD from oldies.com

A Three Mesquiteers film that happens at a particular time and place: Texas after the Civil War. In this case, the Union Army have the evil carpetbaggers and the Texan "bushwhackers" are the heroes. It would seem this film really was designed for the southern audiences in 1941.

The film is more than a bit problematic in 2025. There is a former slave character played by Cordell Hickman in broad stereotype terms who is helping the former Confederates. One black character is named "Rastus." To add insult to injury, Davis gets into blackface and sings a song about watermelons in an effort to save the boys from hanging at the hand of the corrupt Union officials.

Tyler gets a chance to play a drunk in the film and pulls it off well.

The Film Daily, December 22,1941, "The Three Mesquiteers ride high, wide and handsome in their latest adventure tale. Not much concern is paid

Bob Steele and Rude Davis help Tyler out by getting the drop on the bad guys, including Roy Barcroft in "West of Cimarron." (author's collection)

An atmospheric still from "West of Cimarron." (author's collection)

to the yarn but director Les Orleback has concentrated on the action phases to carry the film along in an effective manner.

"Story has The Three Mesquiteers arriving in Texas shortly after the Civil War. The commander of local army post is unaware of the fact that his civilian aide is a crook and that one of the chief officers is responsible for robbing and murdering the ranchers.

"Leader of the ranchers is holding out against two of the Mesquiteers. It takes some convincing for the Mesquiteers to show they are really helping the ranchers. After the commander shot in the back considerable shooting goes on until The Three Musketeers subdue the villains.

"Bob Steele and Tom Tyler adequately supplied the action for the triumphant with Rufe Davis furnishing the laughs. Lois Collier, James Bush, Guy Usher, Hugh Prosser offer capable support. Direction has a good pace and action and well photographed."

Code of the Outlaw
Directed by S. Roy Luby

The Exhibitor Feb. 11, 1942,

"The Three Mesquiteers are deputy sheriffs charged with running down a gang of highway robbers ended by Weldon Heyburn. After a gun battle the only outlaw they can capture alive is young Benny Bartlett, Heyburn's son but can't they get the lad to talk. Melinda Layton, newspaper girl accuses the boys falsely of using third degree methods, so he's sent to an orphanage. Through a ruse, they get custody of him, even though he's reluctant to accompany them. Kindness on the part of the Mesquiteers later almost has young Bartlett ready to talk. Untimely arrival of Miss Layton and the orphanage principal forces the boy to run away, and outlaw Donald Curtis gets him to claim a $98,000 deposit of stolen money in a neighboring town, planning to kill him later. But the Mesquiteers get there in time to round up the remaining

The odds aren't in Tyler's favor in this scene from "Riders of the Range." (author's collection)

criminals. This is a satisfactory western. The Mesquiteers turned in their standard performance. There is a minimum of dialogue and the action is continuous."

Riders of the Range
Directed by John English
Showman's Trade Review April 4, 1942,

"The villainous owner of the town saloon is holding second rights to an oil well being drilled and is anxious to prevent its completion before his option takes effect. The country doctor, who heads the band of ranchers financing the drilling, sends for The Three Mesquiteers to put a stop to the efforts being made to sabotage the well. He falls victim to a scheme of the saloon keeper and, when threatened with imprisonment, is rescued by the trio who perfect a plan that forces the guilty parties to expose themselves and implicate the saloon keeper. The bulk of the action is staged in the background of an oil drilling operation and there are some good shots of roughneck drillers and a gusher being blown in. There is a goodly supply of bar room brawls and the

It's time for Stoney to step in – a scene from "Riders of the Range." (author's collection)

usual amount of shoot-em-up horse riding action punctuating the drinking bouts and sabotage efforts among the oil drillers to give good variety of camera range. The inclusion of murderers through poisoning furnishes complications that helped both the plot and story relation. There is a total absence of romance and only a smattering of comedy in the interlude."

Westward Ho!

Directed by John English
Can be seen on YouTube under the title "Riders for Justice"

This film benefits from the hard-edged performance by Evelyn Brent as the bank owner/gang leader. Brent was a major star in the silent period, appearing in films directed by such talents as Josef Von Sternberg. Although she made the transition to sound well, she went from starring to supporting roles.

The script is also hard-edged with the idea of real bank robbers setting up innocent people as thieves, then shooting them to collect a reward.

Film Bulletin, June 1,1942, "A novel plot, involving a female menace, puts this among the best of the Mesquiteers westerns. The action of 'Westward Ho' never lags and director John English has injected shootings aplenty, fast riding and stagecoach hold-ups and finally a bang-up fist fight to set the cowboy devotees cheering. One of the more logical westerns and one which wastes no time in nonessential romantic complications, this will please wherever outdoor action is favored. Playing up the lady outlaw angle may also attract some of the regular patrons.

"In this story Evelyn Brent, president of a small western bank, is the secret leader of a gang of bandits who robbed banks in nearby towns with the $5,000 reward posted by the Bankers Association, Miss Brent and her partner workout a cowardly scheme whereby an innocent bystander is suspected of the hold up and they collect the money for the killing. When the Mesquiteers come to town, Lullaby is made a victim of Miss Brent's scheme but his two pals, Stoney and Tucson, rescue him in time. The Mesquiteers are then classed as outlaws and in this manner they tie up with Miss Brent's bandits and eventually expose her.

"Evelyn Brent looks attractive in costumes of the old West and gives a fine performance portrayal of the crafty female banker. Donald Curtis gives a smooth performance as the associate villain and The Three Mesquiteers do stock heroic acting jobs."

The Phantom Plainsman

Directed by John English
Can be seen on YouTube

As a kid seeing westerns on TV, I was always confused when the action took place in some sort of "wild west" that looked like contemporary times. Did people really drive cars and ride horses?

This film takes the Mesquiteers out of the 19th century and places them about 1938 or so. It's done very well and, of course, matches the tone of the times.

Toward the end of the film there is a great fight scene with Bob Steele being doubled by David Sharpe.

The cast's "brains" villain is one of the movies' favorite choices to play a Nazi, Rudolph Anders. He fled the Nazis from his native Germany, only to play them in movies here.

Film Bulletin, Nov. 16, 1942, "This lively western which has The Three Mesquiteers fighting Nazi villains makes good entertainment for the cowboy fans. The 'Phantom Plainsmen' of the title are German agents engaged in the undercover buying of horses for the use of their country's military machine. "Although the plot has a few novel twists the greater part of the footage is devoted to the riding, shooting and fistic encounters in which the stars excel. Bob Steele and Tom Tyler each have several realistic settos with the bad men, while Rufe Davis takes care of the comedy department.

"The picture keeps up a fast pace and is sure to satisfy in action spots. Taking place before the outbreak of the war, the story has The Three Mesquiteers working for a kindly old rancher, Charles Miller, who sells his horses to Alex Callam of the Cattlemen's Exchange. Knowing that Miller whose son is studying in a German university, is against the use of his horses for military use, Callam has concealed the fact that he is secretly in the employ of Nazi agents. "When the Mesquiteers learned the truth about Callum he forces Miller to continue selling him horses under the threat of placing his son in the custody of the Gestapo. The Mesquiteers then organized as an outlaw band and prevent the shipment of the horses and by breaking into Callam's office they get a message through to the Nazis which releases Miller's son. When the Nazi agent arrives out West, he and Callam are captured and their plan is exposed. Robert O. Davis is an excellent Nazi type and Alex Callam does well as his hireling of the cattlemen's exchange. Lois Collier makes a pleasing heroine."

Shadows on the Sage
Directed by Les Orlebeck
On DVD from VCI
This is the first film for Jimmie Dodd, adding the potential for music in the series. A device that occurs fairly regularly in B westerns is for the hero to have a twin who is an outlaw. Bob Steele has the double duty in this production. There is an inside joke in this film as the outlaw that looks like Tucson is named "Curley Joe," clearly a reference of the character "Curley" who Steele played in "Of Mice and Men."

Much of the comedy (and drama) is caused by "Uncle Lippy," a blowhard whose exaggerations get him into trouble with the townspeople who out of desperation appointed Lippy to the job. Harry Holman did a fine job as the elderly braggart.

The illusion of the two look-alikes is well done and Steele seems to relish the dual role.

There is a clever – but unbelievable– gag at the end.

The Exhibitor Sept. 23, 1942, "When the sheriff of Holbrook is murdered by the bandit Bob Steele, Harry Holman is selected to carry on. He realizes the job is more than he can handle, and calls in The Three Mesquiteers who, on their own way to town, see bandit Steele rob Griff Barnett, rich mine owner, and Holman, were conveying a gold shipment. Mesquiteer Steele gives chase, trails the bandits and surprises them in their hideout but is captured. When banker Bryant Washbourne, brains of the gang notes that the bandit and the Mesquiteers are almost identical in appearance, he dresses the bandit in the other's clothes, and sends him to Barnett's home, where he robs and then kills Barnett. The crime is witnessed by Cheryl Walker and Freddie Mercer, the miner's children. Washburn holds a mortgage on Barnett's mine and, in order to foreclose, has systematically been robbing his gold shipments. After rope work, fights, writing, and gun fights the double identity is revealed, the Mesquiteers round up the entire gang. Action, suspense and fun are well worked out here. Steele in a dual role, handles his assignment nicely, Tyler is excellent and Jimmy Dodd sings two cowboy numbers."

"What the Picture did for Me, "Motion Picture Herald, Feb, 6, 1943, "Fair western for Friday and Saturday. Believe the new star [Dodd] will be OK. Melville Danner Kozy Theatre, Granite, OK.

Valley of Hunted Men

Directed by John English

Can be seen on YouTube

Another time travel film in which once again the Three Mesquiteers are fighting Nazis. It also is another role for Edward Van Sloan. Set in 1941 before the USA entered the war, the film believably puts our cowboy heroes into modern times.

This film has a hard edge to it. The three escaped Nazis have no qualm to shoot unarmed people and folks in the back. While Republic often portrayed violence in a subdued manner in its action films, the studio was clearly making a point here.

The studio also managed to incorporate the attack on Pearl Harbor into the script.

A well-written film that was very topical when it was released and by the way culebra is a real plant.

The Exhibitor, Nov. 4, 1942, "Three Nazi Flyers headed by Roland Varno escaped from a Canadian concentration camp, head for the US and, after committing murder, stealing horses and guns, they arrive in Valley City, Montana, where The Three Mesquiteers head a manhunt. They tracked down and killed two of the Nazis.

"Varno having thumbed a ride, kills the driver, takes his clothes and papers, and discovers the dead man is the nephew of Edward Van Sloan, a German refugee and scientist who induced ranchers to raise culebra plants from which he will extract rubber by a secret formula. Posing as the nephew, Varno escapes detection long enough to get in touch with a Nazi council who instructs him to stick it out and get possession of the formula.

"He all but succeeds in wrecking the crop by pouring a volatile liquid into a liquid which is being sprayed from a plane when the Mesquiteers get wise, crack down on him and save the formula. This one is a deviation from the cattle rustling theme and is well done. Acting as above par, there is plenty of riding interspersed and a good performance by Varno. It should set well with action fans."

Thundering Trails
   Directed by John English
   The Exhibitor, Jan. 27, 1943,
   "The Three Mesquiteers are all set up when official red tape seems to stand in the way of equipping the Texas Rangers of which they are a part to cope with increased lawlessness. One of the boy's dad, Charles Miller, is captain of the Rangers, and he shares their impatience. Not knowing that his friend, Judge Sam Flint, is secretly allied with an outlaw gang which poses as a county police force, he tells the judge that after protecting an incoming stage load of gold, he is going to Austin to bring pressure to bear to have additional funds allocated to the Rangers so they will have more men and arms to protect the territory. Flint tips off his henchman and arranges for them to hold up the gold shipment and kill Miller. He does not reckon on the Mesquiteers arriving on the spot at the right moment to frustrate the brigandage. Miller is shot in the back. On the stage is rancher's daughter pretty Nell O'Day, the lady in distress. From there on, it is plot and counterplot and sleuthing with the Mesquiteers falsely accused of banditry, incarcerated and delivered from jail. With a final smash bang battle, it ends okay. This is in the usual series tradition, the story being familiar. However, there is plenty of action throughout and the western addicts will probably be satisfied."
   "What the Picture did for Me," Motion Picture Herald, May 29, 1943," Nice

western that got by on a weekend. Seemed to satisfy. Harland Rankin, Centre Theatre, Chatham, ON, Canada."

The Blocked Trail
Directed by Elmer Clifton
Can be seen on YouTube in a colorized version

An interesting film built around a trained dwarf horse in a role usually reserved for a dog. Perhaps a little convoluted, but still a fast-moving and fun who-done-it, the central idea is that a miner going blind has trained his dwarf horse as a seeing-eye animal. I can only wonder if someone at Republic knew about this trained horse and wrote the story around it.

By the way, if you think a seeing-eye horse is a bit of a stretch, the web has quite a few entries of people training small horses as support animals today.

And, of course, the title had no relation to the plot of the story.

Motion Picture Herald, April 3, 1943, "This is among the better offerings in the Three Mesquiteers series produced by Republic with Bob Steele, Tom Tyler and Jimmy Dodd in the title roles. This time the trio encounters a mine mystery. After a blind miner is murdered, a town lawyer sets his gang of bandits on the trail of a dwarfed horse which apparently carries the clue to the location of a gold mine. As is the case in westerns, the heroes are blamed for crimes committed by bandits and the lawyer is highly respected in the town. There's plenty of riding and shooting before the Mesquiteers round up the bandits and the horse leads the way to a rich gold strike. 'Brilliant,' the dwarf horse, tops an able cast."

Santa Fe Scouts
Directed by Herbert Bretherton
April 7, 1943. The Exhibitor

"The Three Mesquiteers who work for Elizabeth Valentine act as wet nurses for her son John James, always in a peck of trouble. To make himself reliant, his ma gives him a ranch to settle down and marry Lois Collier. After James has left for his ranch, the mother decides to give him 50 head of choice cattle. The Three Mesquiteers are delegated to drive and deliver them. Arriving at a water hole near the ranch we find old Tom London and tricky Bud Buster trying to charge a dollar ahead for herds to drink. They challenge London's right and are referred to the owner of the property who turns out to be James. The latter is furious at the deception being practiced on him by London who has lived for years on the ranch as caretaker. James goes to shifty lawyer Tom Chatterton who has been tipped off that the squatter rights law has been passed and arranged with London to stick on the property 'till midnight the next day. During a quarrel in the lawyer's office, Collier fires and apparently kills Buster. London and Chatterton say they will protect Collier and advise James to go away while London then takes the apparent corpse away in his wagon. The Three Mesquiteers who learned of the new law rush to take possession of James's ranch and find the pass is blocked with a wagon guarded by a bunch of cutthroats. They grab off a big herd of cattle, stampede them up the pass and either kill or capture all the bandits, restoring the ranch to its rightful owner. This stacks up with the better westerns. It has hard riding, plenty of fights, plus the wild stampede is plenty exciting. While no epic, it will more than satisfy western fans."

"What the Picture did for Me," Motion Picture Herald, May 29, 1943, "Good western which pleased on Friday, Saturday, May 14 and 15. from E. M. Freiberger, Paramount Theatre, Dewey, OK."

Riders of the Rio Grande
Directed by Howard Bretherton
Can be seen on YouTube (colorized); On DVD from VCI

This film benefits from a different departure in story and a fine performance from veteran character actor Edward van Sloan, best known perhaps as Van Helsing in the 1931 production of "Dracula." This was his second appearance in the series.

It takes a while before the Mesquiteers appear in the story, but the build-up is well done. The story is the ultimate mistaken identity plot for a western.

While Jimmie Dodd might not have been the funniest sidekick, he could sing well and performs an enjoyable blues number original for the film.

This was the last film in the series.

Motion Picture Herald, May 15, 1943, "There is little to recommend in the summing up of 'Riders of the Rio Grande,' latest in the Three Mesquiteers series. A story unusually involved for cowboy pictures, some hammy acting and unaccountable time lapses all conspire to throw it for a loss. Where they are prime favorites their fans should take the new adventures of the Mesquiteers in stride, but 'Riders of the Rio Grande' doesn't appear to be of a caliber to win any new friends for the series.

"The story opens strongly. It looks for a while as if it's going to be a good show, with accent on drama not usually found in westerns. But soon it takes a familiar turn as the Mesquiteers ride onto the screen, are confused with the notorious Cherokee Boys and ordered out of Owensville. They should be rounding up the gang that robbed the bank and teaching a lesson to young

Tom Owens, whose father knows he had a hand in the holdup. Instead, the father hires gunman to kill him so the insurance money can recover the bank's loss and protect the son's name. The Mesquiteers are further prevented from righting matters when they are jailed trying to rescue the son from the real robbers and the heroine throws in with the villain.

"Howard Bretherton directed the original screenplay by Albert Diamond. It is a Lewis Gray production. Tom Tyler, Jimmy Dodd, and Bob Steele play their Mesquiteer characters satisfactorily but the strides that Rick Vallin has been making in several appearances lately come up against some obstacles in this job. Lorraine Miller is the heroine and there is an interesting, if overplayed, character created by Edward van Sloan."

Wagon Tracks West
Directed by Howard Bretherton

Tom plays the tribe's medicine man who is in opposition to the young doctor in this Bill Elliot western.

Showman's Trade Review, July 31, 1943, wrote, "When a young Indian doctor tries to help a fever ridden white man on his reservation, he finds himself up against a lawless element. These men had refused to permit the purification of the water in the native village in order to drive the Indians out and nab their land. After Bill Elliott takes a hand, everything is straightened out and the doctor receives a public apology. This is good cowboys and Indian stuff, with action and speed; With Wild Bill Elliott doing some nice shooting to save the young Indian chief which Rick Vallin plays nicely. George 'Gabby' Hayes contributes his usual good performance that has made him an institution, and his type a must for all westerns. It's good screen fair for the action and western addicts. Lou Gray's production shows the appreciation for story and timing that these horse operas need. Credit Howard Bretherton with direction on a well-paced fast moving outdoor picture."

In 1950, Tyler returned to Republic for a guest appearance in a Roy Rogers production.

Trail of Robin Hood
Directed William Witney
Can be seen on Tubi

Jack Holt plays a version of himself – a retired movie star – who is now in the Christmas tree business (!) and intends to give trees away to needy kids but the rival tree farmer wants to stop him. Roy Rogers decides to help Holt and rounds up a bunch of current and former cowboy stars – all Holt's friends, supposedly – including Rex Allen, Monte Hale, Allan Lane, Tom Keene, Ray Corrigan, Kermit Maynard and Tyler to help bring in Holt's tree harvest and foil the bad guys.

The film has nothing to do with Robin Hood as near as I can tell, but it has a sweetly nostalgic feel to it with the appearances by the older stars, all of whom get a line or two. It's an enjoyable and somewhat off-beat Rogers vehicle with the usual more-than-competent direction by William Witney. Seek it out.

Tyler is dressed in a very atypical outfit for him – his western wear was always more functional than decorative – and he looks gaunt. This was his last credit for Republic and my guess is he was pleased to be included.

(Jan. 15, 1951) "An ordinarily routine Roy Rogers western 'Trail of Robin Hood' packs an extra box office wallop for the Saturday matinee crowds and faithful devotees of cowboy films. The additional attraction lies in the presence of much old-time boots and saddle favorites as Jack Holt, William Farnham and Tom Tyler as well as present day Republic stars Rogers, Rex Allen, Allan "Rocky' Lane and Monte Hale. The marquee value of these names plus the Trucolor photography and an action-full cow country yarn makes certain good grosses for the above-mentioned situations."

What a line-up from "Trail of Robin Hood!" Left to right (standing) Tyler, Ray "Crash" Corrigan, Allan "Rocky" Lane, Monte Hale, George Chesebro, Kermit Maynard and crouching, Tom Keene, Roy Rogers, and William Farnum. (author's collection)

THE 3 MESQUITEERS
"CODE OF THE OUTLAW"
featuring
BOB STEELE
TOM TYLER
RUFE DAVIS
WELDON HEYBURN - BENNIE BARTLETT
MELINDA LEIGHTON
JOHN ENGLISH Director
A REPUBLIC PICTURE

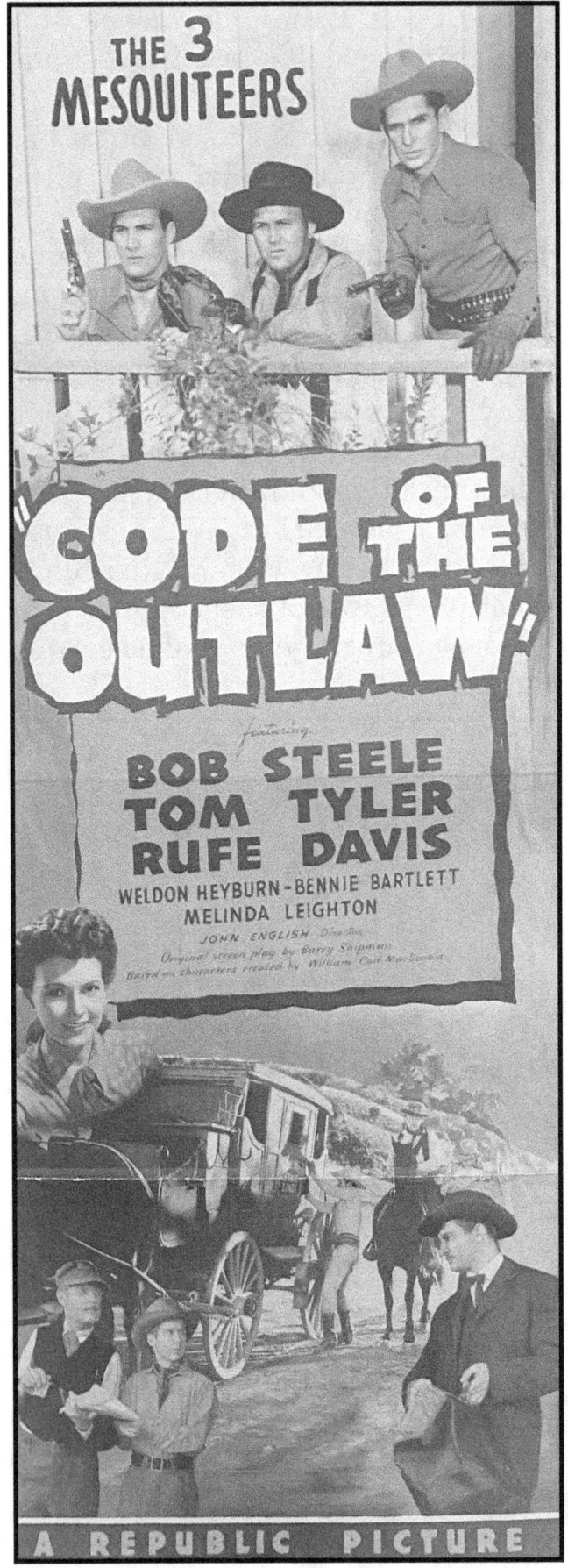

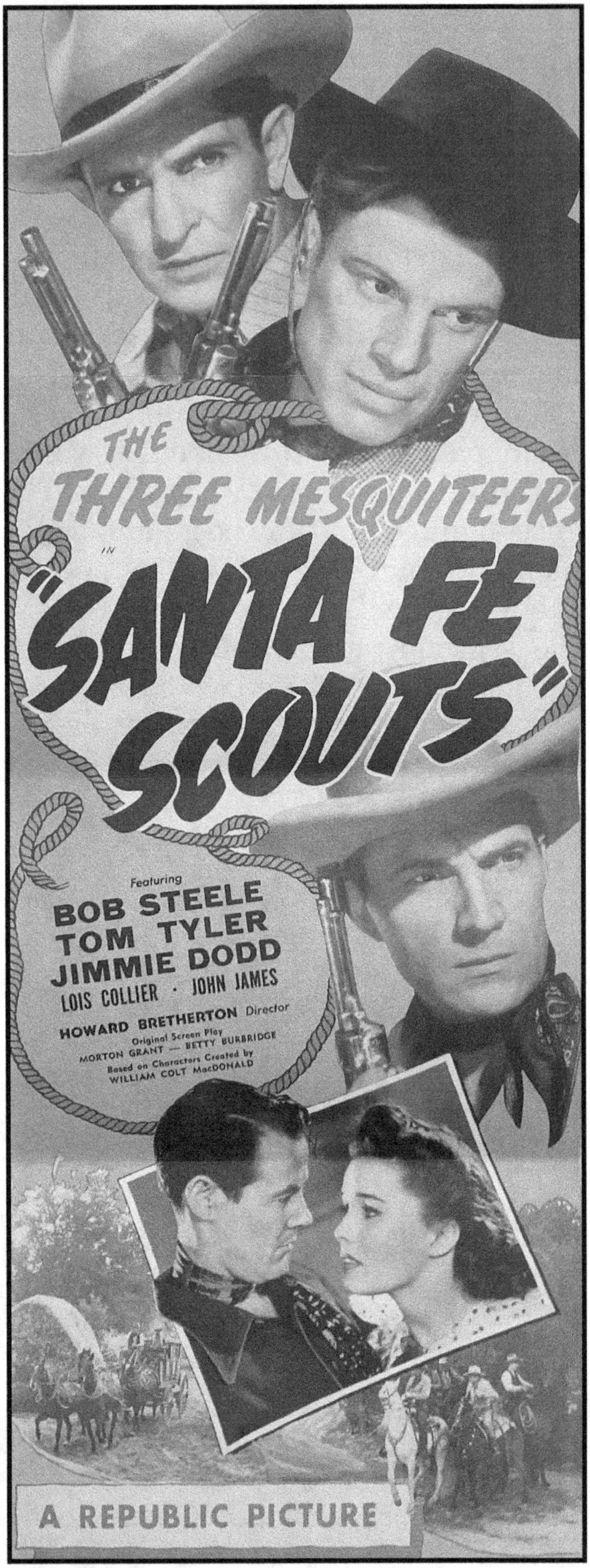
THE THREE MESQUITEERS
in
"SANTA FE SCOUTS"
Featuring
BOB STEELE
TOM TYLER
JIMMIE DODD
LOIS COLLIER · JOHN JAMES
HOWARD BRETHERTON Director
Original Screen Play
MORTON GRANT — BETTY BURBRIDGE
Based on Characters Created by
WILLIAM COLT MacDONALD
A REPUBLIC PICTURE

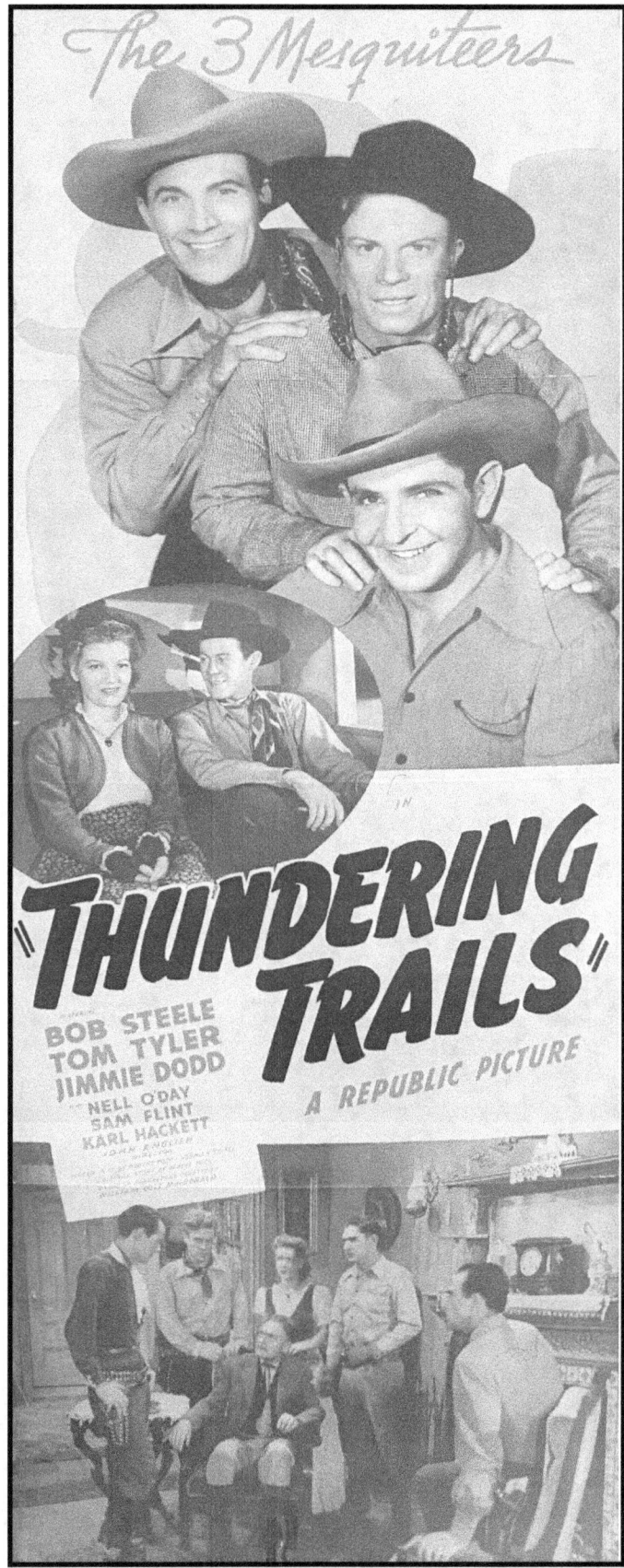

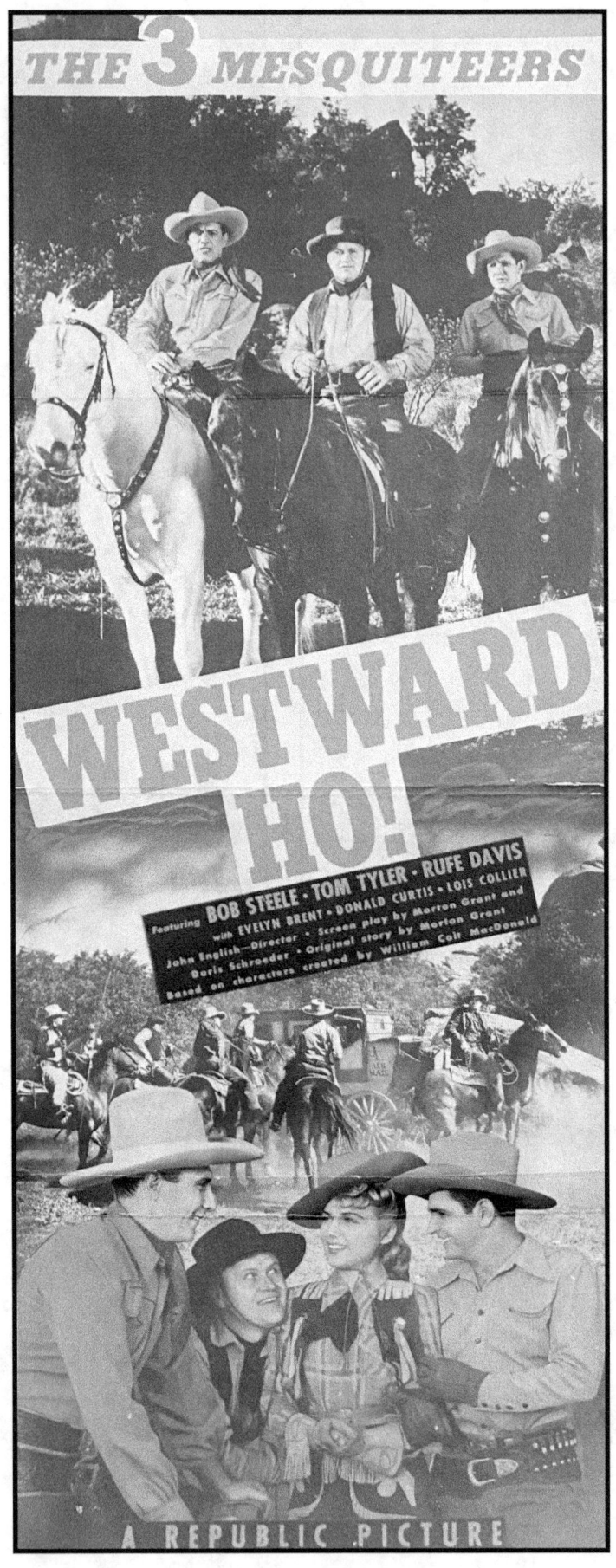

G. MICHAEL DOBBS

"RETURN OF CAPTAIN MARVEL"

(Formerly entitled "Adventures of Captain Marvel")

A REPUBLIC SERIAL IN 12 CHAPTERS

(Chapter Synopses For Exhibitors Only. NOT FOR PUBLICATION)

111A

"CURSE OF THE SCORPION"

EPISODE ONE

To a remote section of Siam, zealously guarded by unconquered native tribes, comes the unwelcome Malcolm Scientific Expedition, seeking knowledge of the ancient Scorpion Dynasty. Billy Batson, assistant to the radio expert, is the only one of the party who does not enter a forbidden chamber. As a result, he is awarded the power to transform himself into a superman, "Captain Marvel," upon uttering the word "Shazam." Meanwhile, the scientists who have entered the sacred tomb have discovered "The Scorpion," a powerful gold weapon the potency of which is brought about by focusing five peculiar lenses. The scientists divide the lenses among themselves so that no one of them will have supernatural power. There is a pitched battle between the native tribesmen and the scientists during which Betty, the expedition's secretary, appears to meet her death by falling into a gorge.

112A

"THE GUILLOTINE"

EPISODE TWO

Billy, disguised as "Captain Marvel," rescues her, and transforms himself back into Billy Batson before she regains consciousness. The party returns to America but is pursued by a sinister gang, headed by a human "Scorpion," who wants to wrest from them the secret of the places where they have hidden the gold weapon. Carlyle, one of the scientists, is captured by the Scorpion's men, who try to force him to tell where he has hidden the lens entrusted to him. Carlyle sends a message to Betty to bring the lens to a rendezvous. Suspecting that Carlyle is the victim of foul play, Billy pursues in his Captain Marvel guise. He allows the Scorpion's henchman to take a false lens, and follows, in order to learn the base of operations. In a struggle there, he is threatened by death from a fiendishly contrived guillotine.

113A

"TIME BOMB"

EPISODE THREE

The guillotine is smashed to bits as it contacts Captain Marvel's superhuman body. He drives the gangsters from the building. Meanwhile, the scientific group, at the home of Malcolm, its leader, has assigned Betty the task of getting the Carlyle lens from the safe at his mountain lodge. Billy insists that she use his car, which is equipped with a two-way radio system. The gangsters abduct Betty, forcing her to drive her car into their moving van. When they attempt to force her to tell the combination of Carlyle's safe, she throws the switch of the radio so that Billy overhears. He transforms himself to Captain Marvel and rescues Betty. As Billy, he flies to Carlyle's mountain lodge to secure the lens and the Scorpion has a bomb placed in his plane, which explodes, trapping him inside.

114A

"DEATH TAKES THE WHEEL"

EPISODE FOUR

As "Captain Marvel," Billy is invulnerable; he soars safely through space to the ground. It is apparent that one of the scientists is the mysterious "Scorpion," but all of them, of course indignantly deny any complicity. The Carlyle lens is stolen by the Scorpion's gang, and in tracing it, Betty is kidnapped and taken to a garage where she discovers a secret room. She attempts to relay this information to the scientists by telephone, but is caught in the act, bound, and threatened with death. Billy, meanwhile, assumes his Captain Marvel character and flies through space to her rescue. Betty, in attempting to make her escape, races her car down a ramp at top speed, is knocked unconscious and lies helpless as the car speeds directly toward a huge building.

115A

"THE SCORPION STRIKES"

EPISODE FIVE

Captain Marvel leaps into the careening car, swerves the wheel and steers it away from danger. Betty recovers, tells him that the gangsters are still within the building. He dashes into the building in pursuit. When the Scorpion gang sees him, they roll a heavy motor down the ramp toward him. His superhuman strength enables him to pick up the motor and hurl it back at them, killing a large number. Those who attempt to escape via the elevator are thwarted when Captain Marvel grabs the cables and hauls the elevator back. Marvel, now transformed back into his Billy character, again tries to force one of the captured thugs to give him information which will enable him to determine the Scorpion's whereabouts. He is led into a trap and is threatened with death by molten lava.

116A

"LENS OF DEATH"

EPISODE SIX

Captain Marvel leaps to safety through an opening in the roof of the mine tunnel. Transforming himself back into Billy Batson, he leaves for the Malcolm home, where the scientists receive a message from the Scorpion, warning them that he has already acquired all the lenses but one, and that death will befall anyone who stands in the way of his securing that. The scientists race for home to make certain of the theft, which is exactly what the Scorpion intended, in order to make them reveal the hiding places. It appears that his plan will be successful, until his gang reaches the home of one of the scientists, who has his wall safe equipped with wires to electrocute any invader. One of the Scorpion's thugs is thus electrocuted; a gun fight ensues, with Captain Marvel appearing, reaching into the safe for the lens, and apparently being electrocuted.

117A

"HUMAN TARGETS"

EPISODE SEVEN

Marvel is stunned but not killed. When he recovers consciousness, he learns that the Scorpion's men have made away with the lens. Meanwhile, Malcolm, because Billy and Captain Marvel seem to be always on the spot whenever the Scorpion's various plottings take place, suggest that perhaps they are in league with the Scorpion. The latter decides to capture Captain Marvel, once and for all, using Billy and Betty as bait. Betty is captured and Billy pursues, assuming the character of Captain Marvel. He rescues her, but a thug hidden in the rescue car overhears him telling Betty that if she is in danger again, she may summon help over a certain radio wave. The Scorpion is tipped off by the hidden thug, and he arranges for Betty to be captured. She calls Marvel by means of the secret radio wave, and he is lured into a trap and seemingly destroyed by bombs.

118A

"BOOMERANG"

EPISODE EIGHT

Before the bombs drop, Billy succeeds in freeing himself from his gag so that he can utter the word "Shazam" which transforms him into Captain Marvel and makes it possible for him to rescue himself and Betty. Betty reveals that in attempting to elude the Scorpion, she wounded him in the hand; Captain Marvel in this way knows that whichever one of the scientists is secretly the Scorpion, will have a wound. The Scorpion knows that inasmuch as Captain Marvel is a superman, nothing will down him but the most powerful weapon on earth — that of the golden scorpion and its five lenses, working in unison. Billy accuses one of the scientists, Lang, of being the Scorpion, since he has a wounded hand. Lang is actually innocent, and tries to aid Billy to escape from the thugs. Together they face death from a bomb exploding in their car.

119A

"DEAD MAN'S TRAP"

EPISODE NINE

Billy is rendered unconscious by the explosion, and as Lang is trying to revive him, the Scorpion's men approach and make them prisoners. The Scorpion tortures Lang until he reveals the hiding place of his lens. Immediately afterward, Lang phones Betty, warning her to remove the lens; but before he can tell her how to avoid a death trap he has set at the safe, the Scorpion overhears him, and shuts him off. Billy transforms himself into Captain Marvel, escapes from all barriers and flies to Betty's rescue, ignorant of the death trap into which he and Betty will walk when they attempt to remove the Lang lens from its hiding place. As they open the safe, two machine guns appear from a secret hiding panel and start to rake the room with a fusillade of death.

120A

"DOOM SHIP"

EPISODE TEN

Betty and Billy miraculously escape the bullets from the machine gun by lowering themselves out of range in front of the safe. The thugs overpower them, however and enter the safe, removing a map of the tomb in Asia where Lang has actually hidden his lens. Billy recovers the document, and goes with it to the scientists. They decide to go to Asia where the lens is hidden, in order to keep it from falling into the possession of the Scorpion. They divide the map into five pieces. On the way to Asia they encounter a storm. Billy, by turning into Captain Marvel, is able to fly to the shore with a line so that a breeches buoy will carry them to safety. He believes that all have been rescued, and does not realize that the Scorpion has knocked Betty unconscious and that she is helpless in a cabin of the sinking ship.

121A

"VALLEY OF DEATH"

EPISODE ELEVEN

Billy rescues Betty and swims to safety with her. The scientific party proceeds inland to find the hiding place of the lens in the secret tomb. By means of a hawk with a message tied to its leg, the Scorpion sends instructions to Rahman Bar, a native tribe leader, to stop the expedition. When Billy learns that Rahman Bar is following the expedition, he turns himself into Captain Marvel and flies to its assistance. A huge tree, blocking the path, is intended to delay the expedition until Rahman Bar, by using explosives, can send the mountain crashing down over them. Marvel, with his superhuman strength, lifts the tree out of the way and the party proceeds to safety, only to face even greater danger when the tribe leader diverts a stream of water into a volcano, making it active, and threatening them with death.

122A

"CAPTAIN MARVEL'S SECRET"

EPISODE TWELVE

A protective arch keeps tons of falling debris from burying the party until Billy, as Captain Marvel, can rescue it. The Scorpion obeserves Billy in the act of transforming himself into Captain Marvel, and realizes that he must be taken by surprise and gagged before he has an opportunity to utter the magic word. Billy is accordingly captured, along with Betty and other members of the party. The Scorpion now has all the lenses fitted into the golden statuette, which makes it the most powerful instrument in the world. He threatens to use it on Billy and his friends, causing their immediate annihilation, unless Billy will reveal the secret of how he transforms himself into a superman. Billy nods agreement, tricking him into removing the gag. Billy utters the magic word, Shazam, becomes Captain Marvel, rescues his friends and rips the hood from the Scorpion, revealing him as none other than Bentley!

The Ad Slugs Appearing On This Page Have Also Been Made in 2 Column Size. SEE AD SECTION.

Publicity

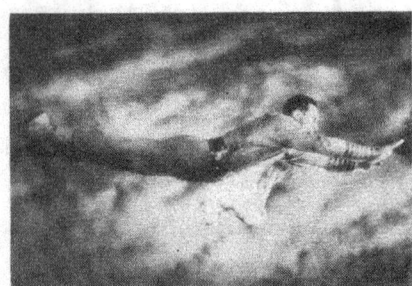

"RETURN OF CAPT. MARVEL" (2B)

SUPERMAN Tom Tyler as he appears in the title role of "Return of Captain Marvel," amazing serial thriller from Republic Studios which begins..................at the .... Theatre.

"Return Of Captain Marvel," Hair-Raising Mystery Thriller

Amazing Feats, Spine-Tingling Adventures Pack Exciting Serial

"RETURN of Captain Marvel," (formerly entitled "Adventures of Captain Marvel"), Republic's excitement-packed serial, got off to a flying start last night with Episode One, "Curse of the Scorpion," leaving its audience in a state of nail-biting, edge-of-the-seat jitters.

This chapter-thriller lives up to the high standard established by Republic, long recognized as masters in the serial field. It brings a fascinating group of characters to a remote section of Siam where they seek knowledge of the ancient Scorpion Dynasty. Billy Baston, one of their number, transforms himself into a superman, and as "Captain Marvel" he is able to perform the most amazing feats.

The expedition is in charge of five scientists who have ascertained that the Scorpion Dynasty is symbolized by a large scorpion of pure gold. In each of this golden image's five claws is a lens, and the five lenses, operated separately, become an instrument of death and destruction such as the world has never seen.

The efforts, on the part of a mysterious villain known only as the "Scorpion" to gain possession of this weapon provide the plot of the serial, and the five scientists, together with Billy in his "Captain Marvel" characterization, are leagued to prevent the Scorpion from thus obtaining world dominion through the unholy use of this fearful instrument.

Cast in the production are Tom Tyler, Frank Coghlan, Jr., Louise Currie, Robert Strange, George Pembroke, Harry Worth, Peter George Lynn, John Davidson, William Benedict and Reed Hadley. William Witney and Jack English co-directed under Associate Producer H. S. Brown, Jr.

"RETURN OF CAPT. MARVEL" (1C)

RUGGED ACTION and thrilling adventure pack Republic's amazing serial, "Return of Captain Marvel," a chapter of which can be seen each.............. afternoon at the...................... Theatre. Pictured above in a scene from the exciting film is Tom Tyler, rugged star who, in the picture, is able to transform himself into a Superman.

"RETURN OF CAPT. MARVEL" (2C)

"THE SCORPION," mysterious murderer and his death-dealing instrument bring chills and thrills to "Return of Captain Marvel," sensational Republic serial playing each .... at the.................. Theatre.

"RETURN OF CAPT. MARVEL" (1A)

ACTION SCENE from "Return of Captain Marvel," Republic serial now thrilling fans each.................... at the.................. Theatre, pictures "The Scorpion" and one of his sinister agents.

Early Days Of Films Recalled By Veteran Player

Jack Mulhall, who has a prominent featured role in Republic's exciting serial, "Return of Captain Marvel," (formerly entitled "Adventures of Captain Marvel"), was one of the first actors in the early days of the industry to receive a weekly salary in three figures. His one hundred dollars a week was considered a small fortune in the early Biograph days. "Return of Captain Marvel," with Tom Tyler in the title role, shows weekly at the.................. Theatre on..................

The serial-thriller was directed jointly by William Witney and Jack English, and includes the following prominent members in its cast: Frank Coghlan, Jr., Tom Tyler, Frank Marlow and Louise Currie.

Many Adventures For Serial Villain

Harry Worth, who enacts the sinister role of Bently in "Return of Captain Marvel," (formerly entitled "Adventures of Captain Marvel"), Republic serial playing every.............. at the.................. Theatre, is a world traveler with a vast fund of anecdotes to narrate to his fellow workers between takes. One of his most hair-raising adventures was being captured by the Riffs when he was crossing French Morocco.

World Record Held By "Superman" Star

For six years, Tom Tyler, virile star playing the title role in Republic's thrilling chapter play, "Return of Captain Marvel," (formerly entitled "Adventures of Captain Marvel"), held the world's record for weight lifting. He appears as a superman in the serial, which plays every................ at the................ Theatre.

Deadly Instrument

A golden scorpion with five lenses in its claws is the sinister and fearful object about which revolves all the spine-tingling action in "Return of Captain Marvel," (formerly entitled "Adventures of Captain Marvel"), Republic serial which shows at the.................. Theatre every........................ Tom Tyler has the title role.

"RETURN OF CAPT. MARVEL" (1B)

"RETURN OF CAPTAIN MARVEL," thrill-packed Republic serial showing each............ at the.............. Theatre, stars Tom Tyler, pictured above in a scene from the exciting film.

STORY

To a remote section of Siam, zealously guarded by unconquered native tribes, comes the unwelcome Malcolm Scientific Expedition seeking knowledge of the ancient Scorpion Dynasty. Billy Batson, assistant to the radio expert, is the only one of the party who does not enter a forbidden chamber; as a result he is awarded the power to transform himself into a superman, "Captain Marvel," upon uttering the word "Shazam." Meanwhile, the scientists who have entered the sacred tomb have discovered "The Scorpion," a powerful gold weapon the potency of which is brought about by focussing five peculiar lenses. The scientists divide the lenses among themselves so that no one of them will have supernatural power.

A sinister gang, headed by a mysterious individual who calls himself "The Scorpion," embarks upon a campaign to steal the five lenses from the scientists so that their combined power will be sufficient to conquer the universe. They inflict various tribulations on the party, from which the members are inevitably rescued by Billy, in the guise of "Captain Marvel." As Marvel, he is invincible and able to overcome any danger. When the Scorpion's men attempt to kill him by means of a fiendishly contrived guillotine, the falling blade smashes to bits as it contacts his superhuman body. When a time bomb is placed in his plane, he becomes "Marvel" and glides safely through the air to the ground.

The expedition returns to America, but it is pursued by the sinister "Scorpion," who is obviously determined to leave no stone unturned in his ambition to attain world dominance. His malevolent influence is directed toward Betty, secretary of the expedition, when he learns that she is intrusted with many of the secrets of the party and undertakes various dangerous missions for them.

The Scorpion acquires all of the lenses but one, without which he is unable to focus the secret weapon. Naturally, he becomes more determined to acquire it, and will stop at nothing.

Billy has reason to believe that the Scorpion is in reality one of the scientists taking part in the Malcolm expedition. The Scorpion decides that it is very necessary to bring about his sudden death — a death so sudden that he will not have time to utter the magic word "Shazam" before it overtakes him. This is attempted; Billy is bound and gagged so that he cannot utter the word. He tricks the Scorpion into releasing the gag in order, as he pretends, to explain to him the secret of his invulnerability. Once released, he cries "Shazam" and becomes Captain Marvel. He is able to free himself and his friends and expose the Scorpion, once and for all, as Bentley himself, leader of the expedition.

Cast

Captain Marvel.................TOM TYLER
Billy Batson....FRANK COGHLAN, JR.
Whitey..............WILLIAM BENEDICT
Betty Wallace..........LOUISE CURRIE
The Scorpion...........THE SCORPION
John Malcolm........ROBERT STRANGE
Prof. Bentley..............HARRY WORTH
Henry Carlyle............
........................BRYANT WASHBURN
Tal Chotali..........JOHN DAVIDSON
Dr. Stephen Lang............
........................GEORGE PEMBROKE
Dwight Fisher............
........................PETER GEORGE LYNN
Rahman Bar................REED HADLEY
Howell........................JACK MULHALL
Barnett................KENNETH DUNCAN
Shazam................NIGEL DE BRULIER
Cowan........................JOHN BAGNI
Martin................CARLETON YOUNG
Major Rawley...LELAND HODGSON
Owens....................STANLEY PRICE
Akbar................ERNEST SARRACINO
Chan Lal................TETSU KOMAI

Credits

Associate Producer............
........................Hiram S. Brown, Jr.
Directed by............
........William Witney - John English
Original Screen Play by............
........Ronald Davidson, Norman S. Hall,
Arch B. Heath, Jos. Poland, Sol Shor
Production Manager............Al Wilson
Unit Manager............Mack D'Agostino
Photography............William Nobles
Film Editors................Edward Todd
........and William Thompson
Musical Score................Cy Feuer

RCA SOUND SYSTEM

A Republic 12-Episode Serial

A WOUNDED SOLDIER NEEDS YOUR BLOOD — TODAY!

ADVANCE STORIES FOR EACH CHAPTER

EPISODE ONE
(First Week)

"Return of Captain Marvel," (formerly entitled "Adventures of Captain Marvel"), Republic's thrill-packed serial, is scheduled to go into the............Theatre to show weekly for twelve weeks, beginning................

A remote section of Siam is the locale of this chapter-thriller, with a scientific expedition, under the leadership of John Malcolm, seeking knowledge of the ancient Scorpion Dynasty.

Billy Batson, radio man connected with the party, refrains from entering a sacred chamber, and as a reward, is given the power to transform himself into a superman by uttering the word "Shazam." This knowledge gives the scripters opportunity to invent the most bizarre and breath-taking situations which will feature in the serial throughout its run.

Tom Tyler portrays "Captain Marvel," with Frank Coghlan, Jr. as "Billy Batson." Louise Currie is the leading lady.

William Witney and Jask English co-directed under Associate Producer H. S. Brown, Jr.

EPISODE TWO
(Second Week)

Episode One of Republic's exciting serial "Return of Captain Marvel," (formerly entitled "Adventures of Captain Marvel"), which plays weekly at the .... Theatre on............ got off to a smashing start, with the Malcolm Scientific Expedition uncovering the secrets of the forbidden Scorpion Dynasty. Billy Batson, one of the radio operators, has acquired the power of turning himself into a superman as a reward for his refusal to enter a forbidden sacred chamber. By uttering the magic word "Shazam" he becomes "Captain Marvel," a man of supernatural strength who has the ability to emerge unscathed from any danger.

All the resources of his "Captain Marvel" characterization will be taxed in Episode Two, playing............... when he must save Betty, the expedition's secretary, from being plunged to her death in a gorge.

EPISODE THREE
(Third Week)

Captain Marvel is threatened with death from a fiendishly contrived guillotine at the close of last week's episode of "Return of Captain Marvel," (formerly entitled "Adventures of Captain Marvel"), Republic serial playing every .... at the............ Theatre. But tomorrow's episode will no doubt extricate him from this danger, as well as it will plunge him into other dangers, more ingenious and more breath-taking.

Tom Tyler is cast in the title role of Captain Marvel, and Frank Coghlan, Jr., portrays Billy Batson, the youth who has acquired the ability to turn himself into Captain Marvel, the superman, by uttering a magic word.

William Witney and John English co-directed under Associate Producer H. S. Brown, Jr.

EPISODE FOUR
(Fourth Week)

The guillotine, which threatened Captain Marvel one week ago, was smashed to bits as it made contact with the superman's deathless body! Thus began last week's episode of "Return of Captain Marvel," (formerly entitled "Adventures of Captain Marvel"), Republic serial which thrills local fans every ....

Betty, the scientific party's secretary, was abducted by henchmen of the sinister Scorpion, but when they attempted to force her to tell the combination of the safe containing the fearful lens, she threw the switch of the two-way radio so that Billy Batson, humble radio man, could become aware of her danger, transform himself into "Captain Marvel" and come to her rescue.

But before he had an opportunity to do so, the Scorpion plotted to bring

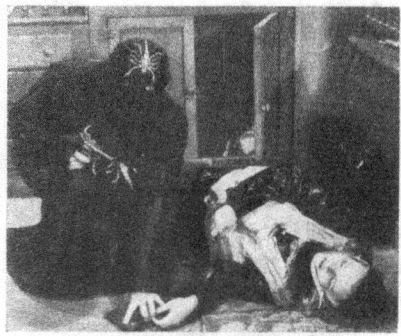

"RETURN OF CAPT. MARVEL" (2A)

"THE SCORPION" and Louise Currie in a thrilling scene from Republic's amazing serial, "Return of Captain Marvel," the first chapter of which will be screened............... at the............... Theatre.

EPISODE FOUR
(Continued)

about his immediate demise by placing a time bomb in his plane, and on this note of suspense and foreboding disaster ended the week's thrilling episode.

Episode Four, showing tomorrow, promises to clear up Billy's difficulties and plunge him into other, far more sinister.

EPISODE FIVE
(Fifth Week)

Billy Batson, as "Captain Marvel," eluded the winged death which haunted him in last week's episode of "Return of Captain Marvel," (formerly entitled "Adventures of Captain Marvel"), Republic serial showing every............... at the............... Theatre.

A secret room figures prominently in this week's episode of the chapter thriller, which features a large name cast including Tom Tyler, Frank Coghlan, Jr., Louise Currie, Robert Strange and William Benedict.

Betty is again kidnapped, and at the close of the episode we see her lying unconscious in her car as it races down a ramp at top speed, directly toward a large concrete building across the street. Will Captain Marvel get to her rescue in time? This problem, with many others, will be settled in Episode Five, which plays...............

William Witney and Jack English, who have directed many famous serials were behind the megaphones on this production. Associate Producer H. S. Brown was in charge of production for Republic.

EPISODE SIX
(Sixth Week)

Betty, the beautiful blonde stenographer accompanying the danger-ridden Malcolm scientific expedition, was saved from a horrible death in last week's episode of the Republic super-thriller, "Return of Captain Marvel," (formerly entitled "Adventures of Captain Marvel"), which shows every............... at the............... Theatre.

Recovering consciousness, Betty is able to tell the superman facts which put him on the trail of the Scorpion, a sinister force of evil who covets the power of world dominion.

Serial fans who see the current episode, opening............... will learn the

EPISODE SIX
(Continued)

unique way in which Captain Marvel thwarts the Scorpion's evil machinations, including a spectacular escape from a horrible death by molten lava.

Tom Tyler, Frank Coghlan, Jr., Louise Currie, Robert Strange, George Pembroke and Harry Worth are featured in the production.

EPISODE SEVEN
(Seventh Week)

"The Lens of Death," Episode Six in Republic's "Return of Captain Marvel," (formerly entitled "Adventures of Captain Marvel"), closed with the intrepid Captain Marvel approaching almost certain death by electrocution as he attempts to extract the coveted lens from the scientist's safe. Captain Marvel, for the benefit of those local fans who missed the earlier chapters of the serial, is a superhuman individual who is able to confer immortality upon himself by uttering the magic word "Shazam," returning again to normal life as "Billy Batson," radio operator on the Malcolm scientific expedition.

He is seeking to prevent the forces of evil, led by a mysterious man calling himself "The Scorpion," from obtaining possession of the five magic lenses which will, when operated in unison, give their owner the power of world dominion.

Tom Tyler has the title role in the production, with Frank Coghlan, Jr., Louise Currie, Robert Strange, Harry Worth, Jack Mulhall and Reed Hadley in supporting roles.

EPISODE EIGHT
(Eighth Week)

Captain Marvel was stunned, but not killed at the opening of Episode Seven of "Return of Captain Marvel," (formerly entitled "Adventures of Captain Marvel"), Republic serial playing every .... at the............... Theatre.

When he recovers consciousness he learns that the Scorpion's men have made way with a powerful lens and, unless halted will have at their command a weapon which will conquer the world.

Marvel's adventures take him into a death trap in which he appears doomed to certain destruction when bombs dropped from the Scorpion's planes above drop on top of him.

William Witney and Jack English co-directed the serial.

EPISODE NINE
(Ninth Week)

Before the bombs, which threatened Billy Batson in last week's episode of "Return of Captain Marvel," (formerly entitled "Adventures of Captain Marvel"), dropped, he succeeded in freeing himself from his gag so that he could utter the word "Shazam" which transformed him into "Captain Marvel" and made it possible for him to rescue himself and the beautiful blonde Betty, secretary with the Malcolm scientific expedition.

This week's episode of the Republic serial, which is scheduled to show............... at the............... Theatre, presents several novel new angles. Captain Marvel, with the aid of Betty, has ascertained that the mysterious Scorpion is in reality one of the five leaders of the expedition. They know, too, that the Scorpion has been wounded in the hand — so it appears that the object of their search will soon be made apparent.

EPISODE TEN
(Tenth Week)

The sinister Scorpion took Billy prisoner in last week's episode of Republic's thrilling serial, "Return of Captain Marvel," (formerly entitled "Adventures of Captain Marvel"), which shows every .... at the............... Theatre. After attempting unsuccessfully to torture various members of the party into disclosing the hiding place of the secret lens, the Scorpion concocted a death trap which, for sheer fiendishness, surpasses any of his wickednesses to date.

Facing the fusilade of death, Billy Batson seems to have met an all time high in the danger that has dogged his path ever since he joined the ill-fated Malcolm scientific expedition.

The all star action cast of the serial includes Tom Tyler, Frank Coghlan, Jr., Louise Currie, Robert Strange and Harry Worth.

EPISODE ELEVEN
(Eleventh Week)

Last week's episode of Republic's exciting serial, "Return of Captain Marvel," (formerly entitled "Adventures of Captain Marvel"), took the Malcolm Scientific party on a voyage to Asia, where their ship was wrecked and Billy Batson, by assuming the immortal character of "Captain Marvel" was able to rescue his friends from being buffeted to death by angry seas.

This week's episode "Valley of Death," which plays............... at the............... Theatre, shows how the invulnerable Captain Marvel, slowly but inexorably, pieces together his damning bits of evidence pointing to the true identity of "The Scorpion," a wicked man who desires to subject the world.

Listed among the popular favorites in the cast are such stellar performers as Tom Tyler, Frank Coghlan, Jr., Billie Benedict and Jack Mulhall. William Witney and Jack English directed under Associate Producer H. S. Brown.

EPISODE TWELVE
(Twelfth Week)

"Return of Captain Marvel," (formerly entitled "Adventures of Captain Marvel"), Republic serial, draws to a smashing climax this............... at the .... Theatre, with Billy Batson, through the aid of his altar ego, "Captain Marvel," revealing the identity of the sinister "Scorpion." Local fans, who have been following the serial since its opening twelve weeks ago, will be genuinely astonished when they learn the identity of the "Scorpion."

The twelve episode serial has attracted much attention locally — has never flagged in interest, and the twelfth and final chapter promises to deliver a smashing conclusion.

Tom Tyler has had the title role, with supplementary roles being ably filled by Frank Coghlan, Jr. and Louise Currie.

LOBBIES

Set of Eight 11 x 14's

ALSO AVAILABLE —
CIRCUS HERALD

MAT for a flash CIRCUS HERALD is available GRATIS.
Size: 4¾" x 12½".

Write to:
REPUBLIC PICTURES, EXPLOITATION DEPT.
1740 Broadway   New York 19, N. Y.

VALANCE

A brilliant flash piece for your marquee or lobby, the valance is printed in several eye-arresting colors on GORGEOUS RAYON SILKOLENE. It measures 9 feet wide by 3 feet deep and is all ready for hanging. Price: $9.75.

Order direct from:
NATIONAL FLAG COMPANY
43 West 21st Street   New York, N. Y.

POSTERS

One Sheet

Three Sheet

ORDER ALL ACCESSORIES FROM NATIONAL SCREEN SERVICE

Entire Contents Copyright, 1953, by Republic Pictures Corporation

ADVERTISING

1 Col. x 80 Lines

1 Col. x 56 Lines

Illustrated above are four of the twelve two-column slugs — numbered from 211A through 222A — one for each episode — on "RETURN OF CAPTAIN MARVEL." The one-column slugs are shown on page 1. Use them in newspapers to bring capacity audiences to your theatre.

321

3 COL. x 90 LINES

2 COL. x 38 LINES

1 Col. x 70 Lines

2 COL. x 56 LINES

2 COL. x 70 LINES

G. MICHAEL DOBBS

Chapter Nine

Tom Tyler in Print

The westerns that starred Tom Tyler were not just limited to the United States for distribution as these appearances in magazines illustrate. Tyler had a world-wide fan base.

In Great Britain, from 1919 to 1940, boys who were movie fans had a weekly magazine of their own, Boy's Cinema.

Each issue had two novelizations of current action movies. Film producers Richard and Alex Gordon, who grew up in London in the 1930s, remembered that publication well and both read it. A number of American cowboy stars were featured including Tom Tyler as these covers noted.

Here are several Boy's Cinema covers of issues featuring Tyler.

And here is an entire story, an adaptation of "Ridin' Through."

THE FILMS AND LIFE OF TOM TYLER

Every Tuesday — BOY'S CINEMA

A range stallion and a crooked foreman—here was the combination responsible for the losses on the Bar L Ranch, and it needed fighting Tom Saunders to crush the menace which threatened his employer's ruin. A smashing tale of romance and adventure in the Far West, starring Tom Tyler and Ruth Hiatt.

RIDING THROUGH

Horse Power.

ON the western skirts of the Sierra Nevada Mountains lies the old stage-coach trail that leads from Fresno to White Bluff, and it was upon this road that two horsemen might have been sighted on a certain morning in the early summer.

They were cowboys wending their way northward through the Californian cattle country, and they had been on the move for several days, neither of them being total strangers to the particular section through which they were now travelling, though they had not visited it in many years.

They were an ill-dressed pair, but were fast friends nevertheless. One of them was a handsome young giant with dark brown hair and clean-cut, sun-burned features—Tom Saunders by name, and by reputation the best rider and roper between the Gila River and the Grand Canyon. The other was a short, stocky fellow known as Barney Tilson, comical in appearance, but a staunch comrade in a tight corner, as Tom could testify.

Meet the boys as they pause for a moment beside a sign-post at a fork in the road. One indicator of that sign-post is pointing to the left, and denotes the route to Fresno. The other bears the following legend:

Turn right for Bar L Guest Ranch.
Proprietor—ELMER BROOKS.

It was the latter arm of the sign-board that held the attention of the cowboys, and they considered it thoughtfully for a few seconds. Then Tom Saunders addressed himself to his companion.

"Old Daddy Brooks must have run into a streak of bad luck all right, or he'd never have turned his place into a dude outfit," he declared.

Barney Tilson nodded gloomily.

"Maybe we won't get jobs as horses' chambermaids, after all," he vouchsafed.

"Don't worry about that," Tom retorted. "When Daddy Brooks says he's got jobs, he's got 'em."

He spoke with conviction, for he knew Elmer Brooks—had worked under him when the old fellow had been manager of a ranch in Arizona. That had been before Brooks had drifted to California to start in business for himself, and all had seemed to go well with him for a year or two. Then out of the blue Tom Saunders had received a letter from him, offering him a billet in the Bar L, and hinting at trouble.

"Things are in bad shape, Tom," he had written, "and I can't seem to get the right men. If anyone can help me, you can. I haven't forgotten that it was you who cleaned out those rustlers that used to bother the outfit I was managing in Arizona. Now, when you get here, I think it would be a good plan if we were to pretend that we don't know each other. Just show up, casual-like, and ask for work. And, by the way, how about fetching along that little runt, Barney Tilson?"

So Tom and Barney were now on the last lap of their journey, both of them looking forward to an early arrival at their destination.

"We ought to be at the Bar L about noon," Tom opined. "Come on, Barney, old-timer, let's go."

They swung away from the sign-post, taking the right-hand fork and pushing farther into the hills, and they had gone about a couple of miles when they suddenly beheld a troop of horses in a pleasant valley some distance ahead of them.

The troop was composed of a small herd of mares, about thirty head, and they were munching peacefully at the mesquite grass.

"Some of Elmer Brook's stock most likely," Tom said. "At any rate, they're not wild ponies. I guess they're about ——"

The sentence was left unfinished, for at that moment a white form dashed into the valley from a cleft among the hills and bore down on the herd of mares at speed. It was the form of a palomino stallion, a magnificent creature with strength and vigour in every line of its body.

"Boy, what a horse!" Barney declared admiringly.

Tom was thinking the same, but all at once his appreciation of the animal's finer points was dismissed from his mind by its remarkable behaviour, for, sweeping down on the bunch of mares, it began to cavort around the herd in circles, tossing its silky mane, stamping its unshod hoofs.

"What's it up to now?" Barney murmured.

He soon had his answer. The mares had become restless, and on a sudden, as the stallion wheeled to make for the cleft in the hills again, the whole herd broke into a gallop and followed it.

Tom and Barney realised that they were witnessing a spectacular piece of enticement on the part of that male palomino. Nor was the circumstance unheard of so far as they were concerned, for both of them knew that some of these wild, outlaw stallions had a trick of coaxing ranch ponies into the remote fastnesses of the hills, the mares obeying the deep-rooted, animal instincts which the appearance of the stallions aroused. It was often a difficult job recovering the stock thus lost.

June 2nd, 1934.

for the broncs quickly fell into the ways of their untamed forbears.

"That palomino sure is a ladies' man," Barney stated. "I'll bet he's got more wives tucked away in these here mountains than King Solomon ever had."

"Let's see where he's bound for," Tom proposed. "If we get near enough to spot the brand those mares are carryin', we'll be able to tell for sure if they belong to the Brooks' outfit."

He clapped heels to the flanks of his mount, and Barney imitated his example, the two friends galloping down into the valley and spurring for the cleft through which stallion and ponies had disappeared. Beyond that cleft stretched a country of peaks and ridges that were separated by lonely ravines — typical mountain scenery abounding with the characteristics of the West—and it was into the heart of this rugged landscape that the cowboys followed the fleeing horses.

The stallion and its decoyed herd had a considerable start, but after covering a mile of ground at top speed, the pursuing riders were appreciably closer to their quarry, and they felt that they had every prospect of tracking the palomino to its lair when an unexpected challenge greeted their advance.

A shot rang out, and a bullet whizzed between them. They drew rein immediately, and looked around in bewilderment, uncertain whence the leaden slug had come, for the hills had taken up the echoes of the report and baffled any attempt to locate the whereabouts of the marksman who had fired. Nor did the punchers discern any white drift of gun-smoke to indicate the position of a foe.

"Somebody's shootin' at us," Barney said superfluously. "Cain't locate the guy—can *you*?"

"He might be up in that belt of brushwood," Tom muttered, indicating a dense mass of thickets that clothed a hillside some distance ahead. "Supposin' we go forward again."

They did so, but their horses had only taken a few steps when a desultory volley ripped the quiet of the hills, signifying that more than one man was disputing the cowboys' approach. This time a regular shower of lead whistled past them and, lending grim emphasis to the warning fusillade, one bullet whipped Barney's sombrero clean off his head.

The little puncher drew up his mount with a jerk, and then, sliding out of the saddle, collected his hat. A neat hole was bored clean through the crown of it.

"Nice friendly neighbourhood," Barney commented sourly.

Tom had also halted again. He was frowning darkly, and his eyes were bent on the vanishing figures of the stallion and the herd of mares. They were skirting the hillside from which he judged that the shooting had come, and presently they passed out of sight in a haze of dust.

"Looks like somebody don't *want* us to follow these critters, Barney," he said. "There's something fishy about this."

His comrade had climbed astride his bronc again.

"Let's get outa here," he urged. "Them bullets told us plain that we was to mind our own business, an' we'd be crazy to argue with a bunch o' guys that we can't even see."

"You're right, Barney," Tom agreed thoughtfully. "Remember the old sayin'—it was curiosity that killed the cat."

They swung around and rode at a trot in the direction from which they

June 2nd, 1934.

had come. As they retired from the scene they had the feeling that several pairs of eyes were watching their departure, as indeed they were—the eyes of three or four men concealed in the tract of brushwood that Tom had noted a few minutes before.

They were ruffianly-looking individuals, armed with rifles and revolvers, and they continued to spy upon Tom and Barney until the cowboys were no longer in view. Then one of the group broke silence—a squarely-built man with a broken nose and a slit of a mouth.

"That fixed them two hombres," he said with a harsh chuckle. "Come on, let's see what the palomino has brung this time."

He led the way through the thickets to where a small bunch of saddle-horses stood tethered. The rogues mounted these and cantered round the hillside, then dipped into a small canyon which was to all appearances blind at one end. In this ravine the stallion and the decoyed herd of mares were "milling" aimlessly.

The armed men spurred towards the horses, and one of the fellows dismounted, running to a mass of brushwood at the far end of the canyon. He dragged at the vegetation, and it proved to be a loose pile of twigs and foliage that cunningly screened a tunnel in the rock.

The other men proceeded to hustle the herd of ponies through the secret cavern, but the rogue with the broken nose singled out the stallion and prevented it from entering. Driving it back, he chased it from the ravine and then returned to the curtain of brushwood that masked the tunnel.

The individual who had shifted the vegetation looked up at him.

"I see you've turned the palomino loose again, Joe," he remarked.

"Yeah!" answered the man with the broken nose. "He might pick up some more strays an' entice 'em here."

"Miss Dolores."

BACK in the valley where they had first sighted the stallion, Tom Saunders and Barney Tilson rejoined the road to the Bar L Ranch, and they had proceeded along it in silence for a mile or two when they swung round a sharp bend and almost collided with an empty car, which had been left somewhat thoughtlessly in the middle of the trail.

The cowboys pulled up sharply and surveyed the automobile, a smart two-seater.

"This is a funny place to leave a car," Tom commented. "It wouldn't be a bad idea to move it off the road. Some other motorist is liable to run into it if they come speedin' around the bend. Why, we almost fouled it ourselves."

"Yeah, but do you think you can handle that outlaw?" growled Barney, to whom all machinery was as diabolical as it was incomprehensible.

Tom swung himself out of the saddle. His familiarity with automobiles was slight, but he had an abundance of confidence.

"Sure I can handle it," he announced. "Just watch me."

He opened the door of the car and climbed in behind the steering-wheel. Then he began to fumble somewhat vaguely with the controls, while Barney looked on dubiously.

Tom located the brake and released it. This done, he proceeded to tamper with various switches on the dashboard, and then, seeing a button-like object, he pressed it in tentative fashion. It was the self-starter, and the engine was set in motion—indeed, the whole car was set in motion with an alarming suddenness, for the puncher's uncertain hand had already engaged the gear lever when he had been searching for the hand-brake, and he had also switched open the throttle during his floundering activities.

The two-seater shot forward as if propelled from a gun, and Tom was thrown back against the upholstery. Blanching, he clutched at the wheel and yawed it round in a frenzy of panic. At the same time he tried to reach the foot-brake, but only succeeded in thrusting down the accelerator pedal.

He drove the car off the road all right, for in the wink of an eye it had swung on to a sweep of grass. Here, under the bewildered guidance of the cowboy, it turned round and round in circles, rocking violently over the uneven ground until by some unorthodox means which he himself could not have described the man at the wheel succeeded in stopping it.

Tom scrambled out of it swiftly, glad to plant his feet on terra firma again. Then he looked at Barney, who had dismounted from his horse and was standing at the roadside with an amused expression on his face.

"I've been watchin' you, pal," he observed. "You sure can handle them ornery automobyles."

"Something went wrong, I guess," Tom grunted in a sheepish tone, and even as he spoke the words his eyes wandered to a glade set amidst some thickets near by.

Two girls were there, and they had apparently been enjoying a picnic. But at the moment they were scrambling up indignantly, and the smaller of them, an attractive young miss whose looks were in no way impaired by her furious expression, suddenly made for Tom in a stumbling run.

"What are you doing with my car?" she demanded, on confronting the puncher.

"Why, I—I'm sorry, miss!" Tom stammered. "When I saw the auto standin' in the middle of the road I figured somebody might run into it, and I thought I'd better move it."

"Oh, you thought, eh?" the girl retorted angrily. "Well, you shouldn't think!"

She pushed past him and climbed into the car, and her rage increased as she discovered that the starter had jammed.

"You clumsy idiot!" she flung at Tom. "Now see what you've done!"

Her friend was approaching, carrying a bag which contained the crockery they had used for their picnic.

"Is the car damaged, Dolores?" the taller girl asked.

Tom was now beginning to recover his composure, and he winked at Barney, who had walked across from the road.

"Pretty name—Dolores," he said. "Don't you think so, pardner?"

"Sure is, Tom," Barney agreed; but before he could proceed further the girl in the automobile broke in on him fiercely.

"Keep quiet, or I'll have you arrested —both of you!" she snapped. "This is an outrage. First you jam up my car, and then I've got to listen to your insults! What are you standing there for like a couple of boobs, anyway? Why don't you help me? Why don't you push the car for me?"

The twinkle of merriment faded from Tom's eyes, for the tone of "Miss Dolores" had been cutting. Sticking out his jaw, he went to the back of the auto and prepared to shove. Barney following his example.

"Come on, Myra," said the girl at the wheel. "Get in."

Her friend entered the machine, and

THE FILMS AND LIFE OF TOM TYLER

Every Tuesday

Tom and Barney heaved with all their might. The car rolled towards the road, and as it was gathering momentum its attractive owner let in the clutch with a jerk, the gear-lever still being in a fixed position.

The engine started up with a roar, and the auto forged ahead, Tom and Barney falling full-length as it shot away. They picked themselves up amidst a haze of oil-fumes, and stared after the car as it swung on to the road and drove off in a northerly direction.

"Nice girl—Miss Dolores," Barney remarked as he brushed himself down.

"Yeah," Tom growled, "for a sister."

* * *

The Bar L ranch had fallen on evil times, and it had been in a fit of sheer desperation that old Elmer Brooks, familiarly known as Daddy, had taken on paying guests in the shape of wealthy city folks, who rode the countryside on tame ponies, or played bridge, or sunbathed in scanty attire.

Elmer Brooks was seated in the comparative privacy of his study, one of the few retreats to which he could make his way without much chance of finding it occupied by some rich loafer in fancy riding-breeches or some simpering debutante in a jazzy beach-suit.

The old man was clutching a stick, on which he had found it necessary to hobble round for the last week or two. Lean, white-haired, he was still normally active, but a bullet in his leg had left him a temporary cripple, a circumstance which was trying to him in the extreme.

Opposite Brooks sat a tall, powerfully-built man, known as Winthrop. He was the rancher's foreman, and he was looking at his employer solemnly, fingering his trim, dark moustache as he listened to what the old fellow had to say.

"I have got to have money, or I'm sunk," Elmer Brooks declared testily. "The cash that I'm making out of these dudes isn't enough to keep the outfit going through the winter months, and, besides, I don't want to depend on these city swells for a living any longer than I can help. I want you to ship those prize mares the day after to-morrow, Winthorp. They ought to raise five thousand dollars."

"That herd's in the corral, Mr. Brooks," the foreman stated, "and they'll fetch top prices all right."

"H'm!" Brooks grunted. "And how many head are left out on the range?"

"Some of the boys are out makin' a tally of them," Winthrop answered. "There ought to be a thousand head, anyway."

Elmer Brooks struck his walking-stick hard against the floor.

"A thousand head," he grated. "There would have been five thousand if those ornery horse thieves hadn't run 'em off!"

"Don't get excited, Mr. Brooks," Winthrop protested, endeavouring to pacify him. "I'm following up some clues."

The old man pursed his lips.

"Get more men to help you," he snapped. "I'm short-handed here at the ranch as well as out on the range. I tell you, Winthrop, I'm almost at the end of my string. What with losing my stock and having to turn this place into a crazy dude ranch, I'm fit to be hog-tied."

"Don't worry, Mr. Brooks," the foreman said reassuringly. "We'll get the better of these horse thieves yet, and you won't have to run your ranch as a hotel much longer."

He rose to go, and, making his way from the room, walked out into a patio, where numbers of the paying guests were seated around little tables, whiling away the time in card games or idle gossip. Passing through this courtyard, Winthrop strolled towards a wicket-gate, and just as he reached this he heard his name spoken.

A man approached him. He was one of the ranch hands, and the chief characteristic of his face was a broken nose. He was the same rogue who had captained the gang responsible for driving off Tom Saunders and Barney Tilson when they had attempted to follow the palomino and the decoyed herd of ponies.

"Hallo, Joe!" Winthrop said to him in an undertone. "What's the news? Any luck?"

"Thirty head more safe in the canyon," Joe muttered.

"No trouble of any kind?" the foreman asked.

"No trouble of any kind?" the foreman asked.

"Not to speak of, boss," was the answer. "A couple o' strangers came snoopin' around, but we scared 'em off good an' plenty."

He paused, for at that moment he had caught sight of two horsemen, riding towards the ranch. With a start, he recognised them as the cowboys to whom he had just referred, and he spoke to Winthrop swiftly.

"Here's the two guys themselves," he said. "Listen! They didn't see us, but watch your step!"

The foreman's eyes had narrowed, and he watched the newcomers as they cantered up to the gate. His attention was still riveted on them when they dismounted and walked forward.

"What do you want?" he demanded of them tersely.

It was Tom who replied.

"We want jobs," he stated. "Do you need any hands?"

"No, we're full up," Winthrop lied. "On your way, cowboys!"

"But, listen!" Tom remonstrated. "We——"

The foreman pulled open the gate savagely and stepped close to them. His accomplice, Joe, moved after him, ready to render assistance in the event of any trouble.

"You heard me!" Winthrop snapped at Tom. "There's no work for you here—so get out!"

"How do you know there ain't no jobs?" put in Barney Tilson with some

"You heard me," Winthrop snapped at Tom. "There's no work for you here, so get out!"

June 2nd, 1934.

heat, one hand resting on the butt of his gun.

"Because I'm the foreman—that's how," came the rash rejoinder. "Now, beat it, you two—and don't come back!"

"Huh! I guess you're a bouncer—not a foreman," Barney remarked ironically.

"I'll bounce one off your chin if you don't keep a civil tongue in your head!" Winthrop rasped, and with that Barney's fighting blood was aroused.

"You and who else?" he taunted violently.

Winthrop swung at him, but, stepping in quickly, Tom knocked up his arm and pounded him heartily on the jaw. Instantly the foreman's broken-nosed lieutenant charged forward, and next moment an ugly scuffle was in progress.

The fracas was fairly at its height when Elmer Brooks appeared on the scene, limping to the gate with the aid of his stick, and calling out in angry tones:

"Here—here! What's going on? Winthrop—Winthrop! What do you think you're doing?"

The combatants separated, and a look passed between Elmer Brooks and Tom; but, remembering that he and Barney were to affect the manner of men who were total strangers to the rancher, the stalwart cowboy gave no sign of recognition.

Winthrop spoke to the elderly horse breeder.

"These cowboys got fresh, Mr. Brooks," he panted. "Joe and I had to set about them."

"I didn't know that lookin' for a job was fresh," Tom drawled, and at that Elmer Brooks glanced at his foreman sharply.

"Why didn't you hire them?" he snapped. "You know we're short-handed."

"I didn't like the looks of 'em," Winthrop grumbled.

"Looks or no looks, put them on the pay-roll," the rancher commanded. "We need every man we can get."

"But, Mr. Brooks——"

"You heard me, Winthrop," the old fellow cut in. "I'm still running this outfit, and you'll do as I say!"

He turned and hobbled off, and, with a heavy scowl on his face, the foreman shot a lowering glance at Tom and Barney.

"All right," he bit out. "Shove your traps in the bunkhouse. You'll find it around the corner."

Smirking in a way that further incensed the foreman, the two cowboys sauntered in the direction that Winthrop had indicated, the pair of them leading their horses by the reins, and en route to their quarters Barney did not fail to notice a bevy of girls in bathing-costumes reclining near a fountain in the middle of the patio.

"Say, this don't look like no ranch to me," he whispered, in an elated voice. "It looks like one o' them million dollar revues you read about. I'm gonna like it here."

"You keep your eyes shut," Tom told him. "We're here on business."

He and Barney were still in full view of Winthrop and Joe, and the foreman and his lieutenant were eyeing the new hands grimly.

"So Brooks wants 'em on the pay-roll, eh?" Winthrop murmured. "Well, I don't. This ranch can stay short-handed so far as I'm concerned. It suits me better."

"You mean you'd like to get rid of 'em?" Joe inquired, with a wealth of meaning in his voice.

"Yeah, but no shootin'," the foreman said. "Just make things hot for 'em, so they'll be glad to quit. Put Red McCord and Beef Kelly on to 'em. Tell 'em we've a couple of new hands, and I want 'em initiated, good an' plenty."

A Renewed Acquaintance.

BACK in his study, Elmer Brooks was reclining in a deep armchair when one of his employees entered the room—a young cowboy who had been working with him for some years, and whose particular job was to carry mail to and from the ranch.

"Well, Slim, what do you want?" the owner of the Bar L inquired.

"There's another saddle and one of those new blankets missing from the store-room through there, Mr. Brooks," the young fellow reported, indicating an apartment connected with the study. "I thought I'd better let you know."

The old rancher ground his teeth together.

"That's them dudes again, I suppose," he said wrathfully. "They seem to think they have the run of this house and can pick up anything they please. Not satisfied with the saddles and blankets that are put at their disposal, they have to appropriate the equipment belongin' to my employees. What I want to know is this: how do they get through to that store-room? For the last two weeks I've spent most of my time in this study."

"But the door leadin' from the study ain't the only way into the store-room, Mr. Brooks," Slim reminded him. "Don't forget the side-door that opens on to the patio."

"You're right," the old man declared. "Slim, we ought to have a lock on that door. It's not had one for years—never needed one before—but from now on I'm keeping it fastened. Get a padlock the next time you're in town."

Slim promised to do so, and made his exit. A moment or two after he had gone there was a light knock on the study door, and as Brooks called out in answer a tall, well-knit figure slipped across the threshold.

It was the figure of Tom Saunders, and, closing the door behind him, the stalwart puncher moved towards the owner of the Bar L. The latter promptly pulled himself to his feet, and the two men met in the middle of the room with outstretched hands, no longer concealing their friendship, but greeting each other genially.

"Gee, I'm glad to see you, Tom," the rancher exclaimed.

"That goes for me, too," the younger man said, "and I hope I can be of some help, Daddy Brooks."

The older man indicated a chair, and Tom sat down. Then the owner of the Bar L outfit broached the subject of his troubles.

"I hinted in my letter to you that things were very far wrong," he began. "Well, Tom, they're as bad as I made them out to be—maybe worse. Horse-thieves are cuttin' down my stock something terrible."

"Do you suspect anybody?" Tom asked.

Old man Brooks drew in a long breath.

"I'm getting so I suspect everybody," he muttered. "That's one reason why I didn't tell a soul that I had a couple of friends comin' here. I even kept it from Winthrop. You know, Tom, I can't get hands. They're either scared off or bumped off soon after I hire 'em. Oh, it's gonna be no picnic for you here, and I wouldn't blame you much if you cried off——"

"Not a chance of that, Daddy Brooks,"

Tom interposed. "Barney and I are here to see the thing through to the finish. You can depend on that. By the way, I see you're lame. How did that happen?"

The older man grimaced.

"The horse-thieves," he replied. "They plugged me from ambush. I tell you, Tom, they're a tough proposition. The sheriff will bear me out in that. He hasn't been able to do a thing against them."

"H'm," Tom mused, "I wouldn't be surprised if Barney and I haven't found a clue already, Daddy Brooks. Something happened this morning—something that concerned a palomino stallion—— But I'll tell you about that some other time. Meanwhile, I'd better steer clear of you. I think it's a good idea to keep up the impression that you and I are strangers."

He stood up, and, nodding to the rancher, made for the door, pulling it open and stepping forth briskly. As he did so he came into sharp collision with a girl who was carrying a tray of food, and she uttered a squeal as the contents of the salver were spilled over her frock.

Recoiling with an exclamation as the tray clattered to the floor, Tom recognised her immediately as the girl whose car he had attempted to drive. The recognition was mutual, and at sight of him the features of "Miss Dolores" were tinged with a heightening colour that spelled resentment.

"You clumsy fool, look what you've done to my dress!" she cried. "How dare you follow me to this ranch, anyhow?"

"Lady, you flatter yourself," Tom rejoined curtly. "I didn't follow you here. I've just been hired."

"Good!" she snapped. "I'll have my Uncle Elmer fire you!"

Tom suddenly recalled that Daddy Brooks had mentioned he was adopting a niece when he had left Arizona to take up ranching in California, and the youngster looked at the girl with new interest. He was still eyeing her frankly when her uncle limped to the doorway, having heard the altercation.

"I'm afraid I can't fire this man, Dolores," Elmer Brooks said in an amused tone. "You see, we need every hand we can get."

"But look—he's ruined my new dress," the girl protested.

"Well, we'll take the cleaning bill out of his wages," her uncle told her, with a sly wink at Tom.

Tom grinned covertly, and was for passing on when Dolores caught him by the sleeve.

"Oh, wait a minute, cowboy," she said sharply; and then, turning to Daddy Brooks: "Do you need this man for an hour, Uncle Elmer?" she asked.

The old fellow shook his head, and the girl looked at Tom again.

"Go to the stable, and groom and saddle my horse," she ordered imperiously. "She has a name-plate over her stall, and it says 'Brown Betty.' In case you can't read, ask any of the boys which is my pony."

Tom ignored her sarcasm.

"Yes, Miss Dolores," he said with polite stiffness.

"Miss Brooks to you, cowboy," she retorted, while her uncle stood chuckling in the background. "And remember—I want that horse properly groomed. I'll be round for her in half an hour."

"Yes, Miss Dolores Brooks," Tom replied.

He strode out of the ranch-house, but if Dolores imagined that she had set him a laborious and unpleasant task she was far mistaken, for it was Barney who was compelled to groom Brown Betty, a spirited mare that was fairly itching to set foot on the open range.

Under the watchful eye and stern directions of the bigger cowboy, Barney worked with a curry-comb until the perspiration was running from his brow, but Tom was a relentless task-master.

"Keep at it, pardner," he said. "I want this horse to look slicker than axle grease when Miss Dolores Brooks shows up."

"Why don't you do something?" Barney demanded, glowering at him.

"I'm workin' harder than you are," Tom answered in a half-jocular, half-serious tone. "Barney, I'm just tryin' to figure where that white stallion fits into the game."

"You mean—in connection with the horse-thieves that are running off the Bar L stock?"

"Sure," Tom muttered. "But you keep workin' on that mare, Barney. Go on, hit that rump again with the curry-comb."

The little puncher swallowed an oath. "Say," he blurted, "ain't we got enough on our minds without you fallin' for this Dolores dame?"

"Me fallin' for her?" Tom echoed indignantly. "Where do you get that stuff? Listen; I wish she'd break her leg so's I'd have an excuse to shoot her."

Barney's face suddenly changed, and he made a warning gesture. He had seen Dolores approaching—earlier than she had been expected.

Tom looked round as the girl came up, and, in contrast to the disgruntled words he had just uttered, he volunteered a piece of well-meant advice.

"Miss Dolores Brooks," he said, "I'm not so sure I'd use this mare if I were you. She's awful frisky—guess she's been in the stable too long."

"Mind your own business, cowboy," Dolores retorted.

Tom shrugged, and fell silent while Barney saddled the pony. Then he helped the girl to mount.

"I hope you have a nice ride, Miss Dolores Brooks," he remarked, as soon as she had set her feet in the stirrups.

"Don't keep saying 'Miss Dolores Brooks'—like a ninny," she snapped.

"No, Miss Dolores Brooks," Tom murmured; and with an angry dig of her heels the girl spurred her horse into a gallop.

Tom and Barney watched her until she had disappeared down the trail, and then the smaller cowboy offered a comment.

"Nice girl—Miss Dolores Brooks," he observed.

"Yeah, for a cousin," Tom grunted.

"Listen; you and I are goin' out to see if we can pick up the trail of that palomino stallion, and this time no amount of lead is gonna stop us."

"All right—Mister Tom Saunders," Barney said with a smirk.

"Aw, shut up," his comrade snapped. "Go get our horses."

Barney strode off, and Tom followed him at a more leisurely pace. He saw his partner turn the corner of a barn, and then, when he himself reached the same spot, he discovered him in the act of being accosted by two burly ranch-hands.

"We hear that you and another guy have been signed on," one of the cowboys was saying to Barney. "Glad to know yuh, friend. My name's Red McCord, an' this is Beef Kelly."

"Howdy," said Barney. "Glad to know you, too."

"Got a match?" inquired the man named Kelly, rolling himself a cigarette.

The unsuspecting Barney dipped into the breast-pocket of his shirt, and as he did so Kelly swung at him in cowardly fashion. Back went Tom's comrade, and he was still staggering from that first blow when McCord jumped at him and struck him a second.

Barney hit the ground and lay still with widespread arms. His assailants looked down at him and leered unpleasantly.

"That wuz easy," said McCord. "There's more to come for him, too.

We'll show him that it ain't no cinch workin' on the Bar L."

"Meantime, let's look for the other hombre," Beef Kelly suggested. "I understand he's bigger."

"He'll fall the harder," McCord stated. "Come on, let's find him."

They had not noticed Tom standing by the corner of the barn, and now he ducked back out of sight. When McCord and Kelly came round the angle of the building he was walking slowly towards them, apparently unaware of the treatment that had been meted out to his partner.

"Hallo, stranger," Kelly greeted him. "Got a match?"

Tom lifted his hand towards his breast-pocket and with that Kelly hit out at him. But the new cowboy was ready for him—threw up his arm to knock aside the other's fist—and in the same instant drove his bunched knuckles to the point of his man's jaw.

The punch landed with a resounding smack, and Kelly was catapulted against the wall of the barn. With a shout McCord sprang at Tom and lashed at him furiously, but the youngster jerked back, and, though the blow caught him, its force was spent.

McCord bundled into him and tried to clinch. Grabbing him under the armpits, Tom hurled him away and then pounced on him in flying style. The next minute or two were hectic ones for Red McCord, for he was the suffering victim of a whirlwind attack that left him battered, breathless and bewildered.

Punches rained on him from every angle, thumping home against face and body, blackening his eyes, bruising his ribs. He went down in the dust, and picked himself up only to be floored again. This time he lay grovelling for a few seconds ere struggling to his feet, but the moment he raised himself Tom was upon him once more.

A pile-driving right scattered McCord's wits completely, and he dropped to the

Neither Barney nor Tom was aware that the two men were lurking in the shadows of the out-building's interior.

ground as if he had been poleaxed. In the meantime Beef Kelly had recovered himself and was advancing to give battle, but he shared the fate of his companion, for Tom buffeted him into oblivion with the same hurricane tactics.

Kelly finished up in a sprawled attitude across the huddled figure of McCord, and the conqueror of the two ranch bullies was standing over the pair of them when Barney stumbled into view nursing a swollen chin.

"They asked me for a match," he mumbled.

"They met their match," Tom rejoined. "Couple o' big punks. Come on, Barney, let's drift. We've got work to do."

A Mistake in Identity.

ONCE in the saddle, Tom and Barney rode southward from the Bar L outfit, and soon they were well out on the open range.

The locality in which they had sighted the white stallion was the objective that they had in mind, and on gaining the valley whence the herd of mares had been enticed, they made for the cleft in the hills, determined to follow the route taken by the palomino.

"You know, I'm pretty well certain that the horse-thieves are makin' use of that stallion," Tom said to Barney. "It's a smart racket, eh? And mighty simple, too. The palomino coaxes the mares away by its natural instincts, and the rustlers steal 'em from him."

"What do you think about Winthrop?" Barney muttered.

"I don't trust him," Tom rejoined. "He knew Daddy Brooks was shorthanded. If he'd been on the level he'd have hired us willingly. I reckon he put those two guys, Kelly and McCord, on to us, too, but I wasn't sayin' anything until we've got proof."

They had now passed through the cleft in the hills, and Tom was about to push ahead when his comrade laid a hand on his arm.

"Hey, look who's here," he said whimsically. "Miss Dolores Brooks."

He was right, for the girl had just appeared on horseback, riding from behind a mass of chaparral about a quarter of a mile away. She had not seen the two cowboys as yet, and was cantering across their path. They watched her, and Tom was about to make some gruff comment in reference to her when a white figure came bounding into view from some thickets that Dolores was approaching.

It was the figure of the palomino, and Tom scarce had time to utter a startled exclamation before the stallion was rearing up in front of the mare known as Brown Betty.

The pony was frisky, as Tom had warned its owner, and his words were borne out now, for the mare began to plunge and curvet wildly. The cowboys saw Dolores striving to control the animal with the bridle, but her efforts were in vain, and as the palomino wheeled to gallop away the saddle-horse dashed in pursuit, regardless of the rein.

The bit was between Brown Betty's teeth, and she was her own mistress. To follow the stallion was the single purpose in her brute brain, and nothing that her rider might do could prevent her. Helpless, Dolores screamed in terror as the mare carried her onward in blind pursuit of the palomino, and the girl's piercing cry reached the ears of Tom and Barney distinctly.

The hills had hardly taken up the echoes of that shriek before Tom was spurring forward, and the fleet hoofs of his bronc pounded over the mesquite grass. With his mount in full career the puncher began to gain on the runaway appreciably, but the pitiful screams of the frantic girl ahead of him caused him to use his spurs even more rigorously.

His horse answered nobly, and the ground seemed to streak away behind its flying limbs. A magnificent creature, trained to perfection, beautifully built, it had earned renown for speed and intelligence wherever Tom had chosen to enter it in a rodeo, but never had it revealed such pace as it did now.

Rapidly overhauling Brown Betty, Tom drew within a few yards of the runaway, which was straining after the half-wild palomino. Dolores was still in the mare's saddle, but she was swaying uncertainly, and all at once, as she turned a white and stricken face towards him, the pursuing cowboy realised that she was on the verge of fainting.

She was in danger of falling to the ground at any moment, and to have done so would have meant a broken limb, perhaps worse.

"I wish she'd break her leg so's I'd have an excuse to shoot her." Tom remembered those foolish words of his, and regretted that they had ever crossed his lips, for now they had taken on the semblance of a curse that might partially come true. Again his heels dug into the bronco's flanks, and with a spurt his gallant mount carried him abreast of Dolores.

He threw his arm around the girl's waist, and in the very instant that his grasp closed around her he slid limply towards him. Taking her weight, he lifted her clean out of the saddle and swung aside—then drew rein and lowered her gently to the ground.

Brown Betty raced on in the tracks of the stallion, but Tom paid no heed to mare or palomino. Dolores had sunk to the grass in an inert heap, and, quickly dismounting, the cowboy knelt beside her anxiously.

He tried to revive her, but failed in his attempts. Then he remembered that there was a stream hard by, and, snatching off his sombrero, he hurried in the direction of the water, presently disappearing from view over the bank of the rivulet.

Barney was riding towards the spot, but he had been left far to the rear, and he was still some distance away when another horseman hove into sight. The man was Winthrop, and from a bluff towards the left the foreman had witnessed all that had occurred. Now he was making for Dolores to see if he could be of assistance, and on reaching her he swung himself from his pony.

He crouched down alongside the girl and pillowed her head on his knee, and he was rubbing her hands vigorously when she opened her eyes and looked at him dully.

"Are you all right, Miss Dolores?" he asked her. "I was out for a canter, and I——"

"Oh, that terrible wild horse!" she broke in. "The moment Brown Betty saw him there was no holding her. Oh, Mr. Winthrop, it was wonderful that you came along just in time. I'd have been killed if it hadn't been for you."

The foreman was taken aback, but the look of gratitude in the girl's eyes was not unwelcome to him, and after a momentary hesitation he made no attempt to deny that he was her rescuer.

"Don't talk about it, Miss Dolores," he said. "I'm glad you're not hurt. Here, let me help you to your feet."

He assisted her to rise, and, standing there a little unsteadily, she passed her hand across her forehead.

"You know," she faltered, "I—I didn't realise it was you who caught hold of me. I had an idea—just before I fainted—that it was that new cowboy who was galloping alongside me——"

"Oh, forget all about it, Miss Brooks!" Winthrop interposed hastily. "Come, I'll take you to the ranch. I'm afraid you've lost Brown Betty, but you can share my saddle."

He lifted her astride his pony and climbed up behind her. Then he rode off in a northerly direction, taking a short cut through the hills, and man and girl were heading for a belt of trees when Barney arrived at the spot where Tom had lowered his employer's niece to the ground.

Tom came struggling up over the bank of the stream at that very moment. He was holding his sombrero in his hands, and the crown of it was filled with water that was spilling over the broad brim. Blundering forward, he suddenly realised that Dolores was no longer where he had left her, and then, looking around in amazement, he saw her riding towards the distant trees with Winthrop.

Barney was grinning at his partner, and, dismounting, he strolled close to his side.

"Nice girl—Miss Dolores Brooks," he remarked.

"Yes—for an aunt," Tom grated, and with the words he emptied the contents of his hat over Barney's head and shoulders.

Drenched by the miniature deluge of water, Barney glared at him in mute anger, and it was Tom's turn to grin, so comical a figure did the little puncher cut.

"I'm sorry, old pal," the big youngster said, clapping his partner heartily on the back. "It was done on the spur of the moment. Your sense of humour seemed a little dry. Sorry, old pal."

Barney pursed his lips.

"That's all right," he stated, "but don't do it again."

"No—never again," Tom answered, shaking the last drips from his hat over him. "Say, let's see if we can pick up the trail of that stallion."

Tom's bronc had originally followed him to the stream, and was still there, slaking its thirst. He whistled the animal, and it came at his signal. Then he mounted, and Barney did the same.

The two friends rode onward through the hills, finally reaching the neighbourhood where they had been fired upon during the morning. Apparently no foes were on the watch now, for not a single shot broke the stillness of the mountains, but, though they examined the ground intently, they discovered no traces of their query.

It was late in the afternoon when they ultimately gave up their quest, returning moodily to the Bar L Ranch.

The Masque Ball.

TO avoid becoming bored with the simplicity of ranch life, the paying guests at the Bar L outfit had organised a carnival dance, and had condescended to invite the employees of Elmer Brooks to attend.

Thus, when evening fell, the Bar L ranch-house resounded with the strains of music and the chatter of many voices, and the dance was in full swing when Sheriff Jim Melville, of Hotham County, dropped in for a quiet talk with old man Brooks.

He found the rancher tricked out as a Russian, and it was with a somewhat sheepish air that the owner of the Bar L accompanied him out into the garden, where the two of them sat down on a rustic bench.

"I wish I'd never given them dudes permission to hold this crazy affair in my home," Elmer Brooks growled. "What's more, I wish I'd never let 'em persuade me into wearin' this fancy dress. How can I enjoy a dance at my age—with a bullet-hole in my leg and my mind all upside-down on account of those horse-thieves."

The sheriff rolled himself a cigarette and began to smoke.

"If only we could lay them rustlers by the heels," he murmured. "You know, I believe there would be a grand neck-tie party, law or no law. Some of your men are pretty sore about friends that have been shot up by that gang——"

Elmer Brooks and Sheriff Jim Melville were not the only ones who were discussing the horse thieves at that moment, for the same subject of conversation was occupying two men who had slipped away from the dance a few seconds previously, and who were now standing in the patio.

They were Tom and Barney, and the bigger cowboy was talking to his partner in an undertone.

"There's five thousand dollars' worth of prize brood mares down in the big corral," he was saying, "and, with everybody at the dance, it might would be a good opportunity for them rustlers to start something. Just in case of trouble, I reckon you and I will stay on our guard, Barney."

"All right," the other agreed, "but this sure is a bad break. I was gettin' along fine with some gal at the shindig in there when you grabbed me and brought me out here. Say, did you notice Miss Dolores Brooks, too? She was in a Spanish costoom. Had a mask on, but you couldn't mistake her."

"I'm not interested in Miss Dolores Brooks," Tom said, with an emphasis that did not ring true.

"I still think she's a very nice girl," Barney declared.

"Yeah—for a grandmother," his comrade retorted, and even as he spoke the words he saw a figure in the dress of a senorita approaching from the ranch-house.

"Talk of angels!" Barney breathed. "Here she comes now!"

"Talk of alley-cats!" Tom grunted. "Listen! You sneak round to the barn, and I'll meet you there in fifteen minutes."

Barney slipped away, and a moment after he had departed Tom was joined by Dolores. She was wearing a mask—indeed, most of the people attending the fancy-dress carnival had done so—but she withdrew it as she confronted the cowboy, and he had to admit to himself that she looked more beautiful than ever to-night.

"I've been trying to find you," she murmured. "I only learned to-night that you were the man who saved me when Brown Betty got out of control, and I—I want to thank you."

Tom shifted his weight from one foot to another.

"You know, Miss Dolores, you should never wear a mask," he said. "Seems kinda wrong to hide that pretty face of yours—especially when it's smilin' and friendly, like it is now."

"Cowboy, I think you're flattering me," she told him. "But listen—supposing you take *your* mask off?"

"Me?" Tom queried. "I didn't have one on. Masque dances and fancy dresses ain't exactly in my line."

"I mean the mask you've been wearing ever since you came to the Bar L ranch," Dolores said significantly. "Oh, I know the truth of the whole matter, Tom Saunders. Uncle Elmer took me into his confidence. You're here to help him break up that gang of horse thieves."

Tom looked at her whimsically.

"Maybe I am," he confessed, "and, that bein' the case, I'm neglecting my job. Miss Dolores, do you think you can pick another horse out of the stable to-morrow mornin' and go ridin' with me? I'll get Barney to groom and saddle one for you."

"That might be arranged," she answered, with a smile.

"Till to-morrow, then," Tom said. "Adios, senorita."

He turned and made his way across the patio, heading for the stable, to saddle his own bronc, and, having accomplished this task, he rode round to the barn, where he had arranged to meet his partner.

He found Barney waiting there by the doorway of the building, and, leaning down from his horse, he spoke to the little puncher briskly.

"I'm going down to watch the big corral," he stated. "You keep right here and give me a whistle if you see anybody slippin' away from the ranch. Don't forget now—if you notice any suspicious-lookin' guys comin' this way, let me know. Is that clear?"

Neither Barney nor Tom was aware that two men were lurking in the shadows of the outbuilding's interior. They were McCord and Kelly, and the latter was reaching for his gun, but his accomplice quickly stayed his hand.

"All right, Tom," Barney was saying. "I'll tip you off if anybody shows up."

The taller cowboy rode off, and, waiting till he had disappeared beyond a belt of brush which extended between the ranch-house and the main corral, McCord drew his six-shooter and clubbed it grimly. Then he stepped through the doorway and struck Barney from behind, the crushing blow knocking the little puncher to the ground.

Barney lay still, and, seizing him, McCord and Kelly dragged him into the outbuilding.

"Now to find Winthrop," jerked Red. "I've got a hunch, an' I think it oughta work a treat. Come on!"

They hurried toward the ranch-house, and it did not take them long to locate the foreman, for he had left the room where the dance was in progress and was loitering in the patio.

"How'd everything work out?" he asked eagerly as Red McCord and Beef Kelly appeared.

"We brought the stallion from the hide-out and opened the corral gate, just like you told us to," McCord reported. "The mares bust out in a mass, an' then we pulled our freight—went to cover in the barn. We hadn't long been there when them two new hands showed up. The big fellow rode off to the corral, but we put the other one out and threw him in the hay."

Winthrop scowled darkly.

"That's bad," he jerked. "What are we gonna do now? Saunders is liable to chase the stallion away and drive back those mares."

"Not a chance," McCord rejoined. "It would take more'n one man to break up that stampede. Listen! Here's where we can get rid of Saunders an' his partner. We can make out that they were responsible for lettin' the mares out of the corral. With that hombre down there right now——"

Winthrop was quick to see his meaning, and he gripped him by the arm with enthusiasm.

"By gosh, Red, you've hit on a sweet hunch for once," he rapped out. "Listen! You and Beef get your horses and pull out of here. Make for the hide-out, and be ready to handle that five-thousand-dollar herd when the palomino brings 'em home to the canyon. Leave the rest to me. I'll find Brooks and the sheriff. They're out in the gardens somewhere."

The crooks separated, Winthrop hurrying off in quest of his employer and Jim Melville. He discovered them in less than a minute, and broke in on their conversation excitedly.

"Get some men, sheriff," the foreman exclaimed. "I'll show you the horse thief!"

"What do you mean, Winthrop?"

He pitched forward lifelessly and crashed to the floor, and for several seconds Tom and the others looked down at his prone form in silence.

June 2nd, 1934.

Daddy Brooks interposed, looking up at him swiftly.

"That guy Saunders is the man who's been stealin' our herds," the foreman answered tersely. "He's at the big corral now. I just saw him. I met his partner on the way back here, and he tried to lay me out, but I knocked him cold."

Elmer Brooks struggled to his feet with the aid of his walking-stick.

"There must be some mistake," he protested. "Those men——"

"Those men are the horse thieves!" Winthrop cried. "Don't you see? They only got jobs here so they could work from the inside! Mr. Brooks, there's no time to argue. Come on, sheriff! We'll round up some of the boys!"

He led Melville from the gardens at the double, leaving the crippled old rancher to hobble along as best he could, and ere long the foreman and the sheriff were galloping from the ranch at the head of a small band of determined cowboys.

Winthrop's lieutenant, Joe, was a member of that group, and another of the foreman's accomplices was included in the party—a man by the name of Lorrimer. The rest of the punchers were honest ranch-hands, eager to act in the interests of their employer.

They swept through the tract of brushwood between the ranch-buildings and the big corral, and as they cleared the vegetation they beheld a mass of ponies wheeling hither and thither in the moonlight. In the midst of them was a solitary rider—Tom Saunders—and he was doing his utmost to prevent the herd from stampeding after a white stallion which was fleeing across the range. But, Winthrop and his hirelings excepted, the newcomers were unaware of his intentions, and firmly believed that he was attempting to drive the mares onward.

With angry shouts they bore down on Tom, and all at once he found himself surrounded.

"Up with your hands, Saunders," the sheriff ordered curtly. "Take it easy now. The boys have got you covered."

The mares from the corral were now streaming over the open ground in the track of the palomino, for the diversion created by the arrival of Winthrop and his party had permitted them to surge forward without restraint. Nor was any effort made to stop them, for Tom was the sole object of attention at the moment.

"It's just as I told you, sheriff," said Winthrop. "This is the man who's been gettin' away with the Bar L stock."

"But listen," Tom ejaculated angrily; "the stallion was running off with the mares, and I only tried to herd them back."

"Tell that to the judge," the sheriff retorted. "We've caught you redhanded, friend."

"You've got to believe me," Tom shouted. "Look at those mares. They're getting away. Why don't you try to stop them and drive them back to the corral?"

"Yeah, and while we're doin' that you can make your own getaway," Winthrop sneered. "No, Saunders, you can't fool us. We'll round up those mares in our own time, but meanwhile you've got a lot of crimes to answer for—the thievin' of stock and the shootin' of men from ambush."

Tom ground his teeth together.

"You're crazy," he blazed. "Take me to Daddy Brooks——"

"We'll take you to the nearest tree," the foreman cut in, "and there's one right handy. Come on, fellers, string him up. We'll settle with his partner later. He's up at the barn."

There were ominous grunts of approval from the Bar L ranch-hands, and they closed in on Tom. Nor was the sheriff able to hold them in check.

"You keep outa this, Melville," Winthrop told him. "We're in the majority, and we mean to handle this thing our own way. Grab him, boys, an' take him over to that tree."

"No, you don't!" a sharp, incisive voice interrupted. "I'll plug the first guy that lays a finger on him. Get back, all of you—get back, d'yuh hear?"

Tom's captors had turned their heads, and on the edge of the brush near by they saw the form of an armed horseman. It was Barney, and his comical face looked set and grim.

The Bar L hands had the advantage of numbers, but Barney's revolver spelled a threat that none of them cared to challenge, and slowly they raised their arms.

"Get their guns, Tom," the little cowboy ordered, "an' then make 'em climb down from their broncs."

Tom lost no time in disarming the band of men and forcing them to dismount. Then he pitched their six-shooters far into the brushwood one by one, and, when the last weapon had gone flying into the thickets, he blazed off a few shots with his own forty-five, scattering the ponies from which sheriff and ranch employees had descended.

A moment later Tom Saunders and Barney Tilson were spurring forth across the range, heading for the hills into which the white stallion and the fivethousand-dollar herd of mares had already disappeared.

Blind Canyon.

IT was morning, and Tom and Barney were preparing to break camp in a hollow where they had rested for the night.

"I got you out of one mess last night," Barney was saying. "If I hadn't come round an' rid down to the corral you'd be under the ground by now. But it strikes me that we're still in a tough spot. Why not go back to the ranch and demand protection from Daddy Brooks? He knows we ain't no hossthieves."

"No," Tom rejoined. "I figure we may as well stay out on the range. There's light enough to see now, an' though we couldn't trail that stallion yesterday, we might have better luck today. Don't forget it was a mighty big herd that followed him last night, and there ought to be plenty of tracks—fresh ones, too."

"And once we've located the stallion we've got the real hoss-thieves, eh?" murmured Barney.

"You said it," Tom answered. "Come on, let's go."

They secured their mounts and swung themselves into their saddles, and once more they set out in the direction of the locality where they had been fired upon during their first attempt to shadow the palomino. Sure enough they espied the imprints of many hoofs in the trampled mesquite grass, which was still soaking wet from a heavy dew that had begun to fall early the previous evening.

Without any incident occurring to check their investigation, they followed the tracks through the hills, and finally entered a small canyon. Here the ground was barren and rocky, and offered no traces of the missing herd, though it seemed pretty clear that the animals must have entered the ravine.

"The tracks lead right up to the mouth of the canyon here," Tom muttered, "but stallion and mares must have come out of it again. See—the ravine is blind."

"Don't appear to be any tracks leadin' away from it, though," mused Barney. "I didn't notice any, did you?"

As many a searcher had doubtless done before him, Tom was prepared to turn out of the canyon and pay no further heed to it, but at Barney's word he pushed farther into the ravine and proceeded to examine it more closely. In a minute or two he and his comrade were near the mass of brushwood at the blind end of it, and it was as he glanced at this that the taller cowboy gave a sudden start.

Spurring towards the vegetation, Tom grasped twigs and foliage and pulled at them lustily. The greenery came away, and the big puncher uttered a sharp exclamation.

"Hey, Barney, this brushwood is nothing but a gate," he called out. "Look, here's a tunnel."

The cavern in the rock was wide and lofty, and the two friends rode into it slowly. For a distance of fifty yards they were in almost total darkness, and then they saw a glimmer of daylight ahead, and presently they were entering a narrow pass with the clear morning sky above their heads.

Ahead of them they could see a hollow tucked away among the craggy hills, which seemed to surround it like colossal ramparts, and they observed a rough shack in the foreground, with corrals adjoining—corrals packed with herds of ponies.

"By golly, what a hide-out," Tom breathed. "Looks as if this is the only way into it, too. With that tunnel screened off you'd never spot it except from an aeroplane——"

"Too bad you didn't come by aeroplane," a voice broke in; and simultaneously two figures jerked into view from behind a group of boulders, two men whom Tom and Barney recognised immediately as McCord and Kelly.

The crooks were armed, and they were covering the intruders with their guns. Taken completely unawares, Tom and his comrade were forced to raise their hands, and then Kelly spoke in harsh accents.

"Saw you ride into the canyon, you mugs," he stated. "We figured we'd stage a little reception for you when you started to tear away that brushwood back there. Red, go forward and take their guns. It's all right, I've got the drop on 'em."

McCord advanced and relieved the two cowboys of their six-shooters. Then he took the reins of their horses and led them through the pass into the hollow, where Tom and Barney were told to dismount.

The prisoners obeyed, and at Kelly's instructions McCord fetched some rope. While Beef continued to threaten the two friends with his revolver, Red trussed them securely.

"That's fixed 'em," the latter said at length, when the captives were lying helpless on the ground. "They're safe now. I wonder what the boss'll want us to do with 'em when we report this to him."

"Fill 'em full o' lead, maybe," Beef Kelly grunted. "Say, we'd better get back to the canyon and cover up the tunnel again."

"Sure," Red agreed. "It's all right to leave these guys. They can't get away."

He emphasised the words by tugging roughly at the bonds which imprisoned the legs and wrists of the punchers. Then he joined Beef as that worthy proceeded to make for the pass leading out of the hollow.

The rogues disappeared in the direction of the tunnel, and they were no sooner out of sight than Tom and

(Continued on page 24.)

"RIDING THROUGH."
(Continued from page 10.)

Barney began to strain at the cords with which they had been tied. Red McCord had done his work skilfully, however, and Tom for one had given up all hope of obtaining his freedom, when suddenly he felt a cold, wet muzzle nudging him.

His horse had moved over to him, and with a gleam in his eyes Tom spoke to the bronc urgently.

"Come on, boy," he jerked. "Take a chew at these ropes. Come on—attaboy, attaboy. Here—quick now!"

While uttering those rapid words of encouragement he had contrived to push his bound wrists against the animal's teeth, and the magnificent creature seemed to understand his meaning, for all at once it started to tear at the hemp. Lying there, Tom prayed fervently that it might succeed in releasing him ere the return of McCord and Kelly, and it was with a gasp of relief that he presently felt the rope around his hands fall loose as a knot became unravelled.

Once his wrists were unfastened he speedily disposed of the bonds that secured his legs. Then he set Barney free, the little puncher looking approvingly at his companion's mount in the meantime.

"That bronc sure knows something besides eatin' oats," he declared.

"Yeah," Tom rejoined. "If you'd eat some oats maybe you'd have some horse-sense, too. Listen, we'll have to pull these cords around us again and make out that we're still tied. We're unarmed, and if McCord and Kelly discover that we've got loose they'll shoot us down like rabbits. We've got to lie low until they're right close to us."

Barney nodded, and the pair of them wound the loose coils of hemp around their limbs again, then lay down in their former positions. To all appearances they were still powerless, but actually they had only to make a movement with their arms and legs to cast off the ropes.

McCord and Kelly showed up again, and, guns in holsters, they swaggered towards the prone forms of their captives.

"Well," Beef Kelly was saying as he came up, "that's everything in order again, I reckon. Now how about bundlin' these guys into that shed over there? I——"

The man got no farther, for at that instant Tom threw off his faked bonds and swung up his legs to grip the crook around the waist in a scissor-lock. Next second he dragged him to the ground, the burly gangster uttering a strident yell as he went down.

McCord sprang forward with a shout, pulling at his gun as he did so, but Barney tripped him smartly with an outflung foot, and in another moment both crooks were grovelling in the dust with the Arizona cowboys a-top of them.

Tom pounded his man into submission heartily, while Barney whipped out McCord's second revolver and stuck the muzzle of it against the back of the ruffian's neck. The cold, deadly contact of the gun was too much for Red, and he lay there without sign of resistance.

It was the crooks' turn to suffer the indignity of being tied up, and when they had been made secure Tom Saunders stood over them menacingly.

"Now," he stated, "you guys are gonna give me the low-down on this outfit. Who else is in the gang?
June 2nd, 1934.

Who's boss of it—Winthrop? Come on, start talkin'."

The gangsters maintained a truculent silence, and Tom bent threatening eyes upon them.

"Tongue-tied, eh?" he ground out. "All right, I'll tell you what I'll do. I'll let you make a choice for yourselves. If you talk, I'll fetch the sheriff, and by turnin' State's Evidence you may go to the pen, nice an' dignified, for four or five years. But if you don't talk, I'll send Barney to the ranch-house. Do you know what that will mean?"

The captives looked up at him nervously, furtively.

"Some of those boys that you've been workin' beside have had their best friends shot up at the hands of you horse-thieves," Tom went on. "That's why they were ready to string me up last night when they thought I was the culprit. By golly, I wouldn't like to be in your shoes if they get hold of you."

With the prospect of a lynching-party looming large in their minds, Beef Kelly and Red McCord did not remain mute much longer, and soon they had revealed the identities of their accomplices and their leader, Tom and Barney listening attentively the while.

The confession complete, the taller cowboy addressed his partner crisply.

"That's all we want to know, Barney," he said. "Go get the sheriff. I'll look after these fellows, but don't waste any time on the trail."

Barney made for his horse, and, vaulting astride the animal, he spurred into the pass that led to the tunnel. A few seconds later he was galloping through the cavern, to charge down the loose brushwood that screened the mouth of it. Then he swung out of the canyon.

He was riding from the ravine when two horsemen topped the crest of a hill and spotted him. They were Joe and the man Lorrimer, and as they espied Barney they drew rein to watch him.

"Say, that's Tilson," Joe snarled. "He came out of the canyon, too. What do you know about that?"

Barney had not seen them, and Lorrimer reached towards his hip, but, observing the movement of his accomplice's hand, Joe spoke gruffly.

"Leave your iron where it is," he snapped. "You'd never hit him from this distance. No use tryin' to catch up with him, either. He's got too big a start, and he sure is burnin' the wind. Come on, let's get down to the canyon an' see if anything's wrong."

They descended the hillside, and in a minute or two they were entering the ravine. On arrival at the cavern they did not fail to notice how the screen of brushwood had been rent asunder, and they looked at each other significantly.

"We'll leave our broncs here," Joe grated. "Follow me, an' don't make a sound. I smell trouble here."

The rogues dismounted and drew their forty-fives. Then they pushed into the tunnel, the man with the broken nose leading the way, Lorrimer moving along at his heels. Presently they were in the pass, and as they approached the end of it they saw Tom Saunders standing over his prisoners.

The young cowboy's back was towards the newcomers, and with wary tread Joe and Lorrimer stole close to him. Unaware of their presence, Tom kept his eyes riveted on Kelly and McCord, and he had no suspicion of his danger until he felt a hand snatch his six-gun from its sheath.

He whipped round then, only to discover the barrel of Lorrimer's revolver levelled at his breast.

"Easy, Saunders," the gangster warned. "Reach for the sky, will yuh?"

Joe was close by, and Tom's "iron" was in his fist. The man slung it to one side and then, laying down his own gun, knelt beside the prostrate figures of Kelly and McCord.

"Keep that guy covered, Lorrimer," he rasped. "I'll cut Beef an' Red loose."

He tugged out a knife and hacked at the ropes which bound the prisoners. The two men struggled up and, once more a couple of swaggering bullies now that circumstances were in their favour, they glared at Tom savagely.

"That hombre tricked us, Joe," Beef Kelly blurted. "Look what he done to my face, too. That's twice he's laid into me, and I aim to pay him back in kind. Watch this!"

He blundered forward to hit out at Tom, but in his angry advance he unsighted Lorrimer and, quick to see his chance, the Arizona cowboy whipped his right into action.

His fist travelled from the hip, and it crashed home on Kelly's jaw with shattering effect, bundling the rogue into the man with the gun. Both gangsters fell, the revolver spinning from Lorrimer's hand and sliding under the raised floor of a shed nearby.

Joe ripped out an oath, and attempted to snatch up the six-shooter that he had set down, but Tom forestalled him, and with a flying kick he sent the weapon after Lorrimer's. Next second, however, Winthrop's lieutenant was barging into him with lowered head, and the youngster's legs were carried from under him.

He went down heavily, and Joe sprawled atop of him, but with an effort Tom heaved him aside and scrambled up—to meet a bull-like rush by McCord.

The stalwart cowboy jumped towards his man, rammed his left into the gangster's mouth. Back went McCord, recoiling with broken teeth and torn lips, and he was still grimacing with pain when a full-blooded right-hander smacked the wits out of him.

He collapsed in a heap, and Tom wheeled to see Lorrimer and Kelly making for him. Beef was foremost, and the youngster from Arizona treated him to an upper-cut that tossed him to the ground and planted him there in a spread-eagled attitude.

Lorrimer tried to grapple, but was pitched to the dust and, on rising again, he made the acquaintance of a fist that struck him like a battering-ram. But in the meantime Joe had picked himself up, and, darting in as Tom disposed of his accomplice, he landed a punch that knocked the cowboy on his back.

Joe came on to follow up his advantage, and tried to throw himself on the younger man, but Tom lifted his feet and shot the ruffian backwards with a powerful thrust of his legs. By the time that Winthrop's lieutenant had recovered himself his antagonist was erect again.

The crook rushed to the attack and swung a mighty blow. It missed, for Tom ducked beneath it and jammed his knuckles into the rustler's fleshy midriff with a force that doubled him up like a clasp-knife. Head bent, knees sagging, Joe began to sink towards the ground, but his opponent hauled him up again and made sure of him with a hard jolt to the chin.

McCord, Kelly, Lorrimer, Joe—the four of them lay in sorry, recumbent attitudes as Tom surveyed them. Nor did they offer much resistance when he began to tie them up, for each time any of them looked like stirring the cowboy quietened the rogue in question with a lusty cuff. In the space of a few minutes the gangsters were utterly powerless, and their captor was recon-

himself once more to a long wait
Barney and the sheriff.
It was almost noon before Tom heard
the clatter of hoofs, and immediately
after the sound reached his ears he saw
his partner riding into the hollow with
Melville and a posse of men.

The sheriff and his party dismounted.
"Looks as if you've been busy,
Saunders," the sheriff remarked. "I
thought your friend said there were only
two of the gang here."

"Two more showed up after Barney
left," was the answer. "There's your
men, sheriff, and there's the Bar L stock
over in those corrals. Now supposin'
we get Kelly and McCord to repeat
their confession in your presence——"

"Sure!" Melville replied. "But let
me tell you something, Saunders.
You'll have five thousand dollars
coming to you from the Stock Raisers'
Association. They've put up that reward
for the capture of the horse-thieves who
have been stealing Brooks' herds.
Daddy Brooks is a member of the association, and is entitled to its protection."

"Great!" Tom declared. "Five
thousand bucks will just be enough to
kick all those dudes off the Bar L
Ranch, I guess."

The Side Door.

ELMER BROOKS was sitting in his
study early that same afternoon
when the young mail-carrier
known as Slim entered the apartments.

"I've just got in from town, Mr.
Brooks," the youth reported. "I
brought that padlock you wanted."

"Padlock!" the old man echoed
vaguely.

"Yes, sir, you remember," Slim continued. "The one for the store-room.
You wanted to keep the side-door
fastened."

"Oh, yes, to be sure," Daddy Brooks
answered. "Thanks, Slim, thanks."

"Shall I put it on right away, sir?"
the Bar L mail-carrier asked.

"No, Slim," the ranch-owner rejoined, "never mind. You go and get
your dinner. I'll put the lock on, myself. Imagine," he added ironically, "I
haven't had to fasten that door all these
years, and now that a pack of swells
are livin' here I have to protect myself
against petty theft—yes, petty theft!
What with horse-thieves and light-fingered city folks——"

He went across the threshold of the
store-room and made for the door that
opened out on to the patio, and he
clasped the padlock to a couple of
staples that had never before been used.
Having thus secured the door, he pocketed
the key of the padlock in his pocket
and stepped back into his study.

Slim had gone, but in the interval
Dolores had entered the apartment, and
she looked at the old man earnestly as
he appeared.

"Uncle Elmer, what do you suppose
has happened to Tom and Barney?" she
said. "They're not horse-thieves, and
you know it."

"Of course they're not," Daddy
Brooks rejoined. "That's what I've
been trying to tell Winthrop ever since
last night, but I can't seem to get hold
of the man. All the same, it beats me
why Tom and Barney struck out across
the range. They should have come
straight to me and demanded protection. You know, my dear——"

He was interrupted by an urgent
knock on the door, and a moment afterwards Winthrop bustled into the room.

"Mr. Brooks," the foreman said
quickly, "the sheriff and his posse are
headed this way. Saunders and Tilson
are with them. They'll have to be
pretty smart to get out of this fix."

The rancher thumped his walking-stick against the floor impatiently.

"Listen to me, Winthrop," he cried;
"you're a sound foreman but a poor
detective. I don't care what you say—
Tom Saunders wasn't bent on mischief
when he was down at the big corral
last night."

"But, Mr. Brooks, I saw him with
my own eyes," the other protested.
"When I went down there again with
the sheriff and the boys we all saw
him."

"Nevertheless I'm convinced that
Tom can explain his actions," the old
man snapped. "Confound it, I sent all
the way to Arizona for him. Yes,
Winthrop, I sent for him——"

He paused, for now there was a stamping of hoofs and a jingling of harness
outside the very ranch-house. A few
seconds later footsteps became audible
in the hall, and immediately afterwards
Tom, Barney and Sheriff Melville
walked through the doorway of the
study.

Winthrop turned to face them. He
was perfectly composed, for he had no
suspicion that his hirelings had been
rounded up and his own duplicity betrayed by them.

"Ah, sheriff," the foreman exclaimed,
"congratulations on catching your men."

If You're a Radio Enthusiast—

you need POPULAR WIRELESS, for
it will help you in countless ways.
Every aspect of wireless is dealt with
week by week in the pages of this
essentially practical journal. If you
have any particular problem, if your
set is not producing the best possible
results, write to POPULAR WIRELESS. A staff of expert contributors
is at your service. In every issue they
will give you particulars of the newest
and latest developments in the world
of radio. This useful paper will help
you to get the best out of your Wireless set.

Every Wednesday at all Newsagents.

Listen, Mr. Brooks seems to find some
difficulty in believing that they're
guilty——"

"Winthrop, it's you we want," Melville interrupted grimly.

The foreman's face changed colour.
Pale and speechless, he looked first at
the sheriff, then at Tom and Barney,
meeting in each case the level gaze of
stern, accusing eyes. He was aware
that something was amiss, and for a
second he almost lost his nerve. Then
he recovered himself with an effort, and
tried to brazen out the situation.

"Is this your idea of a joke, Melville?" he demanded.

"It's no joke," the sheriff retorted in
a sharp voice. "We've got your men
and Daddy Brooks' stock—and the white
stallion thrown in."

The owner of the Bar L Ranch
hobbled towards the officer of the law
and laid a hand on his arm. The old
man was wearing a look of blank amazement, with which anger was beginning
to intermingle.

"Do you mean to say that Winthrop
is the man who's been stealing my
stock?" he ejaculated.

"Yes," came the reply. "Thanks to
Tom Saunders here, we have the confession from Winthrop's own men."

Daddy Brooks drew in his breath. He
seemed shocked, yet he did not discredit
the sheriff's story, as he had discredited
the accusations levelled against Tom.

"Winthrop, what have you got to say
for yourself?" he grated.

"There's nothing he can say," put in
Melville, "except to admit his guilt.
We've got him dead to rights. And
he's the man that was going to make
an example of Tom Saunders by lynch-law!"

Winthrop was as white as a sheet, but
he affected an air of gloomy calm.

"I know when I'm licked," he said.
"I guess you win."

The sheriff stepped towards him, and
it was then that the expression on the
foreman's features changed. His
assumed resignation had been a blind to
throw his captors off their guard, and
it worked, for none of them was ready
with a gun when Winthrop became
transformed into a hunted creature, galvanised by desperation.

A savage thrust from the scoundrel's
hand and Melville was reeling backwards. Next second Winthrop had
leaped to the store-room door, and as
he jumped for it he clutched Dolores,
pulling her close to him and swinging
round so that her body protected him
from his foes.

The girl screamed, and tried to
struggle free, but he held her tightly,
backing now in the direction of the
store-room. Meanwhile, Tom, Barney
and the sheriff had reached for their
irons, only to stay their hands as they
saw that the crook was shielding himself effectively with his employer's niece.

Winthrop drew a gun from a holster
at his hip and thrust it past the arm
of Dolores.

"Stick 'em up, all of you!" he
snarled. "You, too, Brooks! I'll plug the
first man that makes a wrong move!"

Baffled, not daring to cross him for
fear of injury to the girl, the four men
raised their arms. Retreating still
further, Winthrop gained the door that
led from study to store-room, and, kicking it open, he slipped across the
threshold.

He pushed Dolores from him as he
darted from view, and the girl reeled
into the middle of the study again.
Simultaneously, Winthrop slammed the
communicating door and wheeled for
the one that opened on to the patio.

Sheriff Melville uttered a cry the instant the fugitive disappeared.

"Outside!" he shouted. "He'll leave
by the side door and get to his horse!"

"He can't!" Daddy Brooks gasped.
"I just put a padlock on that door ten
minutes ago. He'll have to break his
way out first——"

Tom sprang forward, waiting to hear
no more. Out came his forty-five, and
next second he was charging through
into the store-room.

He saw Winthrop crouching at the
far wall—trapped—one hand clenched on
the padlock—a man at bay, nevertheless, with a deadly weapon in his right
fist.

The gang-leader swung up his "iron"
viciously at sight of Tom. The cowboy
ducked, and let fly from the hip in the
self-same moment. The crook's revolver
and his foe's, they belched in unison,
and the shadows of the store-room were
rent by flame, while the walls seemed
to hurl the double roar of the guns
back into the two men's ears.

A leaden slug grazed Tom's shoulder
and smacked into the swinging door
behind him. Then he straightened, and
beheld the figure of Winthrop tottering
towards him, the man's revolver clattering to the floor as he came on with
uncertain steps and glazing eyes.

Watching him grimly, Tom backed
(Continued on page 28.)
June 2nd, 1934.

"RIDING THROUGH."
(Continued from page 25.)

out into the study, and as he appeared there he heard Dolores give vent to a relieved cry. Next moment Winthrop staggered into view.

His lips moved, and his voice sounded in a husky whisper.

"You win," he breathed. "I mean it—this time. Yeah—you got me—dead to rights——"

He pitched forward lifelessly and crashed to the floor, and for several seconds Tom and the others looked down at his prone form in silence. Then Daddy Brooks took Tom and Dolores each by an arm and led them from the room.

"Tom," he said hoarsely, when they were out in the hall, "would you consider a permanent job here—as manager of my ranch? There would be a billet for Barney as well, of course."

Tom looked at Dolores, and in her eyes he seemed to read a plea to accept her uncle's proposal.

"Well, Daddy Brooks," he murmured, "I kinda hate steppin' into a dead man's shoes, but right now I don't know any other place where I'd rather be—than the Bar L outfit."

Dolores was pale and wan, and was overwrought by the drama that had taken place in the room from which she had just emerged. It was at her uncle's suggestion that she made her way to her boudoir to lie down and rest, and she was ascending the stairs that led to the upper floor of the ranch-house when Barney Tilson came out of the study.

Barney joined Tom, and the latter informed him of Elmer Brooks' offer.

"We're stayin' here for keeps, partner," the taller cowboy added. "I don't think we could do better."

Barney eyed him knowingly, and then glanced towards the staircase.

"Nice girl—Miss Dolores Brooks," he mentioned.

"Yeah," Tom answered fervently, "for a sweetheart."

(By permission of Universal Pictures, Ltd., starring Tom Tyler and Ruth Hiatt.)

The News Reel

(Continued from page 2.)

Saved by a Good-bye.

Had it not been for a good-bye, Monroe Owsley would have lost his life as the result of a motor-car accident. This strange intervention of Fate on his behalf happened when he was on his way to take part in a race.

Monroe, it may as well be explained here, has always been tremendously keen on motor-racing. When a boy, he used to haunt the race-tracks near his home and soon got to know the names and achievements of the speed kings who came there. In later years he turned to acting as a means of livelihood, but the roar of a racing car continued, as before, to sound like music in his cars. Whenever opportunity offered, he would go to Ascot, which is a racing-track near Hollywood, and thrill to the sport in which men flirted with death under the lure of speed.

One day Monroe persuaded Les Spangler, a speed demon, to let him ride as his mechanic in a big race at Indianapolis. The actor was on holiday at the time, and packing his bags, left for that State to achieve a lifelong ambition. The route took him past a friend's address, and he decided to step off and say good-bye.

"And that decision," smiled Monroe grimly, "saved my life. I found a 'phone call waiting for me from a studio offering me a part in a coming film. I replied I was on holiday and was on my way to take part in a motor race. The studio people, however, urged me to cut short my holiday, forego the trip to Indianapolis and accept the part. Somewhat reluctantly I agreed, after a lot of talking, to do so, and turned back towards Hollywood."

The next day Monroe read with horror and amazement in a paper that the car in which he was to have ridden as mechanic crashed, killing Les Spangler and another man, "Monk" Jordan, who had taken the actor's place. That good-bye to a friend and the subsequent change of plan had saved Monroe from a similar fate.

Answers to Questions.

You are right in thinking, L. V. (Dublin) that Tom Keene is taller than George O'Brien. The latter's height is 5 ft. 10½ ins. and Tom is 6 ft. tall. The cast of "Ghost Valley" is as follows: Tom Keene (Jerry Long), Myrna Kennedy (Jane Worth), Mitchell Harris (Judge Blake), Billy Franey (Scrubby), Harry Bowen (Marty), Kate Campbell (Aunt Susan), Ted Adams (Gordon).

Don't be afraid to give your name. "Inquisitive" (Glamorgan), which will not be published. Frank and Ralph Morgan are brothers, their real surname being Wupperman. Frank studied at the American Academy of Dramatic Art and then made his acting début on the stage in 1911. Among his film appearances are "When Ladies Meet," "Reunion in Vienna" and "Ring Up the Curtain." Ralph was intended for the legal profession, but after a time changed his mind and went on the stage. His screen career followed in 1931, and since then his pictures include "Doctor Bull," "Shanghai Madness" and "Power and Glory." Madge Evans was born in New York on July 1st, 1909, and Ginger Rogers on July 16th, 1911, in Independence, Missouri.

Fred Thompson died in December, 1928, after an operation for appendicitis, G. J. M. (Derby). Both your favourites, Tom Brown and Richard Cromwell, are 5 ft. 10 ins. in height. As Wally Reid, jun., is still a growing lad, his height has not been made known.

The youngsters in "Sooky" were as follows, B. N. (London, S.W.): Jackie Cooper ("Skippy"), Robert Coogan ("Sooky"), and Jackie Searle (Sidney Saunders). The part of Dr. Skinner in the same film was taken by Willard Robertson, and Enid Bennett played as his wife.

Clarence Muse is a coloured actor who first appeared as a circus artiste and, later, on the American vaudeville stage, R. F. (Crewe). Charlie Murray was also at one time a circus clown, and it was in the sawdust ring, too, that Robert Emmett O'Connor first made his début when he was twelve years of age.

DON'T BE BULLIED!
Some splendid illus. lessons in JUJITSU. Articles and full particulars Free. Better than Boxing. 2d. stamp for postage. Learn to fear no man. Or send P.O. 1/- for First Part to:
"A.P.," "Blenheim House," Bedfont Lane, Feltham, Middlesex

BE STRONG I promise you Robust Health, Doubled Strength, Stamina, and Dashing Energy in 30 days or money back! My amazing 4-in-1 Course adds 10-25 ins. to your muscular development (with 2 ins. on Chest and 1 in. on Arms), also brings an Iron Will, Perfect Self-control, Virile Manhood, Personal Magnetism. Surprise your friends! Complete Course, 5/-. Details free, privately.
STEBBING INSTITUTE (A), 28, Dean Rd., LONDON, N.W.2.

BE TALL Your Height increased in 14 days or Money Back. Complete Course, 5/-. Booklet free privately. STEBBING SYSTEM, 28, Dean Road, LONDON, N.W.2.

HANDSOME MEN ARE SLIGHTLY SUNBURNT. "SUNBRONZE" remarkably improves appearance. 1/6, 2/9. 10,000 Testimonials. (Booklet, stamp).—SUNBRONZE LABORATORIES (Dept. A.7), Colwyn Bay, Wales. (Est. 1902).

George GROSE & Co., 8, New Bridge St., London. LUDGATE CIRCUS
SPURPROOF TENTS
Size 6ft. x 4ft. 3in. x 3ft. 6in. high with 6in. wall. Made from Proofed Canvas Complete with 3-piece Jointed Poles, Pegs and Runners, Overhanging Eaves, Ventilators. Packed in Holdall with handle. 7/9 each, Carriage Paid. 7/9 Carr. Paid.
Send for Art Illustrated List, Post Free.

BLUSHING, Shyness, Nerves, Self-consciousness, Worry Habit. Unreasonable Fears, etc., cured or money back! Complete Course 5/-. Details—L. A. Stebbing, 28, Dean Rd., London, N.W.2.

BE TALLER! Ross System is Genuine. Watch Yourself Grow! INCREASED my own height to 6ft. 3¾ins.! T.H., age 16½, to 6ft. T.F., age 21, from 5ft. 5 to 5ft. 10! B.P., age 20, 3¾ins. in 16 days! A.G., age 19, 5ins. in 6 weeks! Fee £2 2s. STAMP brings FREE Particulars. P. M. ROSS, Height Specialist, Scarborough, Eng.

STAMMERING! Cure yourself as I did. Particulars Free.—FRANK B. HUGHES, 7, Southampton Row, London, W.C.1.

STAMMERING, Stuttering, New, remarkable, Certain Cure, Booklet free, privately.—SPECIALIST, Dept. A.P., 28, Dean Road, London, N.W.2.

VENTRILOQUISM TAUGHT. Wonderful System. Failure impossible. 3d. stamps for First Lesson.—"VALMONDE STUDIOS," 17, Balmoral Road, London, N.W.2.

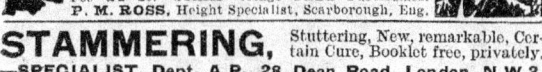

Printed in Great Britain and published every Tuesday by the Proprietors, THE AMALGAMATED PRESS, LTD., The Fleetway House, Farringdon Street, London, E.C.4. Advertisement Offices : The Fleetway House, Farringdon Street, London, E.C.4. Subscription Rates : Inland and Abroad, 11/- per annum ; 5/6 for six months. Sole Agents for Australia and New Zealand: Messrs. Gordon & Gotch, Ltd.; and for South Africa ; Central News Agency, Ltd. Registered for transmission to Canada at Magazine Rates. S.G.
June 2nd, 1934.

> 194 POWDERSMOKE RANGE
>
> quietly, "I didn't know I'd be needin' your guns so soon."
>
> At that moment Sundown threw his body in front of Tucson. The bullet from an outlaw sharp shooter's gun struck Sundown's chest, instead of Tucson at whom it had been aimed. With a moan of pain the famous killer sent one last bullet straight to its mark, the outlaw's body. Then he slid down into the arms of Tucson.
>
> Slowly Sundown opened his eyes
>
> A Bullet Struck Sundown

Tyler only had one appearance in a Big Little book. These mini hardcovers aimed at kids featured adaptions of comic strips, radio shows and movies. Tyler appeared in the one that was a novelization of "Powdersmoke Range." Here is the cover and one of many illustrations in the book.

Tyler's FBO westerns were novelized and translated in Spanish for the movie fans in Spain. There are quite a few of these releases.

This 1961 French photo comic reconstructs Tyler's 1935 "Rio Rattler."

Afterword

When I was a kid discovering movies, watching every film I could, reading film history books, and buying Variety every week I could, the subject matter was generally mainstream directors, actors and studios.

It was only when I discovered the holy grail of film genre reporting, Famous Monsters of Filmland magazine in 1969, that I truly understood there was an underground scholarship about movies seldom touched by the few film people who were writing about the industry. Fanzines such as Photon, Midnight Marquee and Little Shoppe of Horrors truly inspired me.

I can say the same thing for animation. There was precious little published in the 1970s about animation unless it was about Disney until the VHS revolution.

The simple truth is the history of American film should not stop at what MGM did or what prestige directors made. The history of American film includes genre films; animation other than Disney; B movies; studios such as Republic; independent filmmakers such as Alex and Richard Gordon; directors such as William Witney; and fringe people working at budget levels well beneath the Bs.

There are so many films that were made from the beginning of the 20th Century right until its end that deserve rediscovery.

Tom Tyler's story is so typically American and seems like something a press agent would create – a son of immigrants wants to act and hitchhikes across the country to Los Angeles for his big break and after much work he actually is employed as an actor! He had a busy career and would have had an even longer one if not cut down by an incurable disease. His story is fascinating, triumphant and sad.

His accomplishments deserve attention and celebration. How many people worked for John Ford, Ron Ormand, George Stevens, Howard Hawks, as well as Ed Wood? How many people gained a certain kind of film immortality by playing a murderous mummy and the first superhero in live action film?

I would have loved to have been able to interview him but he died 28 days before I was born. I truly wonder what kind of stories he could tell. I bet they were amazing.

This book was made possible because of Internet services that certainly didn't exist when I started the project in the 1970s. Back in the day, at the University of Massachusetts library, I used to go through microfilm of a movie trade magazine frame by frame to gather information. I rented 16mm prints of some of Tom's films in order to see them and traveled to the library at the Lincoln Center in New York City to go through its archives. Years ago, researching film history was not an easy task if you didn't live in New York or Los Angeles, but now the playing field has been leveled through home video, YouTube, The Lantern Media Project and Newspapers.com.

    Do you have a film topic that should see the light of day? Now is your time. Go for it.

Made of Pen & Ink: Fleischer Studios

Take a trip back to yesteryear and read about the forefathers of animation.

Join G. Michael Dobbs, noted animation historian, as he concisely details in Volumes One & Two, the rise of the of the Fleischer Studios in New York and Florida!

Michael introduces you to the cast of characters with in-depth research and interviews with the people who were there!

Buy them now at your favorite online retailer, or ask for it at your local corner bookstore.

inkwell productions

COMING THIS FALL

THE HOOK

A SEQUEL TO BLOOD IN THE WATER

MARK MASZTAL

NOT DOG BOOKS

www.ingramcontent.com/pod-product-compliance
Lightning Source LLC
Chambersburg PA
CBHW080322080526
44585CB00021B/2435